Microsoft®

Data Warehousing with

Microsoft®

SQL Server™ 7.0

Technical Reference

Jake Sturm

PUBLISHED BY
Microsoft Press
A Division of Microsoft Corporation
One Microsoft Way
Redmond, Washington 98052-6399

Library of Congress Cataloging-in-Publication Data
Sturm, Jake, 1961-
    Data Warehousing with Microsoft SQL Server 7.0 : Technical Reference / Jake Sturm.
        p. cm.
    Includes index.
    ISBN 0-7356-0859-8
    1. Data warehousing.   2. SQL server.   I. Title.

    QA76.9.D37 S87   1999
    005.75'85--dc21   99-046101

Printed and bound in the United States of America.

1 2 3 4 5 6 7 8 9   WCWC   5 4 3 2 1 0

Distributed in Canada by Penguin Books Canada Limited.

A CIP catalogue record for this book is available from the British Library.

Microsoft Press books are available through booksellers and distributors worldwide. For further information about international editions, contact your local Microsoft Corporation office or contact Microsoft
Press International directly at fax (425) 936-7329. Visit our Web site at mspress.microsoft.com.

Acquisitions Editor: David Clark
Project Editor: Maureen Phillips
Technical Editor: Dennis Peterson

Contents

5 Introducing Multidimensional Extensions 119

8   ADO Multidimensional   209

Tables

Acknowledgments

I wish to thank my wife, Gwen Sturm, who has contributed countless hours to the editing of this book. She has also acted as my partner, contributing ideas, suggestions, and recommendations for the book's content. I would also like to thank our children, Will, Maya, Lynzie, and Jill, for giving up some of their time with my wife and me so that this book could be completed.

Introduction

Proper management of corporate information is perhaps the most critical issue facing successful corporations in the new millennium. Technology, the market, and the entire way corporations do business can radically change within months or even weeks. A corporation that yesterday sold only through chain stores may today need to sell through the Internet as well to stay in business. To make the decisions necessary to keep the corporation on top of this wave of change, a company must have accurate information that it can manipulate effectively.

Corporations often have a great deal of the right information but lack knowledge management techniques that allow them to easily access important data affecting planning and decision-making. Knowledge management involves using systems that allow employees to access information that exists within a wide array of document formats. This information can include lessons learned, documentation of current and prior development projects, data within databases, documentation of the networking architecture, best practices, and so forth. Any information that is used to make decisions in the corporation should become part of the knowledge management system. When information is trapped within text documents, databases, mail servers, and other reservoirs of data, getting the right information often becomes a difficult, if not impossible, task. Decisions made without sufficient information in this environment of intense competitive pressure and rapid change can be very damaging to a company's success.

Sometimes the problem is not too little information but too much. Anyone who has had hundreds of results returned from an Internet search knows that too much information is as useless as too little. Once the data is made available, it must be properly filtered so that only the information that is required is actually returned. A Microsoft SQL Server 7.0 data warehouse, combined with a set of client applications, can apply this filtering and offer the right information at the right time to the right people—now essential for corporate success.

Microsoft offers four powerful resources to allow corporations to create knowledge management systems: object linking and embedding database (OLE DB), Data Transformation Services (DTS), Microsoft SQL Server 7.0 OLAP Services, and PivotTable Services. OLE DB provides a way to communicate to any data store. With OLE DB, you can access data from text files, Microsoft Exchange Servers, SQL Server 7.0 databases, Microsoft Access databases, and Oracle 8 databases. As long as there are OLE DB providers for your data store, you can access the data. As this book goes to print, there are already OLE DB providers for nearly all the major data stores. The ability to access data is the first step in building knowledge management systems.

Because data can be scattered across the corporation in many formats, managers need a tool to move data around and to transform it into a standardized format that, when necessary, can provide corporate-wide usability. DTS, which is part of SQL Server, provides users with the ability to move, transform, clean, and validate data.

Once you are able to access and move data, you need sophisticated tools to query and analyze the data and then present it in an accurate, useful format. OLAP Services performs queries and analyzes data in data warehouses, while PivotTable Services presents data to the user. The combination of OLE DB, DTS, OLAP Services, and PivotTable Services provides extremely powerful systems that allow you to get the right information to the right place at the right time. This kind of information management affords managers the ability to make more knowledgeable decisions in a shorter amount of time. This book provides information about how to use the four powerful resources to build an enterprise-wide system to manage knowledge using a Microsoft SQL Server 7.0 data warehouse.

Who Should Use This Book?

This book was written for anyone who wants to develop an understanding of data warehousing using SQL Server 7.0. For the SQL Server data warehouse administrator there is material covering everything from the basics of creating and designing the data warehouse to advanced topics such as optimizing the data warehouse. For developers there is a chapter on ADO MD and an extensive Visual Basic code sample in one of the appendices. For both the developer and the administrator there are three chapters on MDX.

What Is In This Book?

This book comprises 13 chapters and 5 appendices. The early chapters cover the essential concepts of building data warehouses and provide readers who are new to data warehousing the foundation they need to build SQL Server 7.0 data warehouses. For the more experienced reader, these chapters can serve as a review. The book explains the new features in SQL Server 7.0 that relate to data warehousing, including DTS, PivotTable Services, and OLAP Services, and how to use them. Readers may read the book from cover to cover, or, with the exceptions of the three MDX chapters, they can read the chapters in an order that suits their interest and knowledge level.

The first chapter looks at the history of corporate knowledge management. Definitions of all the major components of SQL Server data warehousing solutions are provided, including OLAP Services, OLE DB, DTS, wizards, and Microsoft Office 2000. This chapter also defines the difference between analytical and operational data and then gives a detailed description of analytical data.

A data warehouse cannot be built without a good design that fulfills the business requirements of the corporation and meets users' needs. You can use Microsoft Solutions Framework (MSF), described in Chapter 2, to determine the goals and design of the system. MSF also helps turn the design into a working system deployed in your enterprise.This chapter shows how to apply MSF to building a data warehouse. Team structure and ways to effectively work as a unified team are also discussed.

Chapter 3 introduces the theory of online analytical processing (OLAP), which forms the foundation for building an analytical data warehousing system. It covers normalized and un-normalized tables, dimensions, informational objects, star schemas, cubes, and other essential OLAP concepts.

The theory of OLAP introduced in Chapter 3 is applied in Chapter 4 to building a data warehouse with OLAP Services. This chapter shows you how to build a data warehouse using the wizards in OLAP Services.

Chapter 5 shows the basic syntax of MDX, the query language that is used to perform analyses of the data in the data warehouse. It then provides examples to illustrate its usage.

Chapter 6 expands the syntax of the MDX language to include calculated members. A calculated member allows you to create new data warehouse members using members already in the data warehouse. This allows you to create any custom members; for example, the ability to calculate the profit from the total sale value and the total cost for goods value.

MDX expressions, discussed in Chapter 7, are an additional part of the language that allow you to perform a wide range of operations on the data in the data warehouse. Using these expressions, you can create powerful queries that provide answers to even the most complex analytical questions.

Chapter 8 covers ADO Multidimensional (ADO MD), an interface that allows development tools, such as Visual Basic, to communicate to the data warehouse through OLE DB. ADO MD enables you to very easily create powerful applications with Visual Basic, Microsoft Office, ASP (Active Server Pages), and other tools. This chapter discusses the object hierarchy of the ADO MD, what information it can retrieve, how it works, and what types of solutions you can build using the ADO MD hierarchy.

The data warehouse is part of a larger enterprise system. The system also contains numerous applications that bring data from the data warehouse and present it to the user. Chapter 9 discusses some common application design issues with which the data warehouse administrator needs to be involved. It also demonstrates various design principles by working through the design of a Visual Basic project.

Chapter 10 covers Data Transformation Services (DTS), a tool you can use to easily move, cleanse, and transform data. Using OLE DB, DTS can move information from one data store to another. In this chapter, you work with a Microsoft Access database containing December 1998 data provided on the CD that accompanies this book. You move this data into a staging database (FoodMart.mdb), and then update the data warehouse with the new information.

Chapter 11 discusses PivotTable Services, which provide a connection between the OLAP server and all external applications that need to communicate with it. ADO MD, Microsoft Excel, and Visual Basic applications all use PivotTable Services. In the chapter, you learn how to use PivotTable Services to build applications and client-side cubes. PivotTable Services have many features, such as client-side caching of data and meta data, that make analytical queries more efficient.

Microsoft SQL Server 7.0 comes with a variety of tools that you can use to optimize the data warehouse. Chapter 12 describes these tools, as well as a set of best practices for optimizing a SQL Server data warehouse.

The final chapter reviews the overall systems that you can create with a SQL Server data warehouse. It discusses the Digital Nervous System and digital dashboards, two concepts that form the basis for a knowledge management system.

Appendix A provides examples of MDX. Appendix B describes how to store information from a broad array of sources in the Microsoft repository in a standard format called OIM (Open Information Model). In Appendix C, you learn how to build the three components to wrap ADO MD. Microsoft SQL Server 7.0 English Query, a tool that allows users to query a database using the English language instead of regular SQL statements, is described in Appendix D. Finally, in Appendix E you learn about Decision Support Objects (DSO), a set of objects, interfaces, collections, and enumerations that you can use to programmatically administer SQL Server data warehouses. You can create your own custom OLAP Manager within DSO with which you can then set cell level security.

Using the Companion CD

The CD contains white papers, Service Pack 1 for SQL Server 7.0, help files, code samples, and a document containing MDX queries. The material provided on the CD is designed to help you understand the material in this book and also provide the resources you need to use Microsoft SQL Server 7.0 as a data warehouse. To use the materials contained on the CD, you need the following system requirements:

- 486 or higher processor.
- Microsoft Windows 95, Windows 98, Windows NT 4.0, or later.
- 32 MB of RAM.
- CD-ROM drive.
- Mouse or other pointing device (recommended).
- For the Visual Basic files you need Visual Basic 6 installed.
- For the .doc files you need Microsoft Word installed.
- For the Foodmart.mdb database file and the MDX files you need SQL Server 7.0 installed on Windows NT 4.0 or later.

Chapter 1
Sharing Information Across the Enterprise

Over the last 10 years, technology has evolved at an extremely fast pace. In today's shrinking global community, there is a whole range of technologies that did not exist just a few years ago, including nearly instantaneous transactions using electronic data interchange (EDI) and Internet commerce (e-commerce). The current market has forced corporations to become fluid and dynamic. To remain competitive, corporations must now be able to do the following:

- Identify all risks to the corporation
- Optimize business processes
- Maximize profit in a very competitive marketplace with educated consumers
- Identify and respond immediately to changes and opportunities in the marketplace that could affect the corporation
- Manage the risks and opportunities in a rapidly changing marketplace
- Adapt to changes in the marketplace and in technology without restructuring the entire corporation

The key to accomplishing the above tasks lies in having the correct information at the right time, using this information to make the correct decisions, and finally, implementing those decisions in a timely manner.

For corporations, the way to get, use, and implement information is through the use of a comprehensive enterprise solution that spans the entire corporation. Corporations that implement enterprise solutions are more likely to maintain a competitive advantage and profitability in the modern economy. Corporations that do not successfully implement an enterprise system may flounder in the current economy.

An enterprise solution incorporates many technologies, different types of computing and operating systems, and different types of data stores. Trying to integrate all of these into a uniform, cohesive system requires the implementation of a carefully planned set of applications and infrastructure that allow the efficient performance of the required tasks of the corporation. At the heart of such a system is the accessibility of all information stored in the various data sources. This information must be consistent, accurate, and carefully defined for it to have any value.

Microsoft SQL Server 7.0 can store, manage, and analyze databases as small as a few megabytes or as large as a few terabytes. Combined with the power of Microsoft Visual Studio and Microsoft BackOffice, you can create an enterprise solution that not only spans the enterprise but also provides the required information when and where it is needed. SQL Server 7.0, Visual Studio, and BackOffice also provide the resources to turn that information into a timely working solution.

This book shows how corporations can create analytical data stores with SQL Server that give them access to any information within the enterprise. Using Microsoft's development tools, applications can be built to access the information and present it in whatever format the user requires. Building these types of data stores is essential for the continuing profitability of corporations. This book provides you with a resource on a topic that is highly important to corporate developers.

The Heart of the Solution: Operational and Analytical Data

There are two types of data that corporations need for informed decisions and good practices: operational data and analytical data. Both of these types of data can be stored in SQL Server 7.0.

Operational Data

Operational data is constantly being changed and updated; it is dynamic. An example of this is the data for current orders in an order entry database. Operational data represents current information at one point in time. Operational data can show the status of a pending order, the current balance of a checking account, or the number of items currently out-of-stock. This type of data tells us the current state of something, and it can change at any moment.

Analytical Data

Analytical data, on the other hand, is historical data and usually remains the same over time and is static. Analytical data should only change if there is an error in the original information. At some point, a sale becomes final and cannot be reversed. At this point, the information becomes static and can be moved from the dynamic data source to the static data source. Analytical data is used to look at information over periods of time. For example, we can look at the total sales in January, the number of flags sold on July 4 in Washington, D.C., or the change in developers' salaries over the last six months.

Analytical data is usually built from operational data and can be used to perform an exhaustive analysis of how the processes of a corporation have functioned over some period of time. The data must be accurate, accessible, and presented in a usable manner. SQL Server 7.0 gives you the ability to create this type of data.

Analytical data does not necessarily have to come from within the corporation. Over the next few years, a wide range of external data marts (probably accessible through the Internet for a fee) will be available to corporations. Additional outside information can then be added to the corporation's data warehouses.

SQL Server can access data across a wide range of data sources, transform that data into a uniform format, verify the integrity of the data, and finally store the data in an online analytical processing (OLAP) server for easy access. Working with the object linking and embedding database (OLE DB) interface, which is an API that allows access to virtually any information in any data store, you can now build SQL Server data warehouses and data marts that allow access to any information required by the corporation.

History of Analytical Data: Spreadsheets to Data Warehouses

Analyzing data has been an essential business practice for corporations for many years. Today's corporations need information faster than ever before in order to compete in the modern marketplace. One thing that has changed dramatically in the past 20 years is the speed of data analysis.

Prior to the 1960s, all analysis was done using paper documents. Simple calculations, such as total sales for a month, could be a long, laborious process. Comparing sales from one region to another was extremely complicated. Many corporations realized that a uniform system must exist throughout the corporation to perform these comparisons. Without this uniform system, there was no way to determine if a store in California was selling more of a product than a store in New York.

Many companies created standard part and product numbers, uniform ways of making reports, and so forth. Once this system was in place, it was easier for people to put the information together into one large report that gave both detailed and summarized information. Using people to process this information was difficult and time consuming, but it was at least possible with a uniform system. Developing a uniform way of representing information in a corporation is still an essential part of analysis and is one of the first things that must be done before you can create an analytical database.

In the 1960s, large corporations started using very expensive computers to perform analyses. These systems were slow and a simple query could take a very long time. Storing and retrieving data was not very efficient, so even in the companies that had these computers, most information was still stored in a paper-based system.

Over the last 20 years, many efficient computer solutions were developed. These include the spreadsheet, executive information systems, and OLAP.

Spreadsheets

The spreadsheet was an excellent tool to present analytical information. The biggest problem with the spreadsheet was the difficulty in entering the information.

In many corporations, the information was entered by hand. This was not much better than the earlier paper-based solutions. The spreadsheet would do the math, but someone still had to put all the information together and place it into the spreadsheet. An improvement on this was executive information systems.

Executive Information Systems

As computers became more common in the corporation and storing data became easier and less expensive, huge amounts of information were stored in databases. Corporations wanted to analyze this data so they could assess the corporation's business process. To perform this analysis, entire applications were built to create a single report that summarized or detailed information in the database. Extremely complicated queries, usually placed in long stored procedures, would be used to generate the information for these reports. These queries ran overnight because of the time it took to perform them and the resources they consumed. Often, specialized software, called executive information systems, was developed to perform the analyses.

It took developers days or weeks to build the sophisticated queries and write the code to place the information into the spreadsheet. Dozens of applications were created to produce reports for different parts of the corporation. To support these applications, individual departments and sections created smaller databases to hold information relevant to their business processes. These smaller databases could be built from the same set of core information, but they often had completely different data formats, different names for the fields and tables, and usually contained specialized fields. Because of these differences in the smaller databases, information could not be shared between the smaller databases, even when they were built from the same larger set of data. This created what are called "islands of data."

These reports from different departments, built from different databases, often came up with different values for the same calculation. Meetings became rather interesting because each department presented its values for critical business processes and the numbers did not match. Often it was impossible to tell whose numbers were accurate and whose were not. These discrepancies usually resulted in more specialized reports and databases and even more conflicting numbers. The first step toward improving this situation was the creation of OLAP tools.

OLAP Tools: Creating Data Marts and Data Warehouses

OLAP tools perform complicated analyses of historical data using a special data structure called a multidimensional structure. These structures are stored in a special database called a data warehouse. A data warehouse, when built properly, provides consistent, historical enterprise data to the entire corporation. You can also use a data mart, which is similar to a data warehouse except that it contains data for only one group (department), or data that pertains to only one business process. We will spend a lot of time talking about these structures in Chapter 3, as we use them to build our data warehouse.

OLAP tools eliminate the need to build specialized applications for every analysis that a user might want to perform. OLAP tools also allow users to submit an analytical request such as, "How many widgets were sold in May in New York and Chicago to customers over thirty years old?" Microsoft's OLAP tool, which is called SQL Server 7.0 OLAP Services, comes with another tool, the PivotTable Services, which can place this information directly into an Excel spreadsheet. There are also many third-party tools that can be used to view data in a spreadsheet format. Thus, the OLAP Services tool gives the user a way to perform any analytical query quickly and efficiently. The PivotTable Services transform the information from OLAP Services to a format with which the user is familiar.

OLAP Services allows you to build one application to do any analytical query instead of building specific applications for every query. OLAP Services also provides a more efficient way to perform these queries than SQL Server stored procedures.

What OLAP Services does not provide for you, though, is a solution to the problem of different departments creating their own islands of data. Islands of data can only be prevented by the entire data warehousing team and all of the corporation's departments working together, communicating and striving toward a consensus on one uniform enterprise system. By using the Data Transformation Services (DTS) you can bring all of the islands of data together into one central data store in one uniform format and build a single common enterprise solution that connects the islands of data into one land mass. So, although OLAP Services does not automatically solve this problem, the team building the data warehouse and the people in the individual departments can provide a solution.

You have to work with the client and derive an enterprise solution that creates bridges between the islands of data. OLAP Services is only a tool. If users are not able or willing to create a uniform enterprise solution, OLAP Services will not magically create one. These issues are discussed in more depth later in this chapter in the DTS section.

Building a data warehouse requires looking at the big picture. On the one hand you have the corporation, which has existing attitudes and hierarchies that must be addressed. On the other hand, you have an enterprise system that includes your data warehouse. You must address both the corporate environment and the technical issues to guarantee the success of your data warehouse project. Let's look at the larger system, called a decision support system, where our data warehouse is the essential component.

Building a SQL Server 7.0 Decision Support System

When we talk about SQL Server 7.0 and building a decision support system, we are not only talking about the analytical database. The analytical database is part of a larger system. This system will include tools to store and manage multidimensional data cubes (OLAP Server and OLAP Manager); tools to present the data (PivotTable Services, Excel, Visual Basic, and so forth) and tools to transform the data if necessary (DTS, described below). This is one of the strong points of the Microsoft solution; the combination of Microsoft BackOffice, Microsoft developer's tools, third party applications for SQL Server, and SQL Server give you all the tools you need to build every element of your decision support system. Our system will look like the system in Figure 1-1.

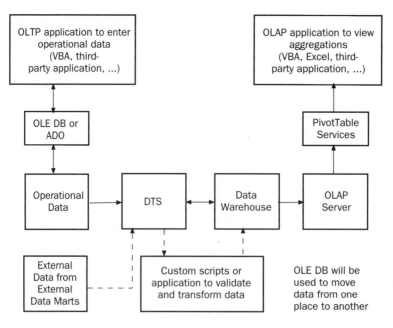

Figure 1-1. *Database and tools that comprise a robust decision support system.*

Decision Support System Goals

Decision support systems can fulfill the following goals of the corporation:

- **Depth of information** The decision support system must allow the user to view information from the highest to the lowest levels. Thus, a user of a decision support system may want to begin with viewing customers on the East Coast, then customers in New York, and then customers in New York City. Once the user reaches the New York City level, he or she can start looking at customers who are male and earning low, medium, or high salaries, and compare them to women earning the same salaries. The user can then compare the same categories in Chicago. This is what a decision support system must offer its users: information at any level that is required.

- **Comparing information** Several comparisons were mentioned in the previous paragraph, such as the comparison between the salaries of men and women in New York City. This is an essential feature of a decision support system: the ability to compare sets of information. One of the most common comparisons is some measure of the business, such as sales during one time period compared to sales during another time period. Thus, a user may want to compare sales during the month of May this year to sales for the month of May last year. Or, a user may want to compare sales prior to a large advertising campaign to sales during and after the campaign. The decision support system must allow the user to make these comparisons with ease.

- **Usable information** Being able to retrieve great quantities of information is useless if the information is not accurate or does not apply to the business problems that need to be solved. Thus, you must build your systems so that they give sufficient valid information to enable the user to make business decisions that will benefit the corporation.

- **Timely information** It does little good to have a system that takes days or weeks to move the data into the analytical data store if the information is needed in hours. Pertinent, accurate information that arrives too late is useless to the corporation. Finding out that a competitor is seizing your market and why they are seizing it, when the competitor has taken only a few percent of your market share, can help the corporation create a plan to protect against this new competition. Finding this out after a quarter of your customers has gone elsewhere, or a large, essential account has been lost, is too late for effective action.

- **Quick analysis** A user may analyze data in many ways to arrive at an analysis of a business process. Each query must be performed quickly so that the user can do dozens of these queries in a reasonable amount of time.

- **Accessible information** Information should be presented in the language of the business, not in the language of analytical systems. The interface should allow the user to perform analyses in words and language with which they are familiar.

A system built in this manner can perform detailed analyses of the sales of the corporation, the status of personnel in the corporation, and the possibility of fraud by customers. It can also identify such things as high-risk customers and buying trends on the Internet. Essentially, a decision support system that meets the above requirements can provide useful, detailed information on almost any business process of the corporation.

Planning a Decision Support System

Building such a system requires careful planning and an understanding of the different options available. A SQL Server 7.0 solution, supported by other Microsoft products, can fulfill all of the above requirements.

One of the most difficult issues you may have to tackle is integrating data from a vast number of potential sources. Some of this data may not be in a very usable format and may require intensive manipulation to be used in a data warehouse. Some of the data will come from data islands built for a specific department, for a specific function. These are all serious issues, and they must be addressed prior to building a data warehouse. Through careful assessment of the enterprise, the use of detailed planning and risk analysis, and tracking, you can identify these problems and create plans to resolve them.

Now let's take a look at the SQL Server features that will help you build your decision support system.

SQL Server 7.0 Decision Support System Tools

A SQL Server 7.0 analytical system will actually use many different components. Microsoft offers the following tools for building decision support systems: OLAP Server, PivotTable Services, OLE DB, SQL Server Data Transformation Services, SQL Server multidimensional database, numerous SQL Server wizards and designers, Office 2000, and a Microsoft Repository. Each of these tools will be discussed in this book. Let's take a quick look at some of these tools.

OLAP Services

As we mentioned above, OLAP Services allows us to perform complicated analytical queries quickly and efficiently. OLAP Services will find the most efficient way to perform the query. With OLAP Services you can often make a choice between the amount of data being stored on the physical hard drive and the speed of analysis by using something called aggregations.

An aggregation is the summing of the data. This is something we often want to do when analyzing data (such as the total sales). OLAP Services can perform the most common aggregations and store them in the database, which will save time when doing analysis of the data. Of course, the more aggregations you save in the database, the larger the database becomes. Thus, we have a trade-off between the size of the database and the time it takes to analyze a query. With OLAP Services, we can easily find the optimum setting between database size and speed of analysis.

PivotTable Services

PivotTable Services allows an application to request a set of data from an OLAP Server, and then return the data so that an application like Excel can display it to the user. PivotTable Services also allows this information to be cached on the client machine. This means that a user can connect, request information, and then view that information offline. PivotTable services can also be accessed from Visual Basic applications, so you can build your own client applications to perform analytical queries.

Object Linking and Embedding Database (OLE DB)

The object linking and embedding database (OLE DB) API is the foundation of universal access. OLE DB is an interface that can be used by database applications to access any type of data that has an OLE DB provider. With OLE DB, we can retrieve and manipulate the multidimensional structures of our data warehouse. OLE DB also allows us to view and manipulate data in other databases, such as ORACLE, data in e-mail files, text files, and so forth. ActiveX Data Objects (ADO) is a tool that allows Visual Basic programmers to access the OLE DB interface; that is, ADO is a wrapper for the OLE DB API. In our coding examples, we will use ADO often.

Data Transformation Services (DTS)

DTS allows us to import, export, and transform data from virtually any data source to any other data source. To do this, DTS will use OLE DB to make the connections to the different data sources. DTS supports many formats, including American Standard Code for Information Interchange (ASCII). DTS transformations can be built using the DTS wizards, or you can code your transformations using scripting languages such as VBScript or JavaScript. You can also write Visual Basic applications that will perform DTS transformations.

SQL Server 7.0 Multidimensional Database

SQL Server 7.0 allows you to either use its relational database to store data for analysis, or to store the information in a special structure called a cube in a SQL Server multidimensional database. As discussed in Chapter 3, the multidimensional database is specifically designed to increase the efficiency of your analytical queries. The differences between the multidimensional database and the relational database are discussed in Chapter 4.

Wizards and Designers

There are numerous design tools included with SQL Server 7.0. These tools allow you to back up the database easily, create aggregations, view the structure of your data warehouse, and create and design cubes. Nearly everything you need to do can be done with easy-to-use graphical user interfaces (GUIs).

Office 2000

With office products such as Excel, you can view cube data in a spreadsheet. You can also write Visual Basic for Applications (VBA) code and create Excel modules to retrieve and manipulate data. This allows you to build customizable front ends for your data warehouse.

Microsoft Repository

The Microsoft Repository provides you with a place to store the structure of your data warehouse in a standard format. Unified Modeling Language (UML) tools, other databases, or any add-on that reads the repository, can read this standard format. Essentially, the repository allows sharing of information, including the structure of your data warehouse.

Conclusion

Combined with other Microsoft products, SQL Server 7.0 provides a powerful set of tools that allows you to build a complete decision support system. This decision support system provides users with the correct information they need, when they need it, and in a format that is easy for them to access. With proper planning, design, and an enterprise view of the project, the SQL Server data warehouse can help drive a corporation's decisions about how to refine and optimize business processes.

Chapter 2
Planning and Designing Enterprise Analytical Systems

Careful planning and management are required to design and properly build an analytical system that includes a Microsoft SQL Server 7.0 data warehouse. Creating an analytical system includes the following steps:

- Designing the structure of the data in the data warehouse
- Designing client applications to view the data in the data warehouse
- Designing the data transformations to move the data from historical or online transaction processing (OLTP) databases into the data warehouse
- Populating the data warehouse
- Deploying the applications and moving data

Usually, the data warehouse is also part of a larger enterprise project that includes building or upgrading an OLTP system, and a front end application to view analytical information. Without a well-defined framework to plan, design, and build your data warehouse, your project will probably fail. A framework is something that provides you with a structure from which to build your solution. A proper framework for building your data warehouse should have three basic characteristics:

- A viewpoint that allows you to make technical decisions for your project
- A measurable reference point that allows you to determine if the project is on time
- The ability to reuse existing knowledge in a flexible manner

The framework that has these three properties is the Microsoft Solutions Framework (MSF). A project that is built using MSF has the additional features listed on the following page.

- The system can be broken down into small projects. These projects can run one after another or concurrently. Thus the system can be implemented over a long period of time but still attain short-term results.

- The system can be built from components, which can be built one after another or concurrently.

- The system is built in cycles. Each cycle completes another part of the system.

- Each project is built by small teams that work together.

MSF breaks the project into four phases: envisioning, planning, developing, and stabilizing. The four phases look like those in Figure 2-1.

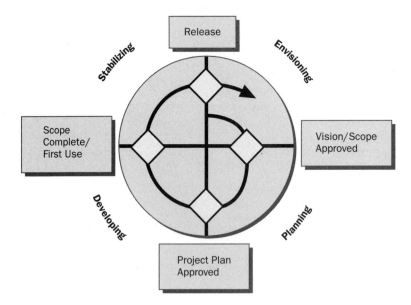

Figure 2-1. *Envisioning, planning, developing, and stabilizing.*

Notice that this process is a spiral and not a circle. This is because an enterprise system is not usually completed in one cycle. Instead, the enterprise system is built over many cycles, with each cycle adding additional functionality.

For example, the solution may involve building a new e-commerce site. The first cycle includes building the Web site with basic order capability. The second cycle includes building a data warehouse to store information on the system's users, such as how they navigate through the Web pages. As the second cycle is occurring, the third cycle, which builds applications to analyze and view the information in the data warehouse, also occurs. The fourth cycle adds additional functionality based on the analysis of the data in the data warehouse. The e-commerce site is built in iterative steps, each step adding more functionality to the overall system.

Once the site is complete, the cycles do not necessarily end. Technology, the marketplace, and the corporation all change over time. These changes may require the addition of new features to the site, so new cycles begin again. In this way, the cycles never end; the system is always evolving and changing to meet current business requirements. Thus, you end up with a never-ending circle of planning, building, managing, planning, and so forth.

Milestones

The completion of each of the four phases is a well-defined, measurable point in the project. Well-defined, measurable points are called milestones. Milestones usually have deliverables and can be used to determine whether a project is on schedule. A milestone is either completed or not completed. Thus, a milestone can be the movement of all data in the data warehouse. You can set a date for this to occur, say May 5. On May 5, the data is either in the data warehouse or it is not. If it is in the data warehouse, you are on schedule; if it is not, you are behind schedule. Meeting milestones ensures meeting your overall schedule.

Once the milestone for a phase has been reached, you can move to the next phase. The only requirement for moving into a new phase is that the previous phase's milestones be completed. The four milestones for each of the four phases are: vision/scope approved, project plan approved, scope complete/first use, and release. All of your milestones should be based on binaries, that is, they are either true or they are false.

In MSF, all team members share responsibility for the project. Every team member is directly responsible for the project's success. MSF allows developers to design a set of components for the project that fulfills the goals of end users and management. MSF requires developers to be creative and use all of their skills to come up with the best possible design for the components within the scope of the project. Designing components or systems based on the needs of the end user and client management is the first goal of the developer.

One of the important advantages of using MSF is that it works both for building software and for implementing infrastructure. Because your analytical system includes the creation of client software, data transformation software, and the building of the data warehouse infrastructure, MSF is ideal for your projects.

General Overview of the Cycles

Envisioning Phase

During the envisioning phase, the system is defined and a vision/scope statement is created. A vision statement defines the goals of the system and provides a direction for the solution. A scope statement defines the limits of the current project. Thus, the vision may be to build a complete e-commerce site that requires many cycles to build the different parts of the system. After the first few cycles create the basic Web site, the scope of the next project may be to build the data warehouse component of the e-commerce site. Future projects might fulfill other parts of the vision statement.

If the project is built with components, additional features can be added at a later time. Vision/scope statements make sure the right problem is solved, which allows you to properly plan the rest of the project. The envisioning phase is complete when both vision and scope are defined and approved.

Planning Phase

The planning phase consists of creating a set of documents that define user requirements, determining the components and services that are required to meet the requirements, and documenting a detailed design of these components. In the case of a data warehousing project, these components could be a Visual Basic project to transform and move the data, an Excel project to view the data, creating the structure of the tables in the data warehouse, and so forth. This phase is complete when these documents are complete. The planning phase ensures that you have properly defined the solution.

Developing Phase

The developing phase consists of building and testing components, and then assembling them into a final, complete system. In the case of a data warehouse, this phase could include building the data warehouse and the client applications. The phase is finished when all new development is complete. This phase gives you the opportunity to implement the best possible solution. After the developing phase is complete, any additions to the project begin a new cycle. It is likely that there will be future additions, since the vision statement extends beyond this cycle. Thus, many cycles result as the project evolves.

Stabilizing Phase

The stabilizing phase focuses on testing the final, completed project and finding and fixing any bugs and deploying components. It also includes moving the data into the data warehouse. This phase is finished when the project is completely tested and released to the operations and support groups.

Goals and Deliverables

Each phase has a set of goals. Each goal should have:

- A purpose
- A set of actions that must be performed to achieve the goal
- A set of deliverables when the goal is complete

Deliverables are the parts of the project that are complete; they can consist of UML diagrams, database schemas, code modules, and so forth, which can be viewed by all members of the team for review and approval.

The Three Groups

There are three basic groups involved in most projects: management, end users, and developers. The project goals for each group are different. Client management goals focus on how the project will improve the corporate mission and profits. Management wants evidence that the project will give a return on investment. End users are interested in final deliverables, such as the software they use to do their jobs, and how they use this software to make their jobs easier. End users are also interested in how this project helps them do their day-to-day tasks. Developers are interested in how to build the project. In a data warehouse project, it is likely that the end users are also the client management.

In the envisioning and planning phases, all three groups—management, end users, and developers—contribute to defining the goals of the project, but each group defines its goals at different points.

During the envisioning phase, the general goal and its purpose is documented, as well as a description of the final deliverables. A detailed description of the set of actions that must be performed to achieve the general goal is documented in the planning phase.

Management

Management's goals focus on the project's impact on business processes, especially on making these processes as efficient as possible. Management's goals also focus on the general goal of the project, the purpose of the project, and the final deliverables of the project. These goals need to be defined and documented in the envisioning phase, therefore it is management's goals that are explored most thoroughly during the first part of the process. End users make contributions to the second half of the envisioning phase by expanding management's goals. End users focus on how the final system will make their jobs more efficient. Developers also make a contribution by setting goals on the general architecture of the system, what platform it should run under, and so forth. In the envisioning phase, management details their vision/scope for the project, and end users and developers add to that vision/scope.

End Users

End users work primarily with the external part of the system, so their goals provide a detailed view of the services provided by this part of the system, usually the user interface. Once the vision/scope and the external part of the system are defined, developers step in and define the details of the internal part of the system.

Developers

Like end users, developers contribute their overall goals to the envisioning phase, such as building the client application of the data warehouse using Excel. Developers' goals complete the documentation of the components and the services the components must perform to accomplish the goals of end users and management.

Once management's, end users', and developers' goals have been defined, developers create a detailed description of the steps required to fulfill these goals. Next, a set of components and services that can fulfill the goals of management, end users, and developers are defined.

In the developing phase, developers build the components defined at the end of the planning phase. The final phase, stabilizing, ensures that the goals of all three groups are actually met. Let's take a closer look at the roles that managers, developers, and end users have when creating a software project.

Your cycle now looks like the one in Figure 2-2.

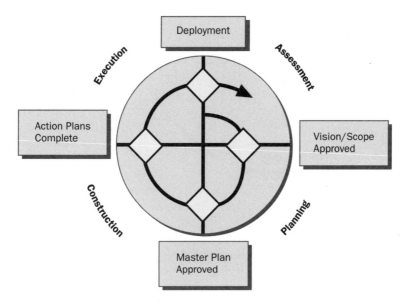

Figure 2-2. *The planning cycle.*

MSF Team Roles

There are six different roles in the software developing team. The first four roles—development, testing, logistics, and user education—will most likely be filled by people in the developers' group. The last two roles—product and program management—will most likely be filled by people in the management group.

The six roles appear in Figure 2-3.

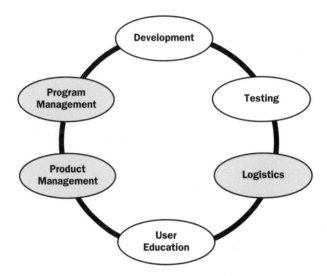

Figure 2-3. *The six roles in the software developing team: development, testing, logistics, user education, product management, and program management.*

Development   Team members in the development role are responsible for building the components defined in the planning phase, as well for assisting in the creation of test applications during this phase. Members in this role also make sure that components are built according to users' requirements, make recommendations for technical solutions, review testing plans, keep the project on schedule, repair bugs in the components, and integrate the components into a working whole.

Testing   Team members in the testing role make sure that all components function appropriately and that there are no bugs in the code. Other responsibilities include making a test plan that will test each component separately and within the entire system, building test cases, developing automated tests, documenting all bugs, and helping to build a high-quality product.

Logistics   Team members in the logistics role are responsible for integrating the finished product into the enterprise solution and moving the project into the support and operations groups.

User education   User education team members make sure that users understand how to use the application, provide user training, and work toward making the application easier to understand and use. These team members are responsible for creating user interface prototypes, setup programs, help files, training aids, and all user documentation.

Product management   Product management team members create a vision for the project, turn users' requirements into a coherent set of scenarios or Unified Modeling Language (UML) use cases, and make sure that the client's requirements are being met. Use cases are documents that explain how a particular group of users, called *actors,* use the system to perform a particular task. Other responsibilities include making business projections, estimating the cost of the project, and defining key business goals and requirements.

Program management   Team members in this role are responsible for creating the right project at the right time, ensuring that the project maintains enterprise standards, managing the master schedule, and managing and documenting project changes. They also work with other team leaders to create the logical and physical views.

In addition to the team members listed above, the following are also members of the software project team:

End users   These are the people who use the project's application on a day-to-day basis.

Sponsors   These are the people who fund the project. Ideally, this should be one person, but it can include several people.

Stakeholders   These are the managers in charge of the end users.

Failure to view end users, sponsors, and stakeholders as members of your team will almost guarantee the failure of your project. Members of all three groups need to be involved in the project from beginning to end.

The involvement of each group will vary throughout the four phases of the project. The level of involvement of each group during the four phases is summarized in Table 2-1.

Table 2-1. Group Level Involvement

Role	Envisioning	Planning	Developing	Stabilizing
Development	low	moderate	very high	high
Testing	low	moderate	very high	high
Logistics	low	low	high	very high
User Education	low	low	high	very high
Product Management	very high	very high	high	high
Program Management	moderate	moderate	moderate	moderate
End Users	high	very high	high	moderate
Sponsor	low	low	low	low
Stakeholders	moderate	moderate	low	low

If there are only a few developers for a project, it is possible that one member can play more than one role. Some roles, however, conflict with each other.

By using MSF to build your project, the project can be broken up into smaller components, which can then each be built by a small team. During the developing phase, several small teams, each consisting of a program manager, developers, testers, and a person from the user education team, can be used to build these components simultaneously or sequentially. Developers, testers, and user education team members should share information with their counterparts on other teams to create a uniform set of components. The ratio of testers to developers on a given team can range from a 1:1 ratio up to a 1:3 ratio, depending on the project. Testers should join the project from the beginning, if possible. The product manager manages the teams. The product manager also puts together the vision/scope statement, based on the consensus meeting and the documents for the conceptual and logical design views, based on documents created by the smaller teams.

Small developing teams allow better communication between team members, lower management costs, faster implementation of the various components, and a higher-quality product. Creating the physical design for these components and building them is the responsibility of the small component groups. Each component group must build their component so that it exposes the methods and properties specified in the logical view. The internal workings of the components should be based on enterprise-wide standards of coding and design.

Component teams should be comprised of peers. Every member should be equally responsible for the quality of the component, meeting schedules, understanding the client's needs, and contributing to the design and creation of the component. The entire team should focus on fulfilling users' requirements, identifying risks, keeping the project within budget and time constraints, and making the best component possible. Each team member has a well-defined role and submits a schedule for his or her component, which becomes part of the master schedule.

In addition to the standard members of an MSF team, a data warehousing project has some additional special members. These include:

Analytical database specialist   This is a person who specializes in data warehouses. This person has an in-depth understanding of SQL Server 7.0 OLAP Server, PivotTable Services, and Multidimensional Extensions (MDX). This role requires a person who is knowledgeable in developing and in infrastructure. It is possible that two people, one who is an expert in infrastructure and one who is an expert in developing, can fill this role. However, the distinction between infrastructure and developing blurs as developers now create code to perform database transformations and to build analytical structures that once belonged to the realm of infrastructure.

Database administrator   This is a person who can assist with general SQL Server 7.0 skills. There may also be a need for database administrators for other databases if data is being brought in from databases other than SQL Server 7.0.

Database modeler   This is someone who is familiar with database modeling tools and can model the database structure. The database modeler should be familiar with the multidimensional database structures discussed in the next chapter.

Four Phases in Building an Analytical System

Envisioning Phase

Perhaps the most important factor in the success of a project is having the correct vision/scope. Without knowing what the project is supposed to be doing and why, it is impossible to design or build the project. Although this may seem obvious, projects often begin without any clear definition of what they are supposed to be doing, and end up moving haphazardly until either a clear definition is created or the project fails.

To identify the vision/scope, complete the following steps:

- Identify and meet with the project's sponsors
- Hold a consensus meeting
- Identify the project's goals
- Make an assessment of the technological resources
- Determine the deliverables of the project

Initial Consensus Meeting

At the first part of this phase, someone from the developing team, most likely the product manager or program manager, has an initial consensus meeting with the sponsors and stakeholders. A consensus meeting is a meeting where everyone works together to establish a set of mutually agreeable goals. Consensus meetings are not described within MSF, but they fit with the general principles of MSF.

Sponsors, who are the people who provide funding for the project, must be involved from the beginning. If the sponsor is unwilling to get involved or is not interested in the project, it is highly unlikely that the project will succeed.

The primary goal of the project's sponsors and stakeholders is to form the vision for the project. This primary goal is broken down into a more detailed set of goals during the initial consensus meeting. The goals to be accomplished within the current cycle will form the scope of the project. The goals defined by management are based on business processes and objectives of the corporation. Attached to each goal should be the reason the goal is important, a method to measure completion, the business processes affected by the goal, and the names of members of the corporation who benefit if the goal is accomplished.

The goals for a data warehouse revolve around performing analysis of data. Any analysis of data has essential measure items called Key Performance Indicators (KPIs). KPIs indicate how well business processes are functioning, as well as show how business processes may be optimized. KPIs can include such items as total sales, total number of an item sold, total number of visits to a particular Web page, and so forth. Users want to use some type of duration or distance information to measure KPIs. For example, a user may want to measure total sales over some time period and over some geographical region. The term "informational object" refers to the duration or distance of objects that you use to measure KPIs.

The primary goal for an analytical application might be:

- Create an analytical database, an application to populate the database, and client applications to analyze the data.

This statement forms the vision for the project. This goal is then divided into a more detailed set of goals by senior management. Some more detailed goals might be:

- The client application should be able to analyze data over geographical regions, customers, and products over different periods of time.
- The database should respond quickly to a request for information.
- The data warehouse should hold two years' worth of data.

A goal should cite the importance of the goal, the business process it affects, and the users who will benefit. You should also have a way of determining if and when the goal succeeds. Here's an example:

The client application should be able to analyze data over geographical regions, customers, and products over different periods of time. This goal will improve the business processes of analyzing sales data, determining future sales, determining customer buying patterns, and matching customer types to product groups. This goal benefits senior management, the different product groups, and advertising. This goal has succeeded if, within six months of project completion, the information can be quickly and easily retrieved from the database and reports can be printed out on the data.

Not every goal can be accomplished right away. Some goals will fall into the scope of the current project, while others will fall within the scope of later cycles. These goals may represent ways of improving business processes, creating new business processes, or filling in areas of the corporate workflow that are currently lacking a needed business process.

Second Consensus Meeting

A second consensus meeting, in which all members of the team are brought together to discuss the project, should be conducted after the initial consensus meeting. This second meeting takes the goals defined in the initial consensus meeting and defines them further.

For example, the goal "The client application should be able to analyze data over geographical regions, customers, and products over different periods of time," can be broken down into many smaller goals, such as:

- The client application will analyze geographical region over countries, states, and cities.
- The client application will analyze time over years, months, days, and quarters.
- The client application will analyze customers by the type of customer.

These goals develop as an expansion of the general goals that were defined in the initial consensus meeting. The product manager should be the facilitator of the second meeting. Ideally, the meeting should take place in a large room. The walls could be covered with large sheets of paper. Begin the meeting with a discussion of the business processes that will be affected by the project. Both good and bad aspects of these business processes should be discussed and listed on the paper sheets.

To help develop these goals, you can look at existing applications, current methods of accomplishing the goal, or review current business processes. If no current system exists, you must work with the end user to determine the steps needed to accomplish their goals. One way to make this easier is to draw a table. Put one of the KPIs into a column. Then ask the end users over what informational objects they want to measure the KPIs at one time. They can include as many KPIs in the rows as they want. Therefore, you could end up with Table 2-2.

Table 2-2. KPIs Table

	Sales
Region, Time, Customer Income, Salesperson	
Geography, Time, Customer Income	

This table indicates that this user wants to see the sales for a region during a period of time, by customer income, and by salesperson. This user also wants to see the sales for a region during a period of time, by customer income. By completing this exercise, we can determine over what informational objects we are going to measure the KPI.

Another technique is to try to ask the questions that the user wants answered. In the above case, you could have asked: "How many items were sold for a region during a period of time, by customer income, and by salesperson?" In this question, you have expanded on the meaning of sales. Sales can be number of units sold, sales revenue, net profit in sales, gross profit in sales, and so forth. It is important to look at the KPIs and determine if they can be expanded or if they can be represented differently.

The goals from the first consensus meeting could also be listed on some of the sheets of paper. Using information from the current state of the business processes, meeting attendees can brainstorm ideas for each general goal defined in the first business meeting. At the end of the meeting, the most important goals that fit within the constraints of the project should be recorded as part of the vision/scope document.

The second consensus meeting should involve the entire team, including end users. If possible, the consensus sponsors and the stakeholders should also attend. When building an analytical solution, it is likely that sponsors and stakeholders will also be users of the application. You may find, though, that many corporations are realizing the importance of making information available to the entire corporation. In this case, end users may be lower level management and nonmanagement personnel. If the users are only higher level management, you can hold one meeting that runs over one or two days. If the users include members of the corporation who are not senior management, there can be two separate meetings, the first with senior management and the second with everyone else.

If it is a large corporation, and there are too many end users to be included in the meeting, then the results of the consensus meeting should be posted on an intranet, if possible. Everyone who might use the project can then review its goals and make suggestions.

A final meeting should be held once the vision/scope document is complete to make sure all team members agree with the contents of the document. If all members of the team agree with the vision/scope document at the second meeting, this phase is finished.

Prioritizing Goals

You will need some way to evaluate which goals are of the highest priority. If you are comparing only two goals, it is fairly easy to decide which goal is more important. Trying to compare dozens of goals can be very difficult. The easiest way to prioritize a large number of goals is to perform comparisons of two goals at a time. This can be accomplished by building a table whose columns and rows contain the goals. For example, if you have five goals, the table will look like Table 2-3.

Table 2-3. Prioritizing Five Goals

	Goal 1	Goal 2	Goal 3	Goal 4	Goal 5
Goal 1	—				
Goal 2		—			
Goal 3			—		
Goal 4				—	
Goal 5					—

Cells containing the symbol "—" should be ignored. Start with the first column and move down; then compare the goal in the column with the goals in the row, as shown in Table 2-4.

Table 2-4. Comparing Goals

	Goal 1	Goal 2	Goal 3	Goal 4	Goal 5
Goal 1	—				
Goal 2	Goal 1 vs. Goal 2	—			
Goal 3	Goal 1 vs. Goal 3		—		
Goal 4	Goal 1 vs. Goal 4			—	
Goal 5	Goal 1 vs. Goal 5				—

In this case the first column is associated with Goal 1, which you compare with Goals 2 through 5 as you move through the rows. As you move down the column, you rank Goal 1 against Goals 2 through 5 as indicated in the above table. If Goal 1 has a higher priority than one of the other goals, place an X in the cell. If it has a lower priority, do not place a mark in the cell. For example, if Goal 1 is a higher priority than Goals 3 and 4, but Goals 2 and 5 are a higher priority than Goal 1, you get Table 2-5.

Table 2-5. Comparing Goals with Different Priorities

	Goal 1	Goal 2	Goal 3	Goal 4	Goal 5
Goal 1	—				
Goal 2		—			
Goal 3	X		—		
Goal 4	X			—	
Goal 5					—

You have now compared the rating of Goal 1 to all of the other goals, which means that you now also have the ranking of Goal 2 versus Goal 1, Goal 3 versus Goal 1, Goal 4 versus Goal 1, and Goal 5 versus Goal 1. Looking at your table, you see the rankings in Table 2-6 across the first row.

Table 2-6. Ranked Goals

	Goal 1	Goal 2	Goal 3	Goal 4	Goal 5
Goal 1	—	Goal 2 vs. Goal 1	Goal 3 vs. Goal 1	Goal 4 vs. Goal 1	Goal 5 vs. Goal 1
Goal 2		—			
Goal 3	X		—		
Goal 4	X			—	
Goal 5					—

So, you can now add the rankings shown in Table 2-7 to the table.

Table 2-7. Two-Goal Comparison

	Goal 1	Goal 2	Goal 3	Goal 4	Goal 5
Goal 1	—	X			X
Goal 2		—			
Goal 3	X		—		
Goal 4	X			—	
Goal 5					—

When you complete the rankings for the second column, Goal 2, you will be able to fill in the second column. This process of filling in the table by comparing two goals at a time is called a *two-goal comparison*. Now, imagine that you do a two-goal comparison for every goal and get a vote from each person on your team to determine which goal is more important. Moving through the columns, you could end up with Table 2-8.

Table 2-8. Reaching Consensus

	Goal 1	Goal 2	Goal 3	Goal 4	Goal 5
Goal 1	—	X			X
Goal 2		—			
Goal 3	X	X	—	X	X
Goal 4	X	X		—	X
Goal 5		X			—

Looking at this table, you can quickly see that Goal 2 is of the highest priority, closely followed by Goal 5. These two goals are the high-priority goals. Goal 1 is a medium-priority goal. Goal 4 is a low-priority goal. Goal 3 is clearly a low-priority goal. Using this method, you can prioritize your goals in a consensus meeting.

Project Costs

Corporations are becoming more cautious about how they spend their money, so it may be necessary to do return of investment (ROI) and total cost of operation (TCO) estimates for the sponsor. It is often very difficult to give accurate estimates of either of these for an analytical system. An accurate estimate for the cost of the software licenses, maintenance, and hardware can be given at the end of the first part of the planning phase, which in turn will provide most of the information on TCO.

The ROI compares the cost of the investment to the additional profit generated by the investment. If the total cost of the investment is less than the additional profit, it is a good investment.

Unfortunately, one of the largest parts of the investment, the cost of development for the entire project, usually cannot be estimated accurately until the end of the planning phase, when all of the details of the project have been determined.

Tip A detailed schedule and cost analysis for any of the four phases of the project can only be done while in the preceding phase. Thus, one can give a detailed cost and time analysis of the planning phase while in the envisioning phase.

Vision/Scope Document

The primary deliverable is the vision/scope document. The vision/scope document should contain the following sections:

- **The vision statement of the project** The vision should be stated in terms of goals of the project.
- **The scope statement of the project** This statement should cite the goals that will be accomplished by this project in this cycle. This statement should

define what will be done in this project and what will be delivered at the end of this project.

- **Assessment of resources**   It is important to determine if there are financial, technological, and personnel resources for the project. A detailed document describing the current state of technology in the corporation, the attitude toward technology in the corporation, and the availability of resources should be created.

- **Team responsibilities**   A list of responsibilities of all team members (including when tasks need to be completed and consequences if tasks are not completed on time) should be created during this phase.

- **Risk assessment**   A complete list of all risks to the completion of this phase should be carefully documented. A complete list of risks to the project should be created. These risks should be tracked throughout the project.

The vision/scope document represents a view of the goals of the project while the system is being developed and shows how these goals will be reached. This document must be accepted and signed off on by the entire team.

Planning Phase

The planning phase translates the general goals described in the vision/scope document into the language of a software/infrastructure project design. All of the components of the system have to be designed and built within the constraints of your project. When designing software for the project, you must be able to create reusable components, build one or more parts of the system at one time, build another part later if necessary, and create a system that is able to be upgraded so that it can include future changes that you cannot now predict.

The client portion of the enterprise solution is built from components. If at some later time a component of the system needs to be upgraded, the component can be redesigned and replaced without redesigning and rebuilding the entire application. If a new component needs to be added, it needs to be added to the project design, built, and added to the project without affecting the existing components.

Parts of the system that are critical for the corporation are built first. Less critical components are added to the system later. As new business requirements are developed, new components are designed and added to the system. This type of enterprise solution can adapt to any changes in the marketplace or technology.

Three Subphases of the Planning Phase

Your planning phase will be broken into three smaller phases. These phases are: conceptual, logical, and physical. During the conceptual phase, the needs of users are defined. In the logical phase, users' needs are transformed into a set of objects that perform services that the project must perform to meet users' requirements. These objects make up the client application. The detailed design of the objects occurs in the physical phase.

Based on the needs of the user and the information required from the database, you will create a schema for your data warehouse in the physical phase. Thus, a data warehouse is not built in isolation from the applications that will use it, but as an integral part of these applications. Because these applications are based on the needs of the user, so is your data warehouse.

The planning phase begins by taking users' goals and converting them into the language of developers and data warehouse administrators (conceptual phase). This is followed by the creation of a set of objects that fulfills users' goals (logical phase). The phase is finished when the developer and data warehouse administrator turn user and management goals into a detailed set of system designs (physical phase).

Projects using these three phases first identify what users want the project to do, then determine what services the project must provide to fulfill user requirements, and finally create a detailed design of components that will perform these services based on available technology. This type of design results in a user-focused project and data warehouse that take advantage of all available technology and are built from components. The most critical components can be built first, and more than one component can be built at any given time (as each component is a separate entity). This also creates a design that takes into consideration the needs of users, the needs of developers, and the possibilities and limitations of the technology.

Iterative Design of the Three Subphases

The three stages of the planning phase create the project design using an iterative process. Each iteration will refine the project's design. Initially, in the conceptual phase, developers meet with users and get a detailed description of the project. Developers then describe the series of steps required to fulfill one of the end user's goals using scenarios. These scenarios can be expanded into UML use cases and user interface prototypes. For the goal, "Analyze sales by region, by customer, over time," one scenario might include the following steps:

- Request first-quarter sales for the United States for customers earning annually over $100,000
- Request first-quarter sales for the United States for customers earning annually between $50,000 and $100,000

- Request first-quarter sales for the United States for customers earning annually between $25,000 and $50,000
- Request first-quarter sales for the United States for customers earning annually less than $25,000

This is a series of steps the user is going to take to achieve the goal. These scenarios define what type of information the user wants to view. You could write three nearly identical scenarios for the second, third, and fourth quarters. You should make your scenarios general enough to identify all of the possible scenarios with just one scenario. Thus, you could rewrite a scenario as follows:

- Request quarter sales for the United States for customers earning annually over $100,000
- Request quarter sales for the United States for customers earning annually between $50,000 and $100,000
- Request quarter sales for the United States for customers earning annually between $25,000 and $50,000
- Request quarter sales for the United States for customers earning annually less than $25,000

You will also have nearly identical scenarios for the different regions, such as the United States, Canada, Europe, New York, Hoboken, and so forth. You may also want to generalize your time measurement even more, since you may want to take measurements over days, months, or years. Thus, you can further generalize your scenarios as follows:

- Request sales for a particular time period for a region for customers earning annually over $100,000
- Request sales for a particular time period for a region for customers earning annually between $50,000 and $100,000
- Request sales for a particular time period for a region for customers earning annually between $25,000 and $50,000
- Request sales for a particular time period for a region for customers earning annually less than $25,000

You need to include a definition of both region and time period. These are usually done using business rules. In your case, a region is a country, state, or city. A time period can be a day, month, year, or quarter.

Looking at your scenarios, you can quickly identify your information objects (a time period and a region) and your KPIs. You can also see that you want to divide your customers into four groups based on income. As shown in the next chapter, this is the information that is essential for designing and building your data warehouse. Thus, you should try to create your scenarios so that they include informational objects and facts. The final scenario was arrived at through several iterations.

The scenarios are reviewed by users, who then add or subtract information from them. It may take several reviews by users before the scenarios fulfill their requirements. Once again, if possible, place the scenarios on an intranet site so everyone can review them.

Once the scenarios reach a point where they seem to meet all of the users' requirements, the design of the project can move on to the logical phase. It is possible that during the logical phase a user requirement will be discovered that was overlooked in the conceptual phase. These missed requirements must be added to the scenarios, refining them even more.

There is a set of users who want to accomplish each goal defined by a scenario. These users can be grouped together into roles. Since you listed the users that want to accomplish each goal in the envisioning phase, it is not too difficult to identify the roles associated with the project.

Roles are very important. Using roles, you can find groups of users that will use the same information, but often for different purposes. For example, you may have a marketing manager and a sales manager. After a major sale they may both review the data. The marketing manager looks at the data to design the next sale. The sales manager looks at the data to determine the profit made during the sale. Knowing that these two different groups will use the same information can prevent you from duplicating data unnecessarily.

The logical phase consists of mapping out all of the services. One common way of doing this is to use UML sequence diagrams. These sequence diagrams identify the project's components and the services these components must perform. Each sequence diagram maps out the steps required to accomplish a system user's goal. These goals connect to one or more business needs. The sequence diagrams can then be refined by adding services that are not visible to users, such as retrieving data from a client object, a client object retrieving data from a middle tier component, and a middle tier component retrieving information from a database. Thus, the design documents created in the logical phase are also refined by many iterations. The sequence diagrams identify the information the data warehouse needs to return to the user.

When components of the system are identified and the communication between the components and the users are mapped, the physical phase begins. A thorough review of the current technology is conducted. The technology solutions that create components that perform services efficiently are chosen. Often, several small test applications are created to find the best technology for a particular project. Test applications can also determine the most efficient way to use the best technology. An initial concept of the final design is created and numerous tests refine and define the physical design. It is likely that some services will be missed and will have to be added to the sequence diagrams created in the logical phase while in the physical phase.

Deliverables and Milestones of the Three Subphases of the Planning Phase

The completion of each of these three subphases represents a measurable, definable point in the project. In this way, the planning phase can be divided into smaller parts, each with a milestone at the end.

The deliverables for the conceptual subphase include a set of documents describing the users' goals for the project, which can be the scenarios. The scenarios can be expanded out into UML use cases.

The deliverables for the physical subphase include a set of documents that identify the components and the services the components need to perform to fulfill users' goals for the project. Since it is the goal of the developer to actually build the components, and it is also the developer who fills in the details of these diagrams, these diagrams represent the developer's goals. The most common way to document these goals is with UML sequence diagrams.

Sequence diagrams show the requests for services between the users and the system, and between one component in the system and another component in the system over time. Sequence diagrams convert the written use case, or scenario, into a visual diagram.

In addition to these documents, the following deliverables may also be part of the logical subphase:

- A user interface prototype
- An evaluation of the user interface prototype
- A user interface specification
- Small test applications to test new technology and new solutions
- An evaluation of the test applications

The deliverables of the physical subphase for the client applications is a set of documents showing how the components of the client applications are coded, built, and distributed. These components should fulfill the goals of all members of the project. The usual method of documenting this is using UML class and activity diagrams.

Activity diagrams can be used to map out the code steps that a component must take to fulfill a request to perform a service. The steps are written in pseudocode. Class diagrams are a set of diagrams that provide a pictorial description of a set of objects with the same attributes, operations, and relationships.

In addition, another possible deliverable for the physical phase is a document analyzing which components should be built and which should come from a third party.

For the data warehouse, the physical phase involves the design of the schema based on the KPIs and informational objects. Also, all of the data transformations are designed at this point.

Each of the three subphases has the following deliverables:

- A set of risk documents
- A detailed schedule for the current phase and the upcoming phase
- A document showing the distribution of resources and the current responsibilities of each of the team members.

Summary of the Planning Phase

From this discussion, you can see that project design must have the following characteristics:

- **An integrated design** The design must reflect the needs of users, fulfill essential business requirements of the corporation, and put reasonable demands on developers. The design must also fit into the existing enterprise solution, as well as help create the future enterprise solution.
- **Iterative design** The design of the project is done in steps, where each step further refines the project.
- **Schedules based on deliverables and milestones** Schedules are based on delivering parts of the projects at a milestone. If the deliverable is ready at the milestone, then the project is on schedule. Likewise, if the deliverable is not ready, the project is not on schedule. The project is therefore broken into small deliverables so it can be monitored throughout its cycles.

- **Communication**   Good communication is the most essential ingredient for success of the project. Communication has to flow between managers, developers, and users. A set of documents that includes design specifications and UML documents can form the basis of good communication. Communication also includes learning certain skills. For a developer, some important communication skills include interviewing users, explaining the scenarios or use cases to the users, and getting management involved in the project.

Developing Phase

At the end of the planning phase, all features planned for this cycle have been developed. A complete set of tests may not have been done in the developing phase, but the product will be stable enough to allow users their first opportunity to use and evaluate the product as a beta version. The infrastructure should also be completely in place at the end of this cycle. There will be a set of internal releases during which all bugs can be found and removed.

The developing phase consists of building the client application based on the design made in the planning phase. Components are built simultaneously or sequentially. After each component is complete, it is tested by itself, and then within part or all of the system. The testing is based on a careful plan made by the testers. Before the components can be built, the design of the system, the schema for the database, and the design of the user interfaces must be frozen. This prevents feature creep, and also prevents rebuilding entire components. Changes that are made once the coding has started are more expensive than those made before any components are actually built. It is fairly easy to change a design document. The further along you are in coding a component, the more expensive any changes become. It is essential that all team members agree on the design before coding begins.

The database is built during this phase. Some data may be placed in the data warehouse so tests can be performed.

Milestones for the Developing Phase

- The design of the user interfaces is frozen. This allows product management and user education to start producing documentation.
- The design of the database is frozen so development of components can begin without making changes due to schema changes.
- Testing of individual components.
- Testing of systems.

- Internal releases.
- Freezing of the specifications and design of the project.
- All features are complete.
- Risk management documents are updated.

Summary of the Developing Phase

The developing phase is where the project is actually coded and built. This is where developers get to be creative and, working with the design documents that reflect the goals of the entire team, find the most effective and efficient way of building the project within the limitations of the current technology. The final outcome of this phase is a project that reflects the best solution to improve the business process.

Stabilizing Phase

The stabilizing phase is where the final testing takes place. Developers fix any problems with the project as they are discovered. Thus, the primary focus of this phase is finding and fixing bugs. Debuggers, and possibly end users, will test the project, and developers will fix any problems found. All of the data will be moved into the data warehouse. When the project is complete, stable, and there are no longer any problems with it, the project is turned over to end users and to operations and support groups. The finished project is the final deliverable for this phase.

Deliverables for the Stabilizing Phase

There are several deliverables that occur in this phase. A few of them (not listed in the order they are completed) are as follows:

- Compiled versions of the code
- Final release notes
- Versioned source code
- Training manuals
- Help files
- A completed bug database
- Risk assessments
- Installation plan/instructions

Conclusion

MSF is based on the idea of breaking the project into four phases: envisioning, planning, developing, and stabilizing. The planning phase can be further divided into three subphases: conceptual, logical, and physical. The members of the team assigned to build projects using MSF all share the responsibility for building and creating the project. Everyone on the team has input on the final project. By using MSF you can build projects that:

- Have a realistic, meaningful vision for the future
- Are centered on the needs of the business
- Are centered on the needs of the end user
- Are built using binary milestones that are associated with a deliverable
- Utilize a team of peers who all contribute to the success of the project
- Fit in with the entire enterprise
- Are built incrementally
- Evolve over time so that they can use the current technology
- Evolve over time to meet new needs in the enterprise

Chapter 3
Online Analytical Processing (OLAP) Systems

An online analytical processing (OLAP) system is a critical enterprise tool that helps corporations pinpoint past successes and failures and predict future successes and failures. It is one of the most important analytical tools of the enterprise.

All of the following accurately describe OLAP systems:

- OLAP systems are tools that can be used to analyze business information.
- OLAP systems can be used by analysts, managers, or executives to gain insight into how the enterprise was functioning over any past time period.
- OLAP systems are fast, consistent, interactive tools that can provide a wide range of refined views of the raw data of the enterprise.

In this chapter, you will learn about the essential elements of an OLAP system. You will also look at multidimensional data structures that can be used by the OLAP system to improve the efficiency of analytical queries.

OLAP Essentials

OLAP systems are very different from online transaction processing (OLTP) systems. The differences between the systems are as follows:

	OLTP	OLAP
Purpose	Real time data entry	Read and analyze historical data
Perform Updates*	Yes	No, read only
Perform Edits*	Yes	No
Source of Data	Data entry	Historical OLTP data
Associated Database	Operational	Analytical, may be operational

*There are some data warehousing applications, such as a budgeting system, that do require edits and updates to the data warehouse. This is not commonly done, but it is an exception to the usual rule that data warehouses contain data that is not updated or edited.

OLAP systems usually consist of two components: a calculation engine and a multidimensional data-viewing tool. Microsoft SQL Server 7.0 has an OLAP calculation engine, a repository, and a viewing tool for the client called the PivotTable Service. The PivotTable Service is covered in Chapter 2 and the Microsoft Repository in Appendix B.

The calculation engine is used to perform nonstandard SQL Server operations such as sums, ratios, time calculations, statistics, and ranking. Some calculation engines can also do custom formulas or algorithms, forecasting and modeling, and perform multiple SQL Server queries.

The calculation engine is specifically designed for high capacity and multiuse. It works most efficiently with special structures called multidimensional cubes. In the structure of these cubes, the cells of the cube conatain measured values and the edges of the cube define the dimensions of the data, such as product, store, customer, and time.

Both the engine and the multidimensional cubes are optimized for fast calculation and transformation of raw data into usable results. The focus of this chapter is to define these multidimensional cubes. The next chapter covers designing and building these multidimensional cubes using Microsoft SQL Server 7.0 OLAP Services.

SQL Server's OLAP system can work with either multidimensional cubes or standard relational databases. There is currently a controversy about whether the proven, relational data structure can be efficiently used by an OLAP system. Before getting into the reasons for this debate, let's do a quick review of what a normalized, relational structure is and then look at why it may not work efficiently with an OLAP system.

Normalized vs. Un-Normalized Data Structures

The relational design model is intended to group related information together. It has been used by OLTP systems for a long time and has proven its ability to keep data consistent. The fundamental ACID rule (atomicity, consistency, isolation, durability), which every operational database must maintain, can be followed easily using a normalized, relational data structure. It is for these reasons that the normalized relational database has dominated the market. Let's take a quick look at the basics of creating a normalized data structure.

Normalizing Data

To better understand normalized data structures, let's look at an example. Ajax Inc. is a small local retailer selling custom accounting software. They have a few employees and less than $100,000 in sales a year. Recently, they created a Web page to sell their product. Within the first week of e-commerce, they sold more software than in the previous two years. They had to increase their staff by over twenty people.

Prior to the Web page, all employee information was entered manually using an Excel spreadsheet. This spreadsheet was basically one huge relational table (all of the information related to an individual employee). Now the company wants to change the structure of the data to allow automatic information updates using a Visual Basic client application (front end).

The original table includes the employee name, address, and hours worked. The employee information would look like Figure 3-1.

	A	B	C	D	E	F	G	H
1	Last Name	First Name	Address	Dept	Dept Location	Jan 1 99	Jane 15 99	Feb 1 99
2	Jones	John	103 Main St	Acct	4th Floor	80	80	80
3	Smith	Joe	1 River Dr	Acct	4th Floor	102	87	88
4	Williams	Bud	3 West St	Acct	4th Floor	56	50	58
5	Rogers	Sally	4 East St	Sales	3rd Floor	80	80	80

Figure 3-1.   *Ajax Inc.'s employee information.*

While this information is all related to an employee, it could never be used to easily update and retrieve information on that employee in an automated Visual Basic application. A data structure that allows automated updates and retrievals should be structured according to these rules:

- The structure should require a minimum amount of space.
- The structure should allow for quick retrieval and updating of the information.
- The structure should show a clear representation of the data.
- The integrity of the data should be easy to maintain.

The current format fails all of these criteria. Let's see why:

- The department location column is redundant. If the accounting department is located only on the fourth floor, you would put in the same 4th floor for every employee working in accounting. If you create a detailed profile listing all attributes of the workers, you will create many redundant columns wasting space.
- Columns F, G, and H represent the number of hours worked for Jan 1, 1999, Jan 15, 1999, and Feb 1, 1999, respectively. To begin with, it is not easy to determine, by looking at the spreadsheet, that these represent hours worked. These numbers could mean anything.
- As the years roll on, the number of columns representing hours worked keeps increasing, expanding the column size indefinitely and forcing the user to scroll further and further out. When adding new rows, it is difficult to determine what column the new hours worked value goes into. If the value of one of the total hours worked entries is incorrect, it will be very difficult to find this value and change it.

Overall, although this is a relational view of the data, it is not very easy to work with if you want to update the information. This data is stored in what is called an un-normalized form, that is, the data is not normalized. Normalizing the structure of the information makes it easier to access and update the information. Let's look at how you can transform this data into third normal form.

First normal form   Information is placed in two-dimensional tables (columns and rows) similar to a spreadsheet, and all repeating groups must be removed. Each cell has one value and represents the intersection of a row and a cell.

A group is a collection of related information. In the example, all of the entries for the hours worked creates a group called "Hours Worked." As the Hours Worked group repeats across columns, it must be changed. To do this, replace the repeating group columns with one single Hours Worked column, and add a column for date. Figure 3-2 shows how this new format looks.

	B	C	D	E	F	G
1	First Name	Address	Dept	Dept Location	Date	Hours Worked
2	John	103 Main St	Acct	4th Floor	Jan 1 99	80
3	John	103 Main St	Acct	4th Floor	Jan 15 99	80
4	John	103 Main St	Acct	4th Floor	Feb 1 99	80
5	Joe	1 River Dr	Acct	4th Floor	Jan 1 99	102
6	Joe	1 River Dr	Acct	4th Floor	Jan 15 99	87
7	Joe	1 River Dr	Acct	4th Floor	Feb 1 99	88
8	Bud	3 West St	Acct	4th Floor	Jan 1 99	56
9	Bud	3 West St	Acct	4th Floor	Jan 15 99	50
10	Bud	3 West St	Acct	4th Floor	Feb 1 99	58
11	Sally	4 East St	Sales	3rd Floor	Jan 1 99	80
12	Sally	4 East St	Sales	3rd Floor	Jan 15 99	80
13	Sally	4 East St	Sales	3rd Floor	Feb 1 99	80

Figure 3-2. *First normal form.*

At first glance, this may not seem like a very big improvement. You just increased the size of the data by a factor of three. Yet, this structure makes it much easier to determine where the hours worked information is going to be stored, which is one of the things required to use this data in an automated process.

If you create a column to give a unique identifier for each employee, you move toward second normal form.

Second normal form In second normal form, keys are created. All non-key values in the table must be dependent on the key value(s).

In second normal form, your table now has the format shown in Figure 3-3.

	A	B	C	D	E	F	G	H
1	EmployeeID	Last Name	First Name	Address	Dept	Dept Location	Date	Hours Worked
2	1	Jones	John	103 Main St	Acct	4th Floor	Jan 1 99	80
3	1	Jones	John	103 Main St	Acct	4th Floor	Jan 15 99	80
4	1	Jones	John	103 Main St	Acct	4th Floor	Feb 1 99	80
5	2	Smith	Joe	1 River Dr	Acct	4th Floor	Jan 1 99	102
6	2	Smith	Joe	1 River Dr	Acct	4th Floor	Jan 15 99	87
7	2	Smith	Joe	1 River Dr	Acct	4th Floor	Feb 1 99	88
8	3	Williams	Bud	3 West St	Acct	4th Floor	Jan 1 99	56
9	3	Williams	Bud	3 West St	Acct	4th Floor	Jan 15 99	50
10	3	Williams	Bud	3 West St	Acct	4th Floor	Feb 1 99	58
11	4	Rogers	Sally	4 East St	Sales	3rd Floor	Jan 1 99	80
12	4	Rogers	Sally	4 East St	Sales	3rd Floor	Jan 15 99	80
13	4	Rogers	Sally	4 East St	Sales	3rd Floor	Feb 1 99	80

Figure 3-3. *Second normal form.*

An EmployeeID key is added to identify each employee.

The data does not have any information that is not related to the employee (the 4th floor is where the employee works, so it is related to the employee). All you need to do to make it second normal form is to add the key. Second normal form just does some cleaning up and prepares the data for the third normal form.

Third normal form   All non-key attributes must be dependent on a key attribute. Any attributes not dependent on a key attribute should be separated out into another table.

This requirement forces some major changes in the structure of the data. Looking at this data, you see that the hours worked column is dependent on the date column and the department location column is dependent on the department column. These four columns must be separated out into two new tables, each with keys. You now split the information into three tables: Department, Employee, and Hours Worked. See Figures 3-4, 3-5, and 3-6.

	A	B	C
1	DeptID	DeptName	DeptLocation
2	1	Acct	4th Floor
3	2	Sales	3rd Floor

Figure 3-4. *Department table.*

	A	B	C	D	E
1	EmployeeID	Last Name	First Name	Address	Dept
2	1	Jones	John	103 Main St	1
3	2	Smith	Joe	1 River Dr	1
4	3	Williams	Bud	3 West St	1
5	4	Rogers	Sally	4 East St	2

Figure 3-5. *Employee table.*

In third normal form, you arrive at a structure that meets all of the requirements to easily retrieve and update information. A normalized database is designed specifically for data that is constantly changing. In Figure 3-6, it would probably be better in relational design not to have the HourWrkdID, and instead use EmployeeID and Date combined as the primary key. The reason for this is because this combination of values is what is supposed to be unique—given a particular date and employee, there is supposed to be only one value for HoursWorkedID. With the HoursWrkdID primary key, you could have multiple HoursWorkedID values for the same employee and date, unless you add an additional unique index to prevent it.

Fourth and fifth normal forms   Fourth normal form requires you to remove many-to-many relationships from within the same table. Fifth normal form rebuilds the original structure from the final structure. Fifth normal form is a check to see if everything was done correctly. The example is already in fourth and fifth normal form.

	A	B	C	D
1	HoursWrkdID	EmployeeID	Date	HoursWorked
2	1	1	Jan 1 1999	80
3	2	1	Jan 15 1999	80
4	3	1	Feb 15 1999	80
5	4	2	Jan 1 1999	102
6	5	2	Jan 15 1999	87
7	6	2	Feb 15 1999	88
8	7	3	Jan 1 1999	56
9	8	3	Jan 15 1999	50
10	9	3	Feb 15 1999	58
11	10	4	Jan 1 1999	80
12	11	4	Jan 15 1999	80
13	12	4	Feb 15 1999	80

Figure 3-6.   *Hours Worked table.*

You now have a normalized data structure. It is important to remember that the driving force for normalizing the data is easy retrieval and updating of the information. Looking at the result, you can see that it is easy to determine where new or updated value needs to go. Normalizing data also helps maintain the ACID rules for the database. Let's now look at a way to represent these table structures using the Entity-Relationship model.

The Entity-Relationship Model

The Entity-Relationship model is a way to model the information in a normalized relational database. Each table is represented by a box, which is called an entity. Above each entity is the name of the table. Inside the box are listed all of the attributes. A horizontal line divides the box. Attributes above the horizontal line are primary key columns, and those below are non-key columns. Microsoft Access uses a similar model for its relationship tool. Instead of using a horizontal line, the Access relationship diagram bolds the primary key. For the Northwind database, the Access Entity Diagram looks like Figure 3-7.

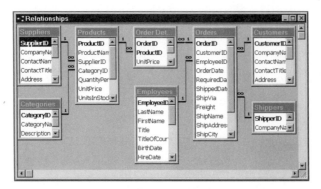

Figure 3-7.   *Northwind Entity-Relationship diagram.*

There can be several types of relationships between entities:

- One to one: A single instance in one table relates to a single instance in the other table.
- One to many: A single instance in one table relates to at least one instance in another table.
- Many to many: A single instance in one table relates to at least one instance in another table and vice versa.
- Zero vs. one: You can replace one to show a zero to relationship, that is, there may be no instances in the table.

Normalized Data and OLAP Systems

Using a normalized relational database structure allows an OLTP system to work fast and efficiently, as well as maintain the ACID rules. This is true even when there are constant updates to the operational database by the OLTP system. Although a normalized data structure works well for an OLTP system, how efficient is it for an OLAP system?

An OLAP system analyzes data that should never be in flux. Analytical data should be static except for occasional updates of new information. Because normalizing the data structure is done to make updates more efficient, and there are usually no updates in an OLAP system, there is no purpose in normalizing the data for an OLAP system.

Note   As will be discussed later in the chapter, normalizing the tables will reduce the total amount of disk space required for the data. If there is a very limited amount of available disk space, a normalized structure may offer you some advantages for your analytical data warehouse.

It is possible that a normalized data structure could work efficiently for an OLAP system, but certainly there is no requirement in the OLAP system for a normalized data structure as there is in an OLTP system. Let's see what happens when you try to use your standard, normalized relational data structure in an operational database for analyzing data.

Analyzing Data Using a Normalized, Relational Design

Imagine that you build an analytical data store by moving the OLTP data into a separate set of normalized relational tables within the same operational database as the OLTP data is stored. You perform a standard set of SQL Server 7.0 queries on these new tables to analyze the data.

These new tables contain information on 100 products sold in 20 different regions. You need to make a stored procedure to calculate the sales for every day in July. In the database are an order details table, a products table, a region table, and an order table. The order details table gives us a productID, quantity sold, date, and regionID. The products table links the productID with the productName. The region table links regionID with regionName, and the order table gives the date for each order.

To get the sales for July, you must complete the following steps:

1. Perform a query on the order details table for all sales on the first day of July for the first product.
2. Perform 20 aggregate query sums for each region and store this information in a temporary table.
3. Repeat this for each of the 100 products.
4. Repeat this for each of the days in July.
5. Scan through the temporary table and perform sums by region for each product.

You can see that even this simple question requires a complicated query that scans the tables many times. This stored procedure is very difficult to debug and takes a considerable amount of processor time.

If you locate the tables and stored procedures in the operational database, this query would takes resources from the updates to the operational data, slowing this system down. Slowing the operational database down slows the entire business down and could seriously affect the corporation. You can improve performance by making a copy of the data on a completely separate server or using a component running on a second server to perform the calculations. Using this second server should prevent slowing down the OLTP database.

Even using a second server, though, you still have to write complicated stored procedures for every type of data analysis your user wants to perform. This means that for every view of the data that the user wants to see, you will write specific, long, complicated queries. Unfortunately, though, when it comes to analytical queries, the user usually does not know what to do until he or she begins.

A user performing analytical queries may start by looking at the sales over five regions. When the user sees that one of the five regions is doing poorly, another query on just that region may be done. Upon looking at the region, the user may perform several queries over the different products, quarters, etc. This is a typical scenario for doing analysis. When you build an analytical database, you will not know exactly what queries the user will want to perform. Therefore, relying on complicated stored procedures for your analysis results in the user only getting a few predetermined ways to analyze and view the data.

You can improve the situation by using an OLAP System that works with a normalized, relational data structure. It is the responsibility of the OLAP system to take a user's request for information and create an efficient query to get this information. Although this is slow, it will allow for ad hoc queries, that is, analytical type queries. The speed of the queries depends on the query, how well they were optimized, and many other factors. How long it will take for a result to come back is completely unpredictable.

> **Note**   One of the main differences between OLTP and OLAP systems is that OLTP systems have a well-defined set of queries that users can perform, whereas OLAP does not. In an OLTP order entry system, you know all of the queries the system will perform when you build it, such as retrieve all customers, retrieve an order with a particular orderID, and so forth. With the OLTP system, you can fine-tune queries to get the maximum performance out of the system. In the OLAP system, you know what type of information the user wants to analyze, but you don't know the exact queries the user will need to perform the analysis. The queries for an analytical system need to be made on demand and optimized by the OLAP system.

We could improve the situation by using an un-normalized, multidimensional relational database structure. Making the tables un-normalized will make the database larger, but also result in queries being performed with fewer joins. Reducing the number of joins will increase the performance time for these queries. We will discuss the advantages of using normalized and un-normalized in the comparison of star and snowflake schemas below.

Analyzing Data Using Dimensions and Facts

The primary purpose of OLAP systems is to perform calculations and do modeling over important business metrics. These metrics are called dimensions. Just as in math and science, where the dimensions of space and time are used, business dimensions can also be treated in time and space. The space dimension is generally referred to as the geography dimension when working with OLAP. In the world of OLAP, there are also other important dimensions, such as customers, salesperson, department, and so forth.

Dimensions are attributes over which to measure a key performance indicator (KPI). As mentioned in Chapter 2, a KPI is a quantitative piece of information that indicates how the business is performing. It tracks information, such as the number of items sold or the total sales in dollars. In a discussion of OLAP Services, we will use the term *measures*, which are either KPIs or values that are derived by performing calculations on one or more KPIs.

When doing an analysis using OLAP, you consider a single measure over several dimensions. If the measure is items sold and the dimensions are time and geography, with time equal to the month of July, and geography equal to New York, the OLAP system calculates the number of an item sold in the month of July in the New York region. OLAP systems almost always analyze measures over many dimensions. That's why OLAP systems are called multidimensional.

Tip In general, when you analyze information, you put it into the following format:

A measure by (over) dimension1, dimension2, … dimensionN.

For example, you might say, "I want to see the total sales **by** region **by** department **over** time." In this case, the measure is total sales and the three dimensions are department, region, and time. When asking end users what information they want from the data warehouse, try to put it into this format.

A dimension is a business metric. The actual metric can be represented in many different ways. For example, you can represent the time dimension as hours, weeks, days, years, or quarters. A grouping of several related representations of a metric make a dimension. Thus, we could create a time dimension consisting of year and month and also make another time dimension consisting of fiscal year and quarter. You might want to see one metric in many different ways and create different dimensions for each representation of the metric.

The members of dimensions often can be grouped into different levels of the metric that are all related to each other. These different levels are called hierarchies. The time dimension can be represented by year and month. These different representations of time are all related to each other (one year is twelve months, a month is twenty-nine to thirty-one days, and so forth). The second time dimension consisting of quarters and fiscal year is also a hierarchy. A geography dimension could have the following hierarchy: regions, states, and cities. OLAP tools can move through these hierarchies to quickly give you more or less detailed views of the corporate information. For example, the OLAP tool could give you a view of sales of widgets in New York State over the month of March. You can use the OLAP tool to view the sales of any city in New York State by selecting the appropriate city and getting the sales of widgets in a particular month for that city.

Using dimensions, and the hierarchies they are built from, and measures, OLAP systems can perform trend analysis over sequential time periods, slice through subsets of data, and quickly create a new view representing this slice. OLAP systems can reach through to underlying detail data, rotate to new dimensional comparisons in the viewing area, and perform a wide range of analytical services.

When analyzing information using an OLAP system, you will ask questions about a measure over several dimensions. For example, "How many widgets were sold in the month of July, August, and September in all 20 regions?" These are multidimensional questions, that is, they query across several dimensions.

You can create a multidimensional view by using a data structure built from tables that contain measures and dimensions. A multidimensional model using measures and dimensions is called a star schema. Star schemas create major tables called fact tables. Fact tables contain measures and represent quantitative or factual information about the business. Fact tables can be normalized or un-normalized and are placed in the middle of the diagram.

The attributes in the fact table almost always have continuous values. Continuous values mean that the attribute in the fact table can have any value, such as 1.1, 1.001, or 1.3.

Star schemas also have much smaller tables called information tables, which contain descriptive data. In the star schema, information tables are un-normalized.

Note You can place the informational tables into third normal form to get something called a snowflake schema, described below.

Information tables contain dimensions. Previously, we gave two representations of the time dimension. The first was year, month. The second was quarters and fiscal year. If the fiscal year corresponds to the regular year, we can put these two dimensions together to get an informational table with the following members: year, month. Because informational tables contain dimensions, they are often called dimension tables. The attributes of information tables generally have values that are discrete, such as 1, 2, 3, and so forth.

Informational tables also include primary keys. The information tables primary keys are usually included as foreign keys of the fact table. If a primary key of an information table is not in the fact table, it is called a degenerate dimension. The primary keys are usually generated by the analytical database.

Note You can think of the informational tables as a large box that contains all of the different representations of a business metric such as time, geography, or customer. To build our dimensions we will go into this "box" and select representations that we will need for our dimensions. For our first time dimension we could reach in and get year, month, and day. For our second we could get year and quarter. For our third we could only get year and month. Thus, we can build many different dimensions from the members in the informational table.

A typical star schema looks like that in Figure 3-8. The name "star" comes from the shape of the structure. Time, customers, sales geography, and products are all informational tables containing attributes that are representations of the essential business metrics. From the attributes in the informational tables we can build all of the dimensions we need to perform analytical analysis of the data.

In Figure 3-8, the table *Order Facts* is the facts table. Notice that the facts table contains not only measures, but also foreign keys to the dimensional tables and a primary key for the fact table. Informational tables also have fields other than the representations of the dimensions. The customer information table contains a primary key and the CustTyp_Desc, Cust_Desc, and City_Desc fields that can be used to provide information about the customer.

Note With the SQL Server 7.0 OLAP system, you build tables in the data warehouse using a star schema.

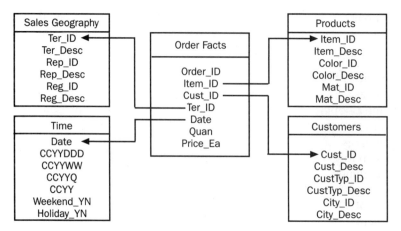

Figure 3-8. *Star schemas.*

When converting a normalized, relational, operational database to a star schema, you must do the following three things:

1.   Determine the measures and dimensions

2.   Design the informational tables

3.   Design the fact tables

The previous chapter on planning and design covered the steps required to determine KPIs and informational objects. Measures are derived from KPIs. The dimensions will be selected from the informational objects. Therefore, the first step is complete.

Let's now look at informational tables in more detail.

Informational Tables

Informational tables are smaller tables that contain data that may change over time. For example, a customer informational table is updated when a customer changes his address. The number of rows in the table is limited to the total number of customers. While there may be many customers, the size of the customer table will be very small in comparison to a sales fact table containing all sales for 1999. Thus, we would consider the customer table, and most of the informational tables, to be small tables in the data warehouse.

There are four types of dimensions: structural, informational, partitioning, and categorical dimensions. The structural dimension is the most common one containing members that can be placed within a hierarchy. Information dimensions contain attributes that need to be calculated. Partitioning dimensions are for comparisons of information, such as planned sales and actual sales. Categorical dimensions are used to create groups based on an attribute in a dimension.

Structural Dimensions

Structural dimensions present information about one metric in the form of a hierarchy. Thus, year, month, and day form a structural dimension.

As an example of how to use a structural dimension, imagine that a department uses total number sold as a measure. Associated with this measure is the product informational table that contains all of the attributes related to the product. One of the dimensions that can be created from the product informational table might be product_name, product_brand, product_category, product_department, and product_family. As you can see, this product dimension forms a hierarchy. You can also add a time informational table. We could build a time dimension from this time informational object that consists of year, month, and day. Using this measure and these two structural dimensions, you could use SQL Server 7.0's OLAP Services to determine the total number sold of a particular product, over a particular period of time.

Some common structural dimensions are:

- **Customer geographic dimension**   This dimension will provide a hierarchy that groups customers together based on where they live. A typical example of a customer dimension would be *customer_city*, *customer_state,* and *customer_country*. This dimension is commonly used to see differences in sales, profit, and other measure for customers living in different geographic locations.

- **Time dimension**   The time dimension will show when an event occurred. A typical time dimension would be year, month, and day.

- **Salesperson geography dimension**   This dimension will provide a hierarchy that groups salespeople together based on where their territories are. This is commonly used to see how sales, profits, and other measures are doing for different sales regions.

- **Product dimension**   The item that was purchased. This hierarchy could include *product_name, product_brand, product_category,* and *product department.* This dimension is used to see the sales, profit, and other measures for the different groupings of products.

All of these structural dimensions contain attributes that are arranged in a hierarchy. The hierarchies in the structural dimensions are so important that we will give them a separate discussion below. First, though, let's look at the other three types of dimensions: information, categorical, and partition.

Information Dimensions

Information dimensions are built from calculated fields. You might want to see the total sales by product by profit. You might expect that the products with greater sales would have greater profits. Yet, if you underprice an item, you may find that sales are very high (especially if you have smart customers), but profit is minimal or even negligible. On the other hand, you might overprice an item and thus make a greater profit. This item may have a fairly high profit margin but sales are probably low. Thus, making profit a dimension and total sales a measure can provide useful information on products.

You can do two calculations on profit. The first is profit per item, which is simply the selling price minus the seller's cost. Once you know the profit per item, you then multiply it by the daily sales of that item to get the total profit per day.

Real World   In a real application, you will probably do this calculation over time, as the selling price and cost may vary from day to day. Thus a table with the daily selling price and the daily cost will be needed. The difference between these two for each day over the time period you are looking at has to be calculated and averaged. The total profit is the profit per item on a particular day multiplied by the sales for the day, summed over the selected time period.

If you create a dimension that includes the profit per item and the total profit, you have an information dimension. Normally, calculated attributes are almost always measures. Yet, if you are creative, you can find ways to use calculated attributes in dimensions.

Informational Tables Made from Partition Dimensions

Partition dimensions are used when two or more dimensions are built from the same structure. For example, you may want to create dimensions for predicted sales and actual sales. The structure of these two dimensions is the same, only the values are different.

Another example is the time dimension. Every year has the same quarters, the same months, and the same days (with the exception of a leap year, which doesn't affect the dimension). In OLAP Services we will frequently use time partition dimensions to partition the data in the data warehouse. For example, we could create two identical dimensions with the following structure:

the_day

the_month

the_year

The data in one dimension will be for 1998 and in the other time dimension the data will be for 1999. When building our fact table, we can then partition the measures into data for 1998 and 1999. This will give us many advantages as we will see in the next chapter.

Caution   Do not use nulls in your dimensions; they will cause errors in your calculated fields.

Categorical Dimensions

A categorical dimension is built by grouping the values of one of the dimension's attributes. If a customer table has a household income attribute, you might want to see the buying patterns of customers based on their income. To do this, you create a categorical dimension that places household income into categories. For example, you may have the following yearly household income categories: $0 to $20,000, $20,001 to $40,000, $40,001 to $60,000, $60,001 to $100,000, and over $100,001. You can now look at measures, such as the number of items purchased within each of these categories to see what people in each income level are buying and in what quantity. Other possible categories are gender and number of people in the household.

Now let's go back to the structural dimension's hierarchies and see some of its special features.

Hierarchical Nature of Structural Dimensions

Structural dimensions contain a set of related members. If you look at these dimensions in the original operational database, you usually find that the attributes that make up the structural dimension have a one-to-many relationship with each other. If you're looking at the Entity-Relationship diagram for the operational database for a department store, you may see that part of the Entity-Relationship diagram looks like Figure 3-9.

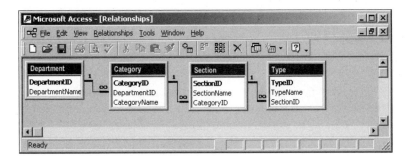

Figure 3-9. *Entity-Relationship diagram.*

Every item in the department store has department, category, section, and type information associated with it. You can see that these tables, related to each other by one-to-many relationships, can be used to create a dimension that gives descriptive information on each item.

A partial view of the information in the original tables may look like Figure 3-10.

DepartmentName	DepartmentID
Clothing	1
Hardware	2
Housewares	3

CategoryName	DepartmentID	CategoryID
Mens	1	1
Womans	1	2
Boys	1	3
Girls	1	4
Wrenches	2	5
Dishes	3	6

SectionName	CategoryID	SectionID
Suits	1	1
Formal	1	2
Informal	1	3
Pants	1	4
Shirts	1	5
Informal	2	6

TypeName	SectionID	TypeID
BlueJeans	1	3
T-Shirts	1	3
Blouses	1	6
Skirts	1	6

Figure 3-10. *Tables for a structural dimension.*

The clothing department is associated with Men's, Women's, Girls, and Boys categories. The Men's category is associated with Suits, Formal, Informal, Pants, and Shirts sections.

These relationships fit the original definition of a hierarchy, which was used at the beginning of this chapter. You can redraw this information in terms of hierarchies. A partial filling in of the data for the hierarchies looks like Figure 3-11.

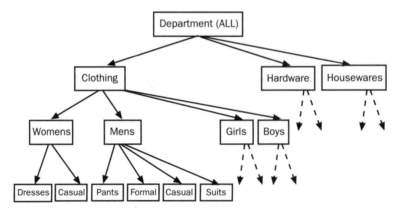

Figure 3-11. *Relational hierarchies.*

There is one important thing to notice about hierarchies. Each item in the category can have certain measures associated with it. For example, you could determine how many dollars worth of one of the sections (such as men's pants) sold during a period of time. This is a special type of measure because it is additive, that is, it is derived by adding the sale price of all men's pants sold during some time period. To arrive at the number of men's pants sold in May, go through the orders for the month of May and sum the dollar sale amount of every item with the category field set to men's (CategoryID=1) and the section field set to pants (SectionID=1). This sum is the total amount in dollars that the men's pants section sold in May. If you perform similar sums for the formal, casual, and suit sections, you find the following:

Sum Men's = (Sum Pants) + (Sum Formal) + (Sum Casual) + (Sum Suits)

This is what makes additive measures so useful when you are working with a hierarchy. If you know the value of an additive measure for all the items in the bottom of the hierarchy, you can calculate the value for every higher level in the hierarchy, as long as you know the structure of the hierarchy. These additive measures are the best attributes for your fact tables. They can be total units sold, gross value sold, net value sold, or any additive quantity. If you use dimensions built on hierarchies and additive facts, you only need to store the values of the facts for the lowest level of the hierarchies. The values of facts at the higher levels can be calculated from lower level information. This idea is discussed in more detail in the next chapter when aggregations are addressed.

Caution   Subcategories with the same name may not be the same thing. There may be a men's informal subcategory that includes slacks and shirts, and a woman's informal category that includes skirts and blouses. The informal subcategory in two different hierarchies could include totally different items.

If we were to use this data to build a products dimension, we would use a dimension with *product_department, product_category,* and *product_subcategory.* To build this dimension, we will first need to create a product informational table that has these three members within it. We need to now determine what is the best way to build an informational table. There are two possible ways of building informational tables: creating consolidated star schemas or creating normalized snowflake schemas.

Informational Tables Built from Star Schemas

In a star schema, all of the dimension information is placed into one informational table. The information in the informational table will include a unique id and the attributes needed for all of the dimensions that are going to be built from this informational table. For example, you could make one product informational table with the following attributes (fields):

ProductID

ProductName

ProductSize

ProductDepartment

ProductCategory

ProductSubcategory

ProductLowFat

From this products informational table, you could create a structural dimension with ProductName, ProductSubCategory, ProductCategory, and ProductDepartment. You could also create a structural dimension with ProductID, ProductSubCategory, ProductCategory, and ProductDepartment. You can also have a categorical dimension with ProductLowFat. All of these dimensions will be built from attributes found in this one un-normalized structural table. We have essentially lumped all of the attributes that we need for all of our products dimensions into one un-normalized table. Taking a close look at this, you will see this results in the star schema we described earlier.

Because this table is not normalized, it takes up more space. Realistically, though, the fact table takes up a far greater amount of space, so, in this case, using an un-normalized structure actually makes the overall size of the structure only a little larger. In addition to the star schema, there is another way we could organize the tables called the snowflake schema.

Snowflake Schema

In the snowflake schema, the informational tables are placed in third normal form. The above example is broken into the following tables:

Product Table

ProductID

ProductName

ProductSize

ProductLowFat

ProductDepartment

ProductCategoryID

Category Table

ProductCategory

ProductSubCategoryID

Subcategory Table

ProductSubCategory

ProductSubCategoryID

When the tables are placed in a diagram, they look like snowflakes. To place the information back together requires numerous joins. These joins will take considerable time. In general, a snowflake schema is less efficient than a star schema.

Snowflake Schema Versus Star Schema

Differences between star and snowflake hierarchies:

	Star	Snowflake
Number of Rows	Higher	Lower
Readability	Easier	Harder
Number of Tables	Less	More
Time to Search Dimensions	Quick	Slow

The snowflake schema offers only one major advantage: it requires less space. Normalizing the informational tables does nothing to improve your analysis of the data, so perhaps the best approach is to leave these tables in a non-normalized format. The extra space required by the non-normalized informational table is actually very small compared to the amount of disk space required by the fact table.

All fact tables have a time informational table associated with them. The time informational table has the following characteristics:

- Attributes in the table represent time divisions and events.
- Most common time dimensions constrain the day, month, and year.
- Special times, such as workdays, weekends, holidays, seasons, fiscal periods, and so forth can also be represented.

Believe it or not, there are still several more dimension topics to discuss. These can wait until Chapter 4, though. For now, let's look at fact tables.

Fact Table

The measures within the fact table contain the business measurements the user needs calculated over several dimensions. The measures are observations in the marketplace and are derived from KPIs. As noted in the discussion of hierarchies, facts are very useful when they are numeric and additive. Additive facts allow the OLAP system to sum hundreds to millions of records.

Fact tables, unlike informational tables, are not supposed to change over time and may become very large. The information in these tables corresponds to measures such as sales, total number sold, and so forth, which should never change. Fact tables can become very large, including millions of records.

Measures do not have to be additive. Some measures do not make sense when you add them together, such as the total units in stock. Yet, it would make sense to take averages of units in stock. Therefore, you can use units in stock as a measure, but you make an average of the values instead of a sum. Measures can also be based on calculated values, such as total profit. Fact tables are usually normalized tables.

Note The star schema is made with small dimension tables and large fact tables. When performing queries on the data in the star schema, OLAP Services begins by selecting the correct record from the informational tables. Because the informational tables are relatively small, this query is quick and efficient, especially if indexes are used. Once the appropriate rows in the informational tables are selected, you can use the primary keys in these rows to find the corresponding record in the fact table. Even though the fact table is large, you perform searches on the fact tables on keyed attributes. This allows for efficient selection of the correct row in the fact table.

Cubes

Once dimensions and measures are defined, you can then define and build cubes. Just as you built a cube in math class from the x, y, and z coordinates' axes to represent the space dimensions, you can build an OLAP cube from the attributes of your business dimensions. The dimension attributes are the coordinate axes of your cube. Thus, you could build a cube with a city axis from your customer dimension, a day axis from your time dimension, and a product name axis from your product dimension.

A point on this cube contains three values: a customer's city, a particular product, and a certain day. A point with multiple values is called a tuple. The values in the tuple are where you want to see the value of a measure. You therefore calculate your measures at points on the cube.

If you have a total product sales measure in your fact table, you can measure the total product sales at a point on the cube. In the above example, this gives the total sales for a particular product on one day in one customer city.

If you remain at the same value for two of the cube's axes and vary the third, you can see how a measure changes over the varying dimension. With the above example, if you keep the product name and the day constant and move along the customer city dimension, you get the values of total product sales for one product on one day in all of the customer cities. In this way, a cube allows you to analyze information across the attributes in the dimensions. This is what OLAP is all about. Moving through an axis of the cube like this is usually called "slicing."

You can do more than just move across an axis of the cube, however. You can exchange the attribute in the dimension you are using for the cube's axes. Thus, you can change days to months to years to quarters, if you need to. This allows you to drill in and out of the data, which is why this process is called drilling. If you change the products attribute from a single product to a product category, the total product sales then represents the sum of the sales of all of the products in this category. This sum is still a single number in the tuple as before, but it now represents a value for many items.

Note   The dimensions and measures in the cube will determine what the user can slice and drill through. OLAP provides the services to perform the slicing and dicing. The PivotTable Services provide the tool that allows the user to make requests to slice and dice data in any way that she wants.

Cubes do not have to only have three axes; they can have up to sixty-four. Only three axes have been discussed thus far because that is all most of us can visualize. The easiest way to understand dimensions, star schemas, and fact tables is to actually see them in action. Now it's time to see what all of this actually looks like in OLAP Server using OLAP Manager.

SQL Server 7.0 OLAP Services

If you did the default install, you now have to open the Microsoft SQL Server 7.0 folder, open the OLAP services folder, and then open the OLAP manager folder. This opens the management console and allows you access to the OLAP Server.

Note   If you like, take a break from the book for a while and look through the Understanding OLAP Concepts application or read the OLAP Manager Tutorial. Or you might want to wait to look at these until after you read this chapter and the next.

Put your cursor over OLAP servers and single-click the plus sign. This should expand out the list and show all available servers. Put your cursor over the correct server and single-click the plus sign. You should see the Connecting To OLAP Server message.

Either double-click the server or single-click the plus sign. You should now see the FoodMart database. Open the FoodMart database and expand the Cubes folder, then the Sales folder, and finally the Dimensions and Measures folders. Your screen should look like Figure 3-12.

What you are looking at on the left side of the management console are the dimensions and measures the user can use to build cubes and the measures that you will need at different points on these cubes. Expand out the customer dimension. Your screen should look like Figure 3-13.

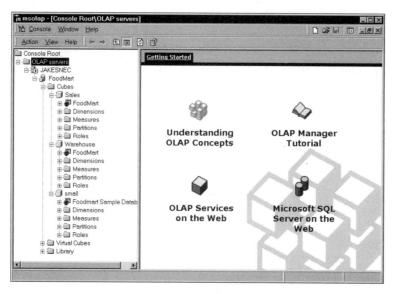

Figure 3-12. *Viewing the FoodMart database.*

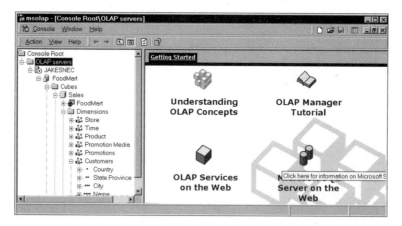

Figure 3-13. *Management console dimensions.*

What you are looking at is a customer geography structural dimension built from a hierarchy. Country is at the top of the hierarchy, followed by State, Province, City, and finally Name. Spend some time expanding the dimensions out to see what choices you made. Some dimensions have only one attribute; others have several. Let's now look at where this cube was built. Place the cursor over the Sales cube, right-click, then select Edit, as shown in Figure 3-14.

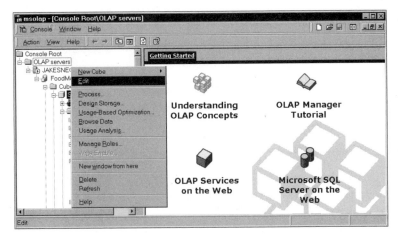

Figure 3-14.   *Dimensions of the Sales cube.*

This brings up the cube editor shown in Figure 3-15.

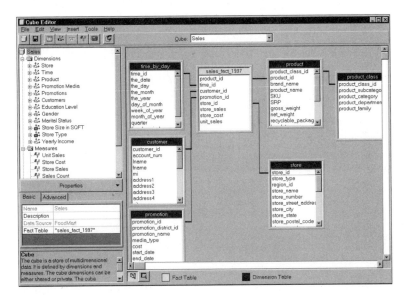

Figure 3-15.   *Cube editors.*

On the right are tables in a snowflake schema from the actual physical database. It is a snow-flake schema because one table's product and product class are normalized. The rest of the tables are in the standard star schema. You cannot edit or change these because they are based on the structure in the data warehouse. In this case, the actual database is an Access database called FoodMart.mdb. You can find this database in the Samples folder located in the OLAP Services folder. You can open the database and view all the data if you like (you may have to close OLAP Services first because it may be locking the database). You can view these tables as a smorgasbord containing all the possible members to build dimensions from. The fact table contains all of the measures you can work with. You can also create your own measures through a mathematical or statistical combination of the non-id attributes in the fact table. From these informational tables numerous dimensions have been created in the FoodMart database, which can be seen on the left side of Figure 3-15.

Caution   In the management console, informational tables are called dimension tables. The term informational tables was used because these tables contain information that you want to measure a fact over, they contain attributes other than the dimensions (such as the primary key), and because it can get confusing talking about dimensions and dimension tables. This has also been done to create a separation between the informational tables, which are in the database, and the dimensions that you build your cubes over. This is also true for fact tables, which are in the database, and measures, which the OLAP system uses to take measurements at points on the cube. In this way, when either fact or informational tables are referred to, you know immediately that the discussion is about the star (snowflake) schema in the physical database. When dimensions or measures are referred to, the discussion is about the attributes that are used by the OLAP system.

The fact table contains the measures. Notice that there are also measures that are calculated. You will go through the cube editor and several other parts of the OLAP Services in the next chapter. For now, just look at the information to get a feel for what the star schema, dimensions, and measures look like.

Conclusion

In this chapter, you looked at the differences between the OLTP systems and the OLAP systems. You found that normalized relational databases are highly efficient for OLTP systems, but produce unpredictable, often long query times for OLAP systems. For this reason, you reorganize the data into an un-normalized structure called the star schema. The star schema contains structural tables that contain dimensions. These dimensions, called measures, are the metrics with which the user will view KPIs. You can assemble the attributes of several dimensions into a cube. You can also take a point on the cube and get the value for a measure at that point. This allows you to slice and drill through the data. The details of building cubes are covered in Chapter 4.

Chapter 4
Building Cubes with the Microsoft SQL Server 7.0 OLAP Services Manager

The last chapter dealt with creating relational data warehouses and cubes. The relational data warehouse was built from a star schema containing fact and informational tables. The cubes were built from dimensions. Measures were calculated on points of the cube. As you will see in this chapter, the cubes can be stored in either a special multidimensional database or they can be stored in the relational data warehouse containing the star schema. There is also a hybrid solution that has features of both of these options.

This chapter explains how tables in the relational data warehouse are arranged into star schemas and how cubes can be built from these star schemas using Microsoft SQL Server 7.0 OLAP wizards. OLAP Services wizards include the Cube wizard, Virtual Dimension wizard, Storage Design wizard, Usage-Based Optimization wizard, Usage Analysis wizard, Dimension wizard, and Virtual Cube wizard. There are also hosts of editors, such as the Cube Editor and the Dimension Editor. All of these wizards and editors can be accessed through OLAP Manager. This multitude of wizards and editors enables you to build cubes and structure star schemas quickly and easily.

Before taking a tour through OLAP Services wizards, let's address a few important OLAP concepts, such as aggregations of the data and the methods for storing data, which include multidimensional OLAP (MOLAP), relational OLAP (ROLAP), and hybrid OLAP (HOLAP); and partitions. Let's begin with these three topics and then show how all of the OLAP Services wizards can be used to build cubes and arrange star schemas.

Aggregations

In the last chapter, you learned that structural dimensions have hierarchies within them. If you use additive measures over these hierarchies, you will find that the value at any level of the hierarchy is the sum of the children in the next level down, as shown in Figure 4-1.

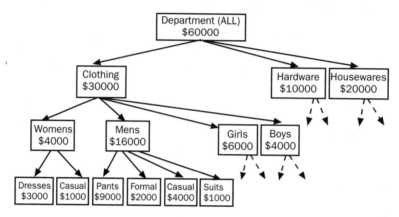

Figure 4-1. *Hierarchy of Chapter 3's sales.*

You can significantly improve the performance of the OLAP tool if you calculate the values of the sums and store these summed values in the data warehouse. Calculating the summed value of a measure across a hierarchy creates an aggregation. Storing aggregate values of the measures allows the OLAP tool to perform queries more quickly. Aggregations are one of the key features of OLAP tools, which give these tools reliable and efficient response times. Storing aggregates does come with a price, though, since these values require more disk storage space. As the number of levels in the hierarchy increases, the possible number of sums increases as well. With large dimensions (about 100 members, which is not uncommon), the amount of space required to store the aggregate information could become huge. This is commonly called data explosion.

Data Explosion

The size of the data explosion depends on what is called the grain of the data. The grain of the data indicates how detailed the information is. There can be many different levels of granularity in a data warehouse. The time dimension can be measured down to days, which is a very fine level of granularity. Or time can be measured in years, which is a very coarse level of granularity. The geography dimension can be measured down to zip code, which is fine, or up to country, which is coarse. When actually building a data warehouse using DTS, you should choose the best grain for the particular situation.

The Size of the Data Grain and Data Explosion

The size of the data grain has a major impact on data explosion. Imagine that you have a product hierarchy that has 50 nodes, where a sum of a measure can be calculated as an aggregate. If the time dimension only includes years and the four quarters (coarse grain), you only have 4 x 50 = 200 values in the data warehouse for each measure. This will represent the measure (such as sales) for each of the four quarters for each of the 50 products. We can aggregate the values for the four quarters into a single value for the year for each of the 50 products. Thus, doing aggregation will result in only 50 more values in the data warehouse. If you then add the 12 months to the time dimension, and the 365 days, you will have 365 x 50 = 18,250 values in the data warehouse. To aggregate a measure over months will require 12 x 50 = 600 aggregates plus 50 aggregates for the year. This results in a total of 650 aggregates. Increasing the grain has resulted in a large increase in both the number of values and aggregates in the data warehouse. This is data explosion.

Things get interesting with three dimensions. Imagine that you now throw in a third dimension—geography—which only has six regions. Figure 4-2 shows how the cube now looks.

Note   While this "cube" is not technically cubical, that is, no sides are equal, it is still referred to as a cube. Even when there are more or less than three dimensions, it is still called a cube in data warehousing.

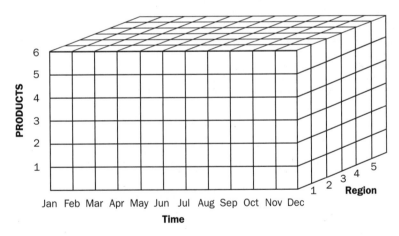

Figure 4-2.   *Hierarchy of a three-dimensional cube.*

In this example, the data warehouse actually stores date values by day. Thus, the month values are actually aggregate values. Cubes can be built from any level in the hierarchy. This example looks at a cube built from a time dimension based on aggregate values.

Now, to perform every possible aggregation, you must perform aggregations for every point on the three-dimensional cube. There would be 7 x 7 x 12 = 588 aggregations. Thus, the total number of points on the cube and the number of aggregations required for the entire cube are found by multiplying all of the number of nodes in each dimension together. If the seven region values are actually aggregates too, there would still be 588 aggregates.

In the real world, you would probably have hierarchies with many levels, and often several hierarchies located in the structural dimensions. You would also have other types of dimensions, such as categorical dimensions, that you could use to create aggregate values. A level in the product dimension could easily reach to over 100 possible values. Let's look at what happens if these 100 possible values for this level are built from an aggregate value. A cube with a product dimension with 100 attributes measured over a time grain of days and a geography grain of city that includes 500 cities would equal 500 x 100 x 365 = 18,250,000 aggregates. Boom! Data explosion! When you put five or six of these large structural and categorical dimensions—each with many attributes, resulting in hundreds of possible values—into a cube, you see how creating aggregations across the entire cube can create an explosion in the size of your database. What you need is a way to perform aggregations on points in your different cubes that will give the largest boost in performance, and a way not to perform aggregations on the rest of the points. As you can imagine, going through thousands of points to find the best ones can be very difficult.

Luckily, OLAP Services offers a tool that gives the minimum number of aggregations while still getting maximum efficiency. The OLAP Services aggregation tool uses the 80–20 rule. The 80–20 rule states that a set of aggregations can be found such that creating only 20 percent of the aggregations gives an 80 percent increase in performance. OLAP Services finds the aggregations that are required to fulfill the 80–20 rule. The aggregation tool is discussed further in the section on the Storage Design Wizard. One of the primary differences between ROLAP, HOLAP, and MOLAP is the way the aggregate values are stored. Let's now look at these three different methods of storing multidimensional data.

ROLAP, MOLAP, and HOLAP

Once you create a data warehouse using a star schema that contains fact and informational tables, you must next build the cubes that contain dimensions and measures that will be used by OLAP Services. You can save these cubes using ROLAP, HOLAP, or MOLAP. Different situations require different methods of storage; there is no one universal answer. This is one of the strong points of SQL Server 7.0; you are not limited to only one method of storage. With SQL Server 7.0, you can choose whichever of the three storage methods is best for your database or a combination of storage methods. Let's begin with a look at ROLAP.

ROLAP

When using a ROLAP storage scheme, OLAP Services places the aggregations in the relational data warehouse and uses the data in the data warehouse to build cubes and aggregations. This means that special multidimensional data structures are not used to store the data. An OLAP tool working with the ROLAP storage scheme must support all of the OLAP functionality (drill down, slicing, quick and uniform response, and so forth) and allow for aggregations. OLAP Services has all of this functionality.

With a ROLAP scheme, OLAP Services uses the tables that make up your star schema to build your cubes and aggregations. This means that the tables are not copied to a multidimensional database. If you store aggregate values, then these are stored in your relational table. Figure 4-3 illustrates a ROLAP solution.

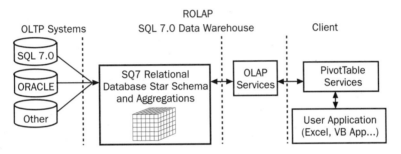

Figure 4-3. *A ROLAP solution.*

Caution   If you are using ROLAP, do not place your data warehouse in your OLTP database without first testing to determine if the OLAP database is degrading the performance of the OLTP database. For the most part, when using ROLAP, combining the OLTP and the OLAP data stores into one database will adversely affect the OTLP system and is generally considered bad design.

Storage Design Wizard

Let's take a look at one of our OLAP Services wizards, in particular, the Storage Design wizard. Before doing anything, though, make a backup of the FoodMart database, because you are about to make some changes to this database. Later, you can replace the modified version with the original. You will find the FoodMart.mdb database at \OLAP Services\Samples, if you installed the samples and used the default OLAP Services directory. Once you locate the database, make a copy of it to another directory. When you open FoodMart.mdb, you see the following tables, as shown in Figure 4-4.

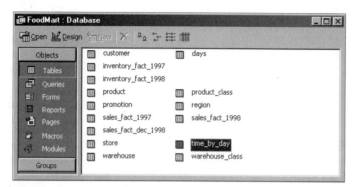

Figure 4-4. *FoodMart schema.*

Close the FoodMart database. Open the OLAP manager. As in the last chapter, open the FoodMart data warehouse. Right-click the Sales cube, and select Design Storage. This brings up the welcome flash screen, as shown in Figure 4-5.

Figure 4-5. *Welcome To The Storage Design Wizard screen.*

You can click Skip This Screen In The Future, as there are no other options on this screen. Click Next. This will bring you to the Select A Partition screen (or the Aggregations Already Exist screen).

Partitions are discussed later. For now, just click Next. You should now be at the screen for selecting data storage. You should have MOLAP selected. Change it to ROLAP, as shown in Figure 4-6. Click Next.

Aggregation Wizard

This now brings us to one of the most amazing wizards in OLAP: the Aggregation wizard. This tool allows you to balance between the amount of space required on the hard drive for the aggregations and the amount of increased performance achieved by the aggregations. You can choose to limit the number of aggregations by the amount of disk space required for these aggregations by selecting Estimated Storage Reaches. The default is 64 MB. Let's reduce that value, just to see how the optimizer works. Change the value to 10. This means that you are allowing 10 MB on your hard drive to store aggregations.

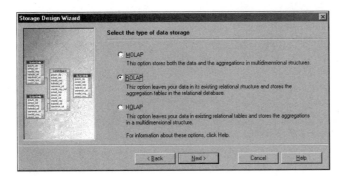

Figure 4-6. *Selecting the ROLAP storage design.*

Click Start and watch what happens. What you see is OLAP Services trying different combinations of aggregations to find the most efficient combination. Each attempt brings you closer to the most efficient combination of aggregations within your 10 MB limit. In my case, I arrived at the following, as shown in Figure 4-7.

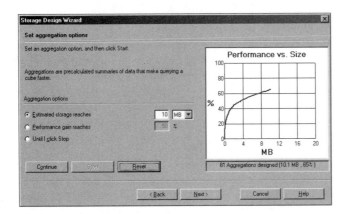

Figure 4-7. *Results after changing the estimated storage to 10 MB.*

By allowing 10 MB of hard drive space to store aggregations, I have given myself a 65% increase in performance over not having any aggregations. The DataMart database is small, so 10 MB goes a long way. Now let's click Performance Gain Reaches and select 80 percent. Click Continue. This time I arrived at the following, as shown in Figure 4-8.

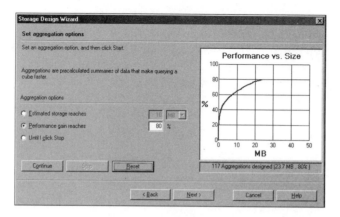

Figure 4-8. *Results after changing the performance gain to 80 percent.*

To achieve an 80 percent increase in performance, I need 23.7 MB of additional hard drive space for 177 aggregations. Finally, I will actually generate the aggregations. So I would not have to wait too long for OLAP Services to build the aggregations, I changed the performance gain percentage to 10 percent. I recommend you also do this.

Click Reset and then Yes when asked if you want to remove all of the designed aggregations. Click Start if you reset your aggregations. When the optimizer is done, note the predicted number of megabytes for the aggregations and click Next.

Note Processing cubes take a great deal of memory. If your machine has less than 100 MB of RAM, it is likely that processing a cube will take some time and will consume all of the resources of your computer.

On the last screen, leave the default Process Now and click Finish. This takes a few minutes, so now is a good time for a coffee break. When you're done, the process screen should look something like the one in Figure 4-9. This log shows the creation of tables in the FoodMart.mdb database for the aggregations requested to be saved to the data warehouse. When the aggregates are created, click Close on the Process screen.

Processing a ROLAP Cube

Once you change the design storage to ROLAP and run the Design Storage Wizard, only the aggregations are created. You can also update a cube by processing the cube. To process the cube, right-click Sales in the OLAP Manager and select Process. Because you don't want to calculate the aggregations again, choose Incremental Update, as shown in Figure 4-10, and then click OK.

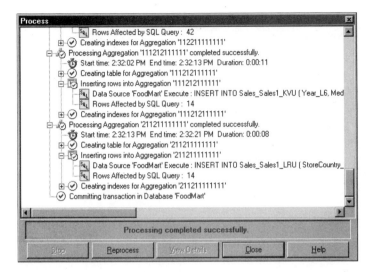

Figure 4-9.   *Log showing creation of the tables in the FoodMart database.*

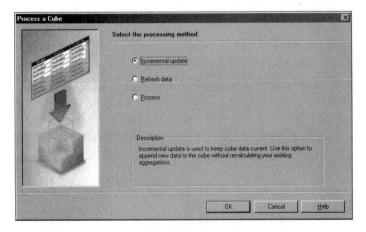

Figure 4-10.   *Choosing Incremental Update.*

You don't need the next splash screen, so you can click Skip This Screen In The Future and click Next.

Go through the rest of the screens clicking Next until you get to the last screen and then click Finish. Once again, you get the Process window, and once again, you are doing aggregations, as shown in Figure 4-11.

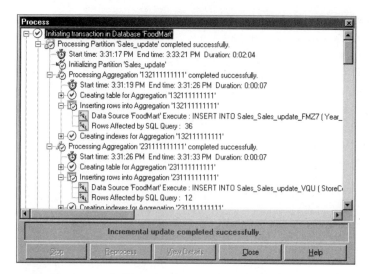

Figure 4-11. *Processing the incremental update.*

Looking through all of the entries, you will only find entries referring to the addition of aggregations. When the cube was processed, no data was copied from the star schema to a multidimensional database. The only way to process a ROLAP cube is to calculate aggregations and save them to the data warehouse.

When you open FoodMart.mdb now, you see additional tables. Figure 4-12 shows how the FoodMart.mdb database now looks.

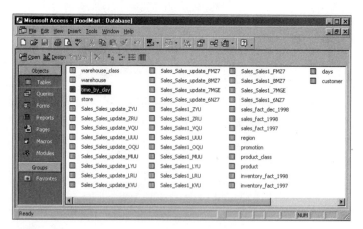

Figure 4-12. *FoodMart.mdb database additional tables.*

A series of sales tables have been added that contain the aggregations. You can open these tables and see what the aggregations look like. Using ROLAP only resulted in the aggregations being added to the relational database.

Look at the size of the FoodMart.mdb file. My aggregation wizard predicted that my database would require roughly 24 MB of space for the aggregations. The actual change was less than 1 MB. The aggregation wizard gives you a conservative estimate. Compare the size of the database with and without aggregations to see if your prediction is correct. Close the OLAP Manager, delete the modified database, and replace it with the original database.

Real World   Restoring the database in this way should never be done in the real world. You get away with this because you put the cube back to MOLAP in a moment and the aggregations are not needed.

It is extremely important to realize that, when using ROLAP, the star schema of your data warehouse is used by OLAP Services to perform your queries. The more you optimize your data warehouse, the quicker OLAP Services performs your analytical queries. One of the most important parts of optimizing your relational data warehouse is using indexes. Before looking at MOLAP, let's look at indexes in the relational data warehouse.

Indexes

Indexes on columns are used in relational databases to improve the efficiency of returning data when performing SELECT queries on the tables. If I place an index on the customer's social security number column in my employee database, the index allows me to find a record with a particular customer name much faster than if no index existed. In a table with thousands of records, the time to find the records with the employee number "000 00 0001," in an un-indexed social security number column, is substantially longer than finding the record when the social security number column is indexed.

In SQL Server 7.0, there are two types of indexes. The first type is called a b–tree (b is for balanced) index. The second type is called a clustered index. The primary difference between the two is that the clustered index actually arranges the data on the hard drive in a particular order. In terms of the social security column, the data is placed numerically.

Indexes and Accessing ROLAP Stored Data

Before you can determine the best type of indexes for your data warehouse, you must step back and think about what type of queries OLAP Services might perform on the data stored with ROLAP. A star schema is designed with small dimensions that have descriptive attributes that could be used by the user to select the value in the dimension that they want to analyze a measure over. When a value of a dimension is selected by a user, OLAP Services searches for the row that has that value, and finds the primary key that is associated with that value. This process is repeated for each of the dimensions, until you have a primary key for each of the dimensions. Once OLAP Services has this, it can then find the record in the fact table that corresponds to the set of primary keys from the dimensions. The fact tables, which can be very large, are then searched by the primary keys of the dimensions to find the entry in the fact table that has a set of foreign keys corresponding to the dimension's primary keys. OLAP Services does something like what is shown in Figure 4-13.

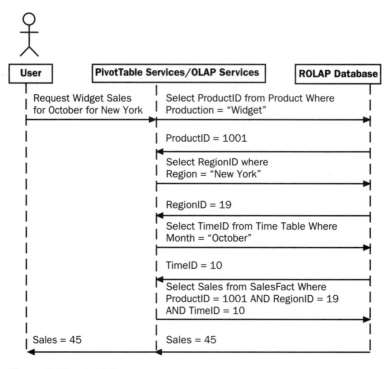

Figure 4-13. *ROLAP request.*

Thus, you can see that dimensions are searched on the descriptive attributes that the user is most likely to select, and the fact tables are searched on the foreign keys that correspond to the primary keys of the dimensions. As these are the attributes of your tables that OLAP Services will search on, these are the attributes that you should put indexes on when using ROLAP to store your data. Certain fields are unlikely to be searched on, such as customer last name. These fields do not need an index. Zip code may be something that is frequently used to divide data up by region and so would be a good candidate for an index. All of the foreign keys in the fact table should have an index placed on them.

Disadvantages of Indexes

One disadvantage of indexes is the increased amount of time it takes to insert data into the database. This is especially true of clustered indexes. With analytical databases, you only do inserts when you update the tables, which could be daily, weekly, or monthly.

This means that the reduced performance with inserts is usually not an issue with a data warehouse. If the time that is required to insert new information into the data warehouse becomes excessive, then it might be necessary to remove some of the indexes or optimize them. If indexes are required and are slowing your updates substantially, you might want to remove them during updates and replace them once the update is done, as SQL Server 7.0 can put an index into the database in a relatively short period of time. SQL Server 7.0 also allows you to create file groups, which can help with slow updates.

File Groups and ROLAP Data Storage

File groups allow you to store relational SQL Server 7.0 database tables on different hard drives on your server. These can be multiple hard drives or multiple RAID devices. By placing your data on several hard drives, you can improve the performance of updates of large tables. The improvement in performance is a result of the writing of information to different tables on different disks at the same time. If you want more details on building SQL Server 7.0 file groups, look at the SQL Server 7.0 documentation or any book on SQL Server 7.0.

File groups bring out one of the major advantages of using ROLAP: with ROLAP, you can use all of the tools for a relational SQL Server 7.0 database for your cube data. When it comes to extremely large amounts of data, especially in the terabyte range, SQL Server 7.0 offers a wide range of options to maximize performance of the data. File groups are designed for very large relational databases, and analytical databases can easily become very large. Thus, ROLAP offers you all of the advantages of a SQL Server 7.0's relational database. This is an important point to remember when building a data warehouse.

Clustered and Nonclustered Indexes

When creating indexes, you have two choices: clustered and nonclustered indexes. These can be single-column or composite indexes (an index on several columns). A clustered index must be unique, that is, the values in the column must be unique for every value. A clustered index stores the data in some order, such as alphabetical or numerical. Nonclustered indexes are not stored in any particular order, but there are references to where the data is stored for quick retrieval.

You should group together the foreign keys in the fact table and make them into an index. The primary keys in the informational tables could be clustered indexes, but they don't have to be. You should also put indexes on the attributes in the informational tables that are frequently searched on. If you are concerned about slowing down inserts by adding the indexes, check the performance.

Using DTS, you cannot insert data into a table without logging if there are indexes and data in the table. Logging will slow the insert down considerably. To insert without logging using DTS you will need to do the following:

1. Remove the indexes by dropping the indexes prior to the insert and recreating them after the insert.

2. Select *Select Into/Bulk Insert* in the properties of the table.

3. Select *Perform Fast load* in the properties of the DTS workflow.

4. Select the Table Lock option in the *Advanced* tab of the transformation.

The proper choice of an index can substantially reduce disk I/O, which greatly improves the performance of record retrieval. Nonclustered indexes are best for the retrieval of a few rows. Clustered indexes are good for scanning over a range of data. Indexes should use a small data type, especially clustered indexes. Placing a nonclustered index on a column in a large table that has only a few unique values will probably decrease performance. Good examples of nonclustered indexes include invoice numbers, unique customer numbers, social security numbers, and telephone numbers. Clustered indexes are for columns used in queries that retrieve ranges that do not have many unique values, such as all values between September and June. Good candidates for a clustered index include states, company branches, date of sale, zip codes, and customer district. Defining a clustered index on the columns that have unique values, such as a primary key, may not be beneficial unless typical queries on the system retrieve large sequential ranges of the unique values. The best choice for the column with the clustered index is the column that is used to retrieve ranges of values. Typically, a clustered index is chosen for a column used in a query in the following way:

```
...WHERE <column_name>  > some_value

...WHERE <column_name> BETWEEN some_value AND some_value

...WHERE <column_name> < some_value
```

Which column is chosen for a clustered index depends on the table and how the table is used. This is another reason why it is so important to have a clear understanding of the business process before building a data warehouse. If users most often perform queries over monthly date ranges, then it makes sense to have a clustered index on the months. If users query on ranges of order numbers, then the order number is a good candidate for a clustered index. Let's now look at MOLAP.

MOLAP

While ROLAP leaves everything in the relational database, MOLAP does the exact opposite. MOLAP places all of the data required for OLAP Services into a special multidimensional database. A MOLAP solution looks like the one shown in Figure 4-14.

When you use the same informational table for identical dimensions in different cubes, the same data is copied into the multidimensional database for all of the cubes using that informational table. Thus, if you have five cubes all using the time informational table to make a time dimension, you will have five copies of the identical time information in your multidimensional databases. This is not only a waste of space, but also a waste of time to transfer the information into the database. Remember how long it took to create the aggregates for this small database. A very large database with gigabytes of data can take hours to process. If each informational table in the data warehouse is transferred only once to the multidimensional database, and then this one copy is used by all of the cubes, the transfer takes significantly less time than if the informational table is copied many times into identical dimensions for each cube. Later in the chapter, virtual cubes are discussed, which allow one copy of a dimension in the multidimensional database to be used by all of the cubes.

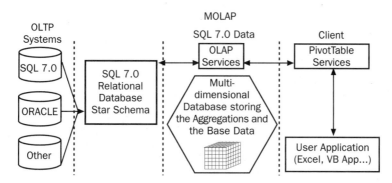

Figure 4-14. *A MOLAP solution.*

Creating a MOLAP Cube

Go back to the OLAP Manager and select the Sales cube. Right-click and select Design Storage. When the Aggregations Already Exist screen comes up, notice that the size of the aggregates created with ROLAP are less than 1 MB (0.74 MB in my case), as shown in Figure 4-15.

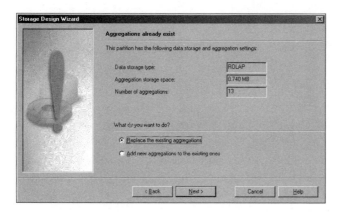

Figure 4-15. *The Aggregations Already Exist screen.*

Leave the default Replace The Existing Aggregations. Click Next. For the type of storage, click MOLAP, as shown in Figure 4-16.

Click Next. In the Aggregation Wizard screen, select Performance Gain Reaches and type in 10, as shown in Figure 4-17.

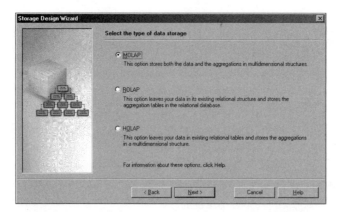

Figure 4-16.   *Selecting MOLAP as the type of data storage.*

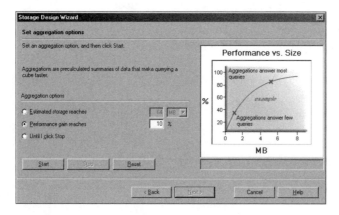

Figure 4-17.   *Changing the performance gain value to 10.*

Click Start to run the aggregation wizard. Click Next, and on the next screen click Finish. Close the Process screen. This time there are no additional tables placed in the FoodMart.mdb. Where did the aggregations go? Go to Program Files\ OLAP Services\Data\FoodMart where you will find files for all of FoodMart's MOLAP dimensions and indexes. Under Program Files\OLAP Services\Data\FoodMart\Sales, you will find the data files related to the Sales cube. All of the data for the cube and the aggregations are stored in the Sales.data file.

Process the cube again as you just did (right-click on the Sales cube and select the Process option). This time, though, instead of creating aggregations, processing the cube moves data from the data warehouse into the multidimensional database. The aggregations are not processed again.

If you open the Storage Design wizard again, you see that only .048 MB was required to improve performance by 10%, which is much less than with ROLAP, as shown in Figure 4-18.

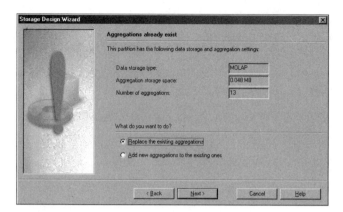

Figure 4-18.   *ROLAP aggregation storage space at .048 MB.*

OLAP Services only creates the aggregations that are required. Close the storage design wizard by clicking Cancel. OLAP Services also reduces the size of your data by not including empty records. For example, there might be 500 products, but a particular store may have only sold 100 products on a particular day. Looking at the sales for that day, you have 400 empty records. These empty records create something that is called sparsity of data. OLAP Services deals with sparse data by not storing the missing values in the database. MOLAP also uses special bitmap indexing. Even though you are copying the data from the data warehouse to a special multidimensional database with MOLAP, the base data—without aggregations in the multidimensional database—should be smaller than the original relational data warehouse.

By choosing MOLAP, all of the data and all of the aggregations are placed into special files in a special multidimensional format. You can only view these special files using OLAP Services. These files are optimized for use with OLAP Services and will result in the best performance for multidimensional queries. Now that you understand what MOLAP and ROLAP are, let's see what each has to offer and when to use each of them.

MOLAP vs. ROLAP

When using ROLAP, data is stored in relational tables. These tables are in a relational database format and can be viewed. Inexperienced system administrators with multidimensional databases can leverage their OLTP relational database skills to maintain and work with the database.

There is no duplication of the data in ROLAP, as the data in the data warehouse is used directly by the OLTP system. Thus, ROLAP uses less disk space.

Because data is in a relational format, and not a multidimensional format, it takes more time to perform analysis on the data. Remember that SQL Server queries are not very efficient for performing analytical queries. With a relational data structure, you have to rely on SQL Server queries for your analytical queries. Drilling down into the data takes a very long time, as SQL Server is very inefficient for this purpose. Using SQL Server to perform queries also means that the amount of time required to return the same query might vary.

MOLAP requires extra disk space, as the information in the data warehouse has to be moved into the multidimensional database in order for OLAP Services to perform queries on the data. Yet, this data is compressed, uses bitmapped indexes, and requires less storage space than the original relational data warehouse.

MOLAP is extremely quick and efficient because it uses a multidimensional database to store the data. The return times for the data are consistent and fast.

MOLAP requires a significant amount of time to transfer the data from the data warehouse into the multidimensional database. This time can range from hours to days, depending on how the data is transferred and how much data is transferred.

Thus, in summary, ROLAP requires less storage space, requires longer query times, and uses relational data stores. ROLAP is an ideal candidate for a data warehouse that contains data that is rarely accessed and/or is extremely large (in the many gigabyte range). Most corporations divide their historical data into two groups, which I call current historical data and archived historical data. Current historical data is frequently used and covers a certain time period, usually two years. Archived historical data is rarely used and covers the time period extending beyond the first group (usually beyond two years). The size of the archived historical data can be very large, because it might span many years, even decades. As there are only occasional queries on this data, the slower performance of ROLAP might not be as important as the savings in database storage or the benefits of using SQL Server's relational database format.

Although it is true that disk space is relatively cheap, there is a lot more involved than the cost of a disk when creating a separate MOLAP copy of the archived historical data. If the archived historical data has to be moved into the MOLAP system from a legacy database, it can take weeks or months—if planning and the actual transference of the data is considered in the time estimate. Once stored in the MOLAP format, this additional MOLAP database has to be backed up on a regular basis (you don't want to transfer all of the data again), properly maintained, and updated. The hardware for a system that can store hundreds of gigabytes with fault tolerance and backup protection can be very expensive in terms of purchase and maintenance costs. When building a data warehouse, the question you want to answer is: "Is it worth the cost of purchasing, building, designing, and maintaining a MOLAP system in order to get extra performance on a set of queries rarely performed?" The answer to that question depends on the situation. These questions are addressed further in the DTS chapter. HOLAP, which is addressed in a moment, is another possible solution.

As for the current historical data and the majority of data warehouses, MOLAP is the best answer. If you are building a data warehouse where frequent queries are expected and performance is an issue, MOLAP will give you the best performance. The investment in a larger system pays for itself when information can be quickly and efficiently retrieved from the data warehouse.

A central idea behind Microsoft's Digital Nervous System is getting the right information to the right person in an efficient, timely manner. A MOLAP system can deliver historical information to anyone in the corporation. Combining the data warehouse with the Internet, you can deliver information to anyone, anywhere in the world. Thus, the manager in charge of inventory in a factory in Asia, working for a company headquartered in the United States, can log on through the Internet and query a data warehouse located in Europe. The manager can look at production in the factory, find which assembly lines have been producing well, and then analyze their techniques to find ways to improve the overall factory. Using a ROLAP system to do queries over the Internet would probably be too slow. The MOLAP system, properly tuned, can return answers in a reasonable time, even over the Internet. MOLAP is not always the right solution, but it is the best solution when the size of the database is less important than the speed and efficiency of performing analytical queries.

You might want a system that doesn't use too much storage space or doesn't require the transference of all of the data into a multidimensional database, but still provides better performance than ROLAP. For these situations, there is a hybrid form of data storage, called HOLAP, which is the middle ground between ROLAP and MOLAP.

HOLAP

HOLAP doesn't move the data from the data warehouse to the multidimensional database. In this way, HOLAP is like ROLAP. The aggregations, though, are stored in a multidimensional database. Figure 4-19 shows what a HOLAP solution looks like.

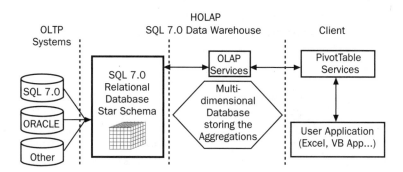

Figure 4-19. *A HOLAP solution.*

Thus far, the discussion on ROLAP and MOLAP has only focused on the storing of aggregates and the data. As mentioned in the last chapter, summing measures does not always yield a meaningful result. With degenerate dimensions you could be taking averages. When using SQL Server 7.0, these are called summary functions and use statements such as AVG, COUNT, COUNT(*), MAX, MIN, SUM, STDEV, STDEVP, VAR, and VARP. In OLAP Services, calculated members are usually used for summary data. Calculated members are stored in memory and recalculated when they are requested. In a database that has a high level of aggregations, the calculated members can be found by OLAP Services very quickly. In a HOLAP database with a high number of aggregations, determining the values of calculated members is very fast, because only aggregations are stored in the multidimensional database. For calculated members, a HOLAP database might be faster than a MOLAP database. Thus, HOLAP can be an efficient storage medium for a fact table comprised of calculated members.

Like ROLAP, HOLAP's drill down is slow. Getting information from aggregations, though, is quick. Overall, HOLAP gives better performance than ROLAP, but, with the exception of calculated members, is slower than MOLAP. If the current historical data is further divided into two groups by time, it is possible to store the older current data as HOLAP, if it is not accessed too frequently. Again, these decisions need to be based on the needs of the corporation and the requirements of the data warehouse. There is no single solution. This is why OLAP Services allows you to save your data in any of the three formats.

Partitions

Important The standard edition of SQL Server 7.0 does not allow you to build user partitions. In this section, we will use a partition to add the 1998 data. This 1998 data will then be used in later examples in the book. To do these examples with the Standard Edition, you will need another way of getting the 1998 data into the Sales cube so you can do the examples.

On the CD, in the folder Standard Edition is a different version of the FoodMart.mdb Access database. This version has both the 1997 and 1998 data in the Fact_1997 table. Close the OLAP Manager if you have it open. Move the original FoodMart.mdb Access database to someplace where you can store it if you need it later. The default location for the database is C:\Program Files\ OLAP Services\Samples. Copy the FoodMart.mdb database on the CD in the Standard folder to the Samples folder on your hard drive. Reopen the OLAP Manager. Expand the tree and right-click on the Sales cube. Select Process. Choose Process on the Select Processing Method screen and click OK. It will take several minutes to process the new data. When the processing is complete, click OK. Right-click on the Sales cube again and select Refresh. You will now have both the 1997 and 1998 data and be able to do all of the examples in the book. You can read the section on partitions if you like, but you cannot do the examples with the Standard Edition. You can also skip down to the virtual cube section.

Another factor that can affect your data storage method type is partitions. Partitions allow you to physically divide your ROLAP cubes into separate smaller pieces on the hard drive. Partitions also allow you to assign one part of your cube to one type of data storage and another part to a different type of data storage. This means that one part of your cube can be stored with HOLAP while another part can be stored with MOLAP. This gives you a very flexible means of data storage, as well as improves overall efficiency of numerous operations.

If you divide your ROLAP cube into two partitions each on different physical hard drives and put half of the data on one partition and half on the other, you can transfer data into the cube in both hard drives at the same time. This substantially increases performance over using only one hard drive.

When partitions are created, each partition has its own aggregations. This means that you can store different dimensions in different partitions and create different types of aggregations for the various dimensions in the cube. In this way, very large dimensions can have an aggregation that best suits the data. You can also set different types of data storage for the different partitions, allowing you to choose the best storage mechanism for the dimensions.

Partition Wizard

Let's look at some of the partitions that already exist in the FoodMart data warehouse. In the OLAP Manager, expand the view for the cubes, and then click Sales and finally Partitions. On the right pane, click Metadata and you should see the following, shown in Figure 4-20.

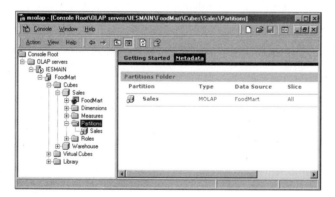

Figure 4-20.   *Sales MOLAP partition.*

The Sales cube has only one partition, the default one that is made when the cube is created. When you click on Metadata, you see the properties of this partition. You see that there is a MOLAP cube and that the slice is called All (the name of the slice for all of the default partitions). Click the Sales partition, and then right-click. Select Edit to see the properties of this cube, as shown in Figure 4-21.

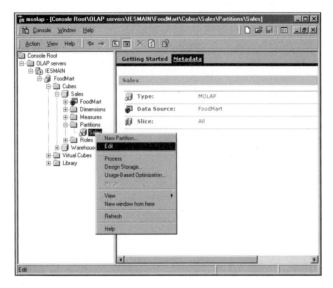

Figure 4-21. *Selecting Edit in the Sales Partition.*

This brings up the Partition Wizard. The Partition Wizard allows you to make new partitions and edit existing ones.

Figure 4-22 shows that this partition is built from Sales_Fact_1997. Thus, this cube currently contains the data from the 1997 fact table. Because it is a MOLAP cube, it means that the data for 1997 has been moved from the relational data warehouse into the multidimensional database. It would be useful to add the information from 1998, too. If you look into the original FoodMart.mdb, you see that there is also a sales fact table for 1998 called Sales_Fact_1998. Let's use a partition to add the 1998 sales data to the cube. Click Cancel in the Partition Wizard.

Click the Sales partition, and then right-click and select New Partition.

If the Welcome To The Partition Wizard screen comes up, click Skip This Screen In The Future, because you don't need this screen to make partitions.

Click Next. This brings you to the first real screen of the Partition Wizard. If the current fact table is Sales_Fact_1997, you need to change this to Sales_Fact_1998. To do this, click the Change button. In the Choose A Fact Table, select Sales_Fact_1998.

Click OK and then Next. The next screen allows you to slice your data by dimension, as shown in Figure 4-23.

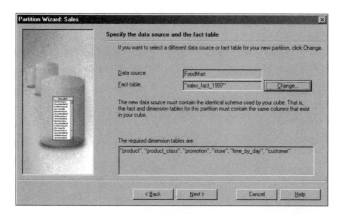

Figure 4-22. *The Specifying The Data Source And The Fact Table screen.*

Tip   When data in a cube is summed, any redundant data elements (the same data element duplicated in more than one dimension) that are present in more than one partition are summarized as if they are different data elements. This can produce incorrect summaries and erroneous data for the user. For example, if a sales transaction for a product is duplicated in the fact tables for two partitions, summaries of this product's sales can include a double accounting of the duplicated transaction. It is important that you properly separate the data when you build the fact tables.

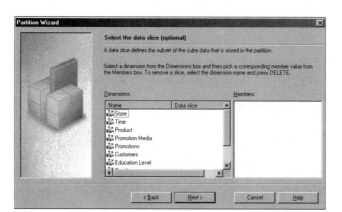

Figure 4-23. *Slicing the data by dimension.*

If you skip this step, all dimensions are selected. Skip this step. Click Next. Type **Sales 1998** in the Partition Name box, and then click Finish.

Storage Design Wizard

You are now in the Storage Design Wizard. To save the sales for 1998 as MOLAP, do exactly as you did before. Select MOLAP on Select The Type Of Data Storage and click Next. You can choose any performance gain. I chose 10% so that the calculations would not take too long. Click Start, then Next, and finally Finish. Click Close in the Process window. You should now see the new Sales 1998 partition listed.

Let's see if the data is there. Click the Sales cube, and click Data on the right window-pane, as shown in Figure 4-24.

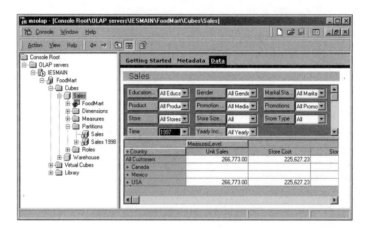

Figure 4-24. *Sales data for 1997 and 1998.*

Click the Time drop-down list box and select 1998, as shown in Figure 4-25.

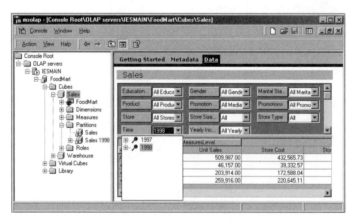

Figure 4-25. *Selecting sales data for 1998.*

Notice that the value of your data has changed. Drag the Time button to the Country button in the grid. Figure 4-26 shows the results of doing this.

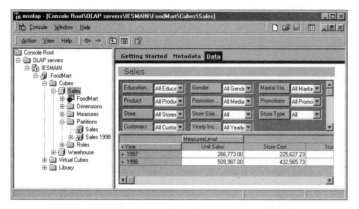

Figure 4-26.   *Results of replacing Country with Time.*

Drill Down

Double-click Year to drill down into the values for the two years. You should see the following, as in Figure 4-27.

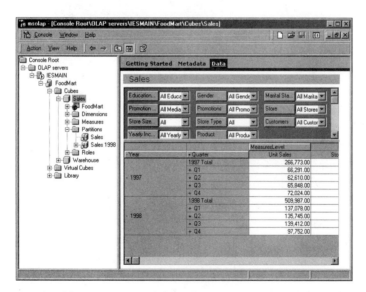

Figure 4-27.   *Values for 1997 and 1998.*

When drilling down is mentioned, moving up and down a hierarchy is usually assumed. You can expand the quarters even more to drill further down the time hierarchy. Yet, drilling down actually has a much broader meaning. To see this, drag the Gender button to the specific Quarter row below the Quarter bar. You should now see the following, as in Figure 4-28.

You have divided the yearly sales by gender. You can now see the value for All Gender, female (F), and male (M). Drill down really adds another column to your view. You can move up and down any of the hierarchies. These hierarchies might or might not be part of the dimension you start with. Looking at the data, you see little difference in sales between men and women. Grab the gender button and drag it back up to the top area. Drag and drop different dimensions, such as store size, to see the patterns (or lack of patterns) in the different measures. This is what drill down is all about. Building partitions does more than break the data into segments (1997 and 1998 in this case). It also allows you to find the most efficient way to store the data. Take some time to drag dimensions into the grid and to expand dimensions.

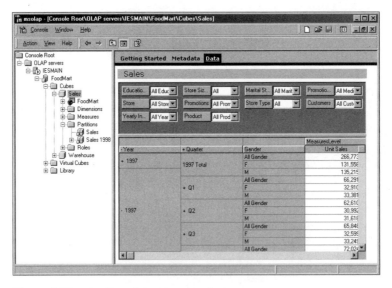

Figure 4-28. *Drilling down into gender.*

Storing Data and Partitions

You have now added the 1998 data into the database. Let's step back in time and say it is January 1, 1999. Let's imagine that in the company, FoodMart, very few people look at data that is over one year old. You have your 1997 data stored in a MOLAP cube, which gives you the maximum performance. Yet, this performance is not really needed, because hardly anyone looks at this data. You could downgrade the 1997 cube to a HOLAP cube (or even possibly a ROLAP cube) and save considerable space on your hard drives. Let's do this. Click the Partitions folder, and then click Sales. Right-click Sales and select De-sign Storage, as shown in Figure 4-29.

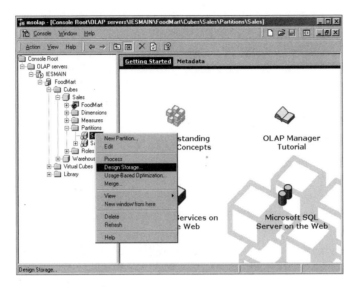

Figure 4-29.   *Selecting design storage for the sales partition.*

You should get the Aggregations Exist screen. Leave the default Replace The Existing Aggregations and click Next. For the data storage type, select HOLAP and click Next. After you enter your performance gain (I have once again selected a performance gain of 10 percent so the aggregations can be built quickly), click Start.

Click Next and then click Finish. Close the Process window. Go to Partitions and right-click, select Refresh and click Metadata in the right windowpane. You should now see HOLAP, as shown in Figure 4-30.

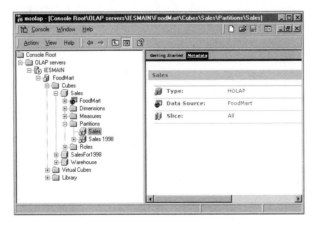

Figure 4-30.   *Sales partition folder.*

Thus, another powerful feature of partitions is the ability to put a portion of the data in one storage format, while putting another portion in another format. Partitions can be used to divide a cube's data, to aggregate different parts of a cube's data, and to store different parts of the cube in different storage formats. There is one more thing to do, and that is spread the cube over several hard drives. Unfortunately, you cannot do this with partitions; partitions can only be saved to the default location. When you go to \Program Files\OLAP Services\Data\FoodMart\Sales you see that there is a new .dat file created for your new partition. Although you must create all of your partitions on the same hard drive because you have no control over where the .dat file is stored, you can divide cubes up between different hard drives using something called virtual cubes.

Virtual Cubes

Virtual cubes are among the more powerful features of SQL Server 7.0 data warehouses. Instead of building one cube with several partitions, you can build several cubes and, using a virtual cube, join these cubes together. Figure 4-31 illustrates this.

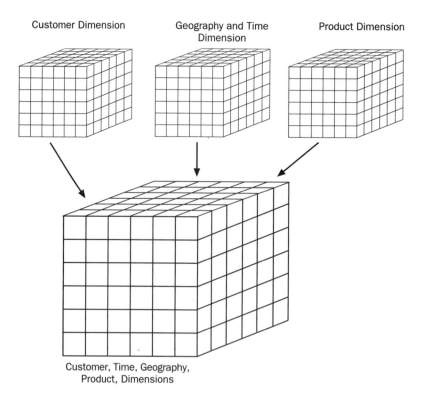

Customer Dimension   Geography and Time Dimension   Product Dimension

Customer, Time, Geography, Product, Dimensions

Figure 4-31. *Creating a virtual cube.*

In this diagram, all of the cubes must have the same fact tables. The three cubes must also all be part of the same data warehouse. You might want to divide a cube up like this if some of the data is extremely large. Providing your server has enough processors and memory, you could update the multiple partitions at the same time. This can substantially reduce the amount of time required to transfer data from the data warehouse to MOLAP cubes. This can also reduce the time it takes to read the data when using ROLAP or MOLAP. Yet, there is a much more powerful use of virtual cubes.

Imagine two departments that both want data marts and that some of the dimensions in both data marts are the same, while others are particular to the mart. By using virtual cubes, you can build the following solutions, as shown in Figure 4-32.

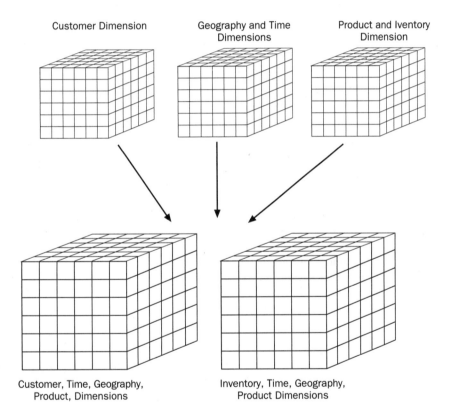

Figure 4-32. *Solutions built with virtual cubes.*

Thus, virtual cubes can solve the problem of creating islands of data. You can create multiple cubes containing dimensions and then share these dimensions across the enterprise. In this way, each data mart can have its own dimensions, but not duplicate dimensions used by other data marts. You can also build one large data warehouse with all of the cubes and then create virtual cubes to provide data marts across the corporation. Each solution requires special considerations. With the flexibility of virtual cubes, partitions, and the ability to create ROLAP, HOLAP, or MOLAP solutions, you can customize your data warehouse to get maximum performance.

There are still other uses of virtual cubes. If you are using ROLAP, you can prevent the copying of the same dimensions into multiple multidimensional databases by creating the dimension once and then using that dimension in multiple virtual cubes. This is useful when the dimension is on one server and will be used by a data warehouse on a separate server. If the dimensions are all in the same data warehouse, then shared dimensions can be used instead. The final use of virtual cubes is security.

Imagine that you want to create one cube, but need different views depending on the role of the person who has logged on. One example is the region dimension. You might not want the Northeast region manager to see sales details for the Southeast, Northwest, and Southwest regions. Yet, you want the manager of the United States, as well as the CEO and other high-level people, to see all regions. You can make one cube that has all four regions and then create four virtual cubes for each region. The Northeast manager only has access to the Northeast region cube, while high-level management has access to the real cube with all four regions. Creating roles for your cubes allows you to create security by using virtual cubes. Now let's look at roles.

Roles

You probably are not surprised to discover that there is a Role Wizard for making roles. Chapter 2 discussed the importance of determining the roles for the different users of your system. The example in Chapter 2 mentions a marketing manager and a sales manager who need to view the same data in different ways. By creating sales and marketing manager roles and defining different cube views for both roles, you can easily give both managers the information they want without building redundant data warehouses or marts.

Viewing Roles

In OLAP Services, the permissions for the roles are based on NT security. You can take the users or groups who have permission in your NT security and assign them to a role in OLAP Manager. In the OLAP Manager, expand Library and then expand Roles. You should find that there is already an All Users role there. Click Metadata on the right pane and you should see the following, as in Figure 4-33.

Notice that there are no virtual cubes listed. To see why the Warehouse And Sales cube is not listed, expand the Virtual Cubes folder, right-click the Warehouse And Sales folder, and select Manage Roles, as shown in Figure 4-34.

This brings us the Manage The Cube Roles screen. At this time, there are no roles assigned to the virtual cube. This is why the virtual cube was not listed in roles.

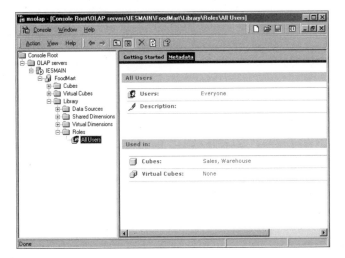

Figure 4-33.   *Viewing roles.*

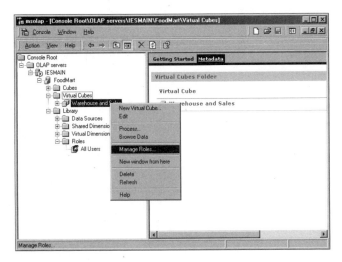

Figure 4-34.   *Manage Roles screen.*

Assigning a Role to the Virtual Warehouse and Sales Cube

There is only one role in this database, All Users. Click the right arrow and move it from the left Database Roles list box to the right Cube Access list box, as shown in Figure 4-35.

Notice that there is a button labeled New Role. You can create a new role here or in the Roles folder under Library. Click New Role. The Create A Database Role window should come up, as shown in Figure 4-36.

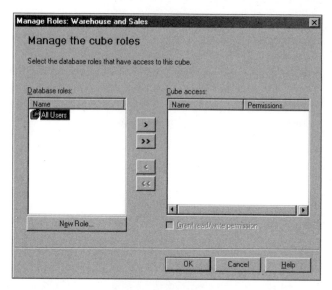

Figure 4-35. *Moving all users to the Cube Access list box.*

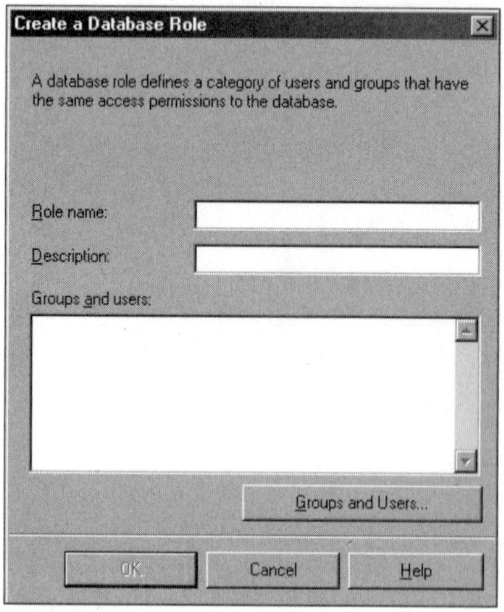

Figure 4-36. *Creating a database role.*

Select Groups And Users. You should now see a list of NT users and groups, as in Figure 4-37.

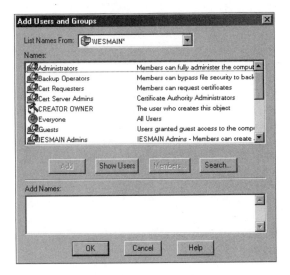

Figure 4-37. *List of NT users and groups.*

Select Cancel on the two new roles screens, and click OK on the Manage Roles screen. Now when you click on the Library folder, Roles folder, and All Users, you should see the virtual cube, Warehouse And Sales.

The OLAP Management Console

You have been using the management console to move through the folder hierarchy and get access to all of the wizards. The Metadata tab on the right window gives details without having to open a wizard. For example, if you click FoodMart and then click Metadata, you see general information on the FoodMart data warehouse, as shown in Figure 4-38.

From this view, you can see that all of the cubes have been processed, when they were processed, the number of partitions, and the size of the data warehouse. As the OLAP Manager is really nothing more than the Microsoft Management Console, you can add other snap-ins to the console.

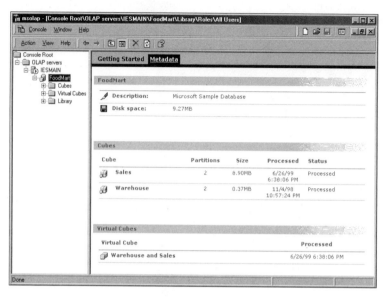

Figure 4-38. *General information on the FoodMart data warehouse.*

Adding Snap-Ins to the Microsoft Management Console

The OLAP Manager is just one of many Microsoft Management Console (MMC) snap-ins. The MMC hosts many administrative tools. These tools can be run in their own instance of the MMC, or multiple administrative tools may be run in the same instance of the MMC. The default is to open one administrative tool at a time in the MMC.

If your database is in SQL Server 7.0, you can add SQL Server 7.0 to the OLAP Manager. Go to the OLAP Manager menu, and select Console/Add/Remove Snap-in.

On the Add/Remove window click Add. This will bring up the Add Standalone Snap-in. Find Microsoft SQL Server Enterprise Manager. Click it and then click Add.

Click Close on the Add Standalone Snap-in screen. Click OK on the Add/Remove Snap-in screen. Your OLAP management console should look like the one shown in Figure 4-39.

There are many snap-ins that can be added. This makes it easier to work with different tools in one place.

There are other wizards that are part of the OLAP management console (such as the Usage-Based Optimization Wizard) which are not discussed in this chapter. They are discussed in the DTS chapter. There is still one more wizard to discuss before leaving this chapter: the Cube Wizard.

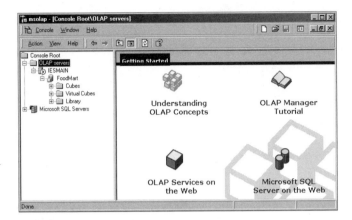

Figure 4-39.   *OLAP management console.*

Cube Wizard

The Cube Wizard is used to build new cubes and edit existing cubes. The Cube Wizard was briefly discussed in the last chapter. Now that you understand what partitions, aggregations, and HOLAP, ROLAP, and MOLAP are, let's take a closer look at the Cube Wizard. In the cube Wizard, you pick the tables in the data warehouse that you are going to use to build the star schema and then join them together into the star schema. Once these tables are selected, choose the dimensions and facts you want to use in your cubes. It's easy to get confused between building the star schema and selecting dimensions and facts, as you begin doing one and then start doing the other. The Cube Wizard really makes no distinction between building the star schema and building the cube. I will point out the applicable process as you proceed.

Creating the Sales 1998 Cube Using the Cube Wizard

Even though you already added the 1998 sales figures to the sales cube, let's create a 1998 sales cube to be used as an example. The schema of the sales cube looks like the one shown in Figure 4-40.

Begin by right-clicking Cubes in the FoodMart folder hierarchy. Select New Cube/Wizard.

If the welcome screen comes up, click Skip This Screen In The Future, as shown in Figure 4-41, and then click Next.

The first thing you must do is select the fact table for your star schema. In the Select A Fact Table For Your Cube, select Sales_Fact_1998, as shown in Figure 4-42.

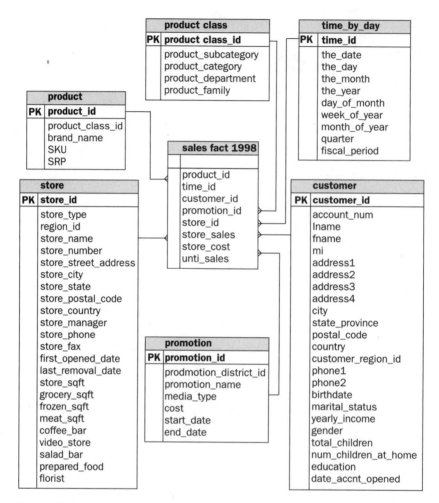

Figure 4-40. *Schema of the 1998 sales cube.*

Click Next. Now you are going to switch from building your star schema to selecting the measures that you want to measure across your cube. Under the Fact Table Numeric Columns list box, select Store_Sales, store_Cost, and Unit_Sales and move them over to the Cube Measures list box, as shown in Figure 4-43. These columns you are choosing in the fact table will be the measures in your cube that you will perform calculations on over your cube.

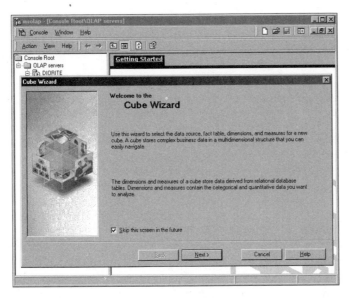

Figure 4-41.   *Welcome to the Cube Wizard screen.*

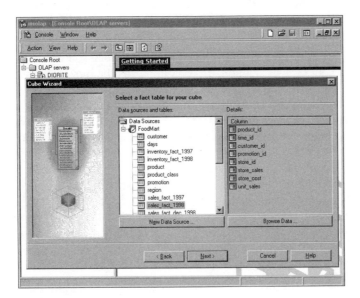

Figure 4-42.   *Selecting the Sales_Fact_1998 table.*

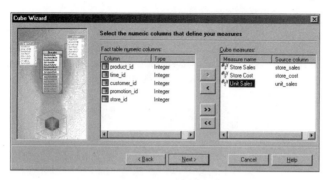

Figure 4-43. *Selecting the measures for the cube.*

Note Notice that you can add additional data sources for your cube, which means that you can build your cubes from multiple data sources. As the data can come from any OLE-DB compliant data source, you can build your cube from any data stored in the enterprise that has an OLE DB provider. If you are storing your data in either ROLAP or HOLAP, you can divide the data across multiple databases by placing the data in multiple databases and choosing multiple data sources for your cube. As mentioned earlier, you can also build one database and spread the data over multiple hard drives using file groups.

For your ROLAP and HOLAP solutions, spreading the data across multiple databases could improve the speed of drilling down into the data. While you can use multiple data sources for your MOLAP solution, this only improves the movement of the data into the MOLAP data warehouse. Once in the MOLAP data warehouse, drill down is done with the multidimensional database, not the original multiple relational data-bases. Thus, placing data in multiple databases and then building your cubes from these multiple sources, can improve drill down performance in HOLAP and ROLAP and improve the efficiency of moving data into a MOLAP cube. On the other hand, creating multiple data sources incurs considerable added expense, maintenance, planning, and effort. For a MOLAP solution, you can also move all of the data in a regular staging relational data warehouse and then move it into the multidimensional database. All transformations and cleansing of the data can be done when moving the data into the staging data warehouse. These solutions should only be considered when the maximum efficiency of the system must be obtained at all costs, such as when there are extremely large tables.

Click Next. What you see on this screen is really a mixture of building the star schema informational tables and building your dimensions. Listed under Shared Dimensions is a list of other dimensions that have already been defined for this fact table in your data warehouse.

> **Note** Remember that you expanded the Sales cube to include the 1998 sales by adding an extra partition (or changing the fact table if you do not have the Enterprise edition) with the 1998 sales data. Because of this, you now have a set of dimensions defined for the 1998 sales fact table.

Instead of redefining these (which is rather time consuming), you can simply reuse the original 1998 dimensions by sharing them. This is the same thing as virtual cubes, except you are now creating a cube with new dimensions as well as using ones already defined and shared. Let's create a new dimension for customers.

For product, store, and promotions, let's use the shared dimensions from the 1998 partition that you created for the other cube. Select Product, Store, and Promotions from Shared Dimensions and click the arrow to move them over to Cube Dimensions, as shown in Figure 4-44. This adds these dimensions to your cube, as well as adding the informational tables required to build these dimensions into your star schema. I realize that this is a bit confusing, but the Cube Wizard does not differentiate between the star schema and the cube, it just mixes them all together. It will be a little clearer when you actually define the customer informational table and dimension.

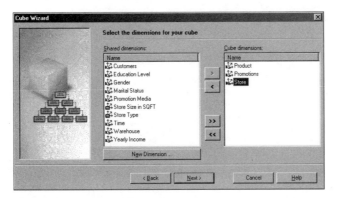

Figure 4-44. *Shared Dimensions.*

Creating a Customer Informational Table and a Customer Structural Dimension

Let's now add the customer informational table to the star schema. Click New Dimension to open the Dimension Wizard as shown in Figure 4-45. Realize that you are actually adding an informational table to the star schema at this point, not a dimension.

Leave the default A Single Dimension Table and click Next. Double-click Customer on the Available Tables list box, as shown in Figure 4-46. The details of the customer table should appear on the right.

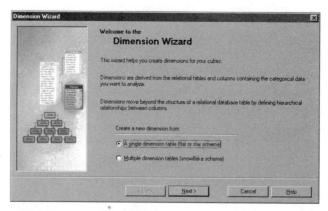

Figure 4-45. *Dimension Wizard screen.*

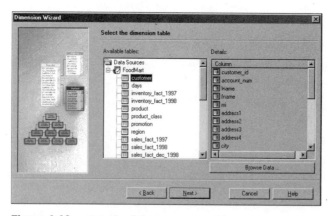

Figure 4-46. *Details of the customer table.*

Click Next. Leave the default of Standard Dimension, and click Next, as shown in Figure 4-47.

You now have reached the select levels for your dimension screen. This switches you from adding an informational table to your star schema to defining the structure of your dimension for your cube. You are now defining the hierarchies that will exist with this dimension. There is a geography hierarchy nested within the customer informational table, so let's use that. Start with the top of the hierarchy, which in this case is Country. Either double-click Country in the Dimension Levels list box or single click and click the right arrow. Do the same for State_Province, City, Postal Code, and Customer ID. Figure 4-48 shows the screen after selecting country.

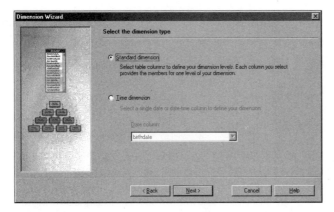

Figure 4-47. *Leaving the default of Standard Dimension.*

Note   It may seem strange that Customer ID is included in this hierarchy. If you stop and think about what the levels in the hierarchy really mean, then it makes sense. Postal Code is not a list of all customer postal codes; it is a list of all customers who are associated with a particular postal code. Geography dimensions usually group some important business element, in this case the customer, according to some geographical boundaries. Thus, geography dimensions represent the grouping of something within the region, not the physical region itself. In this case, you are grouping customers. At the bottom of the customer hierarchy (the leaf level of the hierarchy), there are individual customers, which are represented by customer IDs.

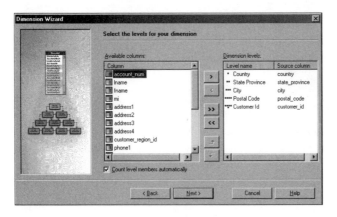

Figure 4-48. *Selecting the levels for your dimension.*

Note RegionID is essentially the same as City, and you have to include the Region table in a snowflake schema in order to include Region. After you are done building the dimension without Region, it's a useful exercise to redo the customer table as a snowflake schema using Region instead of City.

Note One interesting thing about this customer hierarchy is that it is very unlikely that someone would actually perform an analysis on the leaves of this hierarchy, such as Customer ID. It is essential that you include Customer ID, especially to create categorical dimensions. A dimension like this would be ideal for HOLAP, because you could store the base data (the customer IDs) in the relational database. Because virtually no one drills down to Customer ID, there is no loss of performance by placing these in a relational database. If there is a high number of aggregations for this HOLAP table, the higher levels of the hierarchy, which are browsed often, are located in a multidimensional data warehouse that has maximum efficiency. Thus, HOLAP is ideal for a table where the leaf level is rarely drilled down to, and the higher levels, which can be stored as aggregations in a multidimensional database, are often drilled through.

Click Next and type the name **Customer1998** in the Dimension Name box. Notice that you can expand the hierarchy to see what the dimension looks like, as shown in Figure 4-49.

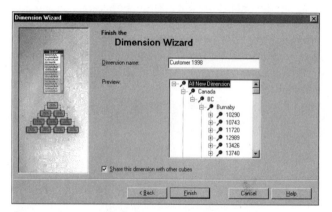

Figure 4-49. *Naming and expanding the hierarchy.*

Notice that there is an option called Share This Dimension With Other Cubes. It is important that you allow this cube to be shared, so leave the default. The importance of this is explained later when virtual dimensions and categorical dimensions are discussed. Click Finish and then click Next. Type the name **SalesFor1998** in the Cube Name box, as shown in Figure 4-50. Click Finish.

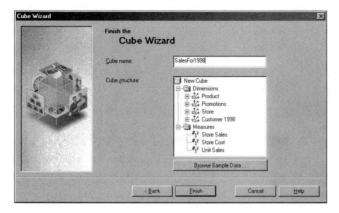

Figure 4-50.   *Naming the cube SalesFor1998.*

Creating a Structural Time Dimension

Let's add a time dimension to your cube using the Cube Editor. Right-click Dimensions and select Dimension Manager. The same screen you saw before comes up again.

On the Select The Dimensions For Your Cube screen, click New Dimension once again. Follow the same steps in the Dimension Wizard as you did before up to the Select The Dimension Table screen. In this case, select Time_By_Day, as shown in Figure 4-51.

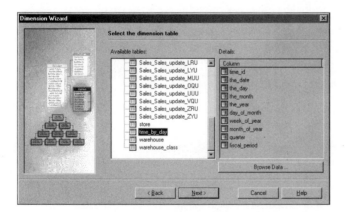

Figure 4-51.   *Selecting Time_By_Day in the Dimension Wizard.*

Click Next. In this case, you have a time dimension, so click the Time Dimension button. The only field listed in the drop-down list box is The_Date. This column is the only column that has a date/time field, and date/time fields are the only types of fields listed in the drop-down list, as shown in Figure 4-52.

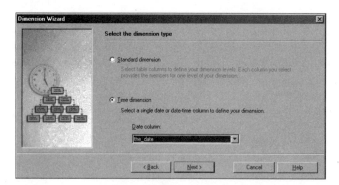

Figure 4-52. *Selecting the Time Dimension as the dimension type.*

Click Next. A hierarchy is automatically created for you for the time dimension. Notice that it has the correct grain for the informational table you are using, that is, the hierarchy only goes down to day, as shown in Figure 4-53.

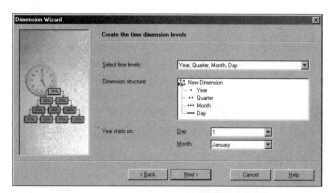

Figure 4-53. *Creating the time dimension levels.*

Note If you want to use the other attributes of the table, you can create additional dimensions based on these attributes.

Click Next. Type the dimension name **TimeDimension1998** (dimension names must begin with a letter). Click Finish. Your screen should look like the one in Figure 4-54.

Click OK and you should land back in the Cube Editor. The star schema with the informational and fact tables is on the right and the measures and dimensions are on the left.

You still need to do a little cleaning up. You can clean up your star schema by moving the tables around. You must now connect the fact table foreign keys to the informational primary keys by dragging and dropping the foreign key from the fact table to the primary key in the informational table, as shown in Figure 4-55.

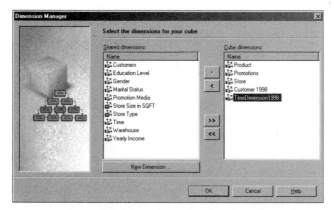

Figure 4-54.   *TimeDimension1998 cube dimension.*

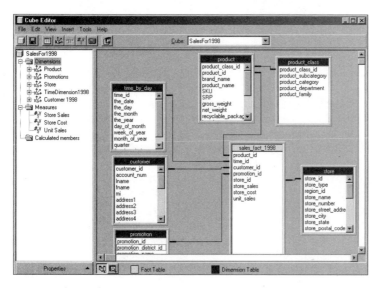

Figure 4-55.   *Connecting the foreign keys to the primary keys.*

Notice that the star snowflake Product/Product_Class informational tables are in your star schema. When you selected the Product dimension, the Product/Product_Class tables, which were used to make that dimension, were automatically brought over into your star schema.

Close the Cube Wizard. You now are prompted to save your cube. Click Yes, and when the message box comes up asking you if you want to set the data storage options now, click Yes again.

The next screen you see is the data storage screen. Select ROLAP (or any storage method you prefer) and click Next. Choose your aggregations and click Start, *then* Next and finally Finish. I will choose my usual 10 percent to keep it quick, but of course this is not what you would use in a real cube.

If you click the SalesFor1998 folder and click Data in the windowpane on the right, your screen will look like the one in Figure 4-56.

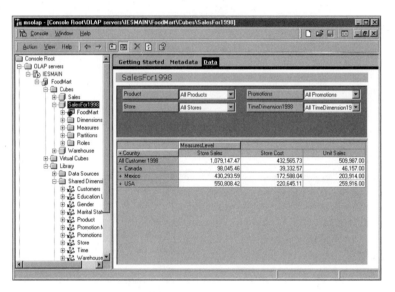

Figure 4-56. *Data for SalesFor1998 cube.*

You should now experiment by adding and removing dimensions to the grid. You should also expand the dimensions. If you click the TimeDimension1998 button and expand All TimeDimension1998, you see that it contains 1997 also. This is because the original Time_By_Day table had both 1997 and 1998 in it. This is wrong, and in a production system, you need to fix this. You could fix it by creating a new timetable with only 1998 values. For this demonstration, though, let's ignore this error.

Information Dimensions

Information dimensions, which are dimensions containing calculated values, can also be created in OLAP Server. In OLAP Server, information dimensions are called calculated members. Each calculated member is associated with either a dimension, including the measures dimensions. If the calculated member is associated with the measures dimension then it is a measure. We will look at some examples of calculated members that are part of the measures dimension.

Note   It can get very confusing when there are so many names for the same thing. I have used the standard naming convention for dimensions, using terms such as information dimensions, because this is how they are referred to in the general database literature. I have also separated the terms for the relational star schema from the terms for the cube. OLAP Services chooses to call various things by their own names, or mixes the cube and star schema information together, which can be confusing. I hope my explanations have allowed you to separate this all out and differentiate between common terminology, my terminology, and OLAP Services terminology.

Let's create two calculated members, profit and average sales. If the Cube Editor is not open, open it (right-click the SalesFor1998 cube and click Edit). Right-click the Calculated Members folder and select New Calculated Member to bring up the Calculated Member Builder. Let's start with profit.

Creating the Profit Calculated Member

Profit is equal to total store sales minus total store costs. Profit is additive across the dimensions. Thus, I could measure the profit for a store for every day in a week and sum the daily values to get the profit for the week. You will use the measure Store Sales and the measure Store Cost to determine the profit. You need to expand the Measures tree to find the measures. Once you expand the Measures Level part of the tree, click the Store Sales measure. Drag Store Sales up to the Value Expression box, as shown in Figure 4-57. Click the minus sign to add it to the Value Expression box.

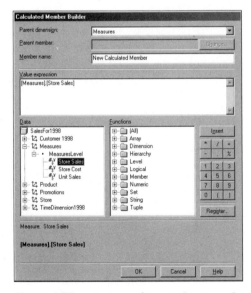

Figure 4-57.   *Dragging Store Sales up to the Value Expression box.*

Next, drag Store Cost up to the Value Expression box. Type in **Profit98** in the Member Name: box, as shown in Figure 4-58. Click OK.

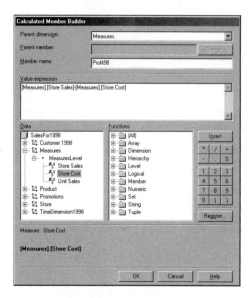

Figure 4-58. *Completing the calculated member for Profit98.*

Now you have a calculated member for the average sale price of each product. Average sales are an average value, and therefore are not additive across dimensions. This means that the average sales per day for a week does not add up to the weekly sales. As long as you use measures to calculate your averages, the values should be correct. The problem is that you do not have a measure for Product Count. The solution for this is to create the new measure.

Creating Calculated Measures

To create a calculated member, go to the Cube Editor and right-click Measures. Select New Measure. This brings up the Select Column window. Select Product_id and click OK. Your new measure should be called ProductID. Click the Product_id measure. If you do not see a Properties window under your hierarchy in the Cube Editor, go to View in the menu and click Properties. In Properties, change the Name of the measure to Product Count. Go to Aggregate Function and click the drop-down list, as shown in Figure 4-59.

Select Count for the *Aggregate Function*. This gives a product count. You have now created a calculated member.

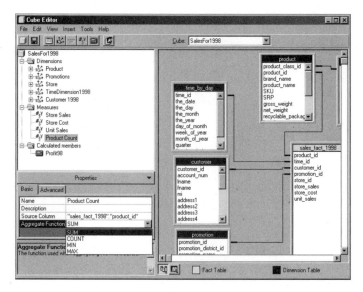

Figure 4-59.   *Drop-down list for Aggregate Function.*

Creating an Average Calculated Member (Information Dimensions)

The calculated member for average sale price for a product can now be created. Right-click the Calculated Members folder and select New Calculated Member. Open the measures part of the tree again and drag Store Sales into the Value Expression box. Click on the "/" sign. Now drag your new Product Count into the Value Expression box. Type **Product Avg Cost** in the Member Name box, as shown in Figure 4-60.

You can create a wide range of information dimensions based on the calculated member tool. Combining this with the ability to make calculated members, you have the ability to present the data in any format that the user needs.

Categorical Dimensions

Several types of dimensions were mentioned in the last chapter. So far, the discussion has been about structural and information dimensions. You can also create a categorical dimension, such as yearly income or marital status. You can create categorical dimensions in the same way as you made structural dimensions, but instead let's use something called virtual dimensions.

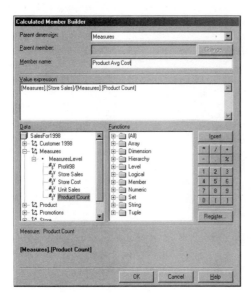

Figure 4-60. *Creating Product Avg Cost.*

Categorical dimensions are descriptive attributes of a dimension. This means that a categorical dimension can be associated with another dimension. As you are using the structural dimensions as the basis of your cubes, you will associate categorical dimensions with a structural dimension. Thus, you would associate the Number Of Children categorical dimension with the Customer1998 structural dimension.

Categorical dimensions should have discrete values, that is, they should be in a range of values. In the FoodMart.mdb data warehouse, marital status has only two values (Married or Single), and Yearly Income has only eight values (0K-30K, 30K-50K, 50K-70K, 70K-90K, 90K-110K, 110K-130K, 130K-150K, 150K+). Both marital status and yearly income are associated with the Customer1998 dimension you just created. You will wait until the cube is completely built to add the categorical dimensions to structural dimensions.

As said earlier, categorical dimensions are associated with a structural dimension. Thus, you must add your categorical dimensions to your structural dimensions. Let's add a categorical dimension, number of children, to the customer structural dimension. To do this, you must first define what OLAP Services calls members.

Members

Members in OLAP Server are any descriptive attributes from the informational table in the star schema, such as marital status, income level, number of children, and so forth. You first define a structural dimension in your cube from the informational table in the star schema, and then associate members with this structural dimension. In this case, you created a structural dimension Customer1998 from the informational table Customer in the star schema you built using FoodMart.mdb data warehouse. Now you need to define members for the Customer1998 structural dimensions, such as marital status, number of children, and so forth. If you are confused, follow along and it should eventually make sense.

Creating Members for the Customer1998 Dimension

To create a member for your Customer1998 dimension, you need to go to the main OLAP manager, open the Library folder and then open the *Shared* Dimensions folder. As you made your Customer1998 dimension shared, it should be listed here. Right-click Customer1998 and select Edit.

This opens the Dimension Editor. Right-click Customer Id and select New Member Property.

This brings up the Select Column window. The columns listed are the columns from the customer table in the star schema, based on the relational data warehouse. You can select any column. Let's begin by selecting Total_Children, as shown in Figure 4-61.

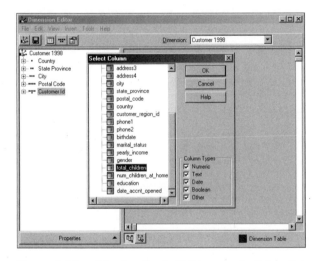

Figure 4-61.   *Selecting Total_Children in the Select Column window.*

Click OK. You should see that Total Children has been added. Click Save or choose File/ Save. Close the dimension editor.

Creating the Virtual Dimension

Go into the OLAP Manager and open the Library folder. Right-click the Virtual Dimensions folder and select New Virtual Dimension.

Click the Skip This Screen In The Future check box in the welcome screen of the Virtual Dimension Wizard. Click Next. Expand Customer1998 in the tree and select Customer Id.Total Children, as shown in Figure 4-62.

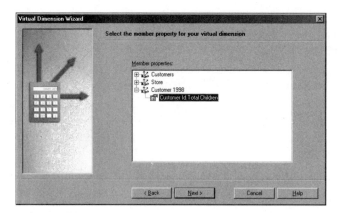

Figure 4-62. *Selecting Customer Id.Total Children.*

Click Next. Type **Customer Total Children** in the Virtual Dimension Name box.

Click Finish. Now under the Cubes folder, right-click SalesFor1998 and select Edit to bring up the Cube Editor. Right-click Dimensions in the Cube Editor and select Dimension Manager. Select Customer Total Children on the left, and click the right arrow to bring it into the right list box, as shown in Figure 4-63.

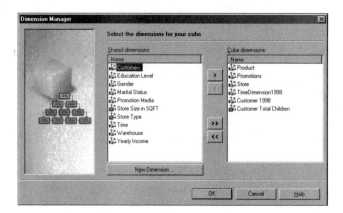

Figure 4-63. *Selecting Customer Total Children.*

Click OK and close the Cube Editor. Save the cube. When prompted to design storage options, resave and re-aggregate the cube.

Storing Categorical Dimensions as Virtual or Real Dimensions

You stored your categorical dimension as a virtual dimension. There is no reason why you could not have saved Number Of Children as a regular dimension instead of making it a virtual dimension. When you look at the original Sales cube that comes with the FoodMart example, you see that Marital Status is created as a regular dimension.

Looking at Store Square Feet, as presented in the FoodMart.mdb database, you see that it is made from continuous values, that is, the square footage of the stores are a value between 0 (value not entered) and 39,696 square feet. This is not a very good design for the square foot information, as there are over twenty different values for square foot. Ideally, it is better to create a new column in which you have different ranges of values, for example, 0-2500, 2501-3000, 3001-3500, and 3501 and above. Doing it this way reduces the number of values for square foot to four values.

If I include the square footage in FoodMart.mdb as a regular dimension, OLAP Server has to make aggregations for over 20 different values of square footage in the FoodMart.mdb data warehouse. These aggregations over these different square footages add a considerable amount of size to the database. You can see that one advantage of creating categories is the reduction of the number of aggregates that exist for a descriptive attribute. In regard to square footage, you could have four categories instead of over 20 values. This could be a substantial savings in the size of the overall database. Regardless of how you build the column, it is quite likely that there will be very few queries done on square footage.

So, what should you do when you have a categorical dimension that is almost never used? Perhaps only one user wants the categorical dimension included in the data warehouse, so it is not used that often. You can go for the more complicated solutions, such as partitions with no aggregations or you can use the simple solution that OLAP Services offers: virtual dimensions. The aggregations for virtual dimensions are not actually stored in the data warehouse; they are calculated in memory when they are needed. Thus, you don't need to worry about exploding your cube by using virtual dimensions. Of course, the penalty for using virtual dimensions is the amount of time required to calculate them. If you were using virtual dimensions with ROLAP or HOLAP, virtual dimensions is a good candidate for an index. Thus, building your categorical dimensions as virtual dimensions makes them calculate more slowly, but they don't take up room in the data warehouse. Some other disadvantages of virtual dimensions are that they can only be one level deep, and you can only define 760 members in a cube. If a structural dimension is used often, it probably should be a regular dimension.

Processing Cubes

There are three ways to process a cube. You can do it incrementally, which only adds new data to the cube; you can refresh the cube, which updates the information but does not delete the aggregations; or you can process the cube, which deletes the aggregation tables and rebuilds them, and also replaces the data. Incremental updates are the fastest, followed by refresh. Processing is the slowest. There is more detail on the Process A Cube Wizard in the DTS chapter. Start by right-clicking SalesFor1998 and select

ProcessThis, which brings up the Process screen. In this case, you select Refresh Data (as the aggregation tables are already made).

Properties of Dimensions in the Cube Editor

In this chapter we have discussed the creation of dimensions, cubes, and measures using wizards. We have also shown how you can view the properties of dimensions, cubes, and measures in the Cube Editor. Below are definitions of all of the properties available for cubes, dimensions and measures in the Cube Editor.

Important If you are working with a shared dimension you cannot edit the dimension properties in the Cube Editor. Instead, you need to go to the Shared Dimensions folder in the OLAP Manager, right-click on the shared dimension that you wish to edit, and select Edit. This will bring up the dimension editor, which can be used to edit shared dimensions.

Cubes

In the Cube Editor, if you click on the name of the cube in the tree you can see properties for the cube. The properties the one can view in the Cube Editor for cubes are listed below.

- **Name** This is the name of the cube. This cannot be edited in the properties window. The name should be unique and make clear what data the cube contains.

- **Description** It is important to include descriptions for your cubes. The description helps determine what type of data the cube contains.

- **Data Source** This is the source of the data for the cube. This cannot be edited in the Cube Editor.

- **Fact Table** This is the fact table associated with the cube. If you change this you will have to recreate the links between the fact table and informational tables and reprocesses the cube.

- **Fact Table Size** This is the size of the fact table. This is based on the size of the fact table when the cube was created. If the fact table size changes substantially from its initial value, you might want to change it.

- **Aggregation Prefix** If you are using ROLAP, the tables that are created for the aggregations are prefixed with the aggregation name.

Important Even when you choose 100 percent aggregations, OLAP Server might not actually perform aggregations on all of your data. OLAP Server looks at the number of records required to make an aggregation. If the number of records required to make an aggregation are less than one-third the size of the fact table, OLAP Server can create the aggregation.

Even when you have set the optimizer to 100 percent aggregations, levels that result in a number of records greater than one-third the size of the fact table will not be included in the aggregations. For example, if the fact table size is 3,000,000, then the number of aggregations for a level can only be included if the number of records to make that aggregation are less than 1000. Thus, an aggregation for customer all, promotion all, and time month, which would be 1 x 1 x 12 = 12 will be included. If there are 500 customers, an aggregation of customerID, month, and store all would be 500 x 12 x 1= 6000. This combination could never be aggregated with a fact table size of 3,000,000.

If you want to increase the number of aggregations that are created, you can increase the size of the fact table to a value larger than the true size of the fact table.

Dimensions and Levels

Using either the Cube Editor or the DSO, you can change the properties of the dimensions, cubes, and measures. Below are the properties that are visible in the cube wizard for each of these.

The following are properties of dimensions and levels:

- **Name**   The name of the level should be something that clearly defines what the dimension is, and is unique for the data warehouse.

- **Description**   It is important to include descriptions for your dimensions and levels. A description not only makes it easier for someone looking at your data warehouse to determine the function of the levels and dimensions, descriptions can also be used by applications to give additional information to the user. You should always include descriptions.

The following are only properties of dimensions:

- **All Level**   The All level is included by default. The All level is an aggregate over all of the members of the dimension. It is especially useful with structural dimensions.

- **All Caption**   This is the name for the All level if you choose to have one. The default is All (dimension name).

- **Type**   The type can be either regular or time. If you define a dimension in the Dimension wizard as being time, the Dimension wizard will set the Type to Time. Time can be useful for applications using the dimension. Setting this value will have no effect on perform of the dimension.

- **Aggregation Usage**   The aggregation usage will determine how the aggregations will be created for the dimension. Standard will let the OLAP Services determine the best way to make aggregations. Top Level Only will result in only the top (usually the All level) having aggregations. Custom will only allow aggregations for levels that have the Enable Aggregations property set to true. Bottom Level Only will allow aggregations only for the bottom level.

The following are only properties of levels:

- **Member Key Column** The member key column determines the column in the informational table that will be used to create aggregations and identify each member of the dimension. The member key does not have to be the primary key that is used as a foreign key in the fact table, though it usually is.

- **Member Name Column** The member name column is a name associated with the member key column. The member key column is almost always a numeric id field. This would have little meaning to the user. Thus, we can also associate the member key column with a text field that would make sense to the user.

- **Member Count** This is the number of members in the level. This is only updated when a level is added to the dimension. Becuase this value is used in creating aggregations, it is important that you make sure this value is correct.

- **Unique Members** If all of the member keys are unique, this should be true. If you selected "Count Level Members Automatically," then OLAP Services will try to determine this automatically. You should verify that this is correct.

- **Disabled** Disabling a level will mean that the level, and all below it, will not be visible to users. Disabling a level essentially moves the leaf level of the dimension to one level above the disabled level.

- **Level Type** The level type allows one to give more information on a time dimension, such as whether a level is month or year.

- **Key Data Size and Key Data Type** This is the size and data type of the member key for the level. If you change the member key for a level, you verify that these values are correct.

- **Order By Key** If this is set to true, the members of the level will be ordered by the key column. If it is set to false, the members will be ordered by the member name column.

- **Enable Aggregations** If you choose custom aggregations for your dimension, you can set this to true to request OLAP Services to aggregate at this level.

Measures Properties

Measures also have a set of properties as listed below.

- **Name and Description** Same as for dimensions and cubes.
- **Source Column** The column in the fact table that this member comes from.

- **Aggregate Function**   You can choose from four types of aggregate functions: SUM, COUNT, MIN, and MAX. SUM is the default.
- **Data Type**   It is important that you choose the right data type for your measures. OLAP Services will provide a default, but you should confirm that this correct.
- **Display Format**   The display format is a standard Office/VBA format string that allows you to determine how you want the measure to be formatted.
- **Internal Setting**   If this to set to true, it makes the measure unavailable to users. You would usually do this when you want to use a measure to calculate other measures.

Calculated Member Properties

Calculated members do have some properties that are worth noting. The following are some of the properties for the calculated members:

- **Parent Dimension**   This is the dimension with which the calculated member is associated.
- **Parent Member**   A calculated member may be associated with a particular level. The parent member would be the level the calculated member is associated with.
- **Solve Order**   This will be discussed in the MDX chapters.

Conclusion

This entire chapter was devoted to building star schemas in the relational data warehouse and then creating cubes based on these star schemas, using the wizards and editors in the OLAP Manager. OLAP Services provides an entire army of wizards to perform the required tasks. In addition, OLAP Server offers an incredible amount of flexibility. You can store your data in a ROLAP, HOLAP, or MOLAP format. You can use partitions to employ different storage and aggregations methods for different parts of your cubes. You can use SQL Server 7.0 relational database tools such as file groups, and you can use virtual cubes to create views of your cube for security purposes and to prevent saving redundant dimensions in MOLAP. I highly recommend spending a few hours more playing around in the OLAP Manager to become more familiar with what it can do. Before you do this, though, I highly recommend that you put all your cubes into MOLAP storage and set your aggregations to at least 80 percent. It takes a very long time to create views of the data at 10 percent performance. Just be prepared for a long break from the computer when you do the new aggregations.

While the OLAP Manager and its army of wizards provide nearly everything you could want in an OLAP solution, they are really only the beginning. In addition to doing everything with interfaces, you can do all of this programmatically. Thus, if you want to create a cube on the client side, or write an application to access cube data and place it into HTML, you can do this, too. There are two additional parts of the solution that you need in order to build cubes and get data programmatically. The first is a set of components that allows you to access cube data. These are discussed in Chapter 6. The second is a new language that goes with the OLAP database, like SQL Server goes with the OLTP database. This new language is called Multidimensional Extensions (MDX) and is the focus of the next chapter.

Chapter 5
Introducing Multidimensional Extensions

Multidimensional Extensions (MDX), developed by Microsoft and other vendors, is an extension of the SQL language. MDX creates views of the data by specifying which points on the cube to use to evaluate measures. You can also use MDX to define temporary dimensions and measures in a cube, which can be added to the data views.

In this book, MDX is discussed in three chapters. In this chapter, an overview of MDX and the syntax for the basic MDX statement are presented. Chapter 6 discusses calculated members, which allow you to create members in your cube based on expressions in your MDX statement. Chapter 7 covers member and set expressions, which allow you to perform various functions on the members of the MDX statement.

MDX and OLAP

MDX is a powerful language that allows you to customize online analytical processing (OLAP) solutions for specific business requirements. While there are good third party tools, such as ProClarity, which give you the ability to create limited customized client solutions without using MDX, using these tools with MDX, or using MDX with Excel, allows you to create any client solution that is required. The entire purpose of a data warehouse is to solve business problems. Real world business problems rarely can be solved using OLAP tools alone; MDX is a required partner.

MDX and Microsoft SQL Server 7.0 Data Warehousing

Understanding MDX is also essential for designing, fine-tuning, and maintaining a Microsoft SQL Server 7.0 data warehouse. The design of the data warehouse can be affected by the very structure of the MDX language and by specific MDX queries against the data warehouse.

For example, field names should be chosen so that MDX queries are easily readable. Using Country as a level name in both the Customer and Store dimensions makes it more difficult to write MDX queries and to read result sets from those queries. Using Milk for a

Product Category and a Product Department in the Products Dimension can wreak havoc on your MDX queries. Does Product Dimension Milk mean the milk category or milk department? There is no way to know. To get the correct result, you must write special queries specifically for this dimension. This prevents developers from writing generic code that works across all dimensions. To handle the Milk dimension, developers have to put special If Statements in their code. This is an unacceptable way to write applications. Good naming conventions may not solve all your data warehouse performance issues, but they will keep your data warehouse applications from becoming a tangle of unreadable queries.

Optimizing the Data Warehouse

Reviewing the MDX queries that will be used against the data warehouse gives the administrator important information on how to optimize the data warehouse. When using relational OLAP (ROLAP) and hybrid OLAP (HOLAP), MDX queries can determine which fields require an index. A virtual dimension might not be acceptable if it is referred to in a large number of MDX queries. Without understanding the MDX queries used to build the client applications, the administrator can only make a guess as to the best design and optimization of the database. The design of client applications and the physical structure of the data warehouse need to be considered at the same time in the design phase.

Designing the Data Warehouse

The administrator should not develop an idea for the data warehouse design and then expect a developer to produce an application based on the design. Instead, the entire team should begin by working directly with users and mapping out their needs in scenarios and use cases. The use cases should be converted into a set of services that the data warehouse application's components can perform using UML scenario diagrams. When this is done, the team can start designing components and the data warehouse administrator can start designing the data warehouse. As the design of the data warehouse application improves through UML activity diagrams, the design of the data warehouse will also improve. By using this design method, the final design primarily reflects the needs of users and only secondarily reflects the needs of the application and the data warehouse. Chapter 9 goes into more detail on making UML diagrams for a data warehouse application.

MDX and SQL Server 7.0 OLAP Services

As a data warehouse administrator, you are expected to be an expert on OLAP Services. Just as the online transaction processing (OLTP) expert is expected to know how to fine-tune and optimize SQL queries, an OLAP Services expert should know how to write and fine-tune MDX queries. If you are a developer, MDX can form the basis of your applications.

There are also many things that you cannot do without MDX. In the last chapter, you defined roles and created security on cubes. But what if you need a more fine-grained security? You can create cell level security, but you can only do it with MDX. Whether you are a developer or an administrator working with a SQL Server 7.0 data warehouse, learning MDX is an important part of your job.

Caution   If you are a SQL Server expert, here is a quick warning. Although MDX is an extension of the SQL Server language, it is a very different language. You should put everything you know about performing SQL Server queries out of your mind while learning MDX. Some of SQL's terms are used in MDX, but their meaning in MDX is completely different. It is best to approach MDX with a clean slate.

Tip   MDX is not something you can learn just by reading about it. To fully understand MDX, you need to try all of the examples in this chapter and expand them when possible. Do every example in this chapter and you will be on your way to becoming an MDX expert.

More Info   The help files for MDX can be found in the Microsoft Data Access SDK 2.0 update. You must first install the Microsoft Data Access SDK 2.0, and then you can install the update. The file for the update is SDKUpd_i.exe, and both the MDAC SDK 2.0 and the update can be found on the CD for this book. The help files can also be found in the current release of the Platform SDK.

Let's begin by looking at the basics of MDX, starting with the five basic elements of MDX: strings, numbers, members, tuples, and sets.

MDX Statements

If we are going to build MDX statements, we need some basic building blocks. The basic building blocks of MDX are a set of elements that form the syntax of object linking and embedding database (OLE DB) for OLAP. These elements give you the ability to specify and create any dataset you need. A dataset is a set of data that is returned by an OLAP Server from an MDX query.

The Five Elements of an MDX Statement

The basic building blocks of MDX are numbers, strings, members, tuples, and sets. They are described below.

Numbers

In MDX, a number can be any type of number. An MDX number can be an exact numeric, such as an integer or decimal, or an approximate numeric such as a float or double. You can apply the usual operations on MDX numbers, such as addition, subtraction, multiplication, and division. Using these operations, you can derive new numbers from existing numbers. The process of creating new numbers from existing numbers is called composition. The expressions for composition are not listed in this chapter because they are the usual operations on numbers.

Strings

An MDX string is a sequence of characters. Strings can have special formatting applied to them within the client side environment.

Members

An MDX member is the value of any attribute belonging to a dimension. For example, for a time dimension that has Year and Quarter as levels, 1998 and Q1 can be valid members. MDX has an existing set of expressions called member expressions that can be used to operate on any member that belongs to the dimension. Member expressions always return either another member of the dimension or zero. For example, one of these member operations is parent. If you have a dimension that includes Country, State, and City and you have the member NY, then Parent(NY) will equal US. Parent(US), though, will return 0, because you have gone beyond the boundaries of the hierarchy. These boundary conditions are discussed in detail later in the chapter. Member expressions allow you to walk up and down a structural dimension's hierarchy.

Caution An MDX member is different from the members you created in the last chapter. When the OLAP Manager was used to create dimensions, members represented descriptive attributes in the dimensions, such as marital status or number of children. These descriptive attributes generally were used to make categorical dimensions using virtual dimensions. In MDX, a member represents any attribute of a dimension, such as USA, Milk, and so forth. The attributes used for MDX members are often part of a structural dimension, because MDX members are usually used to move through the structural dimension's hierarchy.

Tuples

An MDX tuple is a collection of members from different dimensions. For example, (Manhattan, [1997]) is a tuple formed by members of two dimensions: Geography and Time. Tubles represent a unique position on a cubes axis consisting of multiple members. No dimension can be represented twice in a tuple. Thus, (Manhattan, Chicago) is not a tuple.

Sets

An MDX set is a collection of set tuple elements. Set tuples are like regular tuples, except that a set tuple is a collection of members from the same dimension or a collection of members from different dimensions. A set consists of the contents of a cube axis.

An MDX statement can contain set expressions, member expressions, and numeric functions. Collectively, these are called MDX expressions. For expample, the MEMBERS set expression returns all members of a set, provided the set does not contain tuples.

One very important set expression is MEMBERS. Using MEMBERS with a dimension's level is the same as creating a set with all of the members of that level in that dimension. Thus, in the FoodMart data warehouse [Customers].[Country].MEMBERS is equivalent to {([Customer].[USA]), ([Customer].[Canada]), ([Customer].[Mexico])}. The MEMBERS set function is discussed in more detail in the section entitled "Set Expressions" in Chapter 7. We will use MEMBERS in this chapter because it will simplify our examples and is often used in MDX queries.

These MDX elements form the basis for this chapter. The discussion begins with the manipulation of tuples. Next, you will create calculated members using MDX in much the same way as you created calculated members with the OLAP Manager. You will also learn how to format the calculated members. Let's now look at the basic structure of an MDX statement.

Basic Structure of an MDX Statement

For an MDX statement to return a dataset, you should include the following elements in the MDX statement:

- The name of the cube or cubes that will be used to get data for the dataset.
- The number of MDX axes. An axis contains the members from one or more tuples, which is a set.

Important   MDX axes are different from the axes we discussed in previous chapters when working with cubes. The cube axes are a set of coordinates in which each axis represents a single dimension. This is very different from the axes that we will talk about when making MDX queries, which represent a set. For the rest of this chapter, we will use the term axis and axes to refer to MDX axis and MDX axes, and specifically state cube axis or cube axes referring to cube axes to be clear.

Normally, you work with only two axes because most tools used to display data can only show two axes. For example, an Excel spreadsheet can show one axis on the x coordinate going across the spreadsheet and a second axis on the y coordinate going up the spreadsheet. Each tuple contains members from different dimensions. Thus, if we have a tuple consisting of [Product].[Product Family].MEMBERS and [Customer].[Country].MEMBERS on our axis, tuples that will be located on this axis will be (Drink, Canada), (Drink, Mexico), (Drink, USA), (Food, Canada), (Food, Mexico), and so forth. The tuples on the axes are used to define points on the cube. These points are where you get values for your measures.

More Info Normally, the term *dimension* is used instead of axis. Using the term dimension, you could say that an Excel spreadsheet results in a two-dimensional answer, so your MDX statements have only two dimensions. However, in OLAP the word dimension is used for cubes. Therefore, to prevent confusion, use the word *axis* in MDX, instead of dimension.

Up to this point, there was a clear separation between dimensions and measures. In MDX, there is a special dimension that is the collection of all measures. It's called the measures dimension. You already saw this dimension when you added calculated measures to your cube in the last chapter. You can access any measure through this dimension. Thus, you can include measures in your tuples, too. This will be discussed shortly.

- The members projected on each axis, and the dimension each member comes from. If you nest members from different dimensions, you must show how these values will be nested. An example of nesting can be created by opening the OLAP Manager, selecting the Sales cube, clicking on Data, and dragging and dropping any of the dimension buttons under the current far left column in the grid. Figure 5-1 shows how this looks if Year is originally in the far left column, and Products is dragged and dropped underneath it. In this case, Products is nested under Year.

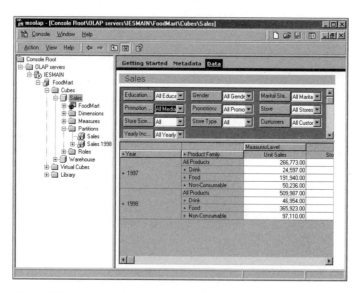

Figure 5-1. *A typical nested hierarchy.*

- You can also sort the members on an axis in a particular order. This sort order can be specified if needed.
- Dimensions that are not being used on the axes should be set to some value. Thus, if you have store sales on the x axis, and the store dimension on the y axis, you still need to set the customer dimension to some value, such as All Customers or USA. This is called slicing.

All of these can be accomplished by the following syntax:

```
SELECT <axis_specification> [,<axis_specification>, …]

FROM <cube_specification>

WHERE <slicer_specification>
```

Let's now look at each piece of the basic MDX statement The MDX Where clause is discussed in detail in the section entitled "Creating Slicer Dimensions."

Specifying the Axes and the Cube

The MDX specifications do not limit the number of axes you can have in an MDX statement.

Caution   Do realize, though, that not all OLE-DB providers allow for an unlimited number of axes. The provider needs to be able to handle at least three axes.

As previously mentioned, normally you only use two axes, as most interface tools can only show two axes. You can call them the x and y axes. In your interface, the x axis forms columns and the y axis forms rows. For this reason, they are called the column and row axes. At least one axis must be specified in an MDX query. Additional axes are optional.

Sample Application

Generally, one of the axes has members from the *measures* dimension and the other axis has members from the regular dimensions. Let's see how some of this actually works. OLAP Services comes with a tool called MDX Sample that allows you to view the results of MDX queries. Go to the Start menu, select Programs, select Microsoft SQL Server 7.0, select OLAP Services, and then click MDX Sample Application, as shown in Figure 5-2.

You will be prompted to choose the server you want to connect to and the provider you want to use, as shown in Figure 5-3.

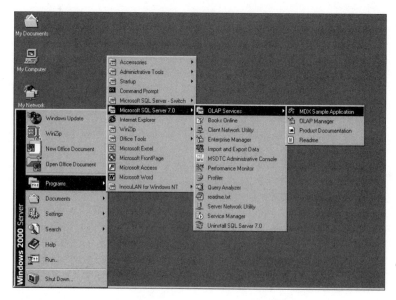

Figure 5-2. *Opening the MDX Sample Application.*

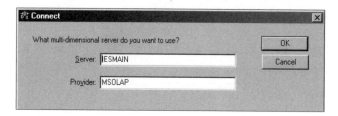

Figure 5-3. *Connecting to the server.*

In my case, this is the main IES server called IESMAIN and I am using the default MSOLAP provider. If the default server that comes up is not the one you want to connect to, change the value in the text box to the correct value. The MDX Sample comes with several sample MDX queries. You can look at them now if you want, but I am going to ignore them, because they are fairly advanced and might actually confuse you. I am also going to ignore the middle frame with cube and syntax examples. The syntax examples are good for basic syntax, but they are not full examples. I have provided a full set of examples in this chapter for all of the essential MDX elements.

Remove the MDX query in the top window and type:

```
SELECT

    {([MEASURES].[Unit Sales])} ON COLUMNS,
```

```
    {(([Time].[Year].MEMBERS)} ON ROWS

FROM Sales
```

Remember that the MEMBERS set expression returns all of the values for that level. In this case, [Time].[Year] has two members, 1997 and 1998. Thus, you could rewrite this query as follows:

```
SELECT

    {(([MEASURES].[Unit Sales])} ON COLUMNS,

    {(([Time].[1997]), ([Time].[1998])} ON ROWS

FROM Sales
```

More Info   Both queries are identical. Because it is easier to write a query using MEMBERS or other MDX expressions, you will use them often. Using MEMBERS in your query would also be good when the current two years are in the data warehouse. The first query always returns the current two years. The second query, which specifies the year, only works when the years in the data warehouse are 1997 and 1998. Unless your data warehouse has a static set of data, general queries like the first one are usually better.

Let's tear this MDX statement apart. I will show all keywords in uppercase, such as columns, rows, and members.

Important   Curly brackets, {}, are used to enclose the sets, which in this case is the axis definition. Parentheses, (), are used to enclose each tuple. Square brackets, [], are used for each level in a member. Do not use square brackets for MDX expressions such as MEMBERS or keywords such as FROM. While the brackets and parentheses are not always required, you should always include them for clarity. Failing to use parentheses and brackets forces OLAP Services to try to determine what the correct placement of brackets and parentheses are. OLAP Services may not always arrive at the result you expect or it will simply give you a mysterious error message because you left out a bracket. If you want to save yourself endless grief, use curly brackets and parentheses!

Starting with the FROM keyword, notice that FROM is used to name the cube from which the data is coming. Let's now look at axes definitions.

In the first way we wrote the example, the query contains a set consisting of members of the MEASURES dimension placed along the columns axis, MEASURES.[Store Sales], and a set consisting of members of the TIME dimension placed along the row axis, [Time].[Year].Members. The set Measures.[Store Sales] has one member, and the set

Time.[Year]. Members has two members. The tuple MEASURES.[Store Sales] has only one member, itself. The tuple [Time].[Year].Members has two members, 1997 and 1998. In our second query, we have two tuples on rows, [Time].[1997] and [Time].[1998], each with one member, themselves.

Each tuple you list in your column axis specification becomes a new column. Each tuple you list in your row axis specification becomes a new row. Thus, {([Time].[Year].MEMBERS)} ON ROWS will have one row for each member of Year. In the case of FoodMart, there are two members, 1997 and 1998, so there will be two rows.

Because most MDX queries are on two axes, MDX defines COLUMNS and ROWS as the first two axes. Thus, you have projected the Unit Sales member onto the columns axis and the Year member onto the row axis. Click the green arrow in the tool bar (or go to the menu and select Query/Run). You should now see the sales for 1997 and 1998, as shown in Figure 5-4.

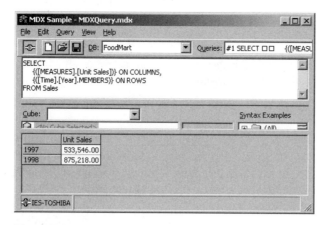

Figure 5-4.   *Unit sales for 1997 and 1998.*

More Info   In addition to COLUMNS and ROWS, the next three axes also have default names. These are PAGES for the third axis, SECTIONS for the fourth axis, and CHAPTERS for the fifth axis. Each axis can also be referred to by AXIS(i) where i is the index of the axis. COLUMNS is index 0, ROWS, 1, and so forth. You must use the axis in the appropriate order or the query will raise an error.

> **Note**   If you did not build the 1998 partition for the Sales cube in the last chapter, you will not see any values for 1998. If you jumped into the MDX chapter first, you must go back to the partition section in the previous chapter. In the partition section, you should add another partition to the Sales cube containing the 1998 data. This data is needed for many of the queries that follow.

Using Dot Operator

Notice that the term Measures precedes the term Unit Sales. The last section mentioned that measures are placed into their own dimension called MEASURES. Using this dimension, you can access any of the measures associated with your cube. If you take the word *measures* out of the statement and run the query over again, it will still work. What has happened is that OLAP Server has searched through the measures and dimensions in the cube and found Unit Sales in the measures dimension. Searching for values is never a very efficient way of doing things. It can lead to serious problems. In the case of Unit Sales, this term is only used once in the Sales cube. Sometimes, though, terms may be used in two or more dimensions.

The dot operator allows you to show which dimension a member comes from. For example, the time dimension might include a FiscalTime dimension with Year, Quarter, and Month, and a DayTime dimension with Year, Month, and Day. In this case, if you simply include Year in your MDX query, the results could be completely unpredictable. You could get year from either dimension. To properly show which year you mean, you need to either use FiscalTime.Year or DayTime.Year.

Using Dot Operator to Retrieve all of the Values of a Member

You can expand your query to show the sales for quarters by redefining rows member as follows:

```
SELECT
    {([Measures].[Unit Sales])} on COLUMNS,
    {([Time].[Quarter].MEMBERS)} on ROWS
FROM Sales
```

You now get sales over all of the quarters as shown in Figure 5-5.

The MEMBERS expression will retrieve all of the values for that level. In the case of Quarter, this results in the values Q1, Q2, Q3, and Q4. You must either include the MEMBERS expression or replace the word Quarter with the particular quarter you want.

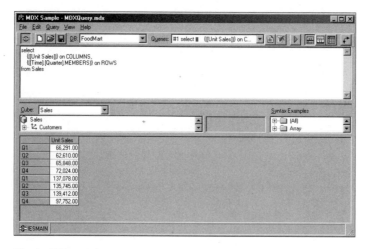

Figure 5-5. *Sales over quarters.*

Real World When trying to retrieve all the members for an attribute in a hierarchy using MEMBERS, first list the name of the hierarchy, next use the dot operator, and then select the name of the level in the hierarchy from which you want to retrieve all the members. Thus, to see all the members for the level Quarter in the Time dimension, use [Time].[Quarter].MEMBERS. When using the MEMBERS expression, you can only specify the dimension name and the level name. In the case of the Product dimension with two levels named Milk, [Products].[Milk].MEMBERS could return either level or an error. There is no way to use the MEMBERS set expression in this case. Thus, a faulty naming convention renders an essential part of the MDX language useless.

Using the Dot Operator to Retrieve Specific Values Within a Hierarchy

Instead of seeing the sales for all of the available years (1997 and 1998 in this case), let's just look at the sales for 1997. Go to the previous query with Year and replace Year with 1997. This gives the sales for 1997. The new query looks as follows:

```
SELECT

    {([Measures].[Unit Sales])} ON COLUMNS,

    {([Time].[1997])} ON ROWS

FROM Sales
```

Make the change and run the query. You will only see the value for sales for 1997.

You can expand this query by adding a specific quarter:

```
SELECT
    {([Measures].[Unit Sales])} on COLUMNS,
    {([Time].[1997].[Q1])} on ROWS
FROM Sales
```

Make this change, and run the query. Finally, you can drill down into the month with the following change:

```
SELECT
    {([Measures].[Unit Sales])} on COLUMNS,
    {([Time].[1997].[Q1].[1])} on ROWS
FROM Sales
```

Run this query and you will have sales for Q1; 1997. Using this technique, you can quickly drill down into specific values for a hierarchy.

Query Errors

It might seem that you should be able to perform the following query to get the sales for the quarters for 1997.

```
SELECT
    {([Measures].[Unit Sales])} on COLUMNS,
    {([Time].[1997].[Quarter].MEMBERS )} on ROWS
FROM Sales
```

Actually, this query results in an error message, as shown in Figure 5-6.

Do not panic; at this point you have barely scratched the surface of MDX. To get the sales for all of the quarters for 1997, you could use the set expression Descendants. The correct query looks as follows:

```
SELECT
    {([Unit Sales])} on COLUMNS,
    {Descendants( [Time].[1997],[Time}.[Quarter] )} on ROWS
FROM Sales
```

This query returns the correct results, as shown in Figure 5-7. You could have also used a WHERE clause.

The details of this and all of the set expressions are discussed in Chapter 7.

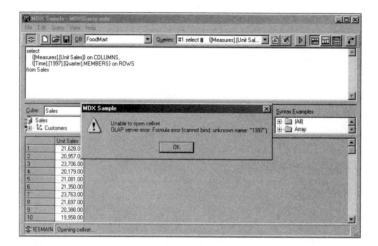

Figure 5-6. *[Time].[1997].[Quarter] query raises an error message.*

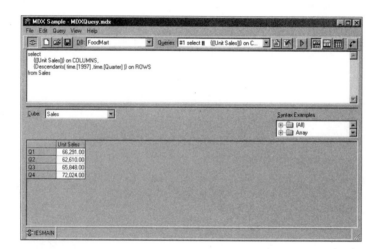

Figure 5-7. *Sales by quarter for 1997.*

Note If you identify a specific value, such as 1997, when drilling down into a structural dimension's hierarchy using the dot operator, all entries for all levels should also be specific values. Thus, 1997.Q1 and 1997.Q1.1 will always work, but 1997.Quarter and 1997.Quarter.MEMBERS will raise an error message as in Figure 5-7.

By just using the most basic part of the MDX syntax, you can retrieve values for specific values of a measure and for all measures. Some additional queries based on this syntax that you can try are as follows:

```
SELECT

    {([Measures].[Unit Sales])} ON COLUMNS,

    {([Customers].[All Customers].[USA])} ON ROWS

FROM Sales
```

This will return sales for all of the customers in the United States.

> **More Info** You could perform the above query without including [All Customers]. OLAP Server will search the Customers dimension and find the correct level. However, it is best to specify all of the dimensions when using values so it is clear what you want. This will make your queries easier to read and guarantee that they are returning the correct value.

The following query will also work:

```
SELECT

    {([Measures].[Unit Sales])} ON COLUMNS,

    {([time].[1997].[Q1].[1]), ([time].[1998].[Q1].[1])} ON ROWS

FROM Sales
```

In this case, there is a set with two tuples consisting of one time dimension member. You know there are two tuples because they are both enclosed in parentheses. An error occurs if you change the query slightly and rewrite it as:

```
SELECT

    {([Measures].[Unit Sales])} on COLUMNS,

    {([time].[1997].[1]), ([time].[1998].[1])} on ROWS

FROM Sales
```

Removing the 1997 will also cause the error.

Name Spaces

This brings up another point about MDX. While using [Customers].[USA] instead of [Customers].[All Customers].[USA] worked in the last sample, this time not explicitly listing all of the dimensions in the hierarchy failed. Thus, when you are listing values for dimension levels, you should list all of the levels. This is called a Fully Qualified Name.

On the other hand, when you are using level names, such as Country, or State Province, and the MEMBERS keyword, you should only list the name of the dimension and the name of the level you want to use.

When you use a name for something, such as a member, OLAP Server will search a certain domain for that name. Usually, the domain is a single cube. This domain is called the **name space.** As long as a name is unique in a name space, there is no problem. If the name is not unique, or OLAP Server cannot resolve the name within the name space, you will get an error as you did in the previous example. If you are wondering why CustomerID was used instead of Customer Last Name when the Customer 1998 dimension was built in the SalesFor1998 cube, this was to ensure a unique value for the name space. It is important to use the rules described in the previous section to ensure a unique name space.

Nesting Dimensions

As mentioned previously, you want the ability to nest dimensions. To do this, you need to use a tuple with more than one member in the select clause. This looks as follows:

```
SELECT

    {([Measures].[Unit Sales])} ON COLUMNS,

    {([Customers].[All Customers].[USA],[Product].[All Products].[Food])}
ON ROWS

FROM Sales
```

In this case, ([Customers].[All Customers].[USA],[Product].[All Products].[Food])} is used as a tuple to return the sales for all customers in the USA who purchased items from the Food category. If you now expand this query as follows:

```
SELECT

    {([Measures].[Unit Sales])} on COLUMNS,

    {

      ([Customers].[All Customers].[USA],[Product].[All Products].[Food]),

      ([Customers].[All Customers].[USA],[Product].[All Products].[Drink]),

      ([Customers].[All Customers].[USA],

      [Product].[All Products].[Non-Consumable])

    } on ROWS

FROM Sales
```

you will get a nested result, as shown in Figure 5-8.

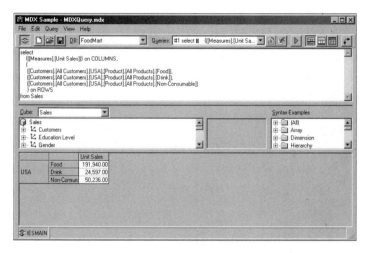

Figure 5-8.   *Products nested within Customers.*

You can further expand this query by adding another country, Canada:

```
SELECT

    {([Measures].[Unit Sales])} ON COLUMNS,

    {

    ([Customers].[All Customers].[USA],[Product].[All Products].[Food]),

    ([Customers].[All Customers].[USA],[Product].[All Products].[Drink]),

    ([Customers].[All Customers].[USA],

     [Product].[All Products].[Non-Consumable]),

    ([Customers].[All Customers].[Canada],

     [Product].[All Products].[Food]),

    ([Customers].[All Customers].[Canada],

     [Product].[All Products].[Drink]),

    ([Customers].[All Customers].[Canada],

    [Product].[All Products].[Non-Consumable])

    } ON ROWS

FROM Sales
```

The results for this query are shown in Figure 5-9.

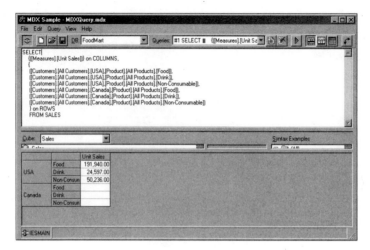

Figure 5-9. *Sales for customers in Canada and the United States for the food, drink, and non-consumable product categories.*

The empty records for Canada do not represent an error; there simply are no values for Canada for 1997. As discussed below, OLAP Server does not raise an error if you try to retrieve a record that does not exist, it returns a 0 value instead.

You might be wondering why these are the 1997 records. All of the measures in the FoodMart data warehouse are time related; they make no sense unless you choose a time period to evaluate this measure over. As OLAP Server was not provided with a date range, it picked one from a default value. In this case, the default is 1997. Whenever you are allowing OLAP Server to choose values for you, you are asking for trouble, because as OLAP Server may or may not pick the values you need. Because all of the queries for FoodMart require a time range, you should be including the time dimension in all of your queries.

Caution   Just because a query returns information does not mean it is returning the information you want. Make sure that your queries include all of the dimensions that are required for the query; do not rely on OLAP Server to use default information.

You can fix your query by changing it to the following:

```
SELECT

    {([Measures].[Unit Sales])} on COLUMNS,

    {

    ([Time].[1997], [Customers].[All Customers].[USA],

    [Product].[All Products].[Food]),
```

```
    ([Time].[1997], [Customers].[All Customers].[USA],
    [Product].[All Products].[Drink]),
    ([Time].[1997], [Customers].[All Customers].[USA],
    [Product].[All Products].[Non-Consumable]),
    ([Time].[1997], [Customers].[All Customers].[Canada],
    [Product].[All Products].[Food]),
    ([Time].[1997], [Customers].[All Customers].[Canada],
    [Product].[All Products].[Drink]),
    ([Time].[1997], [Customers].[All Customers].[Canada],
    [Product].[All Products].[Non-Consumable]),
    ([Time].[1998], [Customers].[All Customers].[USA],
      [Product].[All Products].[Food]),
    ([Time].[1998], [Customers].[All Customers].[USA],
    [Product].[All Products].[Drink]),
    ([Time].[1998], [Customers].[All Customers].[USA],
    [Product].[All Products].[Non-Consumable]),
    ([Time].[1998], [Customers].[All Customers].[Canada],
    [Product].[All Products].[Food]),
    ([Time].[1998], [Customers].[All Customers].[Canada],
    [Product].[All Products].[Drink]),
    ([Time].[1998], [Customers].[All Customers].[Canada],
    [Product].[All Products].[Non-Consumable])
    } ON ROWS
FROM Sales
```

You have now nested the Customers dimension within the Time dimension, and the Products dimension within the Customers dimension. This will give you the correct set of information.

Drilling Down into Nested Queries

Although identifying the specific information in the tuples might seem like a lot of work, it fits naturally with what the user is doing. The user is looking at the data and selecting a value, such as Drink for USA customers in 1998, to expand. Based on this selection, you can get all of the children of the Drink group and expand the query. This new query looks as follows:

```
SELECT

        {([Measures].[Unit Sales])} on COLUMNS,

        {

        ([Time].[1997], [Customers].[All Customers].[USA],[Product].[All
Products].[Food]),

        ([Time].[1997], [Customers].[All Customers].[USA],[Product].[All
Products].[Drink]),

        ([Time].[1997], [Customers].[All Customers].[USA],[Product].[All
Products].[Non-Consumable]),

        ([Time].[1997], [Customers].[All Customers].[Canada],[Product].[All
Products].[Food]),

        ([Time].[1997], [Customers].[All Customers].[Canada],[Product].[All
Products].[Drink]),

        ([Time].[1997], [Customers].[All Customers].[Canada],[Product].[All
Products].[Non-Consumable]),

        ([Time].[1998], [Customers].[All Customers].[USA],[Product].[All
Products].[Food]),

        ([Time].[1998], [Customers].[All Customers].[USA],[Product].[All
Products].[Drink].[Alcoholic Beverages]),

        ([Time].[1998], [Customers].[All Customers].[USA],[Product].[All
Products].[Drink].[Beverages]),

        ([Time].[1998], [Customers].[All Customers].[USA],[Product].[All
Products].[Drink].[Dairy]),

        ([Time].[1998], [Customers].[All Customers].[USA],[Product].[All
Products].[Non-Consumable]),

        ([Time].[1998], [Customers].[All Customers].[Canada],[Product].[All
Products].[Food]),

        ([Time].[1998], [Customers].[All Customers].[Canada],[Product].[All
Products].[Drink]),

        ([Time].[1998], [Customers].[All Customers].[Canada],[Product].[All
Products].[Non-Consumable])

        } on ROWS

from Sales
```

The results of this query are shown in Figure 5-10.

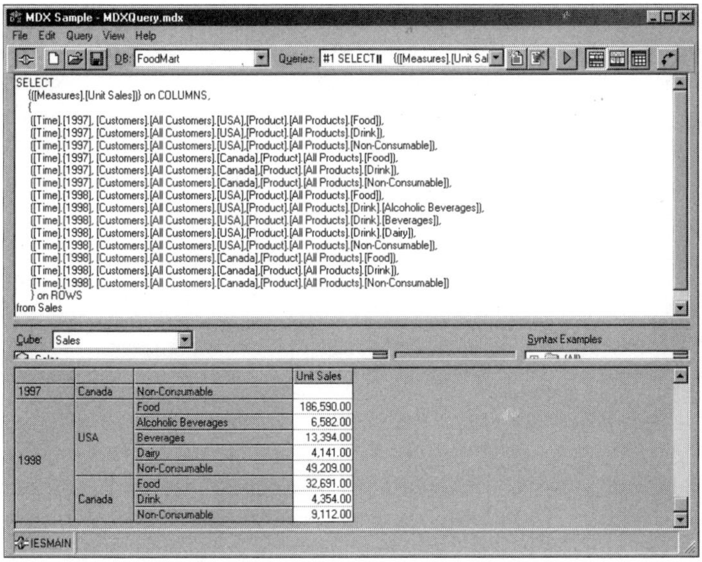

Figure 5-10. *Drilling down into USA drink sales.*

Rules for Creating Tuples in the Select Clause

Figure 5-10 shows that the levels nested vertically. Although the OLAP Manager nested the information horizontally and this nests vertically, it is still easy to read.

However, there is now a column that is a combination of two different levels of one dimension, that is, Product Family and Product Department. This could be confusing for a user. It seems that what you should do is change your product tuple to the following:

```
    ([Time].[1998], [Customers].[All Customers].[USA], [Product].[All
Products].[Drink],

        [Product].[All Products].[Drink].[Alcoholic Beverages]),

    ([Time].[1998], [Customers].[All Customers].[USA], [Product].[All
Products].[Drink],

[Product].[All Products].[Drink].[Beverages]),

    ([Time].[1998], [Customers].[All Customers].[USA], [Product].[All
Products].[Drink],

[Product].[All Products].[Drink].[Dairy]),
```

However, this will fail for two reasons. First, when using multiple tuples on one axis (rows in this case), each tuple must have the same number of dimensions in the tuple and the tuples must be in the same dimension order. Thus, just by adding this into the query, you now have three tuples that have Time, Customer, and Product dimensions and the rest of the queries will be Time, Customer, and Product. Some rows have three members and some rows have four members. This will not work in MDX. You could fix this by adding another Product dimension to the rest of the tuples, but this will fail because of a second problem. A tuple is made up of members from unique dimensions. What you are trying to create is a tuple where one dimension, Product, is contained in the tuple twice. It makes no difference that the dimension is referenced from two different levels; this violates the rules of tuples and MDX.

It helps to step back and think about what a tuple is. The members in your tuples represent points on the cube. A tuple is a point on the cube where you usually want to get values for your measures. By including two members from the same dimension, you are defining two different values for that dimension's point on the cube. Obviously, this cannot be the case. Thus, when nesting using basic MDX syntax, you can only have one value associated with each dimension.

Note When creating tuples in the SELECT statement, for each axis each tuple must have the same number of dimensions, in the same order. With the exception of the measures dimension, the dimensions in the tuple must all be unique.

If you do vertical nesting uniformly, the information can easily be read. Place the following query in the MDX sample and run it. You will see that it is very easy to read:

```
SELECT

MEASURES.MEMBERS ON COLUMNS,

{

( [Time].[1998], [Product].[all products]),

( [Time].[1998], [Product].[all products].[Drink]),

( [Time].[1998], [Product].[all products].[Food]),

( [Time].[1998], [Product].[all products].[Non-Consumable]),

( [Time].[1998].[Q1], [Product].[all products]),

( [Time].[1998].[Q1], [Product].[all products].[Drink]),

( [Time].[1998].[Q1], [Product].[all products].[Food]),

( [Time].[1998].[Q1], [Product].[all products].[Non-Consumable]),

( [Time].[1998].[Q1].[1], [Product].[all products]),

( [Time].[1998].[Q1].[1], [Product].[all products].[Drink]),

( [Time].[1998].[Q1].[1], [Product].[all products].[Food]),
```

```
( [Time].[1998].[Q1].[1], [Product].[all products].[Non-Consumable]),
( [Time].[1998].[Q1].[2], [Product].[all products]),
( [Time].[1998].[Q1].[2], [Product].[all products].[Drink]),
( [Time].[1998].[Q1].[2], [Product].[all products].[Food]),
( [Time].[1998].[Q1].[2], [Product].[all products].[Non-Consumable]),
( [Time].[1998].[Q1].[3], [Product].[all products]),
( [Time].[1998].[Q1].[3], [Product].[all products].[Drink]),
( [Time].[1998].[Q1].[3], [Product].[all products].[Food]),
( [Time].[1998].[Q1].[3], [Product].[all products].[Non-Consumable]),
( [Time].[1998].[Q2].[4], [Product].[all products]),
( [Time].[1998].[Q2].[4], [Product].[all products].[Drink]),
( [Time].[1998].[Q2].[4], [Product].[all products].[Food]),
( [Time].[1998].[Q2].[4], [Product].[all products].[Non-Consumable]),
( [Time].[1998].[Q2].[5], [Product].[all products]),
( [Time].[1998].[Q2].[5], [Product].[all products].[Drink]),
( [Time].[1998].[Q2].[5], [Product].[all products].[Food]),
( [Time].[1998].[Q2].[5], [Product].[all products].[Non-Consumable]),
( [Time].[1998].[Q2].[6], [Product].[all products]),
( [Time].[1998].[Q2].[6], [Product].[all products].[Drink]),
( [Time].[1998].[Q2].[6], [Product].[all products].[Food]),
( [Time].[1998].[Q2].[6], [Product].[all products].[Non-Consumable]),
( [Time].[1998].[Q3].[7], [Product].[all products]),
( [Time].[1998].[Q3].[7], [Product].[all products].[Drink]),
( [Time].[1998].[Q3].[7], [Product].[all products].[Food]),
( [Time].[1998].[Q3].[7], [Product].[all products].[Non-Consumable]),
( [Time].[1998].[Q3].[8], [Product].[all products]),
( [Time].[1998].[Q3].[8], [Product].[all products].[Drink]),
( [Time].[1998].[Q3].[8], [Product].[all products].[Food]),
( [Time].[1998].[Q3].[8], [Product].[all products].[Non-Consumable]),
```

```
    ( [Time].[1998].[Q3].[9], [Product].[all products]),

    ( [Time].[1998].[Q3].[9], [Product].[all products].[Drink]),

    ( [Time].[1998].[Q3].[9], [Product].[all products].[Food]),

    ( [Time].[1998].[Q3].[9], [Product].[all products].[Non-Consumable]),

    ( [Time].[1998].[Q4].[10], [Product].[all products]),

    ( [Time].[1998].[Q4].[10], [Product].[all products].[Drink]),

    ( [Time].[1998].[Q4].[10], [Product].[all products].[Food]),

    ( [Time].[1998].[Q4].[10], [Product].[all products].[Non-Consumable]),

    ( [Time].[1998].[Q4].[11], [Product].[all products]),

    ( [Time].[1998].[Q4].[11], [Product].[all products].[Drink]),

    ( [Time].[1998].[Q4].[11], [Product].[all products].[Food]),

    ( [Time].[1998].[Q4].[11], [Product].[all products].[Non-Consumable]),

    ( [Time].[1998].[Q4].[12], [Product].[all products]),

    ( [Time].[1998].[Q4].[12], [Product].[all products].[Drink]),

    ( [Time].[1998].[Q4].[12], [Product].[all products].[Food]),

    ( [Time].[1998].[Q4].[12], [Product].[all products].[Non-Consumable])

}

ON ROWS

FROM SALES
```

This query is shown in Figure 5-11.

There is an easier way to do this using CROSSJOIN. Just as MEMBERS is shorthand to list out all of the members of a dimension's level, CROSSJOIN is shorthand for nesting dimensions. It is important, though, that you first understand what nested dimensions look like in MDX when written completely.

As a final note on simple MDX and nesting, the following query will not work:

```
SELECT

    {([Measures].[Unit Sales])} ON COLUMNS,

    {([Customers].[Country].MEMBERS ,[Product].[Product Family].MEMBERS)}

     ON ROWS

FROM Sales
```

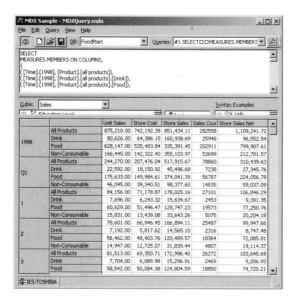

Figure 5-11. *Nested time and product dimensions.*

When listing multiple members in a tuple, you must list specific values, not general dimension level names.

Nesting is an important part of presenting information to the user. Another important way to do so is by creating slicer dimensions.

Creating Slicer Dimensions

Slicer dimensions cut into the cube and give you a view across the data. In general, when you are slicing, you are holding all but one dimension constant. The value of one or more measures is taken across points on the cube. The points of the cube have values where all dimensions but one are held constant. If you have three cube axes and slice the cube over one cube axis, all of the points on the slice will be constant for the two dimensions. Thus, what you are doing is slicing the cube open and taking values across one dimension. This is done using the WHERE clause.

The MDX WHERE Clause

The MDX WHERE clause is very different from the WHERE clause in SQL. In MDX, the WHERE clause defines which dimensions are being held constant and at what value you want to hold those dimensions. Let's look at a typical slicer MDX query. Type the following query into the MDX Sample window:

```
SELECT

  { ([MEASURES].[Unit Sales]) } ON COLUMNS,

  [Product].[Product Category].MEMBERS  ON ROWS

  FROM Sales

  WHERE ([Customers].[All Customers].[USA].[WA], [Time].[1997])
```

The WHERE clause results in the Customer dimension being held constant on the value WA, and the Time dimension on the value 1997. The Unit Sales is measured over all of the values of the Product Category for customers in WA during the year 1997. The result of this query is shown in Figure 5-12.

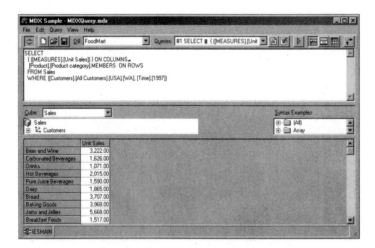

Figure 5-12. *Unit Sales for 1997 for WA customers for all of the product categories.*

If you want to see the Store Cost, Store Sales, and Stores Sales Net for the Dairy category in the year 1997, over the different countries where products are sold, you can use the following query:

```
SELECT

  {([MEASURES].[Store Cost]),([MEASURES].[Store Sales]),

  ([MEASURES].[Store Sales Net]) } ON COLUMNS,
```

```
{([Store].[Store Country].MEMBERS)} ON ROWS
```

```
FROM Sales
```

```
WHERE ([Product].[Drink].[Dairy], [Time].[1998])
```

This query will return the results shown in Figure 5-13.

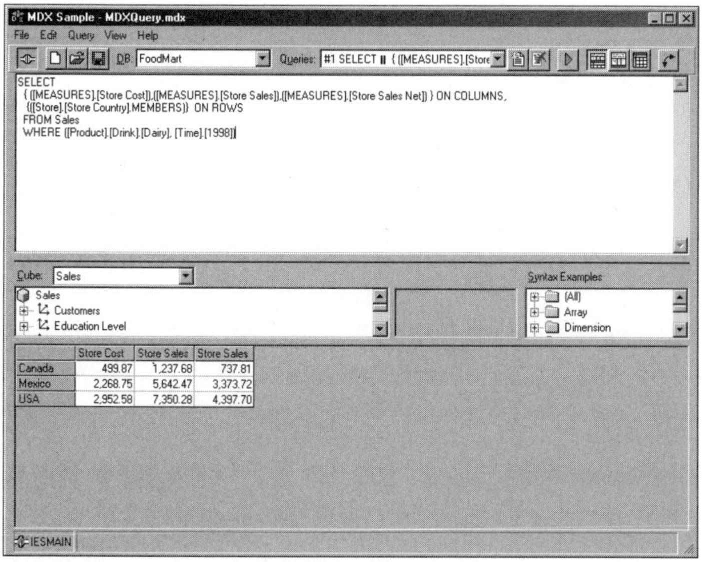

Figure 5-13. *Store Cost, Store Sales, and Stores Sales Net for the Dairy category in the year 1997 by country.*

These queries are beginning to look more like the typical analytical queries you want to perform. If you want to drill down even further, you can perform the following query:

```
SELECT
```

```
{ ([MEASURES].[Store Cost]),([MEASURES].[Store Sales]),([MEASURES].[Store
Sales Net]) } ON COLUMNS,
```

```
[Store].[Store Country].MEMBERS  ON ROWS
```

```
FROM Sales
```

```
WHERE ([Product].[Drink].[Dairy].[Dairy].[Milk], [Time].[1998])
```

Enter and run this query and you will get the sales for milk over the three countries. Notice how dairy is listed in two levels. Using the fully qualified name is the only way to work with this dimension.

Change the category in the WHERE clause and the Time dimension. Spend some time getting used to using the WHERE clause, because it is one of the basic structures of MDX.

Incorrect WHERE Clauses

If you remember that the values in the WHERE clause represent holding one or more dimensions constant at some value, which slices the cube, you will have no trouble with these queries. For example, the following cannot work:

```
SELECT

  { ([MEASURES].[Store Cost]),([MEASURES].[Store Sales]),([MEASURES].[Store
Sales Net]) } ON COLUMNS,

  {([Store].[Store Country].MEMBERS)}  ON ROWS

  FROM Sales

  WHERE

  ([Product].[Drink].[Dairy].[Dairy].[Milk], [Time].[1998], [Time].[1997])
```

This cannot work because you cannot hold the time dimension constant at both 1997 and 1998; you must hold it constant at one value or the other. The items in the WHERE clause form a tuple, and a tuple is defined as being made from different dimensions. The following query also cannot work:

```
SELECT

  { ([MEASURES].[Store Cost]),([MEASURES].[Store Sales]),([MEASURES].[Store
Sales Net]) } ON COLUMNS,

  {([Product].[Product Family].MEMBERS)}  ON ROWS

  FROM Sales

  WHERE ([Product].[Drink].[Dairy].[Dairy].[Milk], [Time].[1998])
```

This will fail because you listed the product dimension in both the SELECT portion of the query and the WHERE portion of the query. The SELECT portion says to measure over the different values of Product Family, and the WHERE clause says to measure over the product Milk; you cannot do both at the same time. Thus, the dimensions listed in the WHERE clause cannot also be listed in the SELECT clause.

Placing Measures into the WHERE Clause

One rather interesting query that will work is the following:

```
SELECT

  { ([Time].[1998)]), ([Time].[1997]) } ON COLUMNS,
```

```
    {([Store].[Store Country].MEMBERS)}   ON ROWS
FROM Sales
WHERE ([Product].[Drink].[Dairy].[Dairy].[Milk])
```

If you type this query in and run it, you will get the results shown in Figure 5-14.

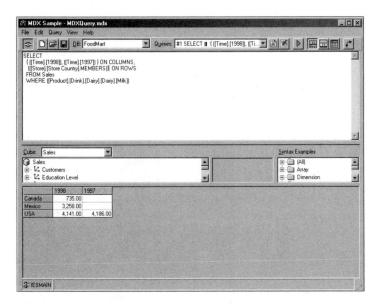

Figure 5-14. *Results of an MDX query with no measures.*

The values that are calculated are for Unit Sales. Because no Measure is listed in the query, OLAP Server chose to use the first Measure in the cube, which is the default, to perform calculations over the listed dimensions. This gives a hint as to what you can do with your MDX query. You will get the Store Sales for the Milk product in the year 1998 for all the countries if you rewrite your query as follows:

```
SELECT
    { ([Time].[1998]) } ON COLUMNS,
    ([Store].[Store Country].MEMBERS)   ON ROWS
FROM Sales
WHERE ([Product].[Drink].[Dairy].[Dairy].[Milk], [MEASURES].[Store Sales])
```

This is exactly what you want.

> **Note** By putting a member of the Measures dimension into the WHERE clause and only regular dimensions into the SELECT clause, you will get values for that Measure over the dimensions.

You now have a basic understanding of the MDX query. Yet, you still have only scratched the surface. You can add more power to your MDX query by adding calculated members to them. In the last chapter, you added Profit98 and Product Avg Cost to your SalesFor1998 cube. You can use calculated members in your queries. For example, the Sales cube has a Profit calculated member, which we can use as follows:

```
SELECT

  { ([Time].[1998]) } ON COLUMNS,

  {([Store].[Store Country].MEMBERS)}  ON ROWS

  FROM Sales

  WHERE ([Product].[Drink].[Dairy].[Dairy].[Milk], [MEASURES].[Profit])
```

You probably notice that when you create a calculated member, it asks the dimension with which to associate the member. The default is Measures and you use this for your calculated measures. Profit from the Sales cube also belongs to Measures, so it is defined as [MEASURES].[Profit] in our MDX query. If the calculated member is created as a member of another dimension, then you have to precede Profit with that dimension.

The problem with calculated members is that everyone wants a personal special calculated member. Perhaps a manager notices that there is a virtual dimension called Total Number of Children and another virtual dimension called Number of Children at Home. The manager believes that the sales of his particular product are affected by the number of adult children who are not at home (perhaps he manages the wedding gifts section). This manager wants to see Number of Children Not at Home, which is the difference between the two virtual dimensions. You could create a calculated Measure, but where would you put a Children Not at Home calculated member? Does it belong with the Customer or the Measures dimension? It really is not a Measure. There is a more serious potential problem here.

The entire idea behind a data warehouse is to allow you to build dynamic applications that can answer whatever query the user wants. This prevents you from making a customized application or customized stored procedures for every view of the data that the user needs. A good design phase will identify the essential calculated measures, such as profit. If you start making calculated measures for every possible combination of the data, you will find yourself making dozens of members and calculated members that will never be used. If you do not create all of the possible combinations, every time a user finds a new combination of the data, you might have to add new measures and calculated measures to the data warehouse. This is no different from making stored procedures for every view the user wants.

Luckily, though, MDX offers a way to create calculated members. Using MDX, you can create applications that allow the user to use the existing dimensions and members to create new calculated members. Basic applications, such as presenting a simple view of the data, can be created without MDX. But when you want to make powerful dynamic applications, you must use MDX.

Conclusion

Even with the most basic syntax, MDX is a powerful language that allows you to create views of the data according to the needs of the user and the business. The next two chapters will extend your basic MDX statements and add more features to them. This will allow you to get the exact data you need in the format you need it. Let's now turn our attention to creating calculated members with MDX.

Chapter 6
Creating Calculated Members

Just as you created calculated members in OLAP Manager, you can also create them in MDX queries. These calculated members enable you to define new members based on existing measures or dimensions within the cube. Thus, you can create a new profit calculated measure from the existing sales and cost measures using the MDX WITH clause.

Using MDX WITH Clause

You create calculated members in MDX using the WITH clause. The format for the WITH clause is:

```
WITH MEMBER parent1.name1 AS 'Expression1',

   [MEMBER parent2.name2 AS 'Expression2', …]
```

Parent refers to the dimension in which the new MDX calculated member belongs. Name is the name for the new member. It should be unique within the name space.

Query Profit and Percent Profit

Profit equals total sales minus cost. Thus, you have the following query to create a calculated member for profit using MDX:

```
WITH MEMBER MEASURES.[Store Profit] AS 'MEASURES.[Store Sales] -

   MEASURES.[Store Cost]'

SELECT

   {([Time].[Year].MEMBERS)} ON COLUMNS,

   {([Product].[Product Category].MEMBERS)} ON ROWS

FROM Sales

WHERE ( MEASURES.[Store Profit])
```

The result of this query is shown in Figure 6-1.

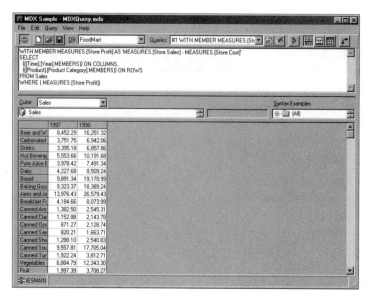

Figure 6-1. *Profit for 1997 and 1998 by product category.*

You can use your new calculated member exactly as you used your regular members. You can also use it to create new calculated members just as you used regular members to create profit. Let's now calculate Percent Profit, which is Profit divided by Store Sales. The new formula looks as follows:

```
WITH
    MEMBER MEASURES.[Store Profit] AS 'MEASURES.[Store Sales] -
        MEASURES.[Store Cost]'
    MEMBER MEASURES.[Store Percent Profit] AS 'MEASURES.[Store Profit] /
                                           MEASURES.[Store Cost]'
SELECT
    {(MEASURES.[Store Profit]), (MEASURES.[Store Percent Profit])}
ON COLUMNS,
    {([Product].[Product Category].MEMBERS)} ON ROWS
FROM Sales
WHERE ([Time].[1997])
```

You created Percent Profit in exactly the same way as you created Profit. Notice that there is no comma between the two calculated members. If you are wondering why the query is completely changed, think back to the previous sections. The list of dimensions in the WHERE clause is a tuple. This means that the WHERE clause has a list of unique dimensions. Since both Store Profit and Store Percent Profit come from the same dimension (measures), you cannot list them both in the WHERE clause. This makes sense, because you can only display one measure in the grids of the grid box. You cannot list 1997 and 1998 in the WHERE clause for the same reason (two members of a tuple from the same dimension).

You can also calculate the difference in sales for 1997 and 1998. This leads you to perhaps one of the most powerful and useful features of MDX—an easy and quick way to calculate the differences between two time periods. Your query looks as follows:

```
WITH
    MEMBER [Time].[1998 1997 Difference] AS '([Time].[1998]) -
                                    ([Time].[1997])'
SELECT
  {([Time].[1998 1997 Difference])} ON COLUMNS,
  { (MEASURES.[Unit Sales])  } ON ROWS
FROM Sales
```

There are some interesting things to notice about this query. To begin with, the parent for your new difference-calculated member is the Time dimension, not the Measures dimension. This had to be done because you are using Unit Sales in your Rows axis, and Unit Sales is from the Measures dimension. Not only are you not allowed to put the same dimension into a tuple more than once, but you also cannot list members of the same dimension on two different axes. This makes sense if you once again remember that tuples are defining points on the cube. Placing the members onto the axis is only for presentation purposes. The cube is defined by values of the dimensions in all the axes and the WHERE clause. Thus, dimensions need to be unique for the tuple definitions in all the axes and the WHERE clause.

Using Additive Calculated Members

To see the store sales, store cost, and store profit for 1997 and 1998 and the difference in profit over the two years, try the following query:

```
WITH
    MEMBER MEASURES.[Store Profit] AS 'MEASURES.[Store Sales] -
                                    MEASURES.[Store Cost]'
    MEMBER [Time].[1998 1997 Difference] AS '([Time].[1998]) -
                                    ([Time].[1997])'
```

```
SELECT
    {(MEASURES.[Store Sales]), (MEASURES.[Store Cost]),
    (MEASURES.[Store Profit] )}ON COLUMNS,
    {(([Time].[1997]), ([Time].[1998]), ([Time].[1998 1997 Difference])}
                                 ON ROWS
FROM Sales
```

The results of the query are shown in Figure 6-2.

The question is, "What is the value in the bottom right cell?" It can either be the difference between the profit for 1998 and the profit in 1997, or the difference in sales between 1998 and 1997 minus the difference in cost between 1998 and 1997. Because both of the calculated Measures are additive (subtraction also counts as an additive type of Measure), both values are the same. Yet, if you change your calculated members slightly, you see what happens with non-additive calculated members.

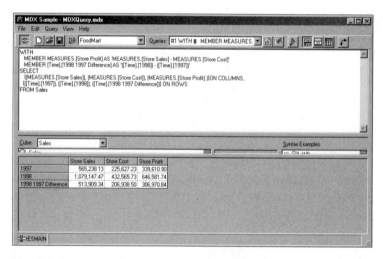

Figure 6-2. *Store sales, cost, and profit differences for 1997 and 1998.*

Calculating Non-Additive Calculated Members

Suppose you want to calculate the ratio between 1997 and 1998. Rewrite your query as follows:

```
WITH
    MEMBER MEASURES.[Store Profit] AS 'MEASURES.[Store Sales] -
                                 MEASURES.[Store Cost]'
    MEMBER [Time].[1998 1997 Ratio] AS '([Time].[1998]) / ([Time].[1997])'
```

```
SELECT
    {(MEASURES.[Store Sales]), (MEASURES.[Store Cost]),
     (MEASURES.[Store Profit] )}ON COLUMNS,
   {([Time].[1997]), ([Time].[1998]), ([Time].[1998 1997 Ratio])} ON ROWS
FROM Sales
```

The results are shown in Figure 6-3.

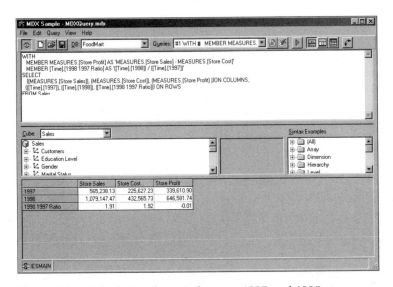

Figure 6-3.   *Calculating the ratio between 1997 and 1998.*

The value in the bottom right cell is the Store Sales ratio minus the Store Cost ratio. This is not what you want. Instead, you want the profit for 1998 to be divided by the profit for 1997. To do this, you need to tell Microsoft SQL Server OLAP Services to do the profit-calculated member first, and then you can take the difference. You do this with the SOLVE_ORDER property.

SOLVE_ORDER Property

There are several properties that you can set using calculated members. SOLVE_ORDER is one of them. When setting properties for a calculated member, you need to place a comma after the definition of the calculated member. SOLVE_ORDER begins with 0. Thus, your new query looks as follows:

```
WITH
    MEMBER MEASURES.[Store Profit] AS 'MEASURES.[Store Sales] -
            MEASURES.[Store Cost]',
```

```
    SOLVE_ORDER =0

    MEMBER [Time].[1998 1997 Ratio] AS '([Time].[1998]) / ([Time].[1997])',

    SOLVE_ORDER =1
SELECT

    {(MEASURES.[Store Sales]), (MEASURES.[Store Cost]),

    (MEASURES.[Store Profit] )}ON COLUMNS,

   {([Time].[1997]), ([Time].[1998]), ([Time].[1998 1997 Ratio])} ON ROWS
FROM Sales
```

Figure 6-4 shows the result of this new query, which is the correct answer.

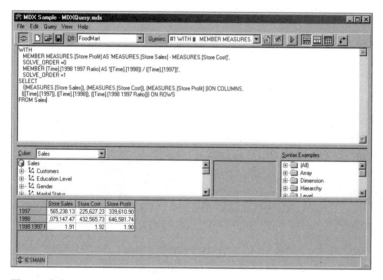

Figure 6-4. *Using SOLVE_ORDER.*

Several other properties belong to calculated members. One of the most important is FORMAT_STRING.

FORMAT_STRING Property

MDX has a wide range of formatting functions so that you can format the results of your calculated member in any way that is required. Format works with character values, strings, and dates.

Formatting Character Values

The format expression for strings can have either one section or two sections. If there are two sections, they are separated by a semicolon (;). See Table 6-1.

Table 6-1. Format Expression for Strings

If you use	The result is
One section only	The format applies to all string data.
Two sections	The first section applies to string data, the second to null values and zero-length strings (" ").

The characters shown in Table 6-2 can appear in the format string for character strings.

Table 6-2. Characters in Format String for Characters

Character	Description
@	Character placeholder. Displays either a character or a space. If the string has a character in the position where the at symbol (@) appears in the format string, it displays the character. Otherwise, it displays a space in that position. Placeholders are filled from right to left unless there is an exclamation point character (!) in the format string.
&	Character placeholder. Displays a character or nothing. If the string has a character in the position where the ampersand (&) appears, it displays the character. Otherwise, it displays nothing. Placeholders are filled from right to left unless there is an exclamation point character (!) in the format string.
<	Forces lowercase. Displays all characters in lowercase format.
>	Forces uppercase. Displays all characters in uppercase format.
!	Forces left-to-right fill of placeholders. (The default is to fill placeholders from right to left.)

Formatting Numeric Values

A user-defined format expression for numbers can have anywhere from one to four sections. If more than one section is used, you must separate the sections by semicolons.

MDX also has predefined named formats. If these format arguments are used, only one section is allowed. See Table 6-3.

Table 6-3. Format Expression for Numbers

If you use	The result is
One section only	The format expression applies to every value the calculated member returns.
Two sections	The first section applies to the positive values and zeros; the second section applies to negative values.
Three sections	The first section applies to positive values, the second section applies to negative values, and the third section applies to zeros.
Four sections	The first section applies to positive values, the second section applies to negative values, the third section applies to zeros, and the fourth section applies to null values.

Table 6-4 below identifies the characters that can appear in the format string for number formats.

Table 6-4. Characters in Format String for Numbers

Character	Description
None	Displays the number with no formatting.
0	Digit placeholder. Displays a digit or a zero.
	If the expression has a digit in the position where the 0 appears in the format string, it displays the digit. Otherwise, it displays a zero in that position.
	If the number has fewer digits than there are zeros (on either side of the decimal) in the format expression, it displays leading or trailing zeros.
	If the number has more digits to the right of the decimal separator than there are zeros to the right of the decimal separator in the format expression, it rounds the number to as many decimal places as there are zeros.
	If the number has more digits to the left of the decimal separator than there are zeros to the left of the decimal separator in the format expression, it displays the extra digits without modification.
#	Digit placeholder. Displays a digit or nothing. If the expression has a digit in the position where the # appears in the format string, it displays the digit. Otherwise, it displays nothing in that position. This symbol works like the 0 digit placeholder, except that leading and trailing zeros are not displayed if the number has the same or fewer digits than there are # characters on either side of the decimal separator in the format expression.
.	Decimal placeholder. (In some locales, a comma is used as the decimal separator.) The decimal placeholder determines how many digits are displayed to the left and right of the decimal separator. If the format expression contains only number signs (#) to the left of this symbol, numbers smaller than 1 begin with a decimal separator. To display a leading zero displayed with fractional numbers, use 0 as the first digit placeholder to the left of the decimal separator. The actual character used as a decimal placeholder in the formatted output depends on the number format recognized by your system.
%	Percentage placeholder. The expression is multiplied by 100. The percent character (%) is inserted in the position where it appears in the format string.
,	Thousand separator. (In some locales, a period is used as a thousand separator.) The thousand separator separates thousands from hundreds within a number that has four or more places to the left of the decimal separator. Standard use of the thousand separator is specified if the format contains a thousand separator surrounded by digit placeholders (0 or #). A thousand separator immediately to the left of the decimal separator (whether or not a decimal is specified), means "scale the number by dividing it by 1000, rounding as needed." For example, you can use the format string "##0,," to represent 100 million as 100. Numbers smaller than 1 million are displayed as 0. Two adjacent thousand separators in any position other than immediately to the left of the decimal separator are treated as specifying the use of a thousand separator. The actual character used as the thousand separator in the formatted output depends on the number format recognized by your system.

(continued)

Table 6-4. Characters in Format String for Numbers *(continued)*

Character	Description
:	Time separator. (In some locales, other characters may be used to represent the time separator.) The time separator separates hours, minutes, and seconds when time values are formatted. The actual character used as the time separator in formatted output is determined by your system settings.
/	Date separator. (In some locales, other characters may be used to represent the date separator.) The date separator separates the day, month, and year when date values are formatted. The actual character used as the date separator in formatted output is determined by your system settings.
E- E+ e- e+	Scientific format. If the format expression contains at least one digit placeholder (0 or #) to the right of E-, E+, e-, or e+, the number is displayed in scientific format and E or e is inserted between the number and its exponent. The number of digit placeholders to the right determines the number of digits in the exponent. Use E- or e- to place a minus sign next to negative exponents. Use E+ or e+ to place a minus sign next to negative exponents and a plus sign next to positive exponents.
- + $ ( )	Displays a literal character. To display a character other than one of those listed, precede it with a backslash (\) or enclose it in double quotation marks (" ").
\	Displays the next character in the format string. To display a character that has special meaning as a literal character, precede it with a backslash (\). The backslash itself is not displayed. Using a backslash is the same as enclosing the next character in double quotation marks. To display a backslash, use two backslashes (\\). Examples of characters that cannot be displayed as literal characters are the date-formatting and time-formatting characters (a, c, d, h, m, n, p, q, s, t, w, y, /, and :), the numeric-formatting characters (#, 0, %, E, e, comma, and period), and the string-formatting characters (@, &, <, >, and !).
"ABC"	Displays the string inside the double quotation marks (" "). To include a string in format from within code, you must use Chr(34) to enclose the text (34 is the character code for a double quotation mark).

The following example has two sections: The first section defines the format for positive values and zeros, and the second section defines the format for negative values.

```
"$#,##0;($#,##0)"
```

If you include semicolons with nothing between them, the missing section is printed using the format of the positive value. For example, the following format displays positive and negative values using the format in the first section and displays "Zero" if the value is zero:

```
"$#,##0;;\Z\e\r\o"
```

You can use this formatting as follows:

```
WITH

    MEMBER MEASURES.[Store Profit] AS 'MEASURES.[Store Sales] -

        MEASURES.[Store Cost]',
```

```
            FORMAT_STRING = '$#,##0;($#,##);\Z\E\R\O'
    MEMBER [Time].[1998 1997 Difference] AS '([Time].[1998]) -
        ([Time].[1997])',
            FORMAT_STRING = '$#,##0;($#,##);\Z\E\R\O'
    MEMBER [Time].[1997 1998 Difference] AS '([Time].[1997]) -
        ([Time].[1998])',
            FORMAT_STRING = '$#,##0;($#,##);\Z\E\R\O'
    MEMBER [Time].[1997 Values] AS '([Time].[1997])',
            FORMAT_STRING = '$#,##0;($#,##);\Z\E\R\O'
    MEMBER [Time].[1998 Values] AS '([Time].[1998])',
            FORMAT_STRING = '$#,##0;($#,##);\Z\E\R\O'
SELECT
    {(MEASURES.[Store Sales]), (MEASURES.[Store Cost]),
(MEASURES.[Store Profit] )}ON COLUMNS,
    {
    ([Time].[1997 VALUES]),
    ([Time].[1998 VALUES]),
    ([Time].[1998 1997 Difference]),
    ([Time].[1997 1998 Difference])
    } ON ROWS
From Sales
```

The results of this query are shown in Figure 6-5.

You could also have written the query as follows and returned the same results:

```
WITH
    MEMBER MEASURES.[Store Profit] AS 'MEASURES.[Store Sales] - MEASURES.[Store
Cost]',
            FORMAT_STRING = '$#,##0;($#,##);Z\E\R\O'
    MEMBER [Time].[1998 1997 Difference] AS '([Time].[1998]) - ([Time].[1997])'
    MEMBER [Time].[1997 1998 Difference] AS '([Time].[1997]) - ([Time].[1998])'
```

```
MEMBER MEASURES.[Store Sales Values] AS 'MEASURES.[Store Sales]',

    FORMAT_STRING = '$#,##0;($#,##);Z\E\R\0'

MEMBER MEASURES.[Store Cost Values] AS '(MEASURES.[Store Cost])',

    FORMAT_STRING = '$#,##0;($#,##);Z\E\R\0'

SELECT

  {(MEASURES.[Store Sales Values]), (MEASURES.[Store Cost Values]),
(MEASURES.[Store Profit] )}ON COLUMNS,

  {

  ([Time].[1997]),

  ([Time].[1998]),

  ([Time].[1998 1997 Difference]),

  ([Time].[1997 1998 Difference])

  } ON ROWS

FROM Sales
```

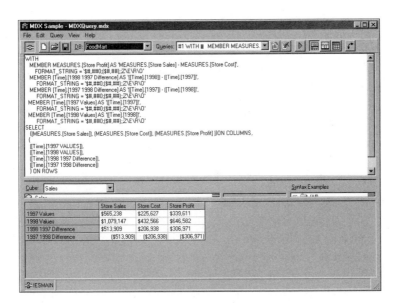

Figure 6-5. *Formatted query.*

The table looks the same either way, but it is much better to actually format the values to be displayed in a formatted fashion. In this case, you are displaying the measures so you should use the second example.

Formatting Date/Time Values

Table 6-5 identifies characters that can appear in the format string for date/time formats.

Table 6-5. Characters in Format String for Date/Time Values

Character	Description
(:)	Time separator. (In some locales, other characters may be used to represent the time separator.) The time separator separates hours, minutes, and seconds when time values are formatted. The actual character used as the time separator in formatted output is determined by your system settings.
(/)	Date separator. (In some locales, other characters may be used to represent the date separator.) The date separator separates the day, month, and year when date values are formatted. The actual character used as the date separator in formatted output is determined by your system settings.
c	Displays the date as ddddd and displays the time as ttttt, in that order. Displays only date information if there is no fractional part to the date serial number. Displays only time information if there is no integer portion.
d	Displays the day as a number without a leading zero (1–31).
dd	Displays the day as a number with a leading zero (01–31).
ddd	Displays the day as an abbreviation (Sun–Sat).
dddd	Displays the day as a full name (Sunday–Saturday).
ddddd	Displays the date as a complete date (including day, month, and year), formatted according to your system's short date format setting. For Microsoft Windows, the default short date format is m/d/yy.
dddddd	Displays a date serial number as a complete date (including day, month, and year), formatted according to the long date setting recognized by your system. For Microsoft Windows, the default long date format is mmmm dd, yyyy.
w	Displays the day of the week as a number (1 for Sunday through 7 for Saturday).
ww	Displays the week of the year as a number (1–54).
m	Displays the month as a number without a leading zero (1–12). If m immediately follows h or hh, the minute rather than the month is displayed.
mm	Displays the month as a number with a leading zero (01–12). If m immediately follows h or hh, the minute rather than the month is displayed.
mmm	Displays the month as an abbreviation (Jan–Dec).
mmmm	Displays the month as a full month name (January–December).
q	Displays the quarter of the year as a number (1–4).
y	Displays the day of the year as a number (1–366).
yy	Displays the year as a two-digit number (00–99).
yyyy	Displays the year as a four-digit number (1000–9999).
h	Displays the hour as a number without leading zeros (0–23).
hh	Displays the hour as a number with leading zeros (00–23).
n	Displays the minute as a number without leading zeros (0–59).
nn	Displays the minute as a number with leading zeros (00–59).

(continued)

Table 6-5. Characters in Format String for Date/Time Values *(continued)*

Character	Description
s	Displays the second as a number without leading zeros (0–59).
ss	Displays the second as a number with leading zeros (00–59).
t t t t t	Displays a time as a complete time (including hour, minute, and second), formatted using the time separator defined by the time format recognized by your system. A leading zero is displayed if the leading zero option is selected and the time is before 10:00 A.M. or P.M. For Microsoft Windows, the default time format is h:mm:ss.
AM/PM	Uses the 12-hour clock. Displays an uppercase AM with any hour before noon; displays an uppercase PM with any hour between noon and 11:59 P.M.
am/pm	Uses the 12-hour clock. Displays a lowercase am with any hour before noon; displays a lowercase pm with any hour between noon and 11:59 P.M.
A/P	Uses the 12-hour clock. Displays an uppercase A with any hour before noon; displays an uppercase P with any hour between noon and 11:59 P.M.
a/p	Uses the 12-hour clock. Displays a lowercase a with any hour before noon; displays a lowercase p with any hour between noon and 11:59 P.M.
AMPM	Uses the 12-hour clock. Displays the AM string literal as defined by your system with any hour before noon; displays the PM string literal as defined by your system with any hour between noon and 11:59 P.M. **AMPM** can be either uppercase or lowercase, but the case of the string displayed matches the string as defined by your system settings. For Microsoft Windows, the default format is **AM/PM.**

Additional Properties of Calculated Members

You can set several other properties for the calculated members. Be aware of the fact that these additional properties do not always display. Even the zero and null replacement strings in the FORMAT_STRING do not always display—it depends on the tool you are using.

The additional properties are as follows:

- **FORECOLOR**   The color value of the foreground.
- **BACKCOLOR**   The color value of the background.
- **FONT_NAME**   The font used for the calculated member.
- **ALIGNMENT**   How the text should be aligned. The values are left, center, and right.

None of these presently works with OLAP Services using the MDX Sample Application. You can set these properties within the OLAP Manager, or the Dimension Manager for shared dimensions. You can also set these properties using the DSO.

There are still two more topics to cover when it comes to calculated members: session-defined calculated members and null values.

Creating Session-Defined Calculated Members

You have been working with the MDX Sample application to test your MDX queries. Although the MDX Sample application is a useful learning and testing tool, MDX belongs in applications. In an application, it is possible that you might want to define a calculated member once and reuse it several times. To do this, MDX enables you to create session-defined calculated members that you can define once and then use in multiple queries. The syntax for session-defined calculated members is as follows:

```
CREATE MEMBER cube1.parent1.name1 AS 'expression1'

[MEMBER cube2.parent2.name2 AS 'expression2' …]
```

Notice that CREATE is used instead of WITH. Also note that the rest of the query is not included with this statement, that is, there is not any SELECT clause following this statement. The session-defined calculated member statement only includes the previous parts.

Once you have created a session-defined calculated member, you can delete it using the following syntax:

```
DROP MEMBER cube1.parent1.name1

[MEMBER cube2.parent2.name2 …]
```

Although you cannot use these in the MDX sample application, you can use them in your code. The final topic, how OLAP Services handles nulls and empty cells when determining the values for calculated members, is covered after member expressions in the next chapter.

Conclusion

Using the calculated members in MDX, you can now create any member you need from existing members. Although having the calculated member in the MDX query means that the values for the member has to be calculated, not having every possible calculated member in the data warehouse makes the data warehouse smaller, faster, and more efficient. If your data warehouse is properly designed, properly optimized, and uses MOLAP, the performance of calculated members in your queries should be within acceptable limits.

Chapter 7
Expressions

In addition to having the full syntax as described in the last two chapters, MDX also has a set of functions called expressions that perform operations on domensions, hierarchies, and levels. The expressions enable you to easily extend the language, and often allow you to simplify a lengthy MDX query.

Member Expressions

Member expressions are functions that apply to members of a dimension, hierarchy, or level and return a member, zero or null. You use these expressions to move up and down the dimension, hierarchy, or level or to move within a dimension, hierarchy, or level. The expressions are as follows:

- **PREVMEMBER**   Returns the previous member in the hierarchy.
- **NEXTMEMBER**   Returns the next member in the hierarchy.
- **FIRSTCHILD**   Returns the first child of a member according to an implicit "natural" order.
- **LASTCHILD**   Returns the last child of a member according to the natural order.
- **PARENT**   Returns the parent of a member.
- **<member>.LEAD(<index>)**   Returns the member that is index positions away along the member's dimension, in the dimension's natural order. The numbering of the positions is zero-based.
- **<member>.LAG**   Similar to **<member>.LEAD(<index>)**, except that it looks in the opposite direction. If index is negative, LEAD becomes LAG and vice versa.
- **<dimension>[.CURRENTMEMBER]**   References the current member of the dimension that is being used in the cube. The concept of "currency" occurs in functions such as GENERATE, where the semantics include some form of iteration through members of a set.
- **<member>.{FIRSTSIBLING | LASTSIBLING}**   Returns the first/last sibling at the parent level of the member. For example, May.FIRSTSIBLING returns April. The expression May.LASTSIBLING returns June (assuming that the parent level is quarters).

- **ANCESTOR(<member>, <level>)**   Returns the ancestor of member at the specified level.
- **COUSIN(<member>, <ancestor_member>)**   This function is best illustrated by an example: COUSIN([1996].March, [1994]) yields the member [1994].March.

You can place these member expressions in two categories. One category moves back and forth in the same level of the hierarchy. This is called horizontal movement. The horizontal category includes PREVMEMBER, NEXTMEMBER, FIRSTSIBLING, and LASTSIBLING. The other category, which moves vertically, allows you to move from one level to another. The vertical category includes PARENT, FIRSTCHILD, LASTSIBLING, and NEXTMEMBER.

CURRENTMEMBER

Once you understand CURRENTMEMBER, you not only have a good understanding of the other member expressions, but also an understanding of how Microsoft SQL Server 7.0 OLAP Server works.

When OLAP Server calculates your queries, it randomly moves through the cube evaluating the measures at each point. The coordinates of the point in the cube that OLAP Server is currently at when solving a query is made up of (dimension1.CurrentMember, dimension2.CurrentMember, …). You can use CURRENTMEMBER to perform very complex problems. Though you did not know it, you have been using CURRENTMEMBER in all your queries.

Look at the query:

```
WITH
    MEMBER MEASURES.[Store Profit] AS 'MEASURES.[Store Sales] -
            MEASURES.[Store Cost]'
SELECT
    {(MEASURES.[Store Sales]), (MEASURES.[Store Cost]),
        (MEASURES.[Store Profit] )}ON COLUMNS,
    {(([Time].[1997]), ([Time].[1998]) } ON ROWS
FROM Sales
```

OLAP Services translates this query into the following:

```
WITH
    MEMBER MEASURES.[Store Profit] AS
'(MEASURES.[Store Sales], [Time].CurrentMember)   -
            (MEASURES.[Store Cost]', [Time].CurrentMember)'
```

```
SELECT

    {(MEASURES.[Store Sales]), (MEASURES.[Store Cost]), (MEASURES.[Store
Profit] )}ON COLUMNS,

    {([Time].[1997]), ([Time].[1998]) } ON ROWS

FROM Sales
```

Though you did not explicitly write the [Time].CurrentMember, OLAP Server put it into your query for you. Imagine you are at a point on the cube with the time dimension at 1997. Your formula now becomes the store sales for 1997—the store cost for 1997. When OLAP Services moves to the next point on the cube where time is 1998, CURRENTMEMBER for time is 1998 and the formula becomes the store sales for 1998—the store cost for 1998. Thus, CURRENTMEMBER is defining where you are on the cube.

You might ask: "What are these total sales based on? Are the total sales for all customers for all stores for all products for all promotions? Or is this total sales for US customers for dairy products for all stores for bag stuffer promotions?" You do not know because you only specified the time dimension. OLAP Server, however, set all the other dimensions for you. OLAP Server turned your query into the following:

```
WITH

    MEMBER MEASURES.[Store Profit] AS 'MEASURES.[Store Sales] -

            MEASURES.[Store Cost]'

SELECT

    {(MEASURES.[Store Sales]), (MEASURES.[Store Cost]), (MEASURES.[Store
Profit] )}ON COLUMNS,

    {([Time].[1997]), ([Time].[1998]) } ON ROWS

FROM Sales

WHERE ([Product].[All Products], [Customer].[All Customers],

        [Store].[All Stores], [Promotions].[All Promotions],

        [Promotion Media].[All Media],

        [Education Level].[All Education Level],

        [Gender].[All Gender], [Marital Status].[All Marital Status]

        [Store Size in SQFT].[All], [Store Type].[All],

        [Yearly Income].[All Yearly Income])
```

These dimensions define the cube. For every dimension in the cube, you should have a member either in your SELECT statement or in your WHERE statement representing that dimension. If you do not include them, OLAP Server does. This is demonstrated in the next chapter. The rest of this chapter focuses on the critical dimensions to define the cube to save space. You should include, however, all the dimensions in your queries. Now, including the other CURRENTMEMBER for your other dimensions, you have the following:

```
WITH
    MEMBER MEASURES.[Store Profit] AS
    '(MEASURES.[Store Sales], [Time].CurrentMember, [Product].CurrentMember,
    [Customers].CurrentMember, [Store].CurrentMember,
    [Promotions].CurrentMember) -
    (MEASURES.[Store Cost], [Time].CurrentMember, [Product].CurrentMember,
    [Customers].CurrentMember, [Store].CurrentMember,
    [Promotions].CurrentMember)'
SELECT
    {(MEASURES.[Store Sales]), (MEASURES.[Store Cost]), (MEASURES.[Store
Profit] )}ON COLUMNS,
    {([Time].[1997]), ([Time].[1998])} ON ROWS
FROM Sales
WHERE ([Product].[All Products], [Customers].[All Customers],
        [Store].[All Stores], [Promotions].[All Promotions] )
```

The following tuple defines the coordinates of the point on the cube where OLAP Server is currently making a calculation.

```
    [Time].CurrentMember, [Product].CurrentMember,
    [Customer].CurrentMember, [Store].CurrentMember,
    [Promotions].CurrentMember)
```

Although you do not have to specify all the CURRENTMEMBER values in your query, you should specify all the dimensions in all your queries. If you do not specify the dimensions in the WHERE clause, OLAP Server gives you default values (in this case, the All values). As always, relying on defaults can result in errors and unexpected results.

Best Practice Always specify all the base dimensions in your query. Set the base dimensions that are not included in the SELECT clause in the WHERE clause.

If you put the previous query into the MDX Sample, you get the same results as you did with the original query, as shown in Figure 7-1.

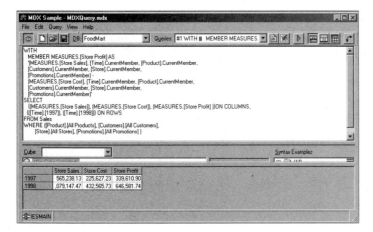

Figure 7-1. *MDX Query with all members explicitly listed.*

While your new query looks very complicated, it is still made from the basic building blocks of an MDX statement.

What CURRENTMEMBER enables you to do is create calculated members based on every point that OLAP Server performs a calculation. Let's look at an example that shows this.

Calculations with CURRENTMEMBER

Using CURRENTMEMBER and other member expressions, you can start doing some powerful calculations. For example, look at this query:

```
WITH MEMBER

 MEASURES.[Sales Difference] As '([Time].CurrentMember, MEASURES.[Store
Sales])-([Time].PrevMember, MEASURES.[Store Sales])'

SELECT

{(MEASURES.[Store Sales]), (MEASURES.[Store Cost]), (MEASURES.[Sales
Difference] )} ON COLUMNS,

{ (Time.[1997]) , (Time.[1998]) }  ON ROWS

FROM Sales

WHERE ([Product].[All Products], [Customers].[All Customers],

       [Store].[All Stores], [Promotions].[All Promotions] )
```

The calculated Measure Sales Difference takes the time coordinate and the value of sales for this value of the time coordinate, and subtracts it from the value of sales for the previous time coordinate. Look at Figure 7-2.

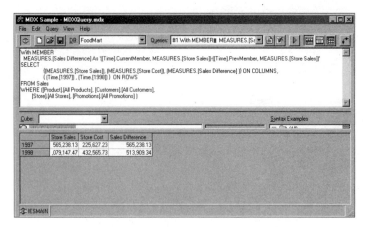

Figure 7-2. *Sales difference by year.*

Notice that the sales difference for 1997 is 565,238.13, the same value as the Store Sales. There is data in our cube for only 1997 and 1998. The sales difference for 1997 is the sales for 1997 minus the sales for 1996. Because there are no sales for 1996, the sales for 1997 are the Store Sales for 1997. Thus, OLAP Server gives the right answer. This happened because of how OLAP Server handles nulls.

Null Members and Empty Cells

When OLAP Server attempted to calculate the sales difference for 1997, it tried to get the sales value for 1996. Store Sales for 1996 is out of the range of our cube, or put another way, falls off the cube. This is called "the problem of non-existing members". Non-existing members are called null members in OLAP. OLAP Server does not raise an error when it reaches a null member—this is because it would make it next to impossible to perform queries because there are always boundary conditions.

Analysts who work with analytical data know about boundary conditions. If they are looking at sales difference by quarter, and they are looking at the first quarter that there were any sales, they know that the value for sales difference is the value of the sales for that first quarter. Thus, the results in the previous query are exactly what analysts expect.

When a null member is reached, the value for any measure at that point is set to zero. Thus, when OLAP Server performed your query, it set Store Sales for 1996 to zero. This is why your results came out correct. You can use this syntax to look at Sales Difference over any time period.

One thing to be careful of with null members is that once something is a null member, it is always a null member. Thus, January.PrevMember.NextMember is not January. Once you do PrevMember and fall off the cube, the answer is always 0, even if you do something (like NEXTMEMBER) that should take you back onto the cube.

A great feature of nulls in OLAP Server is that they are ignored with the AVG function. (This function is covered later in the chapter.) Thus, null members do not affect your set expressions, either.

Besides having null members, you can also have empty cells. Empty cells are ones that are within the cube but the value of the measure is 0 on the cell. This relates to sparsity of data. If you want to check if a cell is empty, MDX supports the IsEmpty function which you can use when coding your OLAP solution.

Additional Calculated Members with Member Expressions

You can now modify your query as follows:

```
WITH MEMBER

   MEASURES.[Sales Difference] As '([Time].CurrentMember, MEASURES.[Store
Sales])-([Time].PrevMember, MEASURES.[Store Sales])'

SELECT

{(MEASURES.[Store Sales]), (MEASURES.[Store Cost]), (MEASURES.[Sales
Difference] )} ON COLUMNS,

{ ( [Time].[Quarter].MEMBERS) }  ON ROWS

FROM Sales

WHERE ([Product].[All Products], [Customers].[All Customers],

      [Store].[All Stores], [Promotions].[All Promotions] )
```

Another query to try is:

```
WITH MEMBER

   MEASURES.[Sales Difference] As '([Time].CurrentMember, MEASURES.[Store
Sales])-([Time].PrevMember, MEASURES.[Store Sales])'

SELECT

{(MEASURES.[Store Sales]), (MEASURES.[Store Cost]), (MEASURES.[Sales
Difference] )} ON COLUMNS,

{ ( [Product].[Product Category].MEMBERS) }  ON ROWS

FROM Sales

WHERE ([Time].[1998], [Customers].[All Customers],

      [Store].[All Stores], [Promotions].[All Promotions] )
```

This gives you the sales by quarter.

Now, imagine that you have to calculate the sales for the stores in each city as a percentage of the sales for the state. Sound impossible? Not with member expressions! If you think about it, state is the parent of city, so you can use the PARENT function to solve this problem. Your query looks as follows:

```
WITH MEMBER

   MEASURES.[Sales By City Percent] As '([Store].CurrentMember,

   MEASURES.[Store Sales])/([Store].CurrentMember.Parent, MEASURES.[Store
Sales])'

SELECT

{(MEASURES.[Store Sales]), (MEASURES.[Store Cost]), (MEASURES.[Sales By City
Percent] )} ON COLUMNS,

{ ( [Store].[Store City].MEMBERS) }  ON ROWS

FROM Sales

WHERE ([Product].[All Products], [Customers].[All Customers],

        [Time].[1998], [Promotions].[All Promotions] )
```

The results of this query are shown in Figure 7-3.

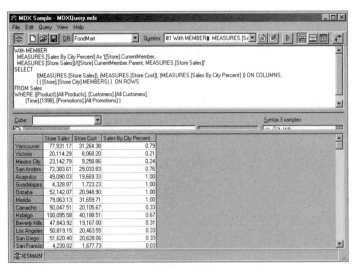

Figure 7-3. *Percentage of sales by city.*

Note You can use the member properties to do comparisons between two members of a dimension, such as time or geography.

You can do many more queries like this. Another query with member properties is:

```
SELECT

MEASURES.MEMBERS ON COLUMNS,

{

([Time].[1998].[Q1]),

( [Time].[1998].[Q1].Children),

([Time].[1998].[Q2]),

( [Time].[1998].[Q2].Children),

([Time].[1998].[Q3]),

( [Time].[1998].[Q3].Children),

([Time].[1998].[Q4]),

( [Time].[1998].[Q4].Children)}

ON ROWS

FROM SALES
```

The results are shown in Figure 7-4.

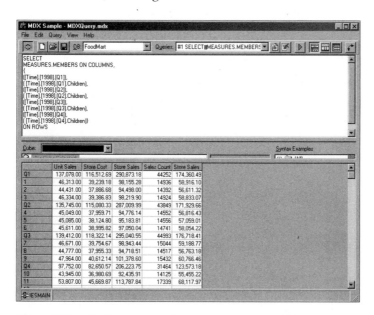

Figure 7-4. *Nesting quarters into years.*

Another query that would be interesting to perform is a comparison of the sales for every time period in a level to the sales in the first member of the level. For example, you can compare the sales for all quarters in 1997 and 1998 to the sales in the first quarter. This calculation allows you to see if the sales are improving, staying the same, or getting worse. To perform this query, use the FIRSTCHILD member expression to get the sales for the first member (Q1 in your case) in the level. Just remember that FIRSTCHILD gives the first child, which is the next level down. You want the first member in the current level, not the next level down. To get around this, take PARENT of the CURRENTMEMBER, and then apply FIRSTCHILD, giving you the first member on the same level as CURRENTMEMBER. The query looks as follows:

```
With MEMBER
  MEASURES.[Sales Compared To Q1] As '([Time].CurrentMember,
  MEASURES.[Store Sales])/([Time].CurrentMember.PARENT.FIRSTCHILD,
MEASURES.[Store Sales])'
SELECT
{(MEASURES.[Store Sales]), (MEASURES.[Store Cost]), (MEASURES.[Sales Compared
To Q1] )} ON COLUMNS,
{ ( [Time].[Quarter].MEMBERS) }  ON ROWS
FROM Sales
WHERE ([Product].[All Products], [Customers].[All Customers].[USA],
       [Store].[All Stores].[USA], [Promotions].[All Promotions] )
```

Figure 7-5 shows how this query looks.

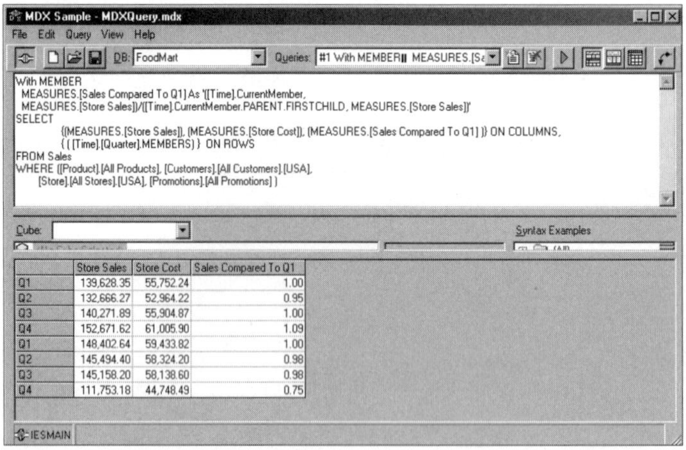

Figure 7-5. *Sales compared to Q1.*

The last part of Q4 1998 does not yet have values, which explains the low value. Q4 1997 shows the best sales. You can change this query to the following:

```
With MEMBER

  MEASURES.[Sales Compared To Q1] As '([Time].CurrentMember,

  MEASURES.[Store Sales])/([Time].CurrentMember.PARENT.FIRSTCHILD,
MEASURES.[Store Sales])'
```

SELECT

```
{(MEASURES.[Store Sales]), (MEASURES.[Store Cost]), (MEASURES.[Sales Compared
To Q1] )} ON COLUMNS,
```

```
{ ( [Time].[MONTH].MEMBERS) }  ON ROWS
```

FROM Sales

```
WHERE ([Product].[All Products], [Customers].[All Customers].[USA],

        [Store].[All Stores].[USA], [Promotions].[All Promotions] )
```

Looking at these numbers, you can see the increase in sales in Q4 1997 was during the months of November and January—perhaps holiday sales? The power of these queries is that by changing one entry, you can drill into the data. These queries can act like templates. Microsoft SQL Server 7.0 Magazine has a section devoted to MDX queries. You can also look at profit as compared to the Q1 by using the following query:

WITH

```
MEMBER MEASURES.[Store Profit] AS '([Time].CurrentMember,MEASURES.[Store
Sales] ) -( [Time].CurrentMember, MEASURES.[Store Cost] )',

    SOLVE_ORDER= 0

MEMBER MEASURES.[Profit Compared Q1] As '([Time].CurrentMember,
MEASURES.[Store Profit])/

        ([Time].CurrentMember.PARENT.FIRSTCHILD, MEASURES.[Store Profit])'
```

SELECT

```
{(MEASURES.[Store Sales]), (MEASURES.[Store Cost]), MEASURES.[Store
Profit],(MEASURES.[Profit Compared Q1] )} ON COLUMNS,
```

```
{ ( [Time].[Quarter].MEMBERS) }  ON ROWS
```

FROM Sales

```
WHERE ([Product].[All Products], [Customers].[All Customers].[USA],

        [Store].[All Stores].[USA], [Promotions].[All Promotions] )
```

It is time to turn your attention to the next powerful feature of MDX: set expressions.

Set Expressions

Set expressions are functions that operate on dimensions, hierarchies, and members and generate sets of members. Set expressions also operate on sets to generate sets of members. These set expressions, combined with the features demonstrated earlier, allow you to create a wide range of results. The following sections cover all the set functions. First, though, a session-defined set is covered.

Session-Defined Sets

Just as you can create session-defined calculated members, you can also create session-defined sets. Unlike a calculated member, session-defined sets are not associated with any dimension and do not have a parent. Like a calculated member, session-defined sets can use WITH or CREATE AND DROP. You can use sets and calculated members together as in the following query:

```
WITH

    MEMBER MEASURES.[Profit] AS

        'MEASURES.[Store Sales] - MEASURES.[Store Cost]'

    SET [AllTheMeasures] AS

        '{ MEASURES.MEMBERS, MEASURES.Profit}'

SELECT

    {[AllTheMeasures]} ON COLUMNS,

    {[Time].[1997], [Time].[1998]} ON ROWS

FROM

        Sales
```

Let's now look at set expressions.

MEMBERS

You can use MEMBERS to return all members of a dimension, all members of a hierarchy, or all members of a level.

All Members of a Dimension

To retrieve all members of a dimension, use the MEMBERS expression as follows:

```
<dimension>.MEMBERS
```

When you use MEMBERS with the name of the dimension, MEMBERS returns all members of a dimension. You can use this with any dimension to return all levels of the dimension. You can change your last query to return all members of the time dimension as follows:

```
With MEMBER

  MEASURES.[Sales Compared To Q1] As '([Time].CurrentMember,

  MEASURES.[Store Sales])/([Time].CurrentMember.PARENT.FIRSTCHILD,
MEASURES.[Store Sales])'

SELECT

{(MEASURES.[Store Sales]), (MEASURES.[Store Cost]), (MEASURES.[Sales Compared
To Q1] )} ON COLUMNS,

{ ( [Time].MEMBERS) }   ON ROWS

FROM Sales

WHERE ([Product].[All Products], [Customers].[All Customers].[USA],

        [Store].[All Stores].[USA], [Promotions].[All Promotions] )
```

The results are shown in Figure 7-6.

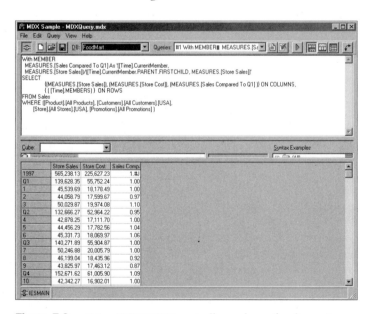

Figure 7-6. *Using MEMBERS to get all members of a dimension.*

One interesting thing to notice is the results for 1997 and 1998. For the year level, PARENT takes you off the cube. Even though FIRSTCHILD should bring you back on the cube, once you fall off the cube, you cannot get back on. Thus, PARENT.FIRSTCHILD is a null member, and returns 0. Because you are dividing by 0, you get an error.

> **Caution** Whenever you are creating a calculated member in which you are dividing and using member expressions, be careful of dividing by zero.

All Members of a Hierarchy

To return all members of one level of a structural dimension, use the following syntax where <hierarchy> is <dimension>.<level>:

```
<hierarchy>.MEMBERS
```

This is how you have been using MEMBERS in your queries throughout this chapter. In this case, MEMBERS returns all members of a dimension at a particular level. In your FoodMart data warehouse, Time.Year.Members returns 1997 and 1998.

All Members of a Level

You can also use MEMBERS with non-structural dimensions in the following format to return all members of a level in a non-structural dimension:

```
<level>.MEMBERS
```

Thus you have the following query on the informational dimension Marital Status:

```
SELECT

{(MEASURES.[Store Sales]), (MEASURES.[Store Cost])} ON COLUMNS,

{ ( [Marital Status].[Marital Status].MEMBERS) }  ON ROWS

FROM Sales

WHERE ([Product].[All Products], [Customers].[All Customers].[USA],

        [Store].[All Stores].[USA], [Promotions].[All Promotions],
[Time].[1997] )
```

CHILDREN

CHILDREN returns a set of all children associated with a member. The format for CHILDREN is:

```
<member>.CHILDREN
```

This returns all children of the member. An example of a query using CHILDREN is:

```
SELECT

{(MEASURES.[Store Sales]), (MEASURES.[Store Cost])} ON COLUMNS,

{ ( [Time].[1997].Children) }  ON ROWS
```

```
FROM Sales

WHERE ([Product].[All Products], [Customers].[All Customers].[USA],

        [Store].[All Stores].[USA], [Promotions].[All Promotions])
```

This returns sales for Q1, Q2, Q3, and Q4.

DESCENDANTS

DESCENDANTS returns all descendants of a particular member at some level in the dimension. The format for DESCENDANTS is:

```
DESCENDANTS(<member>, <level> [, <desc_flags>])
```

By default, only members at the specified level are included. This is associated with the default *desc_flag* value of SELF. By changing the value of *desc_flag* from SELF, you can return the children before (above) the specified level or the children after (above) the specified level (until the leaf).

For example, the following query returns the sales for all quarters for 1998, as shown in Figure 7-7.

```
SELECT

{(MEASURES.[Store Sales]), (MEASURES.[Store Cost])} ON COLUMNS,

{ ( DESCENDANTS([time].[1998], [Time].[Quarter]) ) }  ON ROWS

FROM Sales

WHERE ([Product].[All Products], [Customers].[All Customers].[USA],

        [Store].[All Stores].[USA], [Promotions].[All Promotions])
```

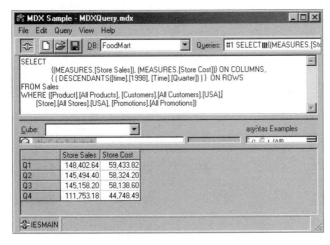

Figure 7-7. *Sales for the four quarters of 1997.*

Some of you might have tried the following query earlier:

```
SELECT

{(MEASURES.[Store Sales]), (MEASURES.[Store Cost])} ON COLUMNS,

{ [Time].[Quarter].MEMBERS ) }  ON ROWS

FROM Sales

WHERE ([Product].[All Products], [Customers].[All Customers].[USA],

        [Store].[All Stores].[USA], [Promotions].[All Promotions],

        [time].[1998])
```

This does not work because you are trying to vary time over quarters in the SELECT statement and constrain time in the WHERE clause. While you could theoretically do this, MDX does not allow you to constrain the same dimension in the WHERE clause and vary it in the SELECT. Thus, to get the sales for the quarters for 1998 you need to use the DESCENDANTS function.

Also, notice that the following query returns the identical results as the first query you did with DESCENDANTS:

```
SELECT

{(MEASURES.[Store Sales]), (MEASURES.[Store Cost])} ON COLUMNS,

{ ( DESCENDANTS([time].[1998], [Time].[Quarter], SELF) ) }  ON ROWS

FROM Sales

WHERE ([Product].[All Products], [Customers].[All Customers].[USA],

        [Store].[All Stores].[USA], [Promotions].[All Promotions])
```

If you change SELF to BEFORE as follows:

```
SELECT

{(MEASURES.[Store Sales]), (MEASURES.[Store Cost])} ON COLUMNS,

{ ( DESCENDANTS([time].[1998], [Time].[Quarter], BEFORE) ) }  ON ROWS

FROM Sales

WHERE ([Product].[All Products], [Customers].[All Customers].[USA],

        [Store].[All Stores].[USA], [Promotions].[All Promotions])
```

...it returns sales for 1998. Using AFTER as follows:

```
SELECT

{(MEASURES.[Store Sales]), (MEASURES.[Store Cost])} ON COLUMNS,

{ ( DESCENDANTS([time].[1998], [Time].[Quarter], AFTER) ) }  ON ROWS

FROM Sales

WHERE ([Product].[All Products], [Customers].[All Customers].[USA],

        [Store].[All Stores].[USA], [Promotions].[All Promotions])
```

...it returns the sales for all months.

ORDER

Often you want to order the results of your queries. ORDER is the set function that does this. MDX does not specify what the default order is for a query, but OLAP Services does provide a sort order for every dimension. Like everything else, you should not depend on defaults and that is where ORDER comes in. The syntax for ORDER is:

```
ORDER(<set>, {<string_value_expression> | <numeric_value_expression>}
[, ASC | DESC | BASC | BDESC])
```

The <set> is any standard MDX set such as [Customers].[USA].CHILDREN. The {<string_value_expression> | <numeric_value_expression>} can be either a typical numeric composition or a string. The string can be a measure that you want to order the query by, such as MEASURES.SALES. For example, if you want to see all sales for all stores in the state of California, do the following query:

```
SELECT

    {MEASURES.[STORE SALES]} On COLUMNS,

    {ORDER([STORE].[USA].[CA].Children, MEASURES.[Store Sales], DESC) }

    ON ROWS

FROM Sales

WHERE (Time.[1997], [Product].[All Products], [Customers].[All Customers],

            [Promotions].[All Promotions] )
```

In this query, you are asking ORDER to list the children of the level CA in descending order of the store sales for each child. This gives you a powerful way to order your results according to any of your measures. The dataset is shown in Figure 7-8.

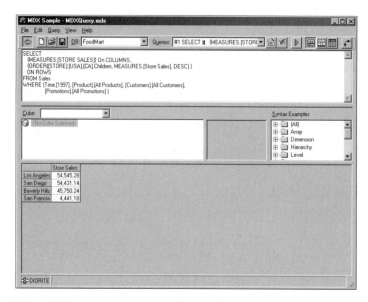

Figure 7-8. *CA stores ordered by sales of 1997.*

Ordering by Hierarchies

You can order the set that is returned by ORDER in two possible ways. The first way is according to hierarchies. It is easiest to see this with the following query:

```
SELECT

    {MEASURES.[STORE SALES]} On COLUMNS,

    {ORDER([STORE].[Store State].MEMBERS, MEASURES.[Store Sales], DESC) } ON
ROWS

FROM Sales

WHERE ( Time.[1998], [Product].[All Products], [Customers].[All Customers],

            [Promotions].[All Promotions] )
```

The results of this query are shown in Figure 7-9.

At first glance, there seems to be something wrong. The sales for BC, which is the last value, seem to belong higher up. Actually, though, this is correct. When you specify DESC, you are asking OLAP Services to order the query by sales for each hierarchy. Thus, this query returns sales for the United States in descending order for sales, then sales in descending order for Mexico, and then sales in descending order for Canada. Using DESC results in the order being separated across hierarchy lines. Both ASC and DESC result in ordering by hierarchies. Try the following query to see this:

Figure 7-9. *Sales by state ordered by sales.*

```
SELECT

    {MEASURES.[STORE SALES]} On COLUMNS,

    {ORDER([STORE].[Store State].MEMBERS, MEASURES.[Store Sales], ASC) } ON
ROWS

FROM Sales

WHERE ( Time.[1998], [Product].[All Products], [Customers].[All Customers],

            [Promotions].[All Promotions] )
```

ASC is the default. If you rewrite the query without ASC you get the same result.

You might not always want to separate the results over hierarchies. In that case, you create sets that "break" the hierarchies.

Ordered Sets that Break the Hierarchies

Ordering members in the set without regard to the hierarchy requires usage of BDESC and BASC. B stands for break the hierarchy. Rewrite your query as follows:

```
SELECT

    {MEASURES.[STORE SALES]} On COLUMNS,

    {ORDER([STORE].[Store State].MEMBERS, MEASURES.[Store Sales], BDESC) } ON
ROWS

FROM Sales
```

```
WHERE ( Time.[1998], [Product].[All Products], [Customers].[All Customers],

               [Promotions].[All Promotions] )
```

The dataset for this query is shown in Figure 7-10. As you can see, the sets are ordered correctly. Now try BASC.

Figure 7-10. *Ordering without regard to hierarchy.*

HIERARCHIZE

HIERARCHIZE orders the members in a level according to their natural order, that is, the default ordering of the members along the dimension when no other sort conditions are specified. HIERARCHIZE always retains duplicates. The format for HIERARCHIZE is:

```
HIERARCHIZE(<set>)
```

For example, the following query orders by the store's state hierarchy:

```
SELECT

    {MEASURES.[STORE SALES]} On COLUMNS,

    {HIERARCHIZE([STORE].[Store State].MEMBERS) } ON ROWS

FROM Sales

WHERE ( Time.[1998], [Product].[All Products], [Customers].[All Customers],

               [Promotions].[All Promotions] )
```

The result of this dataset is shown in Figure 7-11.

Figure 7-11. *Ordering by hierarchy.*

TOPCOUNT and BOTTOMCOUNT

We are now getting to a set of functions that enables you to find the best (or worst) performers. Because there can be thousands of products and hundreds of categories, analysts often just want to see the best and worst selling products. TOPCOUNT enables you to get the best performers. The TOPCOUNT set expression sorts on the numeric value expression (if any) and lists the top items. The format for TOPCOUNT is:

```
TOPCOUNT(<set>, <number to return> [, <expression>])
```

The entry <number to return> is the number of top items to return. TOPCOUNT set expression always breaks the hierarchy. The entry <number to return> is the number of members to return. OLAP Services has optimized the TOPCOUNT and the BOTTOMCOUNT functions.

The BOTTOMCOUNT set expression works the same way as TOPCOUNT, except that it returns the bottom items. Let's look at some queries using these expressions. The entry <expression> can be a measure just like you used in ORDER.

The following gives the customer cities in all sites that had the largest change in sales between 1998 and 1997:

```
WITH MEMBER

[Time].[97 98] As '[Time].[1998]-[Time].[1997]'

SELECT

TOPCOUNT([Customers].[City].Members, 20,

          (Measures.[Store Sales],[Time].[97 98]))
```

```
ON ROWS,

{ Time.[1997] , Time.[1998], [97 98] }   ON COLUMNS

FROM Sales

WHERE ([Product].[All Products],

    Measures.[Store Sales], [Store].[All Stores])
```

This query starts to give you a hint as to the power of MDX. It uses both the TOPCOUNT and the calculated member [97 98]. The dataset for this query is shown in Figure 7-12.

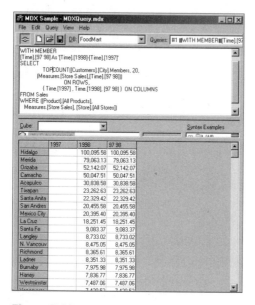

Figure 7-12. *Twenty customer cities with the largest change in sales between 1997 and 1998.*

This brings you to an interesting point. Change your query slightly to the following:

```
WITH MEMBER

 [Time].[97 98] As '[Time].[1998]-[Time].[1997]'

SELECT

TOPCOUNT([Store].[Store City].Members, 20,

         (Measures.[Store Sales],[Time].[97 98]))

ON ROWS,
```

```
{ Time.[1997] , Time.[1998], [97 98] }  ON COLUMNS

FROM Sales

WHERE ([Product].[All Products],

   Measures.[Store Sales], Customers.[All Customers])
```

You are now doing the same query by store city. Do you think the results are the same? The dataset is shown in Figure 7-13.

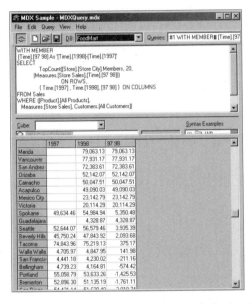

Figure 7-13. *Twenty store cities with the largest change in sales between 1997 and 1998.*

Looking at the two datasets, you see that the results are different. This is because customer city represents where the customer lives, and store city represents where the customer shops (that is, where the store is). These are two different values. The store dimension is properly named. The customer dimension, however, should have levels named Customer Country, Customer City, and so forth.

Best Practice Always name your dimensions in a way that easily identifies the dimension. Country is ambiguous. If it is the customer's country, call it something like CustomerCountry or Customer_Country.

Another interesting point to notice is that your numbers are not very meaningful, because many of the stores that had the biggest changes are those that did not exist in 1997. You will learn how to filter these out in a later section.

Change your query to BOTTOMCOUNT:

```
WITH MEMBER

[Time].[97 98] As '[Time].[1998]-[Time].[1997]'

SELECT

BOTTOMCOUNT([Customers].[City].Members, 20,

            (Measures.[Store Sales],[Time].[97 98]))

ON ROWS,

{ Time.[1997] , Time.[1998], [97 98] }  ON COLUMNS

FROM Sales

WHERE ([Product].[All Products],

   Measures.[Store Sales], [Store].[All Stores])
```

We now get the dataset shown in Figure 7-14.

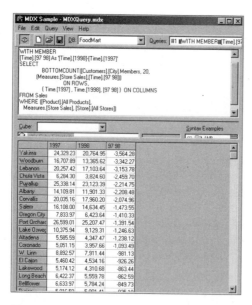

Figure 7-14. *Twenty customer cities with the smallest change in sales between 1997 and 1998.*

This query shows the twenty cities in which customers spent less in 1998 than they did in 1997 (only the first few can be seen in the screenshot). The customers living in Yakima spent $3,564 less in 1998 than they did in 1997. This is the type of information that management needs to know. Let's change the query to see the stores that had the greatest loss:

```
WITH MEMBER

 [Time].[97 98] As '([Time].[1998])-([Time].[1997])'

SELECT

BOTTOMCOUNT([Store].[Store City].Members, 20,

            (Measures.[Store Sales],[Time].[97 98]))

 ON ROWS,

{ Time.[1997] , Time.[1998], [97 98] }  ON COLUMNS

FROM Sales

WHERE ([Product].[All Products],

   Measures.[Store Sales], [Customers].[All Customers])
```

Notice that this gives you the cities with the greatest loss. The Salem store sold more than $12,000 less in goods in 1998 than it did in 1997. That is certainly worth looking into.

Store Profit might be more interesting to look at. You can modify the query to look at store profit instead of sales with the following:

```
WITH MEMBER

MEASURES.[Profit] AS '([Time].CurrentMember, MEASURES.[Store Sales]) -

    ([Time].CurrentMember, MEASURES.[Store Cost])',

    SOLVE_ORDER =0

MEMBER [Time].[97 98] As '([Time].[1998])-([Time].[1997])'

SELECT

TOPCOUNT([Store].[Store City].Members, 20,

            (Measures.[Profit],[Time].[97 98]))

 ON ROWS,

{ Time.[1997] , Time.[1998], [97 98] }  ON COLUMNS

FROM Sales

WHERE ([Product].[All Products],

   Measures.[Profit], [Customers].[All Customers])
```

Once again, you can do BOTTOMCOUNT with this query. Using BOTTOMCOUNT you again find that the Salem store had the greatest losses, with a loss in profit of more than $7,000.

Another query you can do with TOPCOUNT is:

```
SELECT

    MEASURES.MEMBERS ON COLUMNS,

    TOPCOUNT( [Product].[Product Category].Members, 10, MEASURES.[Sales Count]
) ON ROWS

FROM Sales

WHERE ([Time].[1997].[Q1],[Customers].[All Customers],

              [Promotions].[All Promotions])
```

This query returns the top 10 selling products for the first quarter. You can change the time slice or the level of products. You can also use BOTTOMCOUNT to get the worst sellers.

Another way to measure is using TOPPERCENT and BOTTOMPERCENT.

TOPPERCENT and BOTTOMPERCENT

TOPPERCENT and BOTTOMPERCENT look at the values of an expression and sort the top or bottom percentage of that expression. These functions always break the hierarchy. The syntax for these is:

```
TOPPERCENT(<set>, <percentage>, <expression>)
```

The following expression finds the stores whose profit makes up 20 percent of the total profit:

```
WITH MEMBER

MEASURES.[Profit] AS '([Time].CURRENTMEMBER, MEASURES.[Store Sales]) -

    ([Time].CURRENTMEMBER, MEASURES.[Store Cost])',

      SOLVE_ORDER =0

MEMBER [Time].[97 98] As '([Time].[1998])-([Time].[1997])'

SELECT

TOPPERCENT([Store].[Store City].Members, 20,

            (Measures.[Profit],[Time].[97 98]))

ON ROWS,

{ Time.[1997] , Time.[1998], [97 98] }  ON COLUMNS
```

```
FROM Sales

WHERE ([Product].[All Products],

    Measures.[Profit], [Customers].[All Customers])
```

Changing this to BOTTOMPERCENT calculates the stores that made the least contribution to the overall profit. This is not equivalent to the stores with the greatest loss. TOPPERCENT and BOTTOMPERCENT are based on percentages, which require division. These results may not be additive across dimensions, so you must do a new calculation for losses.

To actually calculate the stores that contributed a certain percentage of loss to sales, use the following query:

```
WITH MEMBER

MEASURES.[Loss] AS '([Time].CurrentMember, MEASURES.[Store Sales]) -

    ([Time].CurrentMember, MEASURES.[Store Cost])',

    SOLVE_ORDER =0

MEMBER [Time].[97 98] As '([Time].[1997])-([Time].[1998])'

SELECT

TOPPERCENT([Store].[Store City].Members, 20,

        (Measures.[Loss],[Time].[97 98]))

 ON ROWS,

{ Time.[1997] , Time.[1998], [97 98] }   ON COLUMNS

FROM Sales

WHERE ([Product].[All Products],

    Measures.[Loss], [Customers].[All Customers])
```

If you put this query in, you find once again that Salem has the greatest losses and has contributed to at least 20 percent of the total loss.

TOPSUM and BOTTOMSUM

TOPSUM sorts a set according to descending order, and then finds the top values whose sum equals a value you set. The syntax for TOPSUM is:

```
TOPSUM(<set>, <value>, <expression>)
```

The query is sorted on <expression> and picks up the top elements such that their sum is at least <value>. This function always breaks the hierarchy. The BOTTOMSUM function is similar. For example, the following query returns the top products whose sum of sales is less than $150,000:

```
SELECT

    MEASURES.MEMBERS ON COLUMNS,

    TOPSUM( [Product].[Product Category].MEMBERS, 150000, [Store Sales]) ON
ROWS

FROM SALES

WHERE ([Customers].[All Customers],

        [Store].[All Stores], [Promotions].[All Promotions] , [Time].[1997])
```

The dataset is shown in Figure 7-15.

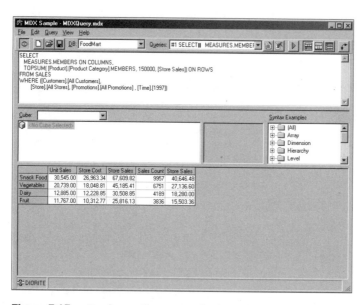

Figure 7-15. *Products whose sum of sales is less than $150,000.*

Notice that the sum of these products does not equal $150,000. TOPSUM only gives the sum of values that is less than $150,000.

TOPPERCENT and BOTTOMPERCENT work in the same way as do TOPSUM and BOTTOMSUM. To find out which products made up at least 30 percent of the sales, do the following query:

```
SELECT

    MEASURES.MEMBERS ON COLUMNS,
```

```
    TOPPERCENT( [Product].[Product Category].MEMBERS, 30, [Store Sales]) ON
ROWS

FROM SALES

WHERE ([Customers].[All Customers], [Store].[All Stores],

 [Promotions].[All Promotions] , [Time].[1997])
```

FILTER

The FILTER function is perhaps one of the more important functions associated with MDX. It enables you to filter out records that you do not want. The syntax is as follows:

```
FILTER(<set>, <condition>)
```

The set that is returned by FILTER is determined by <condition>. You can use the following query to find all products that had higher sales in 1998 than in 1997:

```
SELECT

   {([Time].[1997]), ([Time].[1998])} ON COLUMNS,

   {

     Filter (

                [Product].[Product Category].MEMBERS,

                (MEASURES.[Store Sales], [Time].[1998]) > (MEASURES.[Store
Sales], [Time].[1997])

                )

   } ON ROWS

FROM Sales

WHERE

     ([Customers].[All Customers], [Store].[USA],

     [Promotions].[All Promotions], MEASURES.[Store Sales])
```

Of course, you should do some cleaning up of these values. For example, you probably want to see these values in descending order. To do this, you need to modify your query as follows:

```
WITH MEMBER

    MEASURES.[1998 - 1997] AS

                   '([Time].[1998] , MEASURES.[Store Sales]) -

                   ([Time].[1997] , MEASURES.[Store Sales])'
```

```
SELECT

    {([Time].[1997]), ([Time].[1998])} ON COLUMNS,

    { ORDER

        (

            FILTER (

                            [Product].[Product Category].MEMBERS,

                            (MEASURES.[Store Sales], [Time].[1998]) >

                            (MEASURES.[Store Sales], [Time].[1997])

                            ) ,

        MEASURES.[1998 - 1997], DESC

        )

    } ON ROWS

FROM Sales

WHERE

    (  [Customers].[All Customers], [Store].[USA],

        [Promotions].[All Promotions] , MEASURES.[Store Sales])
```

Notice how the different sections are aligned so it is easy to see each part of the query. You can arrange your query in any way that is readable. As you can see, you have once again used much of the material from this chapter to build this into a usable query. You would probably also format the sales numbers with a dollar sign. The dataset for this query is shown in Figure 7-16.

You can further refine the query by filtering out the products whose change in sales is less than $150 with this query:

```
WITH MEMBER

    MEASURES.[1998 - 1997] AS

                        '([Product].CurrentMember, [Time].[1998] ,
MEASURES.[Store Sales]) -

                        ([Product].CurrentMember, [Time].[1997] ,
MEASURES.[Store Sales])'

SELECT

    {([Time].[1997]), ([Time].[1998])} ON COLUMNS,

    { ORDER
```

```
(   FILTER (

        FILTER (

            [Product].[Product Category].MEMBERS,

            (MEASURES.[Store Sales], [Time].[1998]) >

            (MEASURES.[Store Sales], [Time].[1997])

                    ) ,

        MEASURES.[1998 - 1997] >150

                ),

    MEASURES.[1998 - 1997], DESC

    )

} ON ROWS

FROM Sales

WHERE

    ( [Customers].[All Customers], [Store].[USA],  [Promotions].[All
Promotions], [MEASURES].[Store Sales])
```

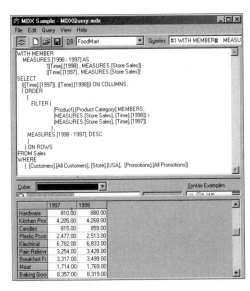

Figure 7-16. *Products with more sales in 1998 than in 1997 in descending order.*

You might be thinking that this is beginning to look very complicated and wondering how long it takes to derive queries of this type. Once you figure out a query like this, you can use it over and over again as a template for any query for which you want to get a comparison between two time periods, order it in a descending manner, and limit it to a specific difference. You just have to change the members. You can also use it as a template in your applications. As a final touch, add the currency onto your Store Sales:

```
WITH
    MEMBER MEASURES.[1998 - 1997] AS
        '([Product].CurrentMember, [Time].[1998] , MEASURES.[Store Sales]) -
        ([Product].CurrentMember, [Time].[1997] , MEASURES.[Store Sales])'
    MEMBER MEASURES.[Formatted Store Sales] AS 'MEASURES.[Store Sales]' ,
        FORMAT_STRING = '$#.##0;; '
SELECT
    {(([Time].[1997]), ([Time].[1998])} ON COLUMNS,
    { ORDER
        (   FILTER (
                FILTER (
                    [Product].[Product Category].MEMBERS,
                    (MEASURES.[Store Sales], [Time].[1998]) >
                    (MEASURES.[Store Sales], [Time].[1997])
                        ) ,
                MEASURES.[1998 - 1997] >150
                ),
            MEASURES.[1998 - 1997], DESC
            )
    } ON ROWS
FROM Sales
WHERE
    (   [Customers].[All Customers], [Store].[USA],
        [Promotions].[All Promotions], [MEASURES].[Formatted Store Sales])
```

This is what MDX is all about. You can build these queries only using MDX and they can do exactly the analysis that the user requires, in the format that the user needs.

UNION

UNION joins two sets by union, that is, including all members of both sets. UNION eliminates duplicates by default. The syntax for UNION is:

```
UNION(<set1>, <set2> [, ALL])
```

The optional ALL flag keeps duplicates in the joined set. You may have not realized that there have been unions in many of your examples. Any time you created a tuple with more than one member, OLAP Services converted it into the union of the two members. This is called an *implicit union*. Thus:

```
{USA.CHILDREN, CANADA.CHILDREN}
```

...is really the same thing as:

```
UNION(USA.CHILDREN, CANADA.CHILDREN, ALL)
```

Duplicated members are always retained in an implicit union.

DISTINCT

DISTINCT deletes duplicate tuples from a set. The syntax for DISTINCT is:

```
DISTINCT(<set>)
```

INTERSECT

INTERSECT finds the intersection of two sets. By default, duplicates are eliminated from both sets prior to intersection. The syntax for INTERSECT is:

```
INTERSECT(<set1>, <set2> [,ALL])
```

The optional ALL retains duplicates. Using ALL returns any elements that are duplicated in both sets.

EXCEPT

EXCEPT finds the difference between two sets. Duplicates are eliminated from both sets prior to finding the difference. The syntax for EXCEPT is:

```
EXCEPT(<set1>, <set2> [,ALL])
```

The optional ALL flag retains duplicates. Matching duplicates in *set1* are eliminated and non-matching duplicates are retained. The <set1> and <set2> must be from the same dimension and at the same level in the dimension. The following query retrieves all the measures for all product families except non-consumables:

```
SELECT

    {MEASURES.MEMBERS} ON COLUMNS,

    {
```

```
    EXCEPT ( [Product].[Product Family].MEMBERS , {[Product].[Non-
Consumable] })

    }ON ROWS

    FROM Sales

    WHERE

       (  [Customers].[All Customers], [Store].[All Stores],

        [Promotions].[All Promotions])
```

Next, let's get the measures for all the categories except Non-Consumable categories. Because it would be tedious to list all members of the Product Department set, you can use the CHILDREN member expression to include all the departments in your query. The query looks as follows:

```
SELECT

    {MEASURES.MEMBERS} ON COLUMNS,

    {

    EXCEPT ( [Product].[Product Department].MEMBERS ,

            {[Product].[Non-Consumable].CHILDREN })

    }ON ROWS

    FROM Sales

    WHERE

       ([Customers].[All Customers], [Store].[All Stores],

        [Promotions].[All Promotions])
```

You can also look at the product categories with the following query:

```
SELECT

    {MEASURES.MEMBERS} ON COLUMNS,

    {

    EXCEPT ( [Product].[Product Category].MEMBERS , {DESCENDANTS
([Product].[Non-Consumable], [Product].[Product Category], SELF) })

    }ON ROWS

    FROM Sales

    WHERE

       ([Customers].[All Customers], [Store].[All Stores],
```

```
[Promotions].[All Promotions])
```

Once again you see how one query can be used as a template to build many more. This query can also be rewritten as follows:

```
WITH

  SET [TEST] AS

'{

  EXCEPT

    (

    [Product].[Product Category].MEMBERS ,

    DESCENDANTS

        (

            [Product].[Non-Consumable], [Product].[Product Category], SELF
              )

    )

  }'

SELECT

    {MEASURES.MEMBERS} ON COLUMNS,

    {

      [Test]

    }ON ROWS

    FROM Sales

WHERE

      ([Customers].[All Customers], [Store].[All Stores],

        [Promotions].[All Promotions])
```

CROSSJOIN

CROSSJOIN generates the cross product of two sets. In MDX sets, the order of the sets matters. Thus, [Customers].[All Customers], [Store].[All Stores] does not always equal {([Store].[All Stores] , [Customers].[All Customers])}. The syntax for CROSSJOIN is:

```
CROSSJOIN(<set1>, <set2>)
```

With the following sets:

```
set1 = {x1, x2,…,xn}
```

```
set2 = {y1, y2, …, yn}, then CROSSJOIN(set1, set2)
```

The order of the tuples in the set returned when using CROSSJOIN with these sets is:

```
{(x1, y1), (x1, y2),,(x1, yn), (x2, y1), (x2, y2),, (x2, yn),, (xn, y1), (xn,
y2),, (xn, yn)}
```

Thus, CROSSJOIN is a very important feature when building user interfaces. What CROSSJOIN actually enables you to do is nest two dimensions together, eliminating the need for you to write all the levels for creating a query that nests information from one dimension into the information in another dimension. Let's see how this works. Use CROSSJOIN to see the difference in the measures between 1998 and 1997 for all the levels in the product dimension. This query looks as follows:

```
WITH

MEMBER [Time].[1998-1997] AS '([Time].[1998]) - ([Time].[1997])'

SELECT

    {MEASURES.MEMBERS} ON COLUMNS,

    {

    CROSSJOIN ( [Product].MEMBERS , { [Time].[1998-1997]} )

    }ON ROWS

  FROM Sales

  WHERE

      ([Customers].[All Customers],

        [Store].[All Stores], [Promotions].[All Promotions] )
```

The dataset for this query is shown in Figure 7-17.

As you can see, there are many ways to get the same dataset. CROSSJOIN is very useful for nesting information for the user. Be careful, though, with CROSSJOIN because it can easily return huge datasets that flow off the screen.

EXTRACT

EXTRACT is the opposite of the CROSSJOIN function. EXTRACT takes a set and removes the dimensions that you list. This function always removes the duplicates. The syntax for EXTRACT is:

```
EXTRACT(<set>, <dimension>[, <dimension>...])
```

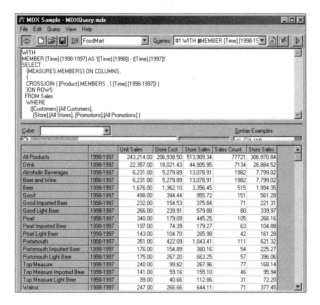

Figure 7-17. *Difference in the measures between 1998 and 1997 for all the levels in the product dimension.*

GENERATE

GENERATE is a very important feature of MDX. It enables you to select only certain members of a dimension's level. With GENERATE, you can only look at the cities in Mexico and the United States or look only at the sales in Q1 1997 and 1998.

GENERATE takes two sets and generates a new set based on the members of set2 that are in set1. Thus, GENERATE filters members out of sets. The syntax for GENERATE is:

```
GENERATE(<set1>, <set2> [,ALL])
```

If the ALL keyword is used, duplicate members are included. Let's see how this works. Imagine you want to see the sales for Q1 for 1997 and 1998. Write the following query to get this result:

```
WITH

SET [1997 and 1998 Q1] AS

  'GENERATE (

          {([Time].[1997]), ([Time].[1998])} ,

          {[Time].[Q1]}

          )'

  SELECT
```

```
     {MEASURES.MEMBERS} ON COLUMNS,

     {

       [1997 and 1998 Q1]

     }ON ROWS

   FROM Sales

WHERE

       ([Customers].[All Customers],  [Promotions].[All Promotions],

       [Store].[All Stores])
```

In this case, you took the set {([Time].[1997]), ([Time].[1998])} and asked the GENERATE function to generate a new set with all the members of the {([Time].[1997]), ([Time].[1998])} set with Q1. In other words, you asked GENERATE to filter out all the Q1 members of the {([Time].[1997]), ([Time].[1998])} set and return a new set with these Q1 members.

A more complicated query using GENERATE is the following:

```
WITH

   SET [USA and MEXICO Stores] AS

   'GENERATE (

                           {[Store].[USA], [Store].[Mexico]} ,

                           {DESCENDANTS([Store].CURRENTMEMBER,

                               [Store].[Store City])}

                   )'

SELECT

   {MEASURES.MEMBERS} ON COLUMNS,

   {

   [USA and MEXICO Stores]

   }ON ROWS

   FROM Sales

WHERE

       (  [Customers].[All Customers],  [Promotions].[All Promotions],
[Time].[1998])
```

This query filters out all the stores at the city level of the store dimension that belong to either the USA or Mexico. Thus, this query returns only the stores in Mexico and the USA. The dataset for this query is shown in Figure 7-18.

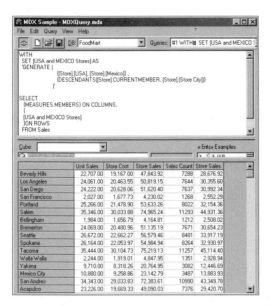

Figure 7-18. *Measures for stores in cities in USA and Mexico for 1998.*

You should create a few more of these GENERATE queries until you understand them completely.

Numeric Functions

There is an entire set of numeric functions, too. The numeric functions are described in the following sections.

SUM

The SUM function calculates the sum of a particular value. The syntax for SUM is:

```
SUM (<set>[, < expression>])
```

This sums the <set>. If the optional expression is included, it sums based on the optional expression. If the optional expression is left off, OLAP Services tries to figure out which measure to calculate the sum on based on information in the query. As stated before, do not rely on OLAP Services to figure out what you want; instead, always include the optional expression.

For example, you might want to calculate the top 10 product categories and compare the sum of their sales to the sum of the sales for all the other product categories. This query looks as follows:

```
WITH

  SET [Top10Products] AS 'TOPCOUNT([Product].[Product Category].MEMBERS,
10, [Store Sales])'

  MEMBER [Product].[Top10Sum] AS ' (SUM ([Top10Products], MEASURES.[Store
Sales]) )'

  MEMBER [Product].[Rest of the Products] AS

     ' ([Product].[All Products], MEASURES.[Store Sales] ) - (SUM
([Top10Products], MEASURES.[Store Sales]) )'

   SELECT

       {MEASURES.[Store Sales]} ON COLUMNS,

       {[Top10Products],[Product].[Top10Sum],

       [Product].[Rest of the Products] } ON ROWS

   FROM

       Sales

WHERE   ([Time].[1997])
```

It is well worth your time to pick this query apart. See how it uses many of the lessons
you learned in this chapter. This query creates a set called *Top10Products* that contains
the top 10 product categories based on store sales. Two calculated members are then
added to the product dimension, *Top10Sum,* which is the sum of the sales for the top
10 products, and *Rest of the Products,* which is the total sales for all the rest of the product categories. The dataset for this query is shown in Figure 7-19.

You can see that the sum of the sales of the top 10 products is nearly the sum of the sales
for all the other product categories.

AGGREGATE

This function uses the "proper" aggregate function based on the context. The proper
aggregate function is determined by the measure the aggregate is being measured over
as follows:

```
AGGREGATE(<set>[, <numeric_value_expression>])
```

An example of a query with AGGREGATE is:

```
WITH

  MEMBER [Store].[Store Total Aggregate] AS 'AGGREGATE( { [Store].[All
Stores].[USA], [Store].[All Stores].[Mexico]  } )'

  MEMBER MEASURES.[Profit] AS 'MEASURES.[Store Sales] - MEASURES.[Store Cost]'
```

```
SELECT

 {MEASURES.MEMBERS, MEASURES.PROFIT } ON COLUMNS,

 {[Store].[USA], [Store].[Mexico],[Store].[Store Total Aggregate]} ON ROWS

FROM

Sales

WHERE ([Time].[1998],[Customers].[All Customers],  [Promotions].[All
Promotions])
```

Figure 7-19. *Top 10 product categories and sum of all other products.*

COUNT

COUNT returns the number of tuples in a set as follows:

```
COUNT(<set>[, INCLUDEEMPTY])
```

The optional INCLUDEEMPTY flag includes empty cells in the count.

AVERAGE, MEDIAN, MIN, MAX, VARIANCE, STDDEV, and RANK

These are a series of functions that perform standard mathematical calculations as follows:

```
AVG(<set>[, <numeric_value_expression>])
```

This function computes the average of the tuples in *set* based on *numeric_value_expression*. Similar numeric functions are:

```
MEDIAN(<set>[, <numeric_value_expression>])

MIN(<set>[, <numeric_value_expression>])

MAX(<set>[, <numeric_value_expression>])

VARIANCE(<set>[, <numeric_value_expression>])

STDDEV(<set>[, <numeric_value_expression>])

RANK(<tuple>, <set>)
```

Each of these functions requires an implicit count of the number of cells, which does not include empty cells. To force the inclusion of empty cells, the application must use the COALESCEEMPTY() function.

This query gives an example of how to use these functions:

```
WITH

MEMBER  MEASURES.[Product Average] AS 'AVG( {([Product].CURRENTMEMBER
,[Time].CURRENTMEMBER), ([Product].CURRENTMEMBER , [Time].PREVMEMBER)} ,
MEASURES.[Store Sales] )'

    SELECT

        { ([Time].[1998]),  ([Time].[1997])} ON COLUMNS,

        {[Product].[Product Category].MEMBERS } ON ROWS

    FROM

        Sales

WHERE ( MEASURES.[Product Average])
```

This gives the average sales for Canada, the USA, and Mexico. You should verify that for 1997, when only the USA had sales, the average did not include Canada and Mexico. Another possible query is the following:

```
WITH

MEMBER  MEASURES.[Store Avg] as ' (AVG( {

                            [Store].[All Stores].[USA], [Store].[All
Stores].[Canada],[Store].[All  Stores].[Mexico]

                            }, MEASURES.[Store Sales]

                    )

            )'
```

```
SELECT

      { ( MEASURES.[Store Avg]) } ON COLUMNS,

      {( [Time].[1998]),([Time].[1997] ) } ON ROWS

   FROM

      Sales
```

Another query could be the following:

```
WITH

MEMBER  MEASURES.[US Store Avg] as ' (AVG( {

                              [Store].[All Stores].[USA].CHILDREN

                              }, MEASURES.[Store Sales]

                    )

              )'

MEMBER  MEASURES.[Canada Avg] as ' (AVG( {

                              [Store].[All Stores].[Canada].CHILDREN

                              }, MEASURES.[Store Sales]

                    )

              )'

MEMBER  MEASURES.[Mexico Avg] as ' (AVG( {

                              [Store].[All Stores].[Mexico].CHILDREN

                              }, MEASURES.[Store Sales]

                    )

              )'

  SELECT

      { ( MEASURES.[US Store Avg]), (MEASURES.[Canada Avg]),
(MEASURES.[Mexico Avg]) } ON COLUMNS,

      {( [Time].[1998]),([Time].[1997] ) } ON ROWS

   FROM

      Sales
```

This query calculates the average for all the stores in each of the three countries. Finally, do the following query:

```
WITH

MEMBER  MEASURES.[Store Min] AS

                    ' (

                    MIN(

                        {[Store].[All Stores].[USA].CHILDREN,

                            [Store].[All Stores].[Canada].CHILDREN,

                            [Store].[All Stores].[Mexico].CHILDREN

                        }

                        , MEASURES.[Store Sales]

                        )

                    )'

    SELECT

            {( MEASURES.[Store Min])} ON COLUMNS,

            {(([Time].[1998]),([Time].[1997] ) } ON ROWS

        FROM

            Sales
```

This query finds the amount of sales for the store with the minimum sales for 1997 and 1998. Experiment with the different functions to see how they work.

Conclusion

As these last three chapters have shown, MDX is a powerful language that enables you to create queries that can be used to return a wide range of datasets. Based on the user's requirements, you can create a set of MDX statements that bring back the data users need in the format they want. Based on these MDX statements, the data warehouse administrator can fine-tune the design of the data warehouse so that these queries can perform with optimum efficiency.

If you are a developer, you can create templates from your MDX queries, and allow your users to select the dimensions and levels of the dimension that will be placed into a standard query. This is covered in Chapter 8.

Chapter 8
ADO Multidimensional

Once you have learned the fundamentals of the multidimensional extensions (MDX) language, the next step is to use the MDX language to develop applications to view the data. Although the system administrator does not build these applications, the administrator is involved in the application's design. Another responsibility of the administrator is to optimize the data according to the needs of the applications using the warehouse. Administrators will also find that many of their required administrative tasks can be done only with a custom application.

The Microsoft SQL Server 7.0 data warehouse administrator does the following administrative tasks using custom code:

- Uses Visual Basic Script (or JavaScript or any scripting language) to write scripts that move data into the data warehouse when using DTS.
- Uses Visual Basic applications to optimize and automate movement of data into partitions.
- Uses MDX to set cell level security.

Don't be concerned if you are not a master of Visual Basic. You do not have to be a Visual Basic guru to be a SQL Server 7.0 data warehouse system administrator. However, you should have at least a basic understanding of what can be done with an application. If you do not have the skills to actually write the application, you should at least know what can be done and how it should be done. Remember, though, that the lines between development and infrastructure are beginning to blur.

The data warehouse administrator should be one of the leaders in finding ways to optimize the data warehouse application. It is only through having some understanding of the basic programming techniques and their limitations that you can make these recommendations.

The administrator should also be involved in discussions about how security is implemented in the application, how MDX queries should be optimized, how much memory is required to perform various operations, and what type of servers the middle-tier components may need.

This chapter begins with an overview of ADO Multidimensional (ADO MD). In the next chapter, you learn how system administrators can be involved with the design of an application, even if they know nothing about coding.

Introduction to ADO MD

ADO MD is the multidimensional extension to ADO. It comes with ADO 2.1 or 2.5. The current hierarchy is shown in Figure 8-1.

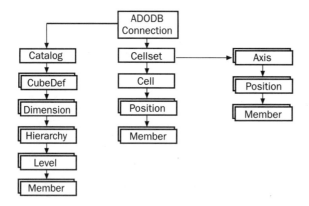

Figure 8-1. *The ADO MD Object Hierarchy.*

Each of the two hierarchies has a purpose. The catalog object hierarchy allows you to get information programmatically on your data warehouse. Using the catalog object, you can get the names of the cubes in the data warehouse, the dimensions and measures in these cubes, and any other information you need on the structure of the data warehouse. This allows you to write generic applications that can gather information on the data warehouse, and therefore work with any data warehouse.

The Cellset object gives you information on a dataset returned from querying the data warehouse with an MDX query. The Cellset object is divided into axes hierarchies and cell hierarchies. The axes hierarchy returns information on what members are on each axis (columns and rows for your examples). The cell hierarchy has data in the individual cells.

Imagine that you pass the following MDX query to the FoodMart data warehouse:

```
{([Customers].[Country].MEMBERS)} ON ROWS
```

In this case, the axes object allows you to determine that on Axis(1) (the row axis), there are the following members:

```
{([Customers].[All Customers].[USA]),

 ([Customers].[All Customers].[Canada]),

([Customers].[All Customers].[Mexico])}
```

In this case, each position on the axis contains only one member. If the axis contained mutiple dimensions, each position would contain multiple members, called tuples. In this case, there are three tuples so there are three positions. In the case of your example, [USA] is at position 0 on axis 1, [Canada] is at position 1 on axis 1, and [Mexico] is at position 3 on axis 1. You use the position object to get information on each position on the axis, such as the position on the axis and the number of members at that position.

Once you know the position on the axes of all the members returned by the dataset, you can then use these positions with the Cell object to return the values at the intersection of all the members on an axis. If you have ([Customers].[Country].MEMBERS) on rows and [MEASURES].[Store Sales] on columns, your axis looks like the one shown in Figure 8-2.

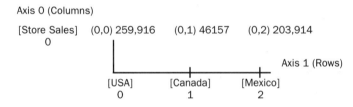

Figure 8-2. *Axes.*

Looking at this figure, you see that at cell (0,0), which is store sales for the USA, the value is $259,916.00. Thus, by using the axis object, you get the coordinates for each axis. Using these coordinates, you get the value at the intersection of the coordinates, which are cells. Let's now go through each of these objects in detail.

Creating an Application to Test ADO MD

In this section, you make a Visual Basic application so you can learn about ADO MD.

Tip Although this application is included on the companion CD under the directory code\Catalog Example, it is highly recommended that you create the application instead of just using the copy on the CD.

Begin by creating a Visual Basic exe application. Name the project prjADOMD. Add a tab control onto the form. Add the following controls with these names onto Tab 1, as shown in Figure 8-3.

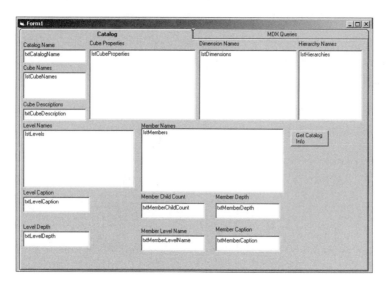

Figure 8-3. *FrmMain Tab 1.*

Add these controls with the following names onto Tab 2, as shown in Figure 8-4. Names starting with 1st are listboxes, names starting with txt are textboxes, names starting with grd are MSFlexGrids; and names starting with cmd are command buttons. The command button is called cmdcatalog.

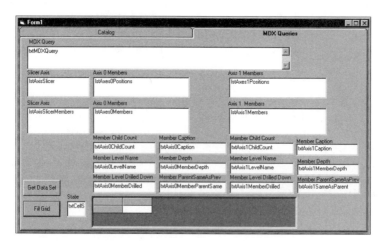

Figure 8-4. *FrmMain Tab 2.*

You can place the controls on the form any way you like. Go to the menu, select Project/References, and then add the Microsoft ActiveX Data Objects 2.0 Library, the

Microsoft ActiveX Data Objects (Multi-dimensional) 2.x Library, and the Microsoft Decision Support Objects (DSO), as shown in Figure 8-5.

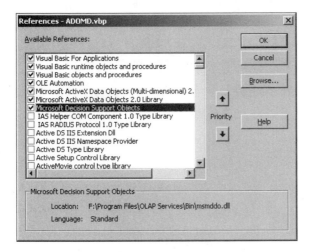

Figure 8-5. *Project References Menu.*

When completed, the first tab looks like Figure 8-6.

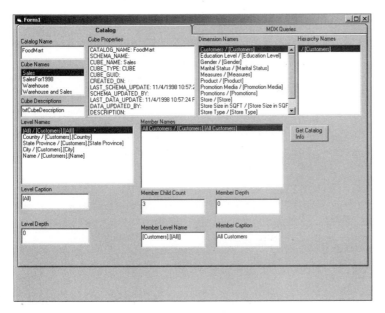

Figure 8-6. *First Tab.*

The second tab looks like Figure 8-7.

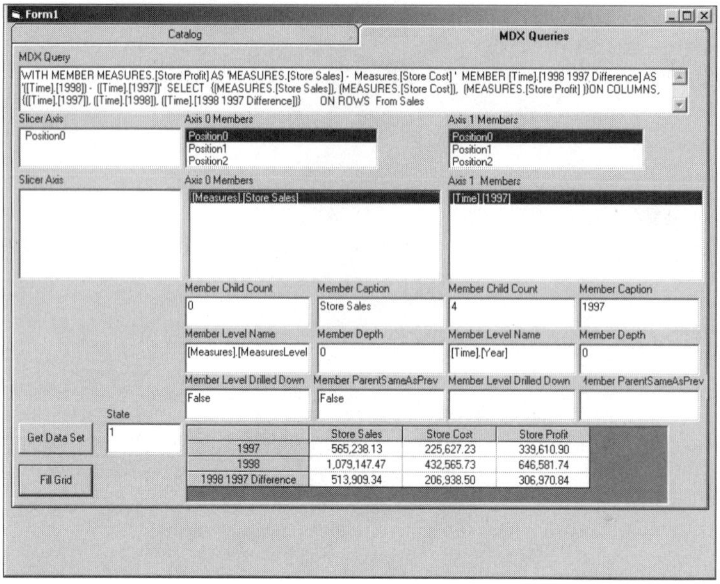

Figure 8-7. *Second Tab.*

Let's now work through the hierarchies and build the application to see how each of the hierarchies works.

ADO MD Catalog Hierarchy

The ADO MD catalog hierarchy gives access to the metadata of the Microsoft SQL Server 7.0 OLAP Services Repository. The Microsoft Repository is explained in Appendix B. Metadata is information about data. In the case of OLAP Services, metadata is information that describes the structure of the data in the data warehouse.

Just as you make a connection to a regular database, you also make a connection to the data warehouse using the ADO Connection object. The ADO Connection object you use for ADO MD is the same as the one you use with the regular ADO. Once the connection object is successfully created, you can use the catalog object to determine the structure of the data in the data warehouse. This means you need both a reference to the ADO 2.x library for the connection object and a reference to ADO Multidimensional in your applications.

Catalog Object

The catalog object has no methods. It has two properties and one collection as shown in Table 8-1.

Table 8-1. Catalog Object Properties

Name	Read/Write	Description
ActiveConnection	Read/Write	The ADO Connection Object.
Name	Read	The name of the catalog.
CubeDef (collection)	Read	A collection of CubeDefs. For each cube in the data warehouse, there is one CubeDef that contains information on the structure of the cube.

Begin by adding the following code to the declarations section of the form:

```
Option Explicit

Const c_ComputerName As String = "JAKESNEC"
```

You have to change the name of the c_ComputerName variable to the name of your OLAP Services server that contains the FoodMart data warehouse. Use the constant c_ComputerName throughout the code to make connections to the server.

You can add the following code to the cmdGetCatalogInfo_Click event to get the name of the FoodMart catalog:

```
Private Sub cmdGetCatalogInfo_Click()

Dim objCatalog As ADOMD.Catalog

Dim objConnection As ADODB.Connection

    Set objCatalog = New ADOMD.Catalog

    Set objConnection = New ADODB.Connection

    lstDimensions.Clear

    objConnection.Open "Data Source=" & c_ComputerName & ";Provider=MSOLAP;"

    Set objCatalog.ActiveConnection = objConnection

    txtCatalogName.Text = objCatalog.Name

    Set objConnection = Nothing

    Set objCatalog = Nothing

End Sub
```

If you run this code, you find this places *FoodMart* in the txtCatalog name textbox when you press the "Get Catalog Info" button. Thus, the catalog is nothing more than the name of the data warehouse.

To initialize your ADO MD objects, make a connection using a regular connection object and then use that connecton in ADO MD. Let's now look at the CubeDefs collection.

CubeDefs Collection

The CubeDefs collection is made up of CubeDef items. Each CubeDef item represents the definition of a cube in the data warehouse. Each cube has one CubeDef associated with it.

The CubeDefs collection has the properties and methods shown in Table 8-2.

Table 8-2. CubeDefs Collection Properties

	Name	Read/Write	Description
Properties	Count	Read	The number of cube definitions (CubeDefs) in the catalog.
	Item	Read	Returns one of the CubeDef objects. It is a zero-based array.
Methods	Refresh		Refreshes the CubeDefs collection.

The main purpose of the CubeDefs collection is to get access to the cube definitions.

CubeDef Object

The cube definitions, which are CubeDef objects, have the properties and methods shown in Table 8-3.

Table 8-3. CubeDef Object Properties and Methods

	Name	Read/Write	Description
Properties	Description	Read	A description of the cube.
	Name	Read	The name of the cube.
(collection)	Dimensions	Read	A dimension object that contains information on all the cube's dimensions.
	Properties (collection)	Read	A properties object associated with this cube. The properties object has a collection of property objects for the cube.

Note Notice that a description is part of all your main ADO MD objects. If you build your data warehouse without putting descriptions in, you deny the programmer the ability to pass this information on to the user. If you take the time to include descriptions using ADO MD, the developers can access these descriptions and pass them on to the user.

If you want to modify your original code to place all the names of the cubes into a list box, you can now rewrite your code as follows:

```
Private Sub cmdGetCatalogInfo_Click()
```

```
Dim lngCubeDefCounter As Long

Dim objCatalog As ADOMD.Catalog

Dim objConnection As ADODB.Connection

    Set objCatalog = New ADOMD.Catalog

    Set objConnection = New ADODB.Connection

    lstDimensions.Clear

    objConnection.Open "Data Source=" & c_ComputerName & ";Provider=MSOLAP;"

    Set objCatalog.ActiveConnection = objConnection

    txtCatalogName.Text = objCatalog.Name

    With objCatalog.CubeDefs

        For lngCubeDefCounter = 0 To (.Count - 1)

            lstCubeNames.AddItem .Item(lngCubeDefCounter).Name

        Next

    End With

    Set objConnection = Nothing

    Set objCatalog = Nothing

End Sub
```

This is the standard way you get information out of ADO MD. You use the count variable to set the maximum value in a For Loop and loop through each value.

There are two objects collections that are properties of the CubeDef: Properties and Dimensions.

CubeDef Properties

CubeDef Properties has the properties shown in Table 8-4.

Table 8-4. CubeDef Properties and Methods

	Name	Read/Write	Description
Properties	Count	Read	The number of Properties.
	Item	Read	Returns a Property Item.
Methods	Refresh	Read	Refreshes the Properties collection.

Property Object

A Property object has the properties shown in Table 8-5.

Table 8-5. Property Object Properties

	Name	Read/Write	Description
Properties	Attribute	Read	A long value associated with the property.
	Name	Read	The name of the property.
	Type	Read	The type of property.
	Value	Read	The value for the property.

You can add code so that when you click on a cube name in the list box, the properties of that cube are placed into the lstCubeProperties list box. Add the following code to the lstCubeNames_Click event:

```
Private Sub lstCubeNames_Click()

Dim lngCubePropertiesCounter As Long

Dim objCatalog As ADOMD.Catalog

Dim objConnection As ADODB.Connection

    Set objCatalog = New ADOMD.Catalog

    Set objConnection = New ADODB.Connection

    lstCubeProperties.Clear

    objConnection.Open "Data Source=" & c_ComputerName & ";Provider=MSOLAP;"

    Set objCatalog.ActiveConnection = objConnection

    txtCatalogName.Text = objCatalog.Name

    With objCatalog.CubeDefs(lstCubeNames.ListIndex)

        With .Properties

            For lngCubePropertiesCounter = 0 To (.Count - 1)

            lstCubeProperties.AddItem .Item(lngCubePropertiesCounter).Name & _

                    ": " & .Item(lngCubePropertiesCounter).Value

        Next

        End With

    End With
```

```
    objConnection.Close

    Set objConnection = Nothing

    Set objCatalog = Nothing

End Sub
```

Dimensions Collection

The dimensions collection has the properties and methods shown in Table 8-6.

Table 8-6. Dimensions Collection Properties and Methods

	Name	Read/Write	Description
Properties	Count	Read	The number of dimensions.
	Item	Read	Returns a dimension item.
Methods	Refresh		Refreshes the dimensions collection.

The dimensions collection manages a collection of dimension objects.

Dimension Object

A dimension object has the properties shown in Table 8-7.

Table 8-7. Dimension Object Properties

	Name	Read/Write	Description
Properties	Description	Read	A description for the dimension.
	Name	Read	The name of the dimension.
	Hierarchies (collection)	Read	A collection of hierarchies objects.
	Properties (collection)	Read	A properties object.
	UniqueName	Read	The unique name for the dimension.

The dimensions include all the dimensions you placed in the database, including the measures.

You can now add the following code to the lstCubeNames_Click event to add the dimension information into a list box:

```
Private Sub lstCubeNames_Click()

Dim lngCubePropertiesCounter As Long

Dim lngCubeDimensionCounter As Long

Dim objCatalog As ADOMD.Catalog
```

```
Dim objConnection As ADODB.Connection

    Set objCatalog = New ADOMD.Catalog

    Set objConnection = New ADODB.Connection

    lstCubeProperties.Clear

    lstDimensions.Clear

    objConnection.Open "Data Source="& c_ComputerName & ";Provider=MSOLAP;"

    Set objCatalog.ActiveConnection = objConnection

    txtCatalogName.Text = objCatalog.Name

    With objCatalog.CubeDefs(lstCubeNames.ListIndex)

        With .Properties

            For lngCubePropertiesCounter = 0 To (.Count - 1)

lstCubeProperties.AddItem .Item(lngCubePropertiesCounter).Name & _

                ": " & .Item(lngCubePropertiesCounter).Value

        Next

        End With

        With .Dimensions

            For lngCubeDimensionCounter = 0 To (.Count - 1)

                With .Item(lngCubeDimensionCounter)

                    lstDimensions.AddItem .Name & " / " & .UniqueName

                End With

            Next

        End With

    End With

    objConnection.Close

    Set objConnection = Nothing

    Set objCatalog = Nothing

End Sub
```

Your dimension object has a properties object with the same structure as the properties object for the CubeDef object. All the rest of your objects are also going to have properties objects, which you will explore in more detail later. The dimension object also has a hierarchies object. A hierarchies object manages a collection of hierarchy objects.

Hierarchies Collection

The hierarchies collection has the properties and methods shown in Table 8-8.

Table 8-8. Hierarchies Collection Properties and Methods

	Name	Read/Write	Description
Properties	Count	Read	The number of hierarchies.
	Item	Read	Returns a hierarchy item.
Methods	Refresh		Refreshes the hierarchy collection.

Hierarchy Object

The hierarchy object has the properties shown in Table 8-9.

Table 8-9. Hierarchy Object Properties

	Name	Read/Write	Description
Properties	Description	Read	A description for the dimension.
	Name	Read	The name of the dimension.
	Properties (collection)	Read	A properties object.
	Levels (collection)	Read	A Levels object that contains all the members of the hierarchy.
	UniqueName	Read	The unique name for the dimension.

Each dimension has a hierarchy associated with it, and within each hierarchy there is a list of levels. Technically speaking, some of your dimensions are not structural dimensions and so they do not have a hierarchy. As far as ADO MD is concerned, all dimensions have a hierarchy, even if there is only one level in the hierarchy.

You can add hierarchies to the lstHierarchies list box when a dimension name is clicked by adding the following code to the lstDimensions_ClickEvent:

```
Private Sub lstDimensions_Click()

Dim lngHierarchiesCounter As Long

Dim objCatalog As ADOMD.Catalog

Dim objConnection As ADODB.Connection

    Set objCatalog = New ADOMD.Catalog

    Set objConnection = New ADODB.Connection
```

```
objConnection.Open "Data Source="& c_ComputerName & _
";Provider=MSOLAP;"
Set objCatalog.ActiveConnection = objConnection
lstHierarchies.Clear
With objCatalog.CubeDefs.Item(lstCubeNames.ListIndex).Dimensions. _
Item(lstDimensions.ListIndex).Hierarchies
        For lngHierarchiesCounter = 0 To (.Count - 1)
            With .Item(lngHierarchiesCounter)
                lstHierarchies.AddItem .Name & " / " & .UniqueName
            End With
        Next
    End With
    objConnection.Close
    Set objConnection = Nothing
    Set objCatalog = Nothing
End Sub
```

The hierarchy object contains a levels object, which manages a collection of level objects.

Levels Collection

The levels collection contains the properties and methods shown in Table 8-10.

Table 8-10. Levels Collection Properties and Methods

	Name	Read/Write	Description
Properties	Count	Read	The number of levels.
	Item	Read	Returns a level object.
Methods	Refresh		Refreshes the level collection.

Level Object

The level object has the properties shown in Table 8-11.

Table 8-11. Level Object Properties

	Name	Read/Write	Description
Properties	Description	Read	A description for the dimension.
	Name	Read	The name of the dimension.
	Properties (collection)	Read	A properties object.
	Levels (collection)	Read	A levels object that contains all the members of the hierarchy.
	Caption	Read	
	Depth	Read	
	Members	Read	
	UniqueName	Read	The unique name for the level.

To see all the levels associated with a hierarchy, add the following code to the lstHierarchies_Click event:

```
Private Sub lstHierarchies_Click()

Dim lngLevelsCounter As Long

Dim objCatalog As ADOMD.Catalog

Dim objConnection As ADODB.Connection

    Set objCatalog = New ADOMD.Catalog

    Set objConnection = New ADODB.Connection

    objConnection.Open "Data Source="& c_ComputerName & ";Provider=MSOLAP;"

    Set objCatalog.ActiveConnection = objConnection

    lstLevels.Clear

    With objCatalog.CubeDefs.Item(lstCubeNames.ListIndex).Dimensions. _

Item(lstDimensions.ListIndex).Hierarchies(lstHierarchies.ListIndex) _

.Levels

        For lngLevelsCounter = 0 To (.Count - 1)

            With .Item(lngLevelsCounter)

                lstLevels.AddItem .Name & " / " & .UniqueName

            End With

        Next

    End With
```

```
    objConnection.Close

    Set objConnection = Nothing

    Set objCatalog = Nothing

End Sub
```

Each level object has a members object that manages a collection of member objects.

Members Collection

The members collection has the properties and methods shown in Table 8-12.

Table 8-12. Members Collection Properties and Methods

	Name	Read/Write	Description
Properties	Count	Read	The number of members.
	Item	Read	Returns a member item.
Methods	Refresh		Refreshes the member collection.

Member Object

The member object has the properties shown in Table 8-13.

Table 8-13. Member Object Properties

	Name	Read/Write	Description
Properties	Description	Read	A description for the dimension.
	Name	Read	The name of the dimension.
	Properties (collection)	Read	A properties object.
	LevelName	Read	The name of the level.
	LevelDepth	Read	A Levels Object that contains all the members of the hierarchy.
	DrilledDown	Read	Returns **True** if there are no child members of the current position member on the axis*.
	Caption	Read	The caption associated with the member.
	Depth	Read	The members level in the hierarchy.
	ParentSameAsPrev	Read	Indicates whether the parent of this position member is the same as the parent of the immediately preceding member*.

Table 8-13. Member Object Properties *continued*

	Name	Read/Write	Description
Properties	Members (collection)	Read	A members object. This returns all the members associated with this member.
	Name	Read	Name.
	UniqueName	Read	The unique name for the level.

*Position members are explained in the axes section.

The members in a level are the possible values for that level. For example, for customer country in the FoodMart database, the members are USA, Mexico, and Canada.

To see information on members, add the following code to the lstMembers_Click event:

```
Private Sub lstMembers_Click()

Dim objCatalog As ADOMD.Catalog

Dim objConnection As ADODB.Connection

    Set objCatalog = New ADOMD.Catalog

    Set objConnection = New ADODB.Connection

    objConnection.Open "Data Source="& c_ComputerName _

    & ";Provider=MSOLAP;"

    Set objCatalog.ActiveConnection = objConnection

    With objCatalog.CubeDefs.Item(lstCubeNames.ListIndex).Dimensions. _

    Item(lstDimensions.ListIndex). _

    Hierarchies(lstHierarchies.ListIndex). _

    Levels(lstLevels.ListIndex).Members(lstMembers.ListIndex)

    txtMemberCaption.Text = .Caption

    txtMemberDepth.Text = .LevelDepth

    txtMemberChildCount.Text = .ChildCount

    txtMemberLevelName.Text = .LevelName

    End With

    objConnection.Close

    Set objConnection = Nothing

    Set objCatalog = Nothing

End Sub
```

ADO MD Cellset Hierarchy

Up to this point, you have been looking at the structure of the cube with the catalog object. The catalog object only requires you to open a connection to the data warehouse. If you now use an MDX query and open a dataset with ADO MD, the results of the dataset are placed into a Cellset object. The Cellset object has the properties and methods shown in Table 8-14.

Table 8-14. Cellset Object Properties and Methods

	Name	Read/Write	Description
Properties	ActiveConnection	Read/Write	The number of dimensions.
	Axes (collection)	Read	The axes objects that contain the data from the MDX query.
	FilterAxis	Read	Returns an Axis object with information on the slicer dimensions.
	Properties (collection)	Read	Returns a properties object.
	Source	Read	The MDX query that defines the source of the data.
	State	Read	Returns 1 if the Cubeset is open, 0 if the Cubeset is closed.
	Item	Read	Returns a Cell Item.
Methods	Close		Closes the Cellset.
	Open		Once the ActiveConnection and Source are specified, the Cellset can be opened to retrieve the dataset.

Before, when you were working with the catalog hierarchy, just setting the connection object in the catalog object initialized the catalog object. With the Cellset object, you must first set the connection object and the source property and then open the connection.

The axes object has the properties and methods shown in Table 8-15.

Table 8-15. Axes Object Properties and Methods

	Name	Read/Write	Description
Properties	Count	Read	The number of Axes.
	Item	Read	Returns an Axis Item.
Methods	Refresh		Refreshes the Axes collection.

The axis object has the methods and properties shown in Table 8-16.

Table 8-16. Axis Object Methods and Properties

	Name	Read/Write	Description
Properties	DimensionCount	Read	The total number of dimensions on the axis.
	Name	Read	The name of the dimension.
	Properties (collection)	Read	A properties object for the Axis.
	Positions (collection)	Read	A positions object.

Positions Collection

The positions collection contains a collection of position objects. It measures the distance of a level from the intersection of the two axes. The positions collection has the properties and methods shown in Table 8-17.

Table 8-17. Positions Collection Properties and Methods

	Name	Read/Write	Description
Properties	Count	Read	The number of positions.
	Item	Read	Returns an Axis Item.
Methods	Refresh		Refreshes the Axes collection.

Position Object

The properties for the position object are shown in Table 8-18.

Table 8-18. Position Object Properties

	Name	Read/Write	Description
Properties	Members (collection)	Read	Information on each position on the axis.
	Ordinal	Read	The position of the value on the axis.

You are now going to code the MDX Queries tab on the Visual Basic application. You are ready to write out code to find out how many position objects exist for each axis. Add the following code to the cmdGetDataSet_Click event:

```
Private Sub cmdGetDataSet_Click()

Dim lngAxes0PositionCounter As Long

Dim lngAxes1PositionCounter As Long

Dim objConnection As ADODB.Connection

Dim objCellset As ADOMD.Cellset
```

```
        Set objConnection = New ADODB.Connection

        Set objCellset = New ADOMD.Cellset

        objConnection.Open "Data Source=" & c_ComputerName & ";Provider=MSOLAP;"

        Set objCellset.ActiveConnection = objConnection

        If txtMDXQuery.Text="" Then

        Exit Sub

        End If

        objCellset.Open txtMDXQuery.Text

        txtCellsetState.Text = objCellset.State

        With objCellset.Axes

            With .Item(0).Positions

                For lngAxes0PositionCounter = 0 To (.Count - 1)

                        lstAxes0Positions.AddItem "Position" & _

                            lngAxes0PositionCounter

            Next

            End With

            With .Item(1).Positions

                For lngAxes1PositionCounter = 0 To (.Count - 1)

                        lstAxes1Positions.AddItem "Position" & _

                            lngAxes1PositionCounter

            Next

            End With

        End With

        objCellset.Close

        objConnection.Close


        Set objConnection = Nothing

        Set objCellset = Nothing

    End Sub
```

Users need to enter an MDX query into txtMDXQuery before they can use this sub. Notice that you have to open a regular ADO connection first, and then you can open the Cellset with the MDX query. You are only moving over two axes in this code. Because the position objects have no names, they are just called Position1, Position2, and so forth. In this way, you can select on Position1 to get all the members of the position object number 1.

Now that you have opened a dataset using an MDX query, let's get all the information associated with that query.

The members collection is the same as described before. The position object can easily confuse someone because for each axis, there can be more than one dimension on the axis. Thus, using a crossjoin you can have the following tuple on the axis:

```
{([Customer].[Country].MEMBERS, [Product].[Product Category].MEMBERS)}
```

In this case, position 0 is held by the customer dimension and position 1 is held by the product dimension. Each position has a set of members associated with it. These members represent the values for each dimension in the tuple and the location of the value on the axis. Thus, customer country would be at position 0, and have members of [USA] located at the 0 coordinate on the axis, [Canada] at the 1 coordinate on the axis, and so forth. Product would be at position 1 and have members of [Dairy] located at the 0 coordinate on the axis, [Meat] on the 1 coordinate, and so forth. When you evaluate measures over the axes, you must evaluate them over all the members of the position's object. In this case, you must get coordinates from both position 1 and position 2, such as [USA], [Meat].

In addition to the axis that you display your data on, there is also a FilterAxis that represents all the members in your WHERE clause. In this example, the information is on the FilterAxis into the slicer list box, because the WHERE clause slices the cube. In cmdGetDataSet_Click, you can add the following code to get information on the FilterAxis.

```
Private Sub cmdGetDataSet_Click()

Dim lngAxes0PositionCounter As Long

Dim objConnection As ADODB.Connection

Dim objCellset As ADOMD.Cellset

Dim lngAxesSlicerCounter As Long

    Set objConnection = New ADODB.Connection

    Set objCellset = New ADOMD.Cellset

    objConnection.Open "Data Source="& c_ComputerName & ";Provider=MSOLAP;"

    Set objCellset.ActiveConnection = objConnection

    objCellset.Open txtMDXQuery.Text

    txtCellSetState.Text = objCellset.State
```

```
        With objCellset.Axes

            With .Item(0).Positions

                For lngAxes0PositionCounter = 0 To (.Count - 1)
                        lstAxes0Positions.AddItem "Position" & _

                                lngAxes0PositionCounter

            Next

            End With

            With .Item(1).Positions

                For lngAxes0PositionCounter = 0 To (.Count - 1)
                        lstAxes1Positions.AddItem "Position" & _

                                lngAxes0PositionCounter

            Next

            End With

        End With

        With objCellset.FilterAxis

            For lngAxesSlicerCounter = 0 To .Positions.Count - 1
                lstAxisSlicer.AddItem " Position" & lngAxesSlicerCounter
            Next

        End With

        objCellset.Close

        objConnection.Close


        Set objConnection = Nothing

        Set objCellset = Nothing

End Sub
```

Now that you have an entry for each position in your list boxes, you can show the members of each position when a position in one of the list boxes is clicked. You start with the slicer axis. Add the following code to the lstAxisSlicer_Click:

```
Private Sub lstAxisSlicer_Click()

Dim lngAxesSlicerMemberCounter As Long
```

```
Dim objConnection As ADODB.Connection

Dim objCellset As ADOMD.Cellset

    Set objConnection = New ADODB.Connection

    Set objCellset = New ADOMD.Cellset

    lstAxes0Members.Clear

    objConnection.Open "Data Source="& c_ComputerName & ";Provider=MSOLAP;"

    Set objCellset.ActiveConnection = objConnection

    objCellset.Open txtMDXQuery.Text

    txtCellSetState.Text = objCellset.State

    With objCellset.FilterAxis

        With .Positions.Item(lstAxisSlicer.ListIndex).Members

            For lngAxesSlicerMemberCounter = 0 To (.Count - 1)

                lstAxisSlicerMembers.AddItem .Item _

                (lngAxesSlicerMemberCounter).Name
                    Next

        End With

    End With

    objCellset.Close

    objConnection.Close


    Set objConnection = Nothing

    Set objCellset = Nothing

End Sub
```

The lstAxes0Positions_Click and the lstAxes1PositionsClick is the same as lstAxisSlicer_Click:

```
Private Sub lstAxes0Positions_Click()

Dim lngAxes0MemberCounter As Long

Dim objConnection As ADODB.Connection

Dim objCellset As ADOMD.Cellset

    Set objConnection = New ADODB.Connection

    Set objCellset = New ADOMD.Cellset
```

```
    lstAxes0Members.Clear

    objConnection.Open "Data Source="& c_ComputerName & ";Provider=MSOLAP;"

    Set objCellset.ActiveConnection = objConnection

    objCellset.Open txtMDXQuery.Text

    txtCellsetState.Text = objCellset.State

    With objCellset.Axes

        With .Item(0).Positions.Item(lstAxes0Positions.ListIndex).Members

            For lngAxes0MemberCounter = 0 To (.Count - 1)

                lstAxes0Members.AddItem .Item(lngAxes0MemberCounter).Name

            Next

        End With

    End With

    objCellset.Close

    objConnection.Close

    Set objConnection = Nothing

    Set objCellset = Nothing

End Sub
```

You now want to see some of the properties of the members of Axis 0 and Axis 1. In the lstAxes0Members_Click event, add the following code:

```
Private Sub lstAxes0Members_Click()

Dim objConnection As ADODB.Connection

Dim objCellset As ADOMD.Cellset

    Set objConnection = New ADODB.Connection

    Set objCellset = New ADOMD.Cellset

    objConnection.Open "Data Source="& c_ComputerName & ";Provider=MSOLAP;"

    Set objCellset.ActiveConnection = objConnection

    objCellset.Open txtMDXQuery.Text

    txtCellSetState.Text = objCellset.State

    With
objCellset.Axes.Item(0).Positions.Item(lstAxes0Positions.ListIndex).Members
```

```
(lstAxes0Members.ListIndex)

        txtAxis0Caption.Text = .Caption

        txtAxis0ChildCount = .ChildCount

        txtAxis0LevelName = .LevelName

        txtAxis0MemberDepth = .LevelDepth

        txtAxis0MemberParent = .ParentSameAsPrev

        txtAxis0MemberDrilled = .DrilledDown

    End With

    objCellset.Close

    objConnection.Close

    Set objConnection = Nothing

    Set objCellset = Nothing

End Sub
```

Axis 1 is basically the same:

```
Private Sub lstAxis1Members_Click()

Dim objConnection As ADODB.Connection

Dim objCellset As ADOMD.Cellset

Set objConnection = New ADODB.Connection

Set objCellset = New ADOMD.Cellset

    objConnection.Open "Data Source="& c_ComputerName & ";Provider=MSOLAP;"

    Set objCellset.ActiveConnection = objConnection

    objCellset.Open txtMDXQuery.Text

    txtCellSetState.Text = objCellset.State

    With
objCellset.Axes.Item(1).Positions.Item(lstAxes1Positions.ListIndex).Members
(lstAxis1Members.ListIndex)

        txtAxis1Caption.Text = .Caption

        txtAxis1ChildCount = .ChildCount

        txtAxis1LevelName = .LevelName

        txtAxis1MemberDepth = .LevelDepth
```

```
        txtAxis1MemberParent = .ParentSameAsPrev

        txtAxis1MemberDrilled = .DrilledDown

    End With

    objCellset.Close

    objConnection.Close

    Set objConnection = Nothing

    Set objCellset = Nothing

End Sub
```

Finally, you have the code to fill the grid with the data. To do this, you have to look at the properties of the cell object.

Cell Object

You use the cell object to get values for each cell. There is one cell for every combination of position members. You add the following code into the cmdFillGrid_Click method:

```
Private Sub cmdFillGrid_Click()

Dim lngColumnCounter As Long

Dim lngRowCounter As Long

Dim lngMemberCounter As Long

Dim objConnection As ADODB.Connection

Dim objCellset As ADOMD.Cellset

    Set objConnection = New ADODB.Connection

    Set objCellset = New ADOMD.Cellset
```

Open the connection object as before:

```
    objConnection.Open "Data Source=" & c_ComputerName & _

    " ;Provider=MSOLAP;"

    Set objCellset.ActiveConnection = objConnection

    objCellset.Open txtMDXQuery.Text
```

Next, you need to adjust the number of columns and rows so that you have enough of them for this query. You need one column for every position on Axis 0. You also want to have fixed columns with the names of the dimensions. The rows are the same except on Axis 1. To set up the proper number of columns and rows, add this code:

```
    With grdDataSet
```

```
.Cols = objCellset.Axes(0).Positions.Count + _

    objCellset.Axes(1).DimensionCount

.Rows = objCellset.Axes(1).Positions.Count + _

    objCellset.Axes(0).DimensionCount

.FixedCols = objCellset.Axes(1).DimensionCount

.FixedRows = objCellset.Axes(0).DimensionCount
```

Next, you want to put the names of the rows and set the width of the rows. Use the caption property of the members object:

```
For lngColumnCounter = 0 To _

  objCellset.Axes(0).DimensionCount - 1

      For lngRowCounter = 0 To objCellset. _

          Axes(1).Positions.Count - 1

          .Col = lngColumnCounter

          .Row = lngRowCounter + .FixedRows

          .Text = objCellset.Axes(1).Positions. _

              Item(lngRowCounter). _

              Members(lngColumnCounter).Caption

          .ColWidth(lngColumnCounter) = 2000

          .CellAlignment = flexAlignCenterCenter

      Next

  Next
```

Now add the captions for the columns:

```
For lngColumnCounter = 0 To _

    objCellset.Axes(0).Positions.Count - 1

    For lngMemberCounter = 0 To _

    objCellset.Axes(0).DimensionCount - 1

        .Col = lngColumnCounter + .FixedCols

        .Row = lngMemberCounter

        .Text = objCellset.Axes(0). _

            Positions(lngColumnCounter). _
```

```
                    Members(lngMemberCounter).Caption
        Next

    Next
```

Loop through the positions on both axes to get the coordinates for the cell object. Using these coordinates, you get the values of each cell. First, though, you move through all the cells in the grid and set the formatting on each grid cell. Add the following code:

```
For lngColumnCounter = 0 To _

    objCellset.Axes(0).Positions.Count - 1

    For lngMemberCounter = 0 To _

        objCellset.Axes(1).Positions.Count

        .ColWidth(lngColumnCounter + .FixedCols) = 1500

        .Col = lngColumnCounter + .FixedCols

        .Row = lngMemberCounter

        .CellAlignment = flexAlignCenterCenter

    Next
```

Finally, you put the values in the cell. If there is no value, put 0 in the grid cell. If there is a negative number, make the grid cell red.

```
For lngRowCounter = 0 To _

    objCellset.Axes(1).Positions.Count - 1

    .Col = lngColumnCounter + .FixedCols

    .Row = lngRowCounter + .FixedRows

    If IsNull(objCellset. _

        Item(lngColumnCounter, lngRowCounter).Value) Then

        .Text = 0

    Else

        .Text = objCellset. _

            Item(lngColumnCounter, _

                lngRowCounter).FormattedValue

        If InStr(.Text, ".") > 0 Then

            .Text = Left(.Text, InStr(.Text, ".") + 2)
```

```
            End If
            If InStr(.Text, "-") > 0 Then
                .CellForeColor = &HFF&
            End If
        End If
    Next
  Next
End With
```

Finally, close the connection and cellset objects.

```
objCellset.Close
objConnection.Close

Set objConnection = Nothing
Set objCellset = Nothing
End Sub
```

Properties for the ADO MD Objects

Many of the objects had a properties object associated with them. The properties associated with these objects are shown in Table 8-19.

Table 8-19. ADO MD Objects Properties

CubeDef	Dimension	Hierarchy	Level	Member
CatalogName	CatalogName	CatalogName	CatalogName	CatalogName
SchemaName	SchemaName	SchemaName	SchemaName	SchemaName
CubeName	CubeName	CubeName	CubeName	CubeName
CubeType	DimensionName	Dimension UniqueName	Dimension UniqueName	Dimension UniqueName
CubeGUID	Dimension UniqueName	HierarchyName	Hierarchy UniqueName	Hierarchy UniqueName
CreatedOn	DimensionGUID	Hierarchy UniqueName	LevelName	LevelUniqueName LevelNumber
LastSchemaUpdate	DimensionCaption	HierarchyGUID	LevelUniqueName	MemberOrdinal

continued

Table 8-19. ADO MD Objects Properties *continued*

CubeDef	Dimension	Hierarchy	Level	Member
SchemaUpdatedBy	DimensionOrdinal	Hierarchy Caption	LevelGUID	MemberName Member
DataUpdatedBy	DimensionType	DimensionType	LevelCaption	UniqueName
Description	Dimension Cardinality	Hierarchy Cardinality	LevelNumber	MemberType
	Default	Default	Level	MemberGUID
	Hierarchy	Member	Cardinality	MemberCaption
	Description	AllMember	LevelType	ChildrenCardinality
		Description	Description	ParentLevel
				ParentUniqueName
				ParentCount
				Description

You have now taken a close look at ADO MD. You can see that it gives you access to everything within your data warehouse. Unfortunately, ADO MD has a few limitations. Let's look at these.

Limitations of ADO MD

There are three basic services: user, business, and data. The data warehouse administrator should be involved in the design and structure of the data services components. This allows the administrator to be involved only with the portion of the application in which the administrator has expertise. Let's take a closer look at these three services.

User, Business, and Data Services

In the usual model of development, projects are divided into three sets of services: data, user, and business. The user services are all the services that relate to the communicaton of the application to the user. User services are usually the user interface. Business services contain the business logics and usually consist of business objects such as a customer object or an order object. Data services components handle the direct communication to the database. Normally, the user services reside on the client, the business services reside on either the client or the server, and the data services are on a server running under Microsoft Transaction Server (MTS) on Windows NT 4 or Component Services on Windows 2000. There are many ways to make connections between the client and server. The most common is DCOM, but a server that has a MS IIS (Internet Information Server) web server on it will allow for a few other options. One can create objects on a server using the RDS (Remote Data Services) with HTTP, DCOM, or COM by passing the requests to the object through an IIS web server. Internet and Intranet sites also provide a powerful means of moving information from the server to the client.

Splitting up the services like this offers you many advantages. Business service components should be reusable. Thus, you can make one product component that is used in a Visual Basic exe application running on the client, in an e-commerce site building HTML tables on a Web server, and on a remote client in a DHTML application. All three applications could use the same product business services component.

Separating the data services also offers advantages. As you will see in a moment, by placing your data services components under MTS, you can make your applications scalable. In addition, many applications require the same data services. By creating one data services component on one (or multiple) server(s), you can now use that one data services component with many business services components.

Creating separate data and business services components also means that you can change the internal workings of these components and keep their external interface the same. If you change components in this way, you only have to upgrade the individual components and not the whole system. This is extremely important, because technology is constantly changing. If ADO MD changes and you do not use a data services component, you might have to upgrade every single one of your applications that uses ADO MD. If you have a data services component, you can upgrade the data services component only internally and not have to change all the applications dependent on the data services component.

Using an OLTP database, you normally work with disconnected ADO recordsets. In this case, the data services component connects to the database, retrieves information from the database into a disconnected recordset, disconnects from the database, and then returns the disconnected recordset to the business services component. The business services component then passes information to the user services component using this disconnected recordset. Finally, the user services component (the user interface) passes information on to the user. This can also go the other way, that is, the user passes information to the user services component (perhaps updates or adds a record), the user services component then passes this information to the business component, which passes it to the data services component, which then connects to the database and updates the record and performs any necessary reconciliations.

Although this works well for your OLTP system, this cannot be done with ADO MD. ADO MD does not retrieve all the information and place it into either the Catalog or Cellset hierarchies. Data is only retrieved when you make a request for the data. If you close your connection to the database with your ADO MD objects, you have nothing in the objects. Thus, with ADO MD, you cannot build a data services component that retrieves the data from the database, fills the ADO MD objects, disconnects from the database, and returns data to the client. ADO MD does not allow you to build applications with data services components.

The ADO MD works in a fundamentally different way than the regular ADO. The PivotTable Services, which are discussed in detail in Chapter 11, will allow data to be cached (stored) on the client computer as it is accessed. If data was previously accessed and cached, the client will not have to go to the server for the data, but instead will retrieve from the client side cache. This can substantially reduce the time involved in retrieving data. The PivotTable Services and data caching can be an essential element in building client data warehouse applications.

Conclusion

The AD MD offers a programmatic solution that, when used with the PivotTable Services client side caching, offers a viable solution for most data warehousing systems. Sometimes, there will be a need to gain more control over the data that is flowing between the client and server. In this case, you can desing and build a component that works more like the traditional ADO disconnected recordsets. This component would use the ADO MD to retrieve data. This custom component wraps ADO MD. With this component you can name the objects anything you like, create separate objects for the structure of the data and for the data, create disconnected datasets, and isolate your application from any future changes to ADO MD. Because building such a component can be difficult, there is one in the Appendix C. This component has all the basic building blocks a developer would need to make a data services component. You will work through the design of this component in the next chapter.

Chapter 9
System Administrator's Role in Design

This chapter explains how you design a data warehouse application using Unified Modeling Language (UML). The contributions a data warehouse administrator must make to the design of a data warehouse application are also covered. You do not need any knowledge of Visual Basic, or any programming language, to understand this chapter.

The data warehouse administrator requires a larger skill set than the administrator of an online transaction processing (OLTP) database. This skill set should include an understanding of application design as well as some basic coding knowledge. Applications built for a data warehouse are far more complex and require the administrator's advice on security, performance, and access technology. Without the administrator's input, an application might have poor security, demand too many connections to the data warehouse, or in some other way compromise the entire performance of the data warehouse. The data warehouse administrator should be involved in the design of any application using the data warehouse from the very beginning of the design process.

This chapter illustrates the design process by leading you through the design of a general component to wrap the ADO Multidimensional (ADO MD). You will also design a component to build a generic control to view data from the data warehouse. You can use this generic control to build an application that acts as a portal, giving high-level managers a view into any data in the data warehouse that they are allowed to see. The actual application is on the CD included with the book under the directory Code\CubeExample. The full discussion of how to design the application is included in the appendixes.

Designing a Generic Application

When creating a data warehouse you need to first talk to the users and find out what types of information they want from the data warehouse. Every aspect of the physical data warehouse depends on the needs of users and the business requirements of the corporation. The database administrator needs to understand the business needs and users' requirements to determine the structure of the data warehouse and what type of information should go into the data warehouse. The best way to do this is to be involved in the design of the applications to be used to retrieve information from the data warehouse. Understanding the design documents for those applications is an essential step in this process.

Creating Scenarios from User Interviews

First, users are usually interviewed and a rough set of criteria for the application is created. These criteria are placed into documents called scenarios. For a data warehouse application, you may find that the user interview has given you the following scenario:

Scenario: Viewing Data from the Data Warehouse

```
User Logs In

User Selects Dimensions for viewing in Grid

User Selects Measures for viewing in Grid

User Drills Down Dimension

User Selects new Dimension for Grid

User Selects new Measure for Grid

User Adds new dimension to grid to nest dimensions
```

Log in would have its own scenario associated with it:

Log In

```
User Selects Server

User Selects Database

User Selects Cube
```

Creating a Use Case

In addition to this information, you also have a set of business rules such as security information, the different roles of the users for the system, and so forth. To keep it simple, we will not look at the business rules at this stage. Once you have created a scenario, next create a use case. In the use case, everything is from the perspective of the user, who is called an actor. For the above scenarios, you end up with the following use cases:

Use Case View Data

OVERVIEW: The purpose of this use case is to view data in any cube in the data warehouse.

Primary Actor: Manager

Secondary Actor: Company Vice President,Company President

Starting Point: The actor has logged in

Ending Point: The actor either builds a view in the grid or cancels

Measurable Result: Data is placed in the grid control

Flow of Events:

Actor Logs In

Actor Drills Down Dimension in Grid

Actor Selects Dimensions for viewing in Grid

Actor Selects Measures for viewing in Grid

Actor Adds new dimension to grid to nest dimensions

Actor Selects new Dimension for Grid

Actor Selects new Measure for Grid

Alternative Flow of Events:

The actor is denied access to the database.

Use Case Log In

Overview: The purpose of this use case is to log an actor into the database.

Primary Actor: Manager

Secondary Actor: Company Vice President,Company President

Starting Point: The actor enters the login information

Ending Point: The actor is either logged in or denied access

Measurable Result: The actor is logged in

Flow of Events:

Actor Selects Server

Actor Selects Database

Actor Selects Cube

Alternative Flow of Events:

The actor enters an invalid userID and password. The user will not be able to view data.

The actor tries to access a cube he or she is not allowed to access. The user will not get access to the cube.

As you can see, the use case is more formal than the scenario. Everything is from the point of view of the user. You can use any format for the sections that works for your corporation. The alternative flow of events gives you the conditions that are considered errors. These are detailed in what is called "constraint business rules." Some of the other business rules are as follows:

- **Definition business rules**   Define the business's terms such as Cube, Server, Manager, and so forth found in the use cases.
- **Factual business rules**   Relate one business term to another. For example, every database has one or more cubes within it.
- **Derivation business rules**   Define any formula or information that is derived from other information. Thus, we could define profit as Total Sales minus cost.

All of these business rules should be created for your system. The business rules that are relevant to a use case should be listed in the use case in a special section called "Business Rules."

> **Note**   You can also use business rules to define business components, formulas, and relationships between objects. For a full discussion of use cases and business rules, look at *VB6 UML Design and Development,* also written by Jake Sturm.

Defining User Groups

If you are a database administrator, there should be certain questions that these use cases immediately raise. The first problem with the View Data use case is that you only know three roles: managers, company vice president, and company president. The manager role is very general.

The system administrator has to define different groups of managers and what data they can view. There are managers from the advertising department who have access to promotions data, managers of the company's warehouse who want to see product information and information on items in the warehouse, and managers of sales who can see sales information on their region.

In this example, the administrator needs to work with the users and the developers to sort out the different types of manager roles that exist for this application. Once these roles are known, the administrator has to design a security scheme for them. Will you use security from the application, Windows NT security, database roles, or a directory? Your answer depends on the application.

If you want to make this a very general application that can retrieve data on any cube in the data warehouse, information on dimensions has to come from the data warehouse instead of the application. Thus, you should put descriptions into your data wherever possible. You should also use good naming conventions.

Using Good Naming Conventions

When building a data warehouse, do not look at the warehouse as a separate entity. The warehouse is part of a larger system that includes the original source of the data (usually an OLTP database), the applications to be used against the data warehouse, and a set of users who will use the data for various reports and decision-making processes. When you view your data warehouse from this perspective, you can begin to design and build it according to the needs of the larger system. Ask essential questions, such as "How can I make this data warehouse meet the performance needs of the user?" or "How can I design the data warehouse to help the developers make the most efficient, reusable components?" These questions can only be answered by the administrator who is involved with the users, the developers, and the entire team building the complete system.

Creating a Sequence Diagram

For the application that allows a user to select any cube in any available data warehouse in the corporation, there is a use case that maps the sequence of steps that are necessary to get this data. Another way to view the data in the use case is by using a UML sequence diagram. A sequence diagram gives a pictorial view of the use case diagram. For your use case diagram, you have the sequence diagram shown in Figure 9-1.

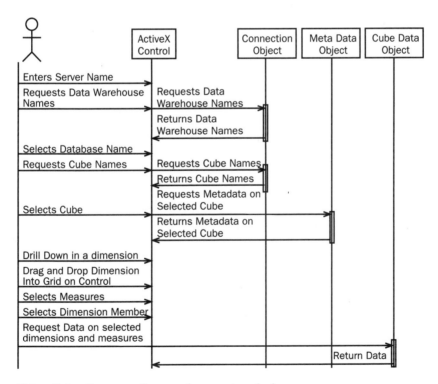

Figure 9-1. *Sequence diagram for generic cube browser.*

In a sequence diagram, each component of the system, including the user, is placed above a vertical dashed line. The vertical lines represent time. Time passes as you move down the vertical line. The horizontal lines represent communications between components. A horizontal line going to the right represents a request for a service or the input of information into the system. A horizontal line to the left is the result of the request for a service.

Exploring Four System Components

In addition to the user, there are four components in the system. The first component is an ActiveX control that is imbedded in a user interface, such as a Visual Basic form or an Internet Explorer browser. This control is part of the user services (the user interface), but contains the business services (the business logic) within it. The three other components make up the data services components.

Connection Object Component

You use the Connection Object component to get the information required to make a connection, such as the database names, server names, and cube names. By looking at the services this component requires and what is returned by this component, you can determine this component's public methods. Thus, Connection Object needs a method for retrieving data warehouse names. This method must return the names. Connection Object also has a method for retrieving Cube names.

Meta Data Object Component

The Meta Data Object component is required to retrieve metadata on a cube. The metadata for a cube contains data on the structure of the cube, such as the dimensions, the members of each dimension, and so forth. You present this information to users so they can choose which dimensions they want.

Cube Data Object Component

The Cube Data Object component retrieves data from the data warehouse based on a Multidimensional Extensions (MDX) query. The MDX query is built from the dimensions, measures, and slicer dimensions the user chooses.

The sequence diagram takes the use case and translates it into a set of services that must be performed by the components of the system. You can add more detail to this sequence diagram by adding the data warehouse into the diagram as an additional object. We have defined a control that will be embedded into a user interface, yet the user interface is not included in the diagram. We could therefore also add the user interface into the diagram. Or, you can keep the diagram simple to see the essential components of the system.

The system administrator needs to look at a sequence diagram and be able to find any issues that might exist in this design. In this diagram, there is no place for users to enter their userIDs and passwords. This needs to be addressed.

Considering Security

As always, security is an issue. What type of security will you place in the Connection component? Can anyone view the names of the data warehouses and cubes on a server, or do you limit it to a certain group of people? Do you allow all of the metadata to be returned to the user so the user can view everything, or do you allow only certain dimensions to be viewed? If you limit a user to certain dimensions, will this limitation be done by the ActiveX Control, the user interface (not shown in the diagram), or the Meta Data Object? How much data will the Meta Data Object return? Could the amount of data being returned overwhelm the client machine or the network? Should you limit the amount of data being returned by the Meta Data Object? By looking at this one diagram, you can come up with a long list of possible questions that have to be answered. The developer is more focused on fulfilling the requirements of the user and building components to fulfill those requirements. It is the job of system administrator to dig into the design and find ways to fulfill the needs of the data warehouse, such as security and performance, while still fulfilling the needs of the user.

Now that you know what components you need and what services they need to perform, let's look at the design of these of components in more detail. Because the three data services components might be useful to the projects your developers are building, this will continue to to be the example for application design. Let's look at the next step in application design.

Designing the Data Services Components

When building a three-tier solution, the data services component will be responsible for all communications to the database or data warehouse. It is essential that the administrator is involved with its design and optimization. Let's look at the data services component for this application.

OLAP Data Services Component

Your development team should manage its projects with a framework such as the Microsoft Solution Framework and go through a thorough design phase for all your projects. If it doesn't yet do so, perhaps it is time to consider using such tools.

There are many ways to document a project. By far the best is by using UML. You already saw the UML use case diagram and the UML sequence diagram. Let's now look at the UML class diagram.

UML Class Diagrams

In this example, you are going to make a class diagram for each class in the project. Each class is represented by a box divided into three sections. The top section is for the name of the class, the middle section is for the properties of the class, and the bottom section is for the methods of the class. Because the example is in Visual Basic, the following are used: a plus sign (+) for public methods and properties, a minus sign (-) for private methods and properties, and a number sign (#) for friend functions. Friend functions are those that can be seen only by classes within the project. Private functions can be seen only by those within the class. Public functions can be seen by any project.

CubeConnection Component

The application will divide ADO MD into three separate components. The first of these three components is a connection object called clsCubeConnection. The connection component will have properties that have information on the connection, such as database, server, user name, and so forth. The connection object also has several methods that provide useful information such as the names of the server, the databases, and the cubes. In the next section clsCubeConnection properties and clsCubeConnection methods are covered.

Using class diagrams, your cube object looks like the one shown in Figure 9-2:

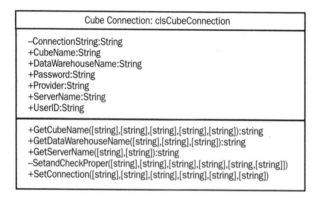

Figure 9-2.   *Cube connection class diagram.*

This diagram gives a great deal of information about your class and can be used by both the developers and the system administrators. When you build this component, it is a class in a Visual Basic dll. The name of the dll is CubeConnection and the name of the class is clsCubeConnection. This information is in the top section of the class diagram.

clsCubeConnection Properties

In the middle section of the class diagram, you find the names of properties and type information on these properties. You can see that clsCubeConnection has six public properties: DataWarehouseName, Provider, ServerName, CubeName, UserID, and Password. All six of these are strings. You can use the public properties of this class to store all the information required to make a connection to Microsoft SQL Server 7.0 OLAP Services.

There is also one private property called ConnectionString, which is the string that is built from these properties to make a connection to the database.

clsCubeConnection Methods

The bottom section of the class diagram gives all the methods. You can see a public method called GetCubeNames that has five string parameters and returns a string. You also have the following public methods: GetDataWarehouseNames, GetServerNames, and SetConnection. There is one private method, SetandCheckProperties.

When we build applications, especially three-tier systems, we will be building stateless and stateful components. Let's take a look at what stateless and stateful components are and how they relate to clsCubeConnection.

Stateless and Stateful Components Methods

The class clsCubeConnection has a bit of a split personality. There are times when a class like this works best as a stateless server component and other times when you may want to use it as a stateful client component. A stateless component has no memory of what happens from one call to the next. With a stateless component, you call one method of the component and ask that method to perform a task for you, passing all the information you need into the parameters of the method. With stateful components, you remember what was done from one call to the next. If you first set a property and then call a method, the component remembers the value you set that property to. A stateless component will have forgotten the value of the property; that is why you must pass everything in as parameters with a stateless component. Stateful components usually set all the properties first and then call methods. You can set the properties one by one or all at once using a method to set all the properties.

Methods of the clsCubeConnection Class

This component allows you to use it as a stateless object or a stateful object. Each method contains optional parameters that can be used when the connection object is used as a stateless component. There is also a method called SetConnection that allows you to set all the properties at once for a stateful component. You also have properties if you want to set the properties first and call a method, or to pass connection information from one object to another by setting the properties of the connection object and passing it from one object to another. This is a very versatile component, and it is built much like the ADO connection object.

GetCubeNames retrieves the names of all the cubes in a database. Although you do not know the exact nature of the parameters because they are only listed as strings, you can figure out what they are. To get cube names, you need to know the name of the database, the name of the server, the provider, the userID, and the password. These are your five parameters. You get a string back separating the names by commas.

Note You could have this method return an array. To keep the example in the appendix simpler, a string is used.

It is fairly simple to parse the string. All parameters are surrounded by brackets ([ ]), which means they are optional. Obviously, the database and server names must be known to get the names of the cubes in a database; thus, if you do not pass the parameter in, you must be using this as a stateful component and have already set the database name and server name properties. This means that your GetCubeNames method needs to check if the optional parameter was passed in, and if it was not passed in, if the property was set. The private function SetandCheckProperties performs these checks and raises an error if the database or server name is not either set through the properties or passed in as a parameter.

GetServerNames and GetDataWarehouseNames work the same as GetCubeNames. Both of these methods have the userID and password as parameters. Although the password and userID information are not used in the code here, you may want to use it to prevent server and data warehouse names from being visible to everyone who has access to this component.

You have now read an exhaustive discussion of this component without looking at a single line of code. This is the advantage of using UML class diagrams. There are many issues that a developer should discuss with the data warehouse administrator (such as security, naming conventions, and the locations of the various components), and the UML diagrams form a bridge between the developer and the administrator. Let's now look at a more complicated component, the CubeMetaData component, which contains data on the structure of the cube.

CubeMetaData Component

The CubeMetaData component gives metadata on the cube. The class diagram looks like the one shown in Figure 9-3.

In Visual Basic, one class can create another class; this is how hierarchies are created. To represent this with class diagrams, connect two classes with a line and a diamond. Place the diamond on the class being created. The star means the creating class has a collection of the other class. Thus, the diagram clsCubeMetaData contains a single clsDimensions object. The clsDimensions object contains a collection of clsDimension objects. Likewise, the clsDimension objects contain a single clsHierarchies object. The CubeData dll has a complicated class hierarchy, but with your class diagrams, it is easy to understand. If you look at the sample code for the dll you see that it would take a long time to figure out this hierarchy by just looking at the code. The class diagram allows you to figure this out in only a few minutes.

This hierarchy is built out of a familiar format for Visual Basic hierarchies. There are two class pairs, a managing class and a managed class.

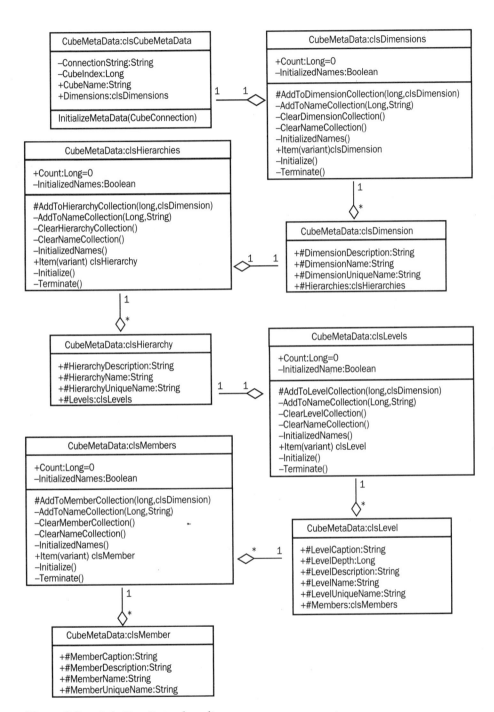

Figure 9-3. *CubeMetaData class diagram.*

Managing and Managed Classes

The managing class has methods to perform actions on the managed class, such as Item, which is used to retrieve one of the managed classes. The managed class is made up primarily of properties. If you look at this class diagram, you can see that clsDimensions, clsHierarchies, clsLevels, and clsMembers are all managing classes. They all share the same basic methods for managing the managed classes. The managed classes are clsDimension, clsHierarchy, clsLevel, and clsMember. They are made up of mostly properties. Thus, if you understand the methods of one managing class, you understand the methods for all of them.

Objects in CubeMetaData

A few of the names in the hierarchy were changed to make it easier to understand what you are working with. At the top of the hierarchy is clsCubeMetaData. The clsCubeMetaData class manages the entire hierarchy and places the appropriate data into the managing classes.

clsCubeMetaData

The clsCubeMetaData class manages the entire hierarchy and is the only public, creatable class in the hierarchy. You use it to initialize the object with the InitializeMetaData method. The IntializeMetaData method has one parameter: a CubeConnection object. The CubeConnection object holds all the information you need to make a connection to the database and retrieve the metadata on the cube. The ConnectionString property is built from the information in the connection object and used internally by the class to make connections.

The CubeIndex is a private property. When you use ADO MD, you do not use the name of the cube to retrieve information on the cube. Instead, use an index number. The CubeIndex number is the index number for the cube you want data on. The cube name property is just the name of the cube. It can be set by the user or set through the clsCubeConnection object.

Starting at the Dimensions object, the clsCubeMetaData object has exactly the same objects as the ADO MD catalog hierarchy. The major difference is that you can place all the data you need into the clsCubeMetaData object on the server, disconnect from the database, and pass the clsCubeMetaData back to the client computer. Thus, you can make data services components with clsCubeMetaData.

The final part of the clsCubeMetaData is the clsDimensions object. This object manages all the clsDimension objects. Let's look at this class.

ClsDimensions Object

This class has the responsibility of managing a collection of clsDimension objects. The Item method returns a clsDimension object. You can pass in either a numeric index or the name of the dimension you want. The Count property returns the number of clsDimension objects in the collection.

You use the index as the key for your dimension objects. You need a way to know what index is associated with each dimension name, because Item also works with dimension names. To do this, use a collection to associate a dimension name with the appropriate index.

There are two private functions, one for adding dimensions to the collection called AddToDimensionCollection and one for adding names to the collection for associating names to IDs called AddToNameCollection. You use these to add new dimensions and names to the collection.

You might be wondering why the function to add dimensions is not public. You place the information on your dimensions into the clsDimensions object from the InitializeCubeMetaData method in the clsCubeMetaData class. The InitializeCubeMetaData method can create a clsDimension object, set all the properties of the clsDimension object, and add it to the clsDimensions dimension collection. It does this by using the AddToDimensionCollection method (if AddToDimensionCollection were public or friend). Instead of doing it this way, you allow InitializeCubeMetaData method to call for an Item. If the dimension does not exist, clsDimensions creates a new dimension and adds it to the hierarchy. Thus, new dimension objects are implicitly added to the collection. All the managing classes are coded this way.

Now let's look at another Visual Basic dll, called CubeData, that allows you to get data from the data warehouse.

CubeData

The class diagram for cube data is shown in Figure 9-4.

You can see that clsCubeData contains one clsAxes object. The clsAxes object contains a collection of clsAxis objects. The clsAxis object contains a single clsTuples object. The clsTuples object contains a collection of clsTuple objects, which contain a collection of clsTupleMember objects.

As you might guess, the clsAxis object contains information on an axis. There are tuples on each axis and your clsTuple object has information on these tuples. Each tuple has members, and these are your clsTupleMember objects. Thus, you have compressed the ADO MD hierarchy down a little bit.

The clsCubeData class is the only public, creatable object. It manages all the other objects. InitializeCubeData takes two parameters, a clsCubeConnection object and a string. The string is the MDX query.

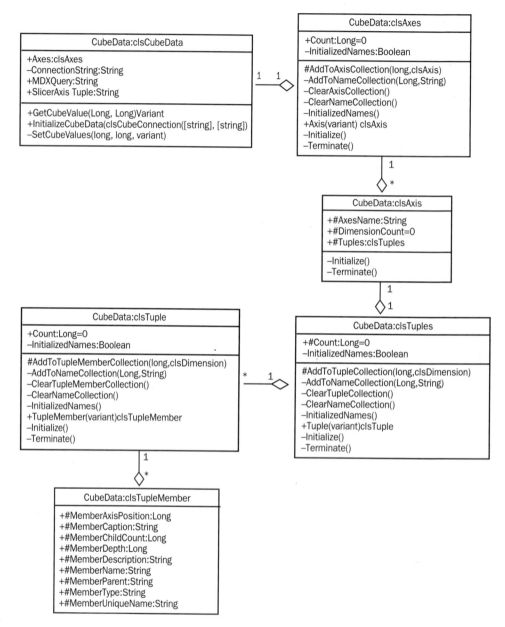

Figure 9-4. *Cube data class diagram.*

Looking at the objects you have designed, you can see there are still quite a few unanswered questions. Security once again is a major issue. If you are placing cube information into your clsCubeMetaData, this could be a great deal of information. The metadata could easily be 10 to 50 megabytes of data. This is a lot of information to drag across the network and might overwhelm the client machine. You need to identify roles and limit the data they are retrieving based on these roles. There is also data that may never be used. For example, it is unlikely anyone will drill down to an individual customer name, therefore, you do not need to drag the customer name information into your database metadata. The location of these components is also an issue that you must decide. Do you place these components on a server or run them on the client? Can you make them scalable? How large must a server be to handle these components? Can the network handle the traffic created by these components if they run on a server? The data warehouse administrator will be heavily involved in these discussions. The answers depend on the available infrastructure, the type of application, and the identified users. Security is not placed with the application because the way you want to implement security will depend on your individual needs You must also make these components flexible enough to run on either the client or server so they can meet your individual needs.

Using Applications to Maintain Security

Now that you have looked at some of the structures of these components, you can address an important issue: security. There are many ways to implement security. People tend to always think first of Windows NT or database security. It is also possible to place security into your code.

Imagine that you have sales managers for five regions. In the data warehouse you have a salesperson dimension whose first level is divided into the five regions ([Sales Person].[Region1], [Sales Person].[Region2], …). You want to limit sales managers' access to just their own data. One way to do this is to implement cell level security and only allow managers to view the cells that include data on their region. There is a much easier way, though.

If the only way the managers could view the data is through custom applications, you can place security into the applications. Your client application has a list of dimensions from which the user can choose. If you define roles for your managers, such as region1 manager, region2 manager, and so forth, and your application logs the sales managers in before they are allowed to view any data, you can limit the information they are allowed to view in the user interface to their own regions. Thus, take the sales region dimension and allow only the sales manager from region1 to view [Sales].[Region 1]. The application filters out the other regions that the region1 sales manager is not allowed to view.

Filtering Security Dimensions

How do you filter out the dimensions you do not want? There are several ways. One way is to place the code directly into your clsTuple class. If you change clsTuple so that it has two additional parameters, userID and password, you can use these parameters to determine what tuples this user is allowed to see. In the case of your sales managers, they would be limited to their particular sales region. If you place the security information into a directory or a database, you can store the userID, password, and what members of the Sales Person dimension they are allowed to see. Based on this information, the Sales Person dimension only has the allowed regions placed in them. The user interface only presents the regions allowed for each manager so managers can choose to view only their own regions.

You might not want to put such limiting code into a general component such as CubeData. Another option would be to create business components that present to the user only the members of each dimension they are allowed to see. This business component can use a security component that contains a list of dimension members the user is allowed to view. This is a better way to code the project, because you are placing the business logic (the restrictions on who can view what data) into the business components where it belongs.

If you use a security component, and the security and business components run on the client, the security component can download the information on the user into memory when the application is first opened. The application can then access it from that component from that point. Of course, the potential danger is that an improperly designed application could allow users to view data they should not be able to view, but this is also true even when you are using Windows NT or database security. If the database administrator is involved in the design of the project from the beginning, choosing to place security within the applications can be as secure as using other forms of security.

The final object covered is a Visual Basic control that provides the functionality for your generic applications. Let's look at this component now.

Building Scalable Components

In the last chapter, you learned that to use ADO MD you have to either hold a connection to the database open, or open the connection every time data is needed. Holding the database open creates a great deal of network traffic and can also create problems if more users want to connect than there are available database connections.

For applications that might have only a few users, the consequences of holding the connection open for the life of the application are minimal on the network. As long as the data warehouse is accessed by only a few people, an application that holds the connection open can be built without adverse effects.

However, if you want to build an application that gets information out to the entire corporation and might require hundreds of simultaneous users, ADO MD may not be very efficient. The design you created earlier allows you to scale for several reasons.

Direct connections between the client computer and the data warehouse can be avoided by doing the following:

- Place the data services components on a server.
- Have the the data services components get the data from the data warehouse.
- Place the data in either a CubeData or MetaData object and pass these objects back to the client.

If only the server connects to the data warehouse, you can create a direct connection between the data warehouse and the server. This means data is not continuously moving across the network as required by ADO MD. Data only flows over the network as the data services components pass data back to the client.

Note   The number of connections can be set by using the SQL Server Manager. You could theoretically set the number of connections to be very high, but connections use resources both on the server and over the network. Eventually, the number of connections will require enough system resources that the performance of the database will begin to suffer. It is for this reason that there must be some limit on the number of connections to the database or data warehouse.

prjCubeGrid

Here you have a project called prjCubeGrid with one Visual Basic control called CubeGridInformation. The control looks like the one shown in Figure 9-5.

You can add this control to a Visual Basic form, or use it in a Web DHTML application or in any container that can use an ActiveX control. This control displays one command button for every available dimension. The measures are listed in a listbox. There is also a treeview control to give the users a way of visualizing the dimension hierarchies. By clicking on a dimension command button, you can move either up or down the hierarchy. Next to the dimension command buttons is the current value for a dimension. This value is used in the WHERE clause. Thus, the user can do many things with this component. Let's look at some views of this component. Figure 9-6 shows the component when the component is first initialized.

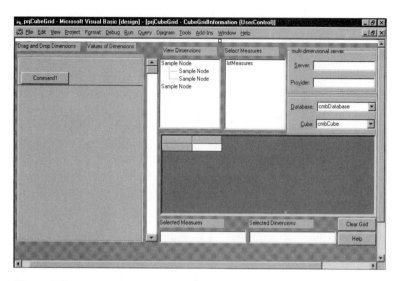

Figure 9-5. *Control in Visual Basic.*

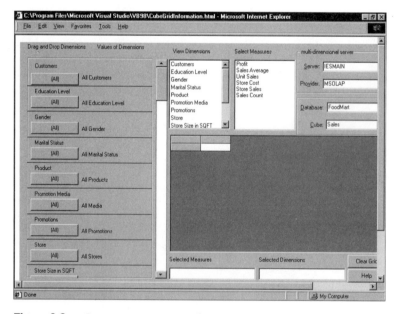

Figure 9-6. *Component upon initalization.*

Figure 9-7 shows the component when dimensions and measures have been selected and the grid is filled with data.

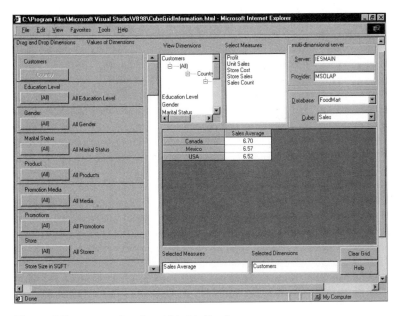

Figure 9-7. *Control with grid initialized.*

This control uses all three objects you created. Let's now look at the code for these components. The class diagram for this component looks like the one shown in Figure 9-8:

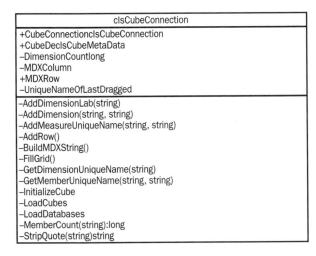

clsCubeConnection
+CubeConnectionclsCubeConnection
+CubeDeclsCubeMetaData
–DimensionCountlong
–MDXColumn
+MDXRow
–UniqueNameOfLastDragged
–AddDimensionLab(string)
–AddDimension(string, string)
–AddMeasureUniqueName(string, string)
–AddRow()
–BuildMDXString()
–FillGrid()
–GetDimensionUniqueName(string)
–GetMemberUniqueName(string, string)
–InitializeCube
–LoadCubes
–LoadDatabases
–MemberCount(string):long
–StripQuote(string)string

Figure 9-8. *prjCubeGrid Class diagram.*

A quick look at your class diagrams tells a great deal about the object. Managing classes is made up of mostly public methods; managed classes is mostly public properties. This class has a few public properties and numerous private methods. The reason there are no public methods is that this component has a user interface that passes information back and forth to the user. Thus, the equivalent of public methods in the control is the control-performing actions on the components of the user interface, such as filling a grid box. This control has two functions. The first function gets information on the database, such as the available dimensions and measures, and presents it to the user. The second function of this control allows users to manipulate this information to select the view of the data they want and get a dataset based on this data.

Presenting Data to the User

The first thing the control must do is initialize the component, which is done by the InitializeCube method once a database, server, and cube are selected. The component tries to find a default cube, server, and database and uses these to initialize the control. If the user needs another database or cube, a list of possible databases and cubes is placed in a listbox using the LoadDatabases and LoadCubes functions. These use the clsCubeConnection object methods to get this information.

Once the database, server, and cube are selected, InitializeCube is called. InitializeCube uses the CubeMetaData object to get information on the server. This information includes the names of the dimensions, which are placed in the treeview control as well as on a command button for each dimension, and the members of the hierarchies for each dimension. The method, AddDimensions, adds a command button for each dimension with the dimension name on the command button. AddDimensionLabel adds a label above each command button identifying the dimension with which the button is associated.

You have to keep track of two pieces of information. The user will be viewing names that are user-friendly, such as Country. For your internal usage, though, you need a unique name like [Customer].[Country]. You need to associate the names on the command buttons, in the treeview, and in the measures listbox with their unique names. To do this you create collections for measures and dimensions. These collections are filled using the two methods, AddMeasureUniqueName and AddDimensionUniqueName.

Returning a Dataset

Once users have all the information on what dimensions and measures are available, they must be able to get a dataset back based on the view of the data the user chooses. The private MDXColumn and MDXRow properties store the current values for the rows and columns part of the MDX query. The BuildMDXString assembles all the parts of the MDX statement, including the WHERE clause. The FillGrid method places the data into the grid.

Conclusion

You have now completed the review of these components. As you can see, using UML diagrams you were able to give an overview of the components without discussing how these components are to be coded. It is important that system administrators understand the design documents so that they can give input on any issues relating to the data warehouse.

For developers reading this book, and system administrators with some Visual Basic knowledge, there is an explanation of the code in Appendix C, and the code for the components designed in this chapter are on the CD under the directory Code\CubeExample. The appendix explains how the design in this chapter is actually implemented.

Chapter 10
Data Transformation Services

If the information in your data warehouse is not accurate, it is useless. You must carefully plan when you are moving data into the data warehouse. You must choose the sources of the data, create a standardized set of names for the fields, and reach a decision on a standard way to present the data with a consensus of those using and developing the data warehouse. Once you do this, it is time to actually build a system to move and transform the data according to your design.

In the previous chapters, you learned how to create a data warehouse from a centralized relational data store. For your example, the centralized data store was the Access database FoodMart.mdb. You can use either ROLAP or HOLAP to use this data store directly or you can use MOLAP and OLAP Manager to move data from FoodMart.mdb into a MOLAP data store.

The centralized relational data store normally gets data from one or more online transaction processing (OLTP) databases or from legacy data stores. Thus, prior to creating your data warehouse, you usually move your data from its original source into one centralized data store. This is shown in Figure 10-1.

You not only move this data, but you also cleanse and filter it so it fits the needs of your data warehouse. To do this, you use Data Transformation Services (DTS). In this chapter, you learn how DTS can fulfill your data transformation needs.

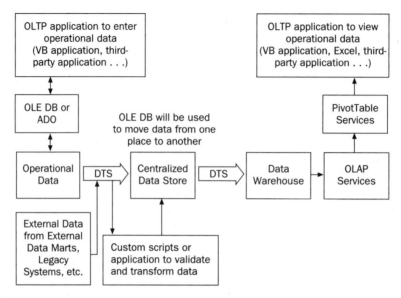

Figure 10-1. *Moving data into the Data Warehouse.*

Overview of DTS

DTS performs numerous functions to allow the movement of data from one data store to another. For simple movements, you can use the wizards to quickly import or export the data. When complicated transformations of the data are required, you need to write scripts of Visual Basic, Java, or scripting language code.

You use DTS both to move data from one data system to another and to scrub and alter the data. The term "data system" represents any possible source of data, such as a database, a text file, a Microsoft Exchange Server, and so forth, because DTS works with any OLE-DB compliant data source. When data is coming from a legacy system, it often needs some cleaning and altering to be usable in the data warehouse.

DTS Features

When it comes to importing and exporting data, the three primary features of DTS you are interested in are extraction, transformation, and loading. These three features give you the ability to move, cleanse, and alter data from one data system to another.

Extraction

Extraction allows you to identify the data elements in the source data system and view the source's metadata (data on the structure of the system). Using extraction, you can get information on the source data system and choose the data you need for transformation.

Transformation

Transformation is mapping data from the source system to the destination data system. Transformation may include altering the data. For example, three sources of data may represent male as "Male," "M," and "0." These may all be transformed into one value, such as "Male." Data may also be summarized and condensed, because the data warehouse does not need all the information in the OLTP system. Validating that the data is correct, and either discarding it or transforming it into a valid format, is part of transformation. Using scripts such as Visual Basic or JavaScript, you can perform these transformations. You can also create COM components, built from programming languages such as Visual Basic or C++, to do these transformations. COM components can be carefully designed, thoroughly debugged, and properly maintained.

For transformations based on simple calculations using data in the OLTP database, you can create views in the OLTP database. An example is the actual sales price being equal to sales price minus the discount.

Loading

Loading involves placing the final cleansed, altered data into the destination data system. DTS helps place the data into the correct data system and allows you to adjust exactly where the data will go in the system. DTS also provides a mapping of the data in the source to the data in the destination data systems.

Using DTS, you can create a data store in one centralized location in a standardized format. You can use this centralized data store as an intermediate database to cleanse and validate data. Data can flow into the centralized data store from sources all through the Enterprise. Once the data has been validated and cleansed, you can move it into the data warehouse.

OLE-DB architecture makes DTS possible. OLE DB provides access to any OLE-DB provider such as Microsoft SQL Server 7.0, Microsoft Access, Oracle 8, or Microsoft Excel, mainframe systems, and so on. OLE DB also works with open database connectivity (ODBC), which gives you access to any data store that does not have an OLE DB provider but does have an ODBC provider. DTS can also access ASCII text files. OLE DB essentially allows DTS to create a communication between virtually any data store.

Another feature you can use with DTS is SQL Server Agent. SQL Server Agent is a SQL Server service that allows you to schedule DTS movements of data. This can be very useful for automating a regularly occurring transformation. The movement of data into the data warehouse can be done during off-peak hours so that it doesn't affect the performance of the OLTP database or the OLAP data warehouse. Let's now look at the basic object of DTS: the DTS package.

DTS Packages

Packages are DTS objects that contain all the steps required to transform data from one data system to another. The package contains a set of tasks that are performed in the transformation. You can create, save, edit, delete, and execute DTS packages.

Packages can have security attached to them that limits who can run them. Packages can also be created to use transactions, thus making the steps in the package completely successful or completely unsuccessful. Packages use three types of objects: connection, task, and step. This is shown in Figure 10-2.

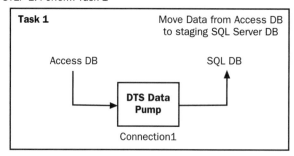

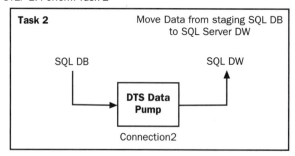

Figure 10-2. *Package objects.*

Connection Objects

A connection object provides the details on all the data stores involved in the transformation. A connection object for a database contains information on server names, user names, passwords, and the format of the data to be retrieved. A connection object for a file contains information on the file locations, file names, and the data format. Using OLE DB and the information in the connection object, DTS can make connections to the data systems and move data in and out of the data systems.

Task Objects

Task objects define a unit of work that is to be performed within the transformation. Thus, a task object can be moving the contents of a text file into a database table, running an ActiveX script, or running a stored procedure.

Step Objects

Step objects define the sequence in which the task objects are executed. Step objects not only determine the sequence of the task objects, but also determine whether one task object depends on the successful completion of another task object. If two steps do not depend on each other, they can be run in a parallel.

Let's now look at how this works using the DTS Import/Export wizards.

Importing and Exporting with DTS

The DTS Import/Export wizards provide an interface to import and export data from one data source to another. The import wizard allows you to create a new target table, or add rows onto an existing table. You can map columns from the source to the destination. You can also adjust data types in the columns, because data types may be different from one data source to another data source. DTS allows you to make these adjustments if necessary.

Exporting Files Using DTS

To do this, use the FoodMartOLTP.mdb Access database included on the CD. You can either move it off the CD into a directory on your computer or use it directly from the CD.

The Source and Destination Data Systems

The FoodMartOLTP database schema is shown in Figure 10-3.

Looking at this schema, you see that Order Details and Orders tables are included. If you look at the original FoodMart Access database, you see that the data for December 1998 is not included in the Sales_Fact_1998 (there is a separate table for December 1998 sales in FoodMart, but that data is not used here). The Orders and Order Details tables in FoodMartOLTP contain the data for December 1998 for FoodMart.

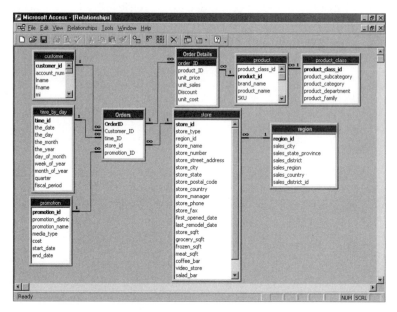

Figure 10-3. *FoodMartOLTP Schema.*

Your job is to move the data for December sales from the FoodMartOLTP database to the FoodMart data warehouse using DTS. Once you move the data into the FoodMart data warehouse, you update the data into a MOLAP data store using DTS with this new information. This allows you to demonstrate both the regular movement of data between relational databases and the updating of data.

Figure 10-4 shows the structure of the fact table for Sales_Fact_1998.

Figure 10-4. *Sales_Fact_1998 table.*

You can find all the information you require for the fact table in the Orders and Order Details tables in the FoodMartOLTP database. This keeps the sample very simple. To make things even easier, there is a query called SalesByLineItem in FoodMartOLTP that gives you all the information for each line item. This query acts as a view, giving you the information you need for your fact table. The query has a calculated field called ActualPrice that takes the sale price of each item and multiplies it by the discount. This is the actual price the customer paid.

Also assumed is that there are no new customers in the database, no customers have changed their information, and that essentially the only thing that has changed is that you have more orders. In the real world, none of these assumptions hold. You will look at all these other issues later. For now, let's focus on just moving data from one relational database to another.

Using the DTS Export Wizard

The DTS Import/Export wizard is not part of the OLAP management console. It is part of the regular SQL Server 7.0 management console. Go to the Start menu and select Program, then Microsoft SQL Server 7.0, and finally Enterprise Manager, as shown in Figure 10-5.

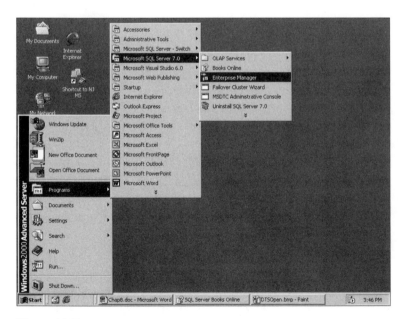

Figure 10-5. *Enterprise Manager.*

This opens the SQL Server Enterprise Manager. Drill down on the left window until you select a database. Go to Tools in the menu and select Data Transformation Services, as shown in Figure 10-6.

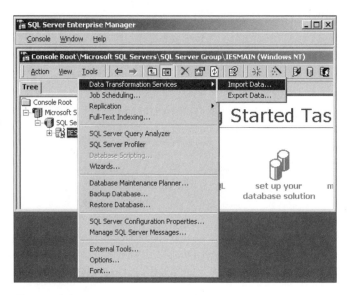

Figure 10-6. *Opening Data Transformation Services.*

Let's begin by looking at importing files. Select Import Data. This brings up the DTS splash screen as shown in Figure 10-7. You can also add the SQL Server snap-in to your OLAP Manager and use one instance of MMC.

Figure 10-7. *DTS Splash Screen.*

Click Next. This brings you to the main DTS import window. If you click the source drop-down list box, you see the wide range of choices from where you can import and export data. This is shown in Figure 10-8.

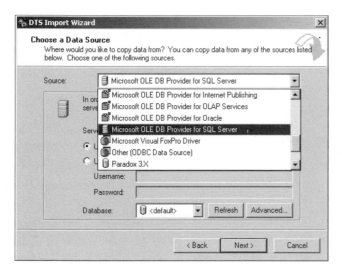

Figure 10-8.   *Source choices.*

In the source drop-down list box, choose Microsoft Access. For Filename, click the button with the ellipsis and select the FoodMartOLTP database, as shown in Figure 10-9.

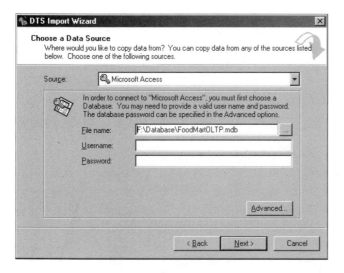

Figure 10-9.   *Selecting FoodMartOLTP as the data source.*

Once you have selected the FoodMartOLTP database, click Next. This brings up the Choose a Destination screen. Your destination is the FoodMart.mdb database. Once again, select Microsoft Access for the Destination. Select FoodMart.mdb for the File Name as shown in Figure 10-10.

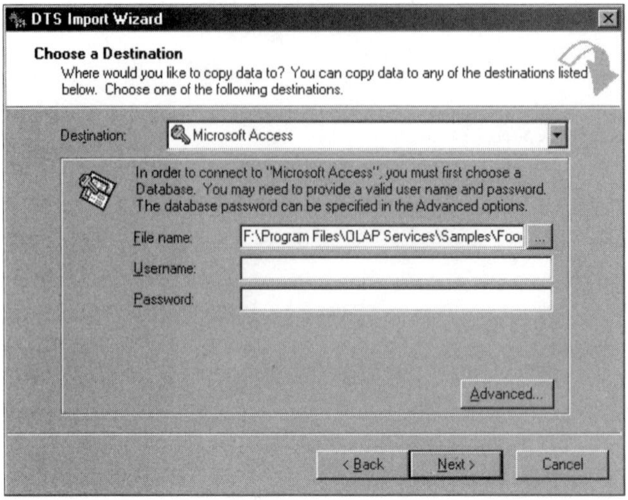

Figure 10-10. *Selecting FoodMart as the data destination.*

Once you have selected FoodMart as your destination, click Next. The next screen allows you to make a choice between moving data from one table in the source to one table in the destination, or using queries to choose what your source and destination data is. Because you are using a view (an Access Query) from FoodMartOLTP, and views are not listed in the DTS list of tables, you must use a query. Click Use A Query To Specify The Data To Transfer, as shown in Figure 10-11. Once you choose Use Query, click Next. This brings you to the Type SQL statement screen, as shown in Figure 10-12.

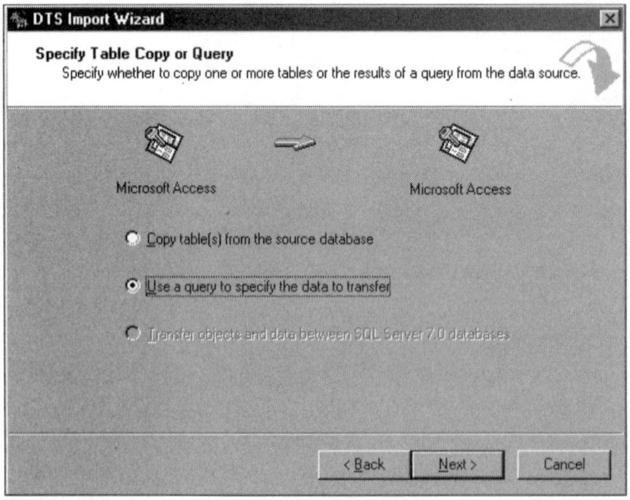

Figure 10-11. *Choosing to use a query.*

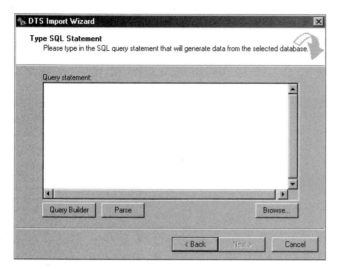

Figure 10-12. *Type SQL statement screen.*

You use this SQL Statement to retrieve data from the source database. You can use the query builder if you are working with tables in the database. Since you are working with a view, you enter the query yourself. Type the following query in the window:

```
Select * From SalesByLineItem
```

This is shown in Figure 10-13.

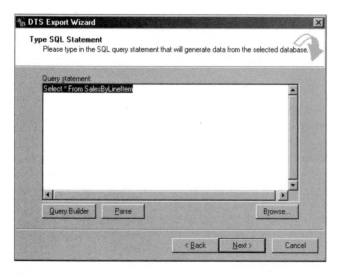

Figure 10-13. *Query entering.*

Click Next. This brings you to the Select Source Tables screen. You need to build the mapping of the fields in your source table to the fields in your destination table. First, you must choose your destination table. In the destination table column, click the drop-down list box and select sales_fact_1998, as shown in Figure 10-14.

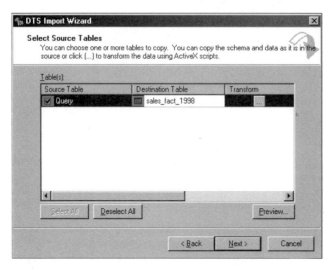

Figure 10-14. *A query as the source table.*

You still need to map the fields from the source to the destination. To do this, click the button with the ellipsis in the Transform column. This brings up the Column Mappings and Transformations screen. Figure 10-15 shows the results of DTS mappings.

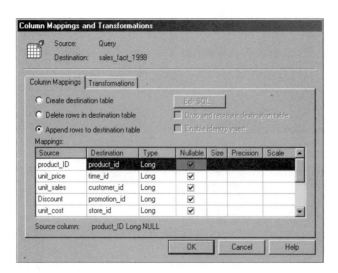

Figure 10-15. *DTS column mapping.*

You need to change this mapping. Go to the source column and click unit_price; you should see a drop-down list box as shown in Figure 10-16.

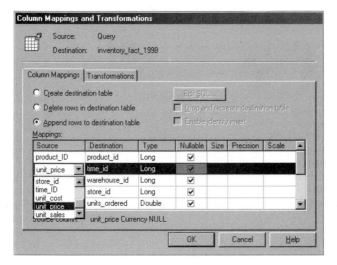

Figure 10-16.   *Drop-down list box of fields.*

The fields should have the mappings shown in Table 10-1.

Table 10-1. Drop-down Field Mappings

Source	Destination
product_ID	product_id
time_ID	time_id
Customer_ID	customer_id
promotion_ID	promotion_ID
store_id	store_id
ActualPrice	store_sales
unit_sales	unit_sales

If you click the Transformations tab and click Transform Information as it is copied to the destination, you can look at the VB Script used to make this package. In your case, the script is as follows:

```
************************************************************************
  Visual Basic Transformation Script
  Copy each source column to the
  destination column
************************************************************************
```

```
Function Main()
    DTSDestination("product_id") = DTSSource("product_ID")
    DTSDestination("time_id") = DTSSource("time_ID")
    DTSDestination("customer_id") = DTSSource("Customer_ID")
    DTSDestination("promotion_id") = DTSSource("promotion_ID")
    DTSDestination("store_id") = DTSSource("store_id")
    DTSDestination("store_sales") = DTSSource("Actual Price")
    DTSDestination("store_cost") = DTSSource("unit_cost")
    DTSDestination("unit_sales") = DTSSource("unit_sales")
Main = DTSTransformStat_OK
End Function
```

This is where you add custom transformations into your package. You do not need any custom transformations for this particular package.

If you clicked Transform Information as it is copied to the destination, click back to the default. Copy the source columns directly to the destination columns because you are not modifying the script. Click OK on the Columns and Mappings window. This returns you to the Select Source window. Click Next. This brings you to the Save, Schedule and Replicate package screen. You want to both run the transformation and save it. On the bottom of the form, select Save DTS Package and select SQL Server as the place to save the DTS package, as shown in Figure 10-17.

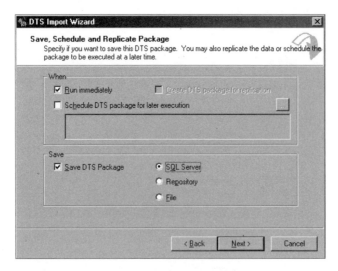

Figure 10-17. *Saving and running package.*

Click Next. The next screen you see allows you to save the package. Call the package FoodMartOLTPtoFoodMart, as shown in Figure 10-18. Click Use Windows NT authentication. Select the server.

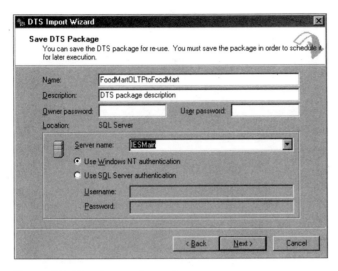

Figure 10-18.   *Saving the package.*

Click Next and the transfer is processed. You are moving more than 70,000 records (FoodMart had the best month ever in December 1998). Remember this when you see how quickly the records are moved!

Viewing the Package

You can look at the package you created and saved in SQL Server. Expand the tree for the database you saved the package to. You see a folder called Data Transformation Services. Expand this folder. You should see the FoodMartOLTPtoFoodMart package you just created, as shown in Figure 10-19.

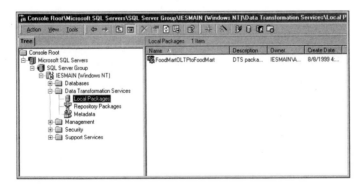

Figure 10-19.   *DTS folder package.*

The Package Designer

Double-click the FoodMartOLTPtoFoodMart package. This opens the DTS designer. The DTS Designer allows you to build or edit packages. The package you created is shown in Figure 10-20.

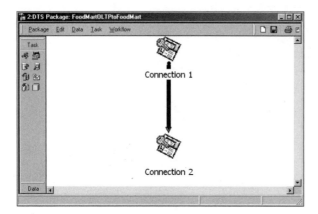

Figure 10-20.   *FoodMartOLTPtoFoodMart package.*

You are actually looking at two connections and one task object. In the DTS designer, a task object is called a Transform Data Task. The Transform Data Task is an instance of a DTS data pump. The DTS data pump is a DTS object that uses OLE DB to import, export, and transform data.

The task object is the line connecting the two connection objects. You can double-click the line to bring up the Data Transformations Properties window. If you look at the tabs, you see many of the transformation properties that we just set. Select the Transformations tab. Figure 10-21 shows the tab.

By clicking a column on the left, clicking a column on the right, and then clicking New, you can define a mapping between two columns. Thus, you could have built this package with the package designer. View the other tabs and then close the Data Transformations Properties windows. Double-click one of the connections and see the properties of the connection. You use the package manager to make connections in the next section. Close the package designer.

This is all there is to moving data from one non-OLAP data source to another. Let's now look at moving data from a relational database to a MOLAP data store.

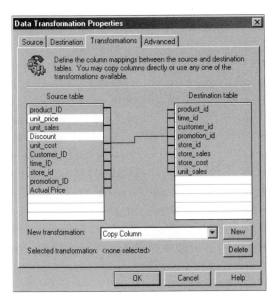

Figure 10-21.   *Transformations Tab (TTab).*

Moving Data into a MOLAP Cube

If you are using FoodMart.mdb as either a ROLAP or HOLAP cube, you are done with building aggregations. You still have to recalculate aggregations, however, because there is new data. If you are using a MOLAP cube, though, you now have to move the data from FoodMart.mdb into the MOLAP cube. Because you do not want to do this manually, use DTS to make this transformation. Once a DTS package is created, you can automate the process of moving data using SQL Server 7.0 Agents.

Before you can use DTS to move data into a MOLAP store, you need to install the DTS tasks. The DTS tasks is an add-on to DTS that gives DTS the capability of working with an OLAP data system. You find DTStasks.exe on the CD. You need to run this to install the OLAP DTS capabilities. Once you install DTS tasks, you can use DTS to work with OLAP.

You want your Sales cube in your FoodMart data warehouse to be set to MOLAP. You also want to make sure you have the Sales 1998 partition.

Note   If you do not have the Enterprise edition, you can use the FoodMart.mdb file located on the CD under the directory FoodMart for Standard Edition. Instead of moving files into the Sales 1998 partition, move them into the Sales partition.

Open OLAP Manager and check that you have done this, as shown in Figure 10-22.

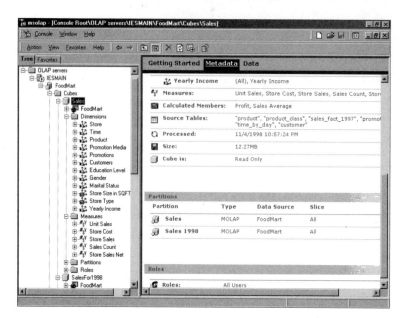

Figure 10-22. *OLAP Manager.*

If you do not have the partition set as MOLAP, change it to MOLAP now. If the Sales 1998 partition has not been created, create it now.

Running DTS OLAP Tasks

In the SQL Server 7.0 Enterprise Manager, right-click Data Transformation Services and select New Package. This opens the package manager. You see a yellow cube on the left. This is the OLAP Services Processing Task, as shown in Figure 10-23.

Click the yellow cube to open the OLAP task manager, and expand the tree, as shown in Figure 10-24.

What you are looking at is all the dimensions in the data warehouse and all the cubes. If the cubes have partitions, such as Sales, these partitions are also listed. You can schedule processing, refreshing, and incremental updating of the different components of the data warehouse. The OLAP Services Processing Task shows you dimensions, cubes, and partitions. Using DTS, you are able to perform a specific set of functions on each of these.

Figure 10-23. *OLAP Services Processing task.*

Figure 10-24. *OLAP Services Processing task.*

Table 10-2 shows what you can do with each of the components of the data warehouse.

Table 10-2. OLAP Services Processing Task Functions

Object or Folder	Option	Description
Database	Process	This processes every cube, partition, virtual cube, and dimension in the database.
Cubes folder	Process	This processes all cubes and virtual cubes in the folder.
Single partition cube	Process	This processes the cube. If there are structural changes, these are processed. This is the most thorough form of cube processing.
Single partition cube	Refresh Data	This reloads the data for the cube and recalculates all aggregations. Only existing data is reloaded or has aggregations calculated. New data is not added using Refresh. This also does not process structural changes to the data warehouse.
Single partition cube	Incremental Update	You use this to add new data to the cube and update aggregations and data. Incremental Update does not process structural changes and does not affect data already in the cube.
Multiple partition cube	Process	This completely processes the cube and recalculates aggregations, including any structural changes.
Multiple partition cube	Refresh Data	This reloads any existing data in the cube and recalculates aggregations. This does not add new data or add new structural changes.
Multiple partition cube - partition	Process	This reloads the data in the partition and recalculates the aggregations associated with the partition.
Multiple partition cube - partition	Incremental Update	This is used to add new data to the partition. This does not have any effect on the parent cube's structure and does not affect data already in the cube.
Virtual cube	Process	This performs a complete processing of the cube.
Dimensions folder	Process	This processes all the dimensions in the data warehouse.
Shared dimension	Rebuild the dimension structure	This completely processes the dimension, including any structural changes made to the dimension.
Shared dimension	Incremental Update	This allows you to add rows to the dimension (that is, new members). This does not process any changes to the structure of the dimension.
Virtual dimension	Rebuild the dimension structure	This completely processes the virtual dimension.

In the first part of the chapter, you moved the data into a central location, that is, into FoodMart.mdb. Because your Sales 1998 partition already is associated with

FoodMart.mdb, you need only to process the Sales 1998 partition to bring the new data into the MOLAP cube.

Change the description to Update Sales 1998. Click Sales 1998 and click Process, as shown in Figure 10-25.

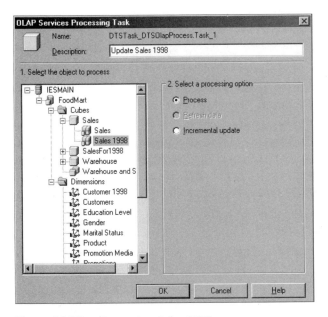

Figure 10-25.   *Processing Sales 1998.*

Click OK. You see that the cube has been added to the package wizard. Click the green arrow to execute the query, as shown in Figure 10-26.

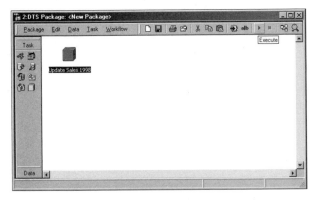

Figure 10-26.   *Executing the package.*

Best Practice When you choose to process a cube you will need to take the cube offline. If this is not acceptable you will need to do an incremental update, which can be done without taking the cube offline.

When this is completed, you get a message saying that the execution has been completed successfully, as shown in Figure 10-27.

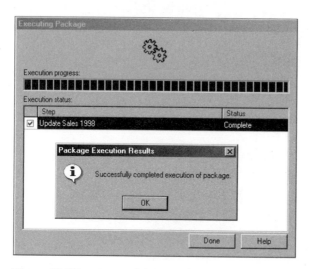

Figure 10-27. *Successful completion.*

Click Done. Go to OLAP Manager and check that the data for December is actually there.

Saving Packages

You can save packages in three places: the repository, a file, and the SQL Server database. Let's look at these three options.

You should still have the DTS designer open. Go to the menu and select Package/Save As. You begin by saving into the SQL Server database. Select SQL Server for the Location and call the package Update Sales 1998, as shown in Figure 10-28.

When a file is saved into SQL Server, it is saved in BLOB format into the SQL Server database file with an msdb extension.

Once again, select Package/Save As. This time select File for Location, and Update Sales 1998f.dts for file name and Update Sales 1998f as the Package Name, as shown in Figure 10-29.

You can easily move a file from database to database or distribute it to other people. You can also add additional package objects to the files without rewriting the files.

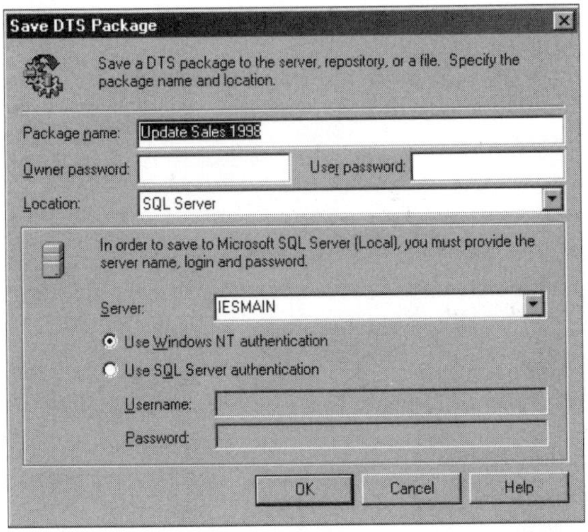

Figure 10-28.   *Saving packages to SQL Server database.*

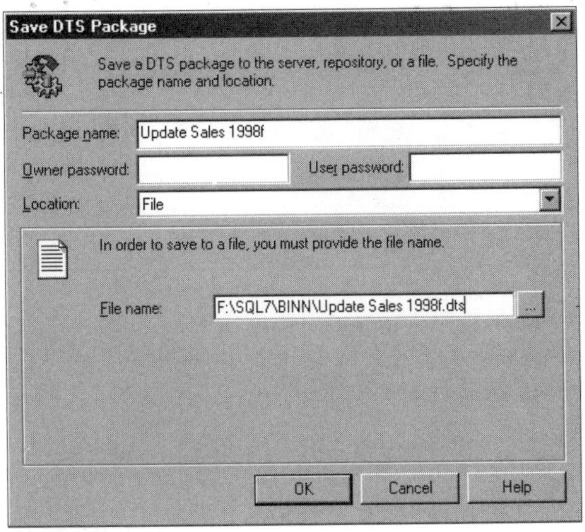

Figure 10-29.   *Saving packages to file.*

Finally, you can save package objects to the repository. Select Package/Save As again. Now, select SQL Server Repository for Location and Update Sales 1998r for the Package name, as shown in Figure 10-30.

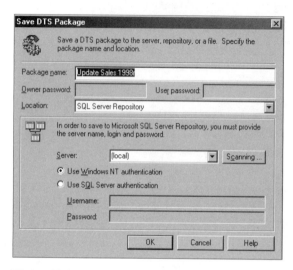

Figure 10-30.   *Saving packages to repository.*

Files stored in the SQL server repository are also stored in an msdb database. Other applications that can read the repository can access the transformations, queries, or scripts you store in the repository. You can also maintain data lineage when you save to the repository. Data lineage allows you to create an audit trail when information is added to the data warehouse. If you close the package designer and click Repository Packages in Enterprise Manager, you see the package added to the repository.

Scheduling Packages

One of the useful features of packages is that they can be scheduled to run at a particular time. This allows you to automate the process of running packages. Go to Enterprise Manager and click Local Packages. Right-click FoodMartOLTPtoFoodMart package and select Schedule. The Edit Recurring Job Schedule form comes up, as shown in Figure 10-31.

You can set the options on this form to schedule your job at an appropriate time. You should do scheduling with planning. You want to make sure your packages do not interfere with other scheduled jobs or the performance of the OLTP system.

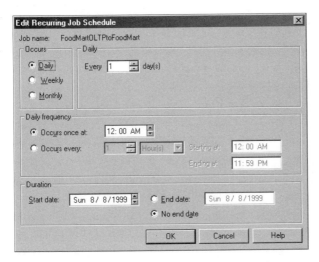

Figure 10-31.   *Edit Recurring Job Schedule window.*

Package Versions

For every package that you create, there are two versions, a package ID and version ID. The package ID is generated when the package is first created. The version ID is generated first when the package is created, and then a new value is generated every time the package is updated or saved.

Go to Enterprise Manager and click Local Packages. After doing this, right-click the FoodMartOLTPtoFoodMart package and select Versions. This brings up the DTS Package Versions, as shown in Figure 10-32.

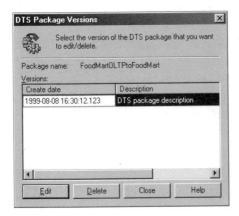

Figure 10-32.   *DTS Package version.*

You can delete versions or edit any version of your package. If you close the versions window, double-click the FoodMartOLTPtoFoodMart package to open it, and save the package again, you see that another version has been added, as shown in Figure 10-33.

Figure 10-33. *DTS Package new version.*

In this way you can have version control over your packages as you update and change them.

General Properties

There are many general properties associated with a package. Once again double-click the FoodMartOLTPtoFoodMart package. Go to the menu and select Package/Properties (make sure none of the objects is selected). The general tab is shown in Figure 10-34.

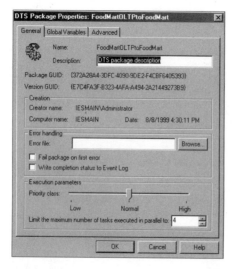

Figure 10-34. *General tab of package properties.*

On this tab you can see the globally unique identifier (GUID) for the package and version, add a description, and change the number of tasks that can be performed in parallel. You can also set the priority for this package.

If you click the advanced tab, you see the options as listed in Figure 10-35.

Figure 10-35.   *Advanced tab of package properties.*

Using the advanced tab, you can turn lineage on for your package, set your package to work with transactions, and determine the transaction isolation level. You can now close the properties window.

Issues with Updating a Data Warehouse

Before you begin to put sales data into the data warehouse, you need to update all the dimensions. If you are simply adding new data into the data warehouse, you can use the techniques outlined here to add data to dimensions.

You can put an entire set of tasks that must be performed regularly into a package. Thus, you could arrange to have the data from the OLTP database moved into the data warehouse once a month. Using tasks, you can update all the dimensions and then the fact table. Finally, you can update the data warehouse. The package designer allows you to easily do this.

There is the possibility that sometimes you will have dimensions that will change over time. These dimensions are called slowly changing. An example of this would be a customer whose name, address, and marital status may all change. How to handle this subject is beyond the scope of this book—however, the CD has a white paper on slowly changing dimensions (Slowlychanging.doc).

Realistically, though, updating your data warehouse can become of the most complex and difficult element of building your data warehouse. Ideally, you will want to automate the entire update process. No matter how you update the data warehouse, you will find yourself facing many issues and problems.

The fields you will need to properly update the data warehouse may not exist within the OLTP database. Often, the OLTP database's structure cannot be changed, making this a difficult problem to solve. Perhaps one of the most difficult problems to deal with is not duplicating data in the data warehouse. There is nothing built into OLAP Server that would prevent you from putting the identical data into the data warehouse multiple times. You also have to make your updates follow the correct pattern. Updating the fact table first with order information and then updating the customer dimension could result in errors. The errors would occur because new customer orders being added to the fact table will not have the new customer in the dimension yet. Thus, order of the updates is another important factor that must be considered when updating the data warehouse.

Though there are many solutions to these various problems, there is no single right answer. The correct solution depends on available resources, current configurations, the possibility of changing the OLTP database, and so on. Finding the right solution requires research and very careful planning. The choices you will make for updating the database can mold and shape the structure of your data warehouse. If you fail to plan and design your methods of updating the data warehouse when you are beginning the project, you may find yourself redesigning it once you have begun building it.

Here are some of many possible solutions: Using staging data warehouses and DTS you can bring data in from an OLTP database and transform it into the appropriate format. Using date and time information you can find what records have changed since the last update of the data warehouse. If the OLTP database does not have a field that includes date/time information, and one cannot be added, another table can be added with this information. This table can be updated with triggers or whatever method works best. Whatever the solutions you decide upon, they should be found during the initial planning of the data warehouse.

Conclusion

You can use DTS to create packages that can be used to move and transform data from the OLTP database to the OLAP data warehouse. These packages can be scheduled to run at the best time. Packages can have Visual Basic script added to them to perform transformations.

Using DTS, you can pull data from many sources and create a uniform set of data for the data warehouse. This data can be cleansed, validated, and put into a standard format for use by the data warehouse. The success of the transformation depends on sufficient planning. Who has access to different packages, when the packages will be run, and what transformations will need to be performed are all questions that must be carefully thought out and planned.

Chapter 11
PivotTable Services

PivotTable Services provides a connection between the OLAP server and all external applications that need to communicate with the OLAP server. Whether you are using Microsoft Excel, third-party software, or a Visual Basic or C++ application, you use PivotTable Services to communicate to the OLAP server.

In this chapter, you look at PivotTable Services and how to use it to build applications and client-side cubes. As you will see, you have already been building applications using one part of the PivotTable Services. Let's now look at how PivotTable Services works.

Overview of PivotTable Services

The relationship between PivotTable Services and the other components of a complete enterprise data warehouse solution is shown in Figure 11-1.

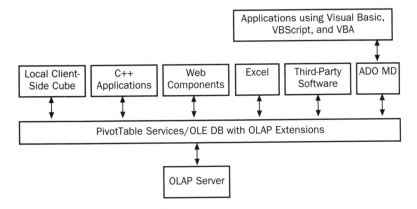

Figure 11-1. *PivotTable Services.*

PivotTable Services usually runs on the client (user's) computer and provides access to the data in the OLAP server. You can see that ADO MD is just a wrapper for PivotTable Services. C++ applications can access PivotTable Services directly. Figure 11-2 shows what you were doing when you created a wrapper object for ADO MD.

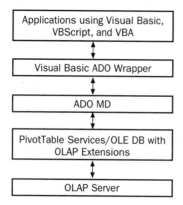

Figure 11-2. *Visual Basic ADO MD Wrapper.*

You can see that you created a wrapper class on ADO MD and that ADO MD is also a wrapper class on PivotTable Services. It is quite likely that you do not lose any efficiency by doing this, but it is a less complicated solution to create a C++ application, as shown in Figure 11-3.

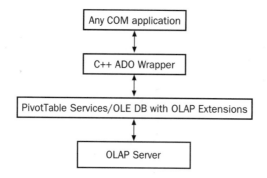

Figure 11-3. *C++ ADO MD Wrapper.*

You might find it interesting that the design you created works with either C++ or Visual Basic. Use case, sequence diagrams, and class diagrams only specify what components are needed in the system and what services they must perform. How you actually make these components is completely up to you. Thus, you can take the same design used to build a Visual Basic ADO MD wrapper and use it to build a C++ PivotTable Services wrapper. This is one of the major advantages of using the Microsoft Solution Framework (MSF) concept of designing components based on the services they perform.

As Figure 11-1 shows, there are many other components that can work through PivotTable Services. The Web components are an add-on that allows you to present data through the Internet in spreadsheet and chart format. Later in this chapter, you will learn about Excel, Web components, and client-side cubes. Just like ADO MD, all of these work using PivotTable Services.

PivotTable Services does more than just provide you with connectivity to the OLAP data store. PivotTable Services also allows you to create a cache of both data and the metadata of your queries, allowing you to work with the same set of data more efficiently. Let's look at this in more detail.

PivotTable Services Client Server Cache

If data is cached on the client (user's) computer, queries can be performed on the data without making another trip to the server. This can make a client application run much faster. Both the data and the metadata from the query are stored on the client computer.

If the data has been cached on the client computer, PivotTable Services can perform aggregations and filtering on the cached data. PivotTable Services can also combine the cached data with data in the data warehouse.

Imagine that data was retrieved for sales by customer state for 1997. When PivotTable Services retrieves this data, it is cached. If the user next wants to view sales by customer country for 1997, PivotTable Services performs an aggregation on the cached data. If the user then wants to view sales for customers in Canada, PivotTable Services allows the cached data to be filtered. If the user then wants to view sales for 1997 and 1998 for customers in Canada, PivotTable Services retrieves the 1998 data and combines it with the cached 1997 data.

The PivotTable Services can do this because it caches the data, the metadata (the structure of the data), and query definitions on the client side. The PivotTable Services contains similar calculation engines as OLAP Server except it takes up much less memory. This allows the Pivot Services to perform such functions as aggregations on the data that is cached on the client side.

The PivotTable Services has what is called intelligent client/server architecture. It is intelligent because the PivotTable Services, using the metadata, can determine what is the most efficient way of getting data, that is, using the cached data, performing aggregations on the cached date, retrieving data from the server, and so on. Thus, if data for 1997 has been accessed and cached, when the next query is made for 1997 and 1998, PivotTables Services will check the metadata, use the cached 1997 data, and retrieve the 1998 data from the server.

You can see that there are many situations in which PivotTable Services uses the cached data to eliminate the delay caused by retrieving data from the OLAP server. When the cached data is used, the response time is very fast. The PivotTable Services provides a robust client solution for many data warehouse systems. Because of the intelligent client/server architecture of the PivotTable Services, the retrieval and analysis of data warehouse information can be done very efficiently using the PivotTable Services.

Note You have already learned about ADO MD, so it is not covered in this chapter.

Excel 9, part of Microsoft Office 2000, uses PivotTable Services. You can use Excel 9 to demonstrate many of the features of PivotTable Services using wizards instead of code. Let's now take a look at the various options available in Excel 9.

Excel 9 and PivotTable Services

Excel 9 allows you to create client-side cubes from a relational database such as FoodMart.mdb or to directly access a data warehouse, such as the FoodMart data warehouse stored in Microsoft SQL Server 7.0. There is a difference between these two options. If you are creating cubes on the client machine using the relational database, you are working with the star schema and using informational tables and fact tables. When you use the data warehouse, you are working with dimensions and measures. Let's look at this in more detail.

Client-Side Cubes

PivotTable Services can create a client-side data cube and load data into the cube from any tabular data store, such as a relational database. Client-side cubes store data either in a multidimensional OLAP (MOLAP) format or in a relational OLAP (ROLAP) format. In either format, the cube data is stored in a .cub file. If a ROLAP cube is chosen, only the metadata is stored in the .cub file. All data must be retrieved from the database for a ROLAP cube. If a MOLAP cube is chosen, the data is stored on the client machine in the .cub file.

Open Excel. In the menu, select Data/Get External Data/New Database Query. This opens the Choose Data Source window. Select FoodMart, as shown in Figure 11-4.

Note If you do not have FoodMart listed, click <New Data Source>, name the data source FoodMart, select Microsoft Access Driver, click Connect, and select the FoodMart.mdb database.

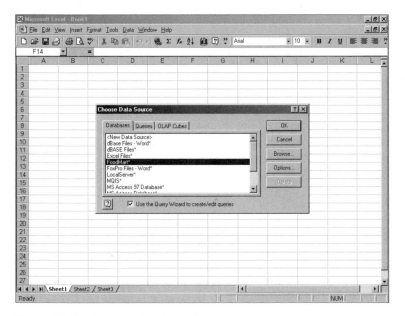

Figure 11-4. *Selecting FoodMart data source.*

Adding Measures to the Cube

Clicking FoodMart and selecting OK brings you to the Choose Columns screen, as shown in Figure 11-5.

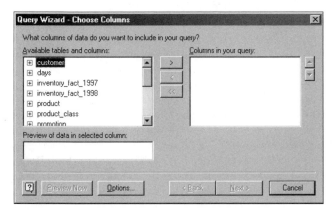

Figure 11-5. *Choose Columns screen.*

Looking at this screen, you see that this is similar to the Cube Wizard in OLAP Manager. The data you are looking at in the Choose Columns screen is the informational and fact tables in your relational database. You must now build cubes with measures and dimensions from these informational and fact tables. The Choose Columns screen allows you to select the fields you want to use to build your dimensions and measures.

Building the Customers Dimension

You begin by selecting the customer information you need for the Customers dimension. Click the plus sign next to customer to expand customer. Click customer_id and click RIGHT ARROW to move it into the Columns In Your Query list box. Move city, state_ province, postal_code, and country over to the Columns In Your Query list box, as shown in Figure 11-6.

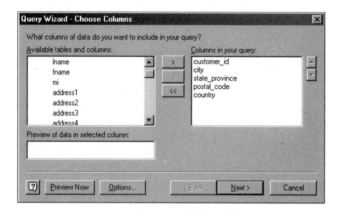

Figure 11-6. *Selecting customer fields.*

The Query wizard differentiates between measures and dimensions. Without expanding Sales Fact 1997, move Sales Fact 1997 over to the Columns In Your Query list box. This moves all the fields in Sales Fact 1997 into the list box.

Click time_by_day and click RIGHT ARROW to move all the time_by_day fields over to the Columns In Your Query list box. Expand Store and move store_id, store_city, store_state, store_postal_code, and store_country over to the Columns In Your Query list box.

Expand Product and select product_name, product_class_id, and product_id. You do not need to expand Product_Class; just click it and move it to move all the fields in Product_Class.

Click Next. This brings up the Filter Data screen. You are not filtering data, so click Next. The Sort Order screen comes up. You are not sorting either, so click Next. This brings you to the Finish screen. Select Create An OLAP Cube From This Query, as shown in Figure 11-7.

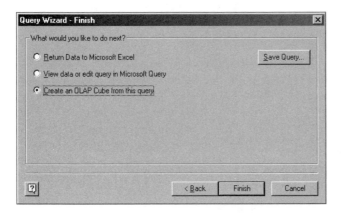

Figure 11-7. *Choosing to save the query as an OLAP cube on the user's computer.*

Click Save Query to save the query. Accept the Query from FoodMart.dqy name and click Save to save the query. On the Final screen click Finish. This brings you to the Welcome To The OLAP Cube Wizard, as shown in Figure 11-8.

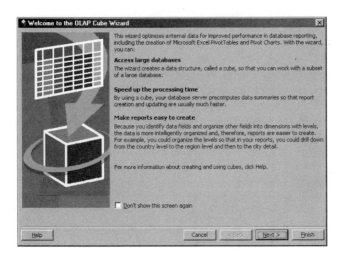

Figure 11-8. *Welcome to the OLAP Cube Wizard.*

Click Next. You find yourself at Step 1 of the Cube Wizard. This step is essentially allowing you to choose measures. Deselect everything except store_sales, unit_sales, and store_cost, as shown in Figure 11-9. These are your three measures.

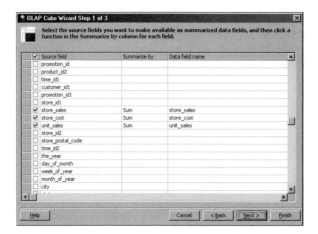

Figure 11-9. *Step 1 of the Cube Wizard.*

Click Next. This section allows you to build dimensions. Begin by creating Customers dimension. To do this, drag country to (Drop Fields Here To Create A Dimension) in the Dimensions list box. A new dimension is created. The default name is the name of the first member of the dimension, country in this case. Right-click the name of the dimension and select Rename from the drop-down list. Rename the dimension Customers, as shown in Figure 11-10.

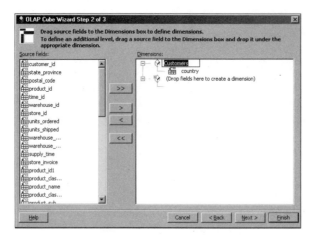

Figure 11-10. *Creating Customers dimension.*

Now drag state_province in the same way, but drop it onto country. This places it below country. Drag city and drop it onto state_province. Drag customer_id and drop it onto city. Your Customers dimension should be the same as shown in Figure 11-11.

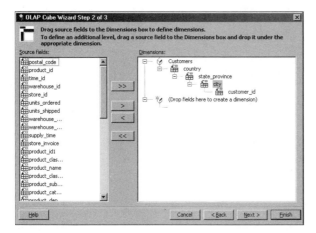

Figure 11-11.   *Completed Customers dimension.*

Caution   You can begin to see how a bad naming convention in the database can make it impossible to use the data. If both the customer informational table and the store informational table used names such as country and state_province, you would end up with country, country1, state_province, and state_province1 in the Cube Builder. There would be no way to be certain which one belongs to customer and which one belongs to store. It is important to make sure that all the names are unique.

Building the Product Dimension

You build your Product dimension in the same way you built the Customers dimension. Drag product_family and drop it onto (Drop Fields Here To Create A Dimension). Rename the dimension Product. Drag product_department onto product_family. Drag product_category onto product_department. Drag product_subcategory onto product_category. Drag product_id onto product_subcategory. If you also have a product_id1, only use product_id. Your Product dimension should look like the one in Figure 11-12.

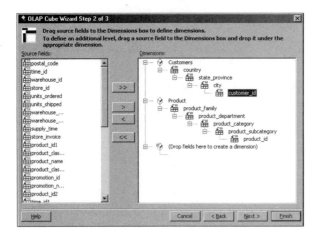

Figure 11-12. *Product dimension.*

Building the Time, Promotion, and Store Dimensions

You build the Store dimension the same way you built the other dimensions. Begin by dragging store_country over to (Drop Fields Here To Create A Dimension). Rename the dimension Store. Drag store_state onto store_country. Drag store_city onto store_state. Drag store_id onto store_city.

With the current name convention, you are really at a loss when figuring out a good Time dimension without looking at the data. Fortunately, you can go into OLAP Manager and see what choices were made in the FoodMart database using the Cube editor. You want the_year, quarter, and month_of_year for your time hierarchy. The FoodMart.mdb database's current naming convention does not make this obvious.

Drag the_year onto (Drop Fields Here To Create A Dimension). Drag quarter onto the_year. Drag month_of_year onto quarter. Name the dimension Time.

Finally, drag promotion_name (or promotion_id) onto (Drop Fields Here To Create A Dimension). Rename the dimension Promotion. The Cube Wizard should look like the one in Figure 11-13.

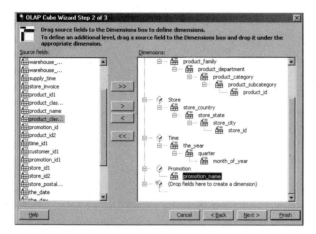

Figure 11-13. *Store, Time, and Promotion dimensions.*

You now have numerous extra fields that you are not using. (You needed the ID fields to build the joins. A few of the other fields were included for demonstration purposes.) You could have not chosen these extra fields when making the query, but their inclusion has no effect on your final cube, so you can ignore them.

Click Next. This takes you to Step 3 of the Cube Wizard.

Real World In a real production environment, you carefully plan the fields you want to use, and only include the needed fields.

Options for Saving a Cube

As you can see, you now have three possible options for saving your cube. The first two options are ROLAP solutions, which rebuild the cube every time a report is opened.

The first option only brings in data if it is needed. The second option brings all the data in when the report (Excel spreadsheet) is first opened. The data is not actually being brought in, however, because this is a ROLAP solution. What this really means is that using the second option results in all the data being cached by PivotTable

Services when the report is open. This creates an initial delay, but speeds up processing time. The first option means that data is cached on the client (user's) computer only as it is viewed.

The first and second options are what you should use when building an application that will give the user the most current data in the data warehouse. You can build your data warehouse with a Time dimension that extends for a year into the future. Data for dates in the future has no data. You can then design your client-side cube to include these future dates in the Time dimension, as well as all other dimensions of interest, such as sales and customers. An Excel spreadsheet can be built from this cube and the user can use the spreadsheet to view the latest data in the data warehouse. Thus, the first two ROLAP options allow you to build a dynamic application that can reflect the latest and most current data in the data warehouse. You will build this type of client-side cube. Because the cubes we will use will contain a large amount of data, let's choose the first option, that is, placing the data in the client-side cache only when you have viewed it.

The third option is to place the data into a MOLAP cube. This creates a static snap-shot of the data. Because older data should not change, you can use this option to create a cube with data from a particular month or week. This cube can then be used offline to analyze the data. This creates a very powerful method to allow a user to get the data online, disconnect from the data warehouse, and then work offline.

Click the first option, as shown in Figure 11-14.

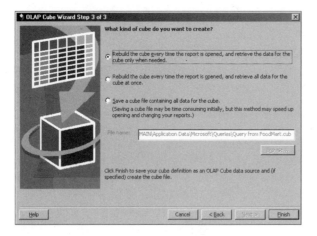

Figure 11-14. *Choosing the first option.*

You have the option to save the cube; click Finish to save your cube definition as an OLAP data source. You should find yourself back in Excel being asked where you want to place the PivotTable, as shown in Figure 11-15.

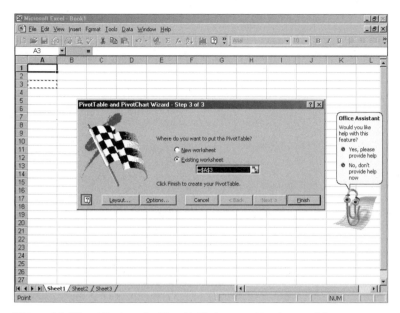

Figure 11-15.   *Placing the PivotTable into an Excel spreadsheet.*

Accept the default and click Finish. You end up with a grid-like PivotTable to display the data and your dimensions on the PivotTable form. Drag Customer from the PivotTable form and drop it onto the Drop Row Fields Here. Drag one of the measures, such as store_sales, from the PivotTable form to the box above Customer, as shown in Figure 11-16.

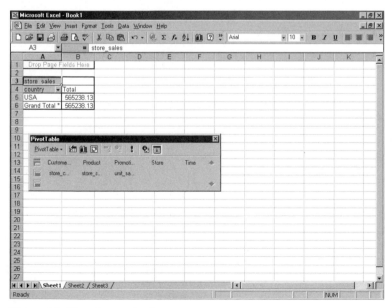

Figure 11-16.   *Store sales by customers.*

> **Note** For those of you who looked at the final solution for the ADO MD wrapper and the final Visual Basic control, you see that the control is very similar to the PivotTable in Excel. Your control has a few more features than Excel does, but they work in a similar way.

If you click the drop-down list box for Country, you see that Mexico and Canada are listed. The reason they are not displayed in the Excel spreadsheet is that there are no values for these countries in 1997. Click OK.

Double-clicking USA expands the view to the next level, as shown in Figure 11-17.

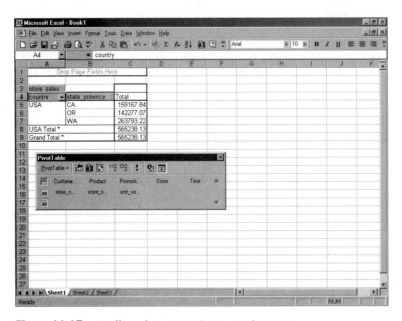

Figure 11-17. *Drilling down into Customer Country.*

The Meaning of Grand Total in Excel

Let's now take a closer look at the Grand Total row on the bottom. The Grand Total is not the total for all visible rows, but instead the Grand Total for all rows, regardless of whether they are visible.

To see how this works, click the Country drop-down list box again. This time, expand USA and clear the check mark out of CA, as shown in Figure 11-18. You might need to click the box twice to clear the check mark. Doing this filters CA out of the Excel spreadsheet.

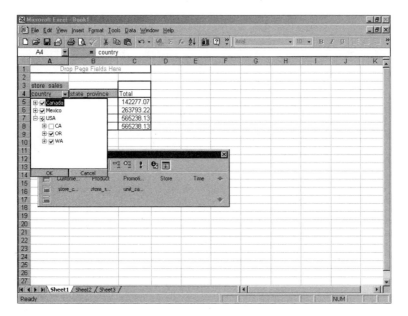

Figure 11-18. *Filtering out CA.*

Click OK and your Excel spreadsheet should look like the one in Figure 11-19.

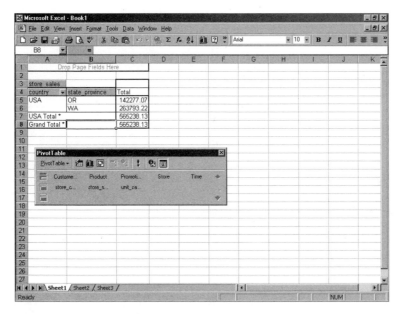

Figure 11-19. *Data with CA filtered out.*

You now have data for OR with a value of 142,277.07 and WA with a sales value of 263,793.22. The sums of these two are 406,070.29, which is clearly not the Grand Total of $565,238.13. This is the way Excel currently works. You cannot change this. If this is not the behavior you want, there are two options.

Customizing the Behavior of Excel

The first option is to use the Web components, described next. The second option is to create your own Visual Basic for Applications (VBA) Excel macros. You can take the code sample you did for the Visual Basic control and change the code to drop the data into Excel cells instead of dropping the data into a grid box. You can even include the control in your Excel spreadsheet and you do not have to code anything. To do this, compile the ADO MD wrapper dlls and the control OLE Custom Control (OCX). Then, open the Control Toolbox, select More Controls, and add the Visual Basic control. This gives you all the required functionality you need. You can even expand the Visual Basic control to pass information from the control to an Excel macro and add specific important information into an Excel spreadsheet. There really are very few limitations to what you can do if you are willing to write code and step outside the wizard box. As a system administrator, even if you cannot write the code, you should know what solutions can be developed with different products. Save the spreadsheet so you can use it later.

Let's now take a look at using Excel to view data from the OLAP cubes using dimensions and measures instead of using client-side cubes.

Viewing OLAP Cubes with Excel

Instead of creating client-side cubes, you can access the information in a data warehouse directly and place that data into Excel. This solution is simpler than building client-side cubes and also allows users to connect directly to the data warehouse. Allowing users to make direct connections into the data warehouse means that you have to be very careful about security and what information people are allowed to view.

Open a new Excel worksheet. Once again select Data/Get External Data/New Database Query. Select the OLAP Cubes tab, as shown in Figure 11-20.

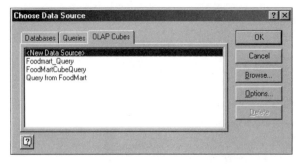

Figure 11-20. *Selecting OLAP Cubes tab.*

Select New Data Source. This brings up the Create New Data Source screen. Call the new query FoodMartQuery and choose Microsoft OLE DB Provider for OLAP Services for the OLAP provider, as shown in Figure 11-21.

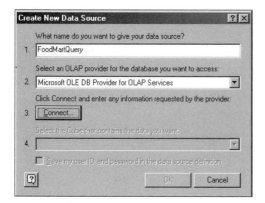

Figure 11-21. *Entering the query name and OLAP provider.*

Click Connect. This brings up the Multi-Dimensional Connection screen. You can select either an OLAP server or local cube file; choose OLAP Server. Type the name of your server, as shown in Figure 11-22.

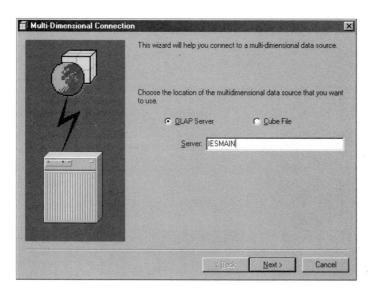

Figure 11-22. *Choosing an OLAP server.*

Click Next. Choose FoodMart as your database and click Finish. This brings you back to the Create New Data Source screen. Notice that FoodMart is now next to the Connect button. Select Sales For 1998, as shown in Figure 11-23.

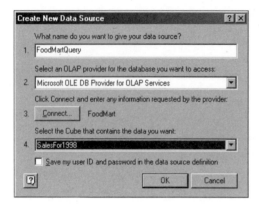

Figure 11-23. *Completing the Create New Data Source form.*

Click OK. You should be back at the Choose Data Source screen with FoodMartQuery selected. Click OK. You are now in the Excel spreadsheet with the PivotTable and PivotChart Wizard Step 3 Of 3 screen. Click Finish in the Step 3 screen. You can now use the data as you did with the cube you created previously.

Now that you have created your Excel spreadsheets, you can use the Web components to publish them as HTML pages.

Office 2000 Web Components

The Office 2000 Web components allow you to create Web pages from your Excel spreadsheets, including spreadsheets that have PivotTables in them, like the ones you created. Web components also work with Microsoft Word, Microsoft Access, and Microsoft FrontPage. Using the Web components, you can create an Excel spreadsheet with a PivotTable and save it as an HTML page. You can thus create a fully working Web application that will give you access to the data warehouse very easily using Office 2000.

Choose either of the spreadsheets you created. Go to the menu and select File/Save As Web Page. This brings up the Save As screen. Choose Selection: Sheet and Add Interactivity. Call the Web page CubeWeb, as shown in Figure 11-24.

Figure 11-24.   *Saving as a Web page.*

Click the Publish button. This gives you additional options. Select PivotTable Functionality, Add Interactivity With, and PivotTable, as shown in Figure 11-25.

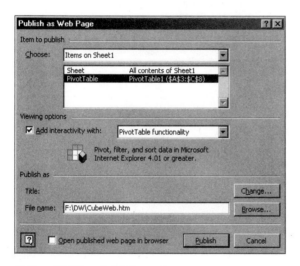

Figure 11-25.   *Publish options.*

Click Publish. Congratulations, you just created an interactive Web page!

Open CubeWeb.htm in Internet Explorer 4.0 or higher. You should find that you now have a Web page with a fully functioning PivotTable. If you do not see the PivotTable Field List, right-click Microsoft Office PivotTable List and click Field List, as shown in Figure 11-26.

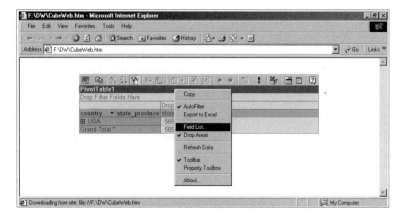

Figure 11-26. *Selecting.*

You should now see all the fields as shown in Figure 11-27.

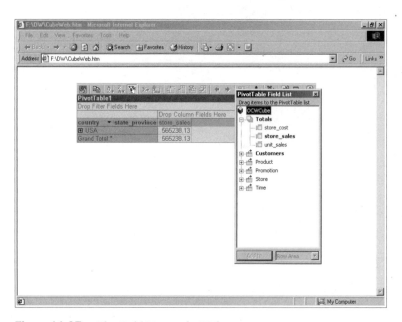

Figure 11-27. *The Field List on the Web page.*

You can now drag fields into the PivotTable. This is a fully functioning Web page.

Conclusion

PivotTable Services allows client applications to have full access to the data warehouse. ADO MD, C++ applications, Excel, Web components, and third-party solutions all use PivotTable Services.

Using Excel 9, you can create powerful applications without writing any code. You can add code to customize any of these solutions to create even more powerful client-side applications. Once you know the requirements of the user, you can use the wide variety of client-side solutions offered by PivotTable Services to create an application that meets those requirements.

Chapter 12
Optimizing a SQL Server Data Warehouse

In this chapter, you learn ways to optimize fact and informational tables in a relational Microsoft SQL Server 7.0 database. You also learn how you can optimize dimensions and measures in relational OLAP (ROLAP), hybrid OLAP (HOLAP), and multidimensional OLAP (MOLAP) partitions and cubes. The chapter therefore has two major sections—optimizing the relational database that contains the star schema and optimizing the cubes (partitions). When the star schema is in a SQL Server 7.0 relational database, you can use the full range of optimization tools that come with SQL Server 7.0. For the cubes, you have tools and a set of best practices that you should use in the design and construction of your cubes. Let's begin with the tools available to optimize the star schema.

Optimizing the Star Schema

Regardless of the storage mechanism for your cubes, you want your star schema to efficiently insert and retrieve data. Retrieval is done through queries. The two areas where you have the most problems with insertion and queries are the queries themselves and the indexes on the table. To improve both of these, SQL Server has the Query Analyzer, Profiler, and the Index Tuning Wizard. With these three tools, you should be able to optimize any relational database and all your queries. Microsoft SQL Server 7.0 OLAP Services has a Cube Schema Optimizer, which you can use to optimize the joins of your star schema.

Using these tools, you can optimize your queries to move data. If you are using a ROLAP or HOLAP solution, you can optimize the indexes of the star schema to increase the efficiency for both insertion and retrieval of data for these storage types. For MOLAP, these tools allow you to decrease the time it takes to update (process) the data warehouse. Let's begin with the Query Analyzer.

Query Analyzer

The Query Analyzer allows you to view the results of queries, optimize the queries, and improve the indexes on the query. The Query Analyzer has a graphical show plan that shows the different steps in the query, along with "fly over" tool tips that give you information on all the steps. Using this information, you can determine what operations are costly and how to improve your indexes. You can also access other tools from the Query Analyzer.

Because FoodMart is not in SQL Server, you will use Northwind to demonstrate the features of these three SQL tools. Open the SQL Server Enterprise Manager. Expand the tree until you see the Northwind database and click Northwind. Click Tools/SQL Server Query Analyzer. In the database drop-down list box select Northwind.

Type the following query in the query window:

```
Select * From Orders join [Order Details] ON [Order Details].OrderID =
Orders.OrderID ORDER BY Orders.OrderDate
```

Click the green arrow to execute the query. You should get the results shown in Figure 12-1.

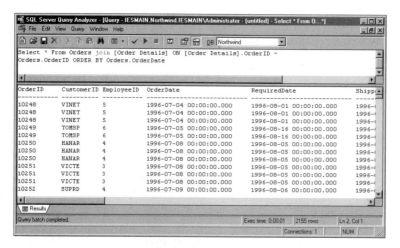

Figure 12-1. *Query Analyzer results.*

Go to the menu and select Query/Display Estimated Execution Plan. The execution plan shows the steps SQL Server must do to perform the query. Read the execution plan from right to left. The thickness of the lines is determined by the amount of data moving between steps, with thick lines representing more data. On the bottom is information on the query, such as how long it takes to execute. In this case, the time was 00:00:01 or .1 milliseconds. Placing the mouse over Order Details on the right shows you the "fly over" tool tips, as shown in Figure 12-2.

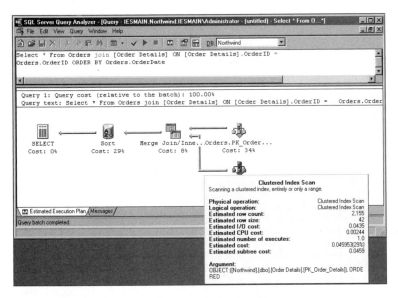

Figure 12-2.   *"Fly over" tool tips in Order Details.*

You can see that the tip provides a great deal of information, including the physical and logical operation. In this case, you are scanning over the clustered index. Two very important pieces of information are the estimated CPU cost and the estimated I/O cost. If the CPU cost is very high, you might need to consider adding another processor. If the I/O is very high, you might need to look at partitioning the data across hard drives, getting better hard drives, or other solutions that might improve hard drive performance. The other valuable piece of information is the cost percentage. In this case, scanning the clustered index was responsible for 29 percent of the time required for the entire query.

Looking at this query, you can see that the sort is taking up 29 percent of the time to perform the query. The sort is on a non-indexed text field. This is very inefficient.

Note   Because the table actually holds very little data, the entire table can be placed into memory to perform the query. When this happens, indexes make little improvement in performance. In a table containing more data, the lack of an index becomes the largest factor in making this query inefficient. With this small amount of data, sorting on a text field is the largest factor.

Let's see what happens when you sort by OrderID. Change OrderDate to OrderID. Click the green arrow. Your time has now become 00:00:00, too quick to be measured. The execution plan is shown in Figure 12-3.

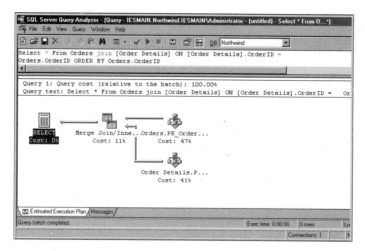

Figure 12-3. *Execution plan.*

You can see the time to perform the sort has dropped to 11 percent of the query. By using the analyzer in this way, you can optimize your queries used to move data into the data warehouse.

In addition to the analyzer, you also analyze the indexes associated with this query. Go to the menu and select Query/Perform Index Analysis. The results are shown in Figure 12-4.

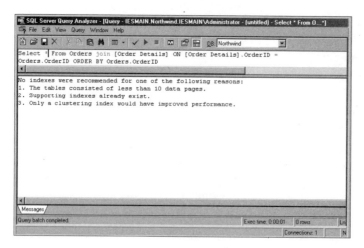

Figure 12-4. *Index analysis results.*

There is already a clustered index on the OrderID field, so these tables already have the appropriate indexes.

If the query returns a large number of rows, SQL Server can use statistics that it has stored to estimate the transfer without actually performing the query. For this to work, though, you must have turned on statistics for your database. If you go back to the Enterprise Manager, right-click Northwind, select Properties, and click Options, you see the options for the table, as shown in Figure 12-5.

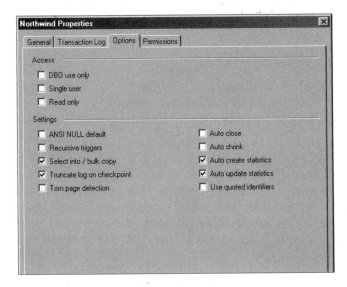

Figure 12-5.   *Options for Northwind.*

Auto Create Statistics and Auto Update Statistics create statistics for your tables. These statistics are highly optimized and if you are performing large queries, you do not need to worry about them affecting performance. SQL Server does not actually create statistics on every action against the database. Actually, only a few percent of the actions on the tables are used to create statistics using averages. By leaving this on, you can quickly do analysis. If you shut this off, you can still use the Query Analyzer, but the Query Analyzer prompts you to calculate statistics. Click Cancel to close the Properties. Leave the Query Analyzer open.

Now that you have seen what the Query Analyzer can do, let's look at Profiler.

Profiler

Externally, the new Profiler might look a little like the old SQL Trace utility, but internally it is a completely different tool. Everything within SQL Server is now an event producer. An event producer writes to the SQL server queue whenever it performs an action. An event producer could be a SQL Server table, and the actions that would result in writing to the queue would be writing, reading, or updating information in the table. Event consumers, such as the SQL Server Profiler, can read from the queue. Other producers are the error log, OLE DB, the query processor, the lock and log manager, and Open Data Services (ODS). ODS is an API that used to be widely used for making a wide range of SQL applications. Now it is primarily used for extended queries. You can also define your own producers. Profiler can trap events from all these producers. There are 68 predefined events that Profiler can monitor.

If Profiler is properly set up, it allows you to do detailed tracing with very little overhead. Profiler can capture a wide range of events. If an event does not occur, there is no cost in profiling it. Warnings and errors should always be profiled, because they cost nothing if there are none. Just as the Query Analyzer used statistics, Profiler also uses statistics.

You can define traces by either using the wizard or doing it directly in Profiler. The wizards have built-in trace definitions that you can select to deal with specific problems. For example, you have a trace for poorly performing queries. This trace returns traces of all the poorly performing queries. You can then feed these traces into the Index Tuning Wizard to optimize these poorly performing queries.

You can also manually make a trace, but you must be very careful. There are many types of traces and if you select too many of them, they could affect performance. You should look at the SQL Server reference materials, such as the SQL Server Books online, to read about all the trace options.

Creating a Profile Using the Wizard

Go to the SQL Server 7.0 Enterprise Manager, and then go to the menu and select Tools/ SQL 7.0 Profiler. In Profiler, go to Tools, and then select Create Trace Wizard. This brings up the wizard to create a trace. On the Welcome screen click Next. This brings you to the Identify The Problem screen. Choose Find The Worst Performing Queries as your problem, as shown in Figure 12-6.

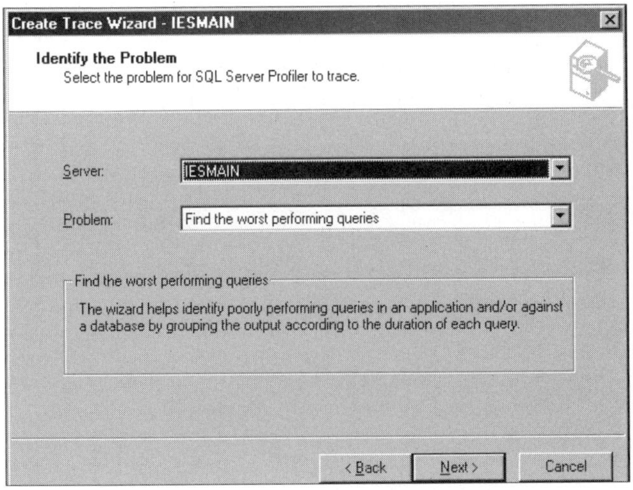

Figure 12-6. *Identify the Problem.*

Click Next. In this screen you set the minimum time a query must run before it becomes profiled. Normally, this is a query running longer than a few seconds. Because you just want to create a trace, type 0 milliseconds. Select Northwind as the database, as shown in Figure 12-7.

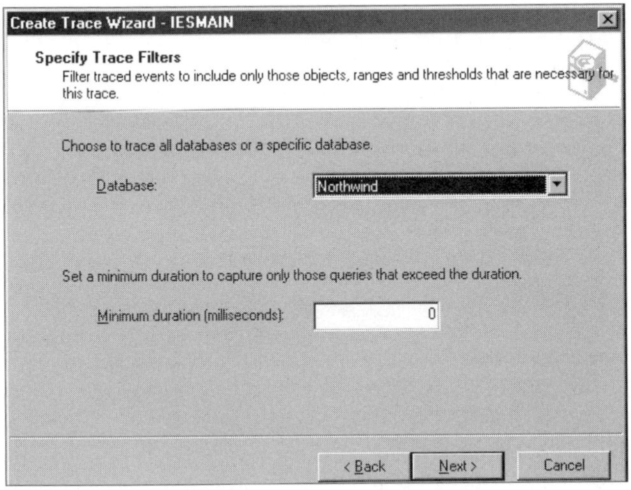

Figure 12-7. *Setting minimum time to zero.*

On the Specify Trace Filters screen, you accept the defaults, so click Next. Click Finish. Now go back to the Query Analyzer and run the query again. If you go back to Profiler, you see that the query has been profiled, as shown in Figure 12-8.

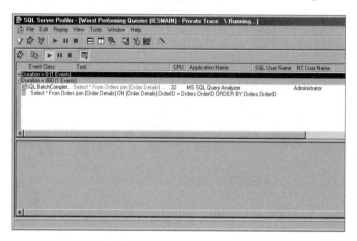

Figure 12-8.   *Profiled query.*

Go to Profiler Menu and select Tools/Performance Monitor. This brings up the Microsoft Windows NT Performance Monitor. Running your query does not even show up on the performance monitor because it uses virtually no resources. Close the Performance Monitor.

You need to save the profile. In Profiler menu select File/Save. Call the file Northwind.

Go to the menu in Profiler and select Tools/Index Tuning Wizard. The Introduction screen comes up. Click Next. It is best to select Keep Existing Indexes, especially when you are using traces on worst performing queries. Select Northwind, as shown in Figure 12-9.

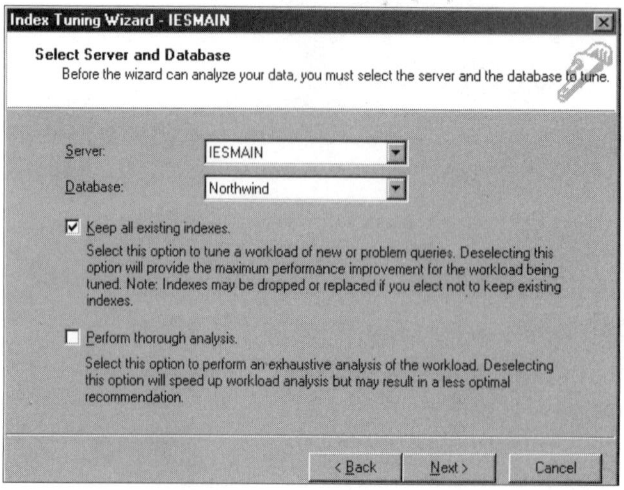

Figure 12-9.   *Selecting Northwind.*

Click Next. This brings you to the Identify A Workload file. You should have a workload file from the profile you created. If I Have A Saved Workload File is not selected, click it. Click Next. In the Specify Workload screen, select the Northwind.trc file you saved in Profiler, as shown in Figure 12-10.

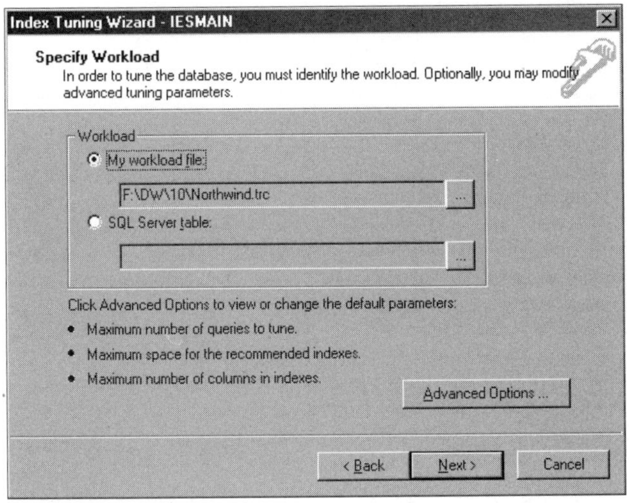

Figure 12-10.   *Selecting the trace file.*

(Notice that there is an Advanced Options button to make modifications to options.) Click Next. This brings you to the Select Queries To Tune screen. You leave the default and do not remove any tables. Click Next. This brings you to the Final Analysis screen.

The query wizard should not find any changes that you can make to these tables that would improve performance. This is what you expect because the table already has clustered indexes defined. You can click Analysis if you want to see more details. If you click Next, you find yourself at the Schedule Index Job screen. You can schedule when you want the change in the indexes to occur. In your case, there is nothing to change, so click Cancel.

Creating a Profile without the Wizard

Go back to Profiler and click the red button to stop the profile. From the menu, select Edit/Clear Trace Window. Now choose Tools/Options from the menu. On the General tab, select All Event Classes and All Data Columns, as shown in Figure 12-11. This allows you to select from all the possible 68 events when you build your profile.

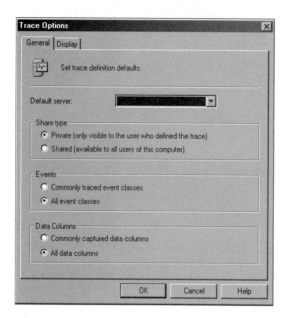

Figure 12-11. *Setting event options.*

Click OK. In the menu select File/New/Trace. This brings up the Trace Properties window. There are four tabs that you can choose from. On the General tab, type the name Error Profile. Click Capture to File and type the path for the profile, as shown in Figure 12-12.

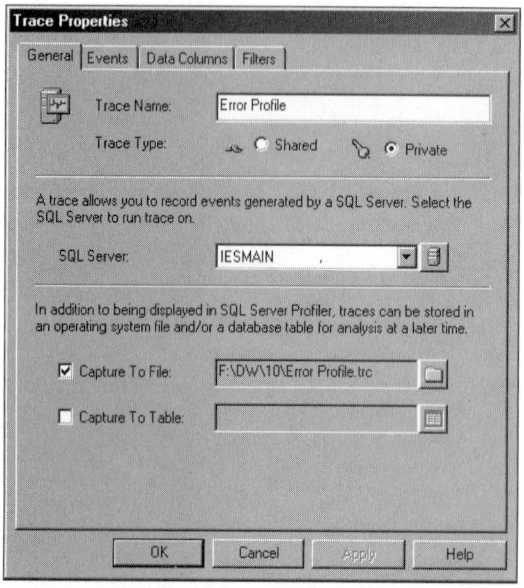

Figure 12-12. *Error profile.*

Click the Events tab. Remove everything that is currently in the Selected events list box by clicking Remove until the list box is empty. Click Error and Warnings and click the Add button. The Events tab should look like the one in Figure 12-13.

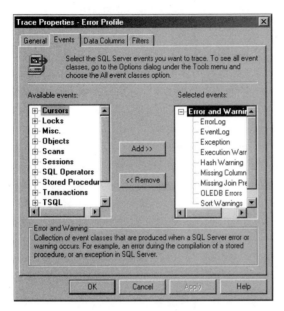

Figure 12-13.   *Events tab with Error and Warnings chosen.*

Click the Data Columns tab, and notice that some of the data columns return different results for different events. A list of the available columns is shown in Table 12-1.

Table 12-1. Data Columns

Application Name *	The name of the client application that created the connection to SQL Server. This column is populated with the values passed by the application, instead of the displayed name of the program.
Binary Data	Binary value that is dependent on the event class being captured in the trace.
Connection ID *	The ID assigned by SQL Server to the connection that is established by the client application. Events produced by system processes might not have a connection ID.
CPU *	Amount of CPU time (in milliseconds) that the event uses.
Database ID *	ID of the database specified by the USE database statement, or the default database if no USE database statement has been issued for a given connection. SQL Server Profiler displays the name of the database if the **Server Name** data column is captured in the trace and the server is available. You can determine the value for a database by using the DB_ID function.

continued

Table 12-1. Data Columns *continued*

Duration *	Amount of elapsed time (in milliseconds) taken by the event.
End Time *	Time at which the event ended. This column is not populated for starting event classes, such as **SQL:BatchStarting** or **SP:Starting.**
Event Class *	The type of event class that is being captured.
Event Sub Class	The type of event subclass that is being captured. This data column is not populated for all the event classes.
Host Name	The name of the computer on which the client is running. This data column is populated if the client provides the host name. To determine the host name, use the HOST_NAME function.
Host Process ID	An ID assigned by the host computer to the process in which the client application is running. This data column is populated if the client provides the host process ID. To determine the host ID, use the HOST_ID function.
Index ID	An ID for the index on the object that is affected by the event. To determine the index ID for an object, use the **indID** column of the **sysindexes** system table.
Integer Data**	An integer value that is dependent on the event class that is being captured in the trace.
NT Domain Name *	Windows NT domain to which the user belongs.
NT User Name *	The Windows NT username.
Object ID	A system-assigned ID of the object.
Reads	The number of logical disk reads that are performed by the server on behalf of the event.
Server Name *	The name of the SQL Server that is traced.
Severity	Severity level of an exception.
SPID *	Server Process ID assigned by SQL Server to the process associated with the client.
SQL User Name *	SQL Server username of the client.
Start Time *	Time at which the event started, if this is available.
Text**	A text value dependent on the event class that is captured in the trace.
Transaction ID	A system-assigned ID for a transaction.
Writes	The number of physical disk writes performed by the server on behalf of this event.

* Events that are available by default

** You can find the values for binary and integer data, along with the text, in the SQL Server Books online that came with SQL Server 7.0. If you installed it with SQL Server 7.0, you should be able to get access to it from Start/Programs/Microsoft Server SQL 7/ Books On Line. Find the topic *Events Monitored by SQL Server Profile*. You can find the values for integer and binary data for each of the events by clicking the Event Category for the event you want to get information on.

If you haven't already done so, move all the items in the Unselected Data: list box over to the Selected Data: list box. Click the Filters tab. You can now place filters on various criteria. You do not create any filters, so click OK on the bottom of the screen.

In the Query Analyzer, type the following incorrect query:

```
Select * From Orders join [Order Details] ON [Order Details].OrderID =
Orders.OrderID ORDER BY Order.OrderDate
```

Run the query so it generates the error. Profiler should look like the one in Figure 12-14.

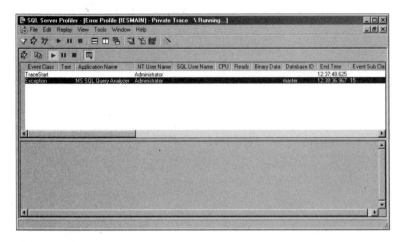

Figure 12-14.   *Error profile.*

All the information you requested is in the trace. You can see how, using the log files, you can track just about anything you need to track to optimize your queries. Let's now look at the Schema Optimizer, which is not part of the SQL Server management console but instead part of OLAP Manager.

Cube Schema Optimization

Creating joins of tables in a relational database is an expensive operation. Regardless of the storage type, you need to retrieve data from the star schema in the most efficient manner possible. Reducing the number of joins improves your retrieval of data from the fact and informational tables.

A join is not needed if your data meets the following characteristics:

- It is a shared dimension (a dimension that can be used by several cubes in the data warehouse).
- The member key column of the lowest level member of a dimension is unique.

- The member key column of the lowest level is the only join between the fact table and the informational table.
- There is a one to one relationship between the member key column and the member name column.

OLAP Services's Optimize Schema Wizard uses this information to remove your joins if they are unnecessary. Open OLAP Manager. Expand the tree for the FoodMart data warehouse. Right-click the Sales 1998 partition and select Edit to bring up the Cube Editor. Go to the menu and select Tools/Optimize Schema from the menu. An OK box appears showing you the changes that were made, as shown in Figure 12-15.

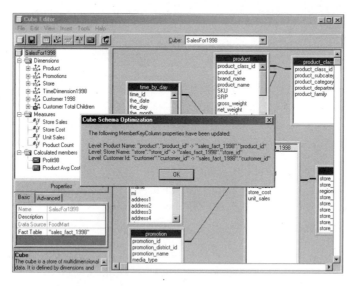

Figure 12-15.   *Results of optimization of Sales 1998.*

At first it appears that nothing has happened. What has actually happened is the MemberKeyColumn was changed from the Product informational table's ProductID to the sales_fact_1998 fact table's ProductID. To see this, click Product, choose the Product Name level, and look at Properties, as shown in Figure 12-16.

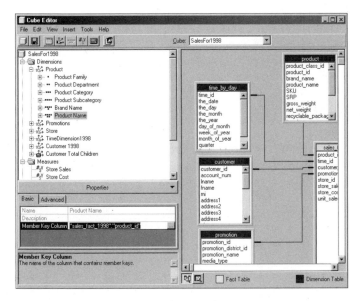

Figure 12-16.   *Product MemberKeyColumn.*

The change made by the Optimizer has eliminated three joins from your table. This can substantially reduce the time to calculate aggregations for ROLAP and HOLAP cubes and reduce the time to move data into a MOLAP cube.

Let's now look at the tools that come with OLAP for optimizing the cubes.

OLAP Performance Tools

OLAP Services comes with two tools to optimize and view queries against the data in your cubes: the Usage-Based Optimization Wizard and the Usage Analysis tool. OLAP Services can monitor the queries to the data warehouse. Based on these queries, the Usage-Based Optimization Wizard optimizes the aggregations of the data warehouse to increase the speed and efficiency of data retrieval, and the Usage Analysis Tool provides reports on the queries performed against the data in the cubes. You begin by making sure that OLAP Services is monitoring the queries.

You cannot just monitor a partition. Monitoring must be done for everything in the data warehouse or for nothing in the data warehouse. Monitoring is on by default. Open OLAP Manager. Expand the tree. Right-click your data warehouse and select Properties, as shown in Figure 12-17.

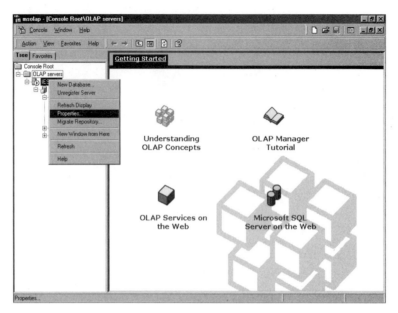

Figure 12-17. *Selecting Properties.*

Select the Query Log tab. Make sure the Sample Frequency (Once Per) is selected, because this turns monitoring of the queries on. Leave the default of once per 10 queries, as shown in Figure 12-18.

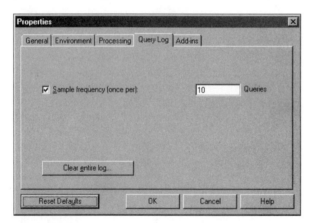

Figure 12-18. *Setting Sample Frequency.*

Let's take a look at the Usage Analysis Wizard.

Usage Analysis Wizard

The Usage Analysis Wizard allows you to view the information gathered on the queries performed against a partition in the data warehouse. Right-click Sales in the FoodMart data warehouse. Select Usage Analysis Wizard. This brings up the Welcome screen of the wizard. You see that there are many types of reports that you can view on the usage of the Sales partition. Using this tool, you can see which queries are taking a long time, what users are making long-running queries, and many other details on the usage of your data warehouse. You can either use the Usage-Based Optimization Wizard to optimize the inefficient or long-running queries or adjust them yourself. Choose Query Run-Time Table as your Report Type, as shown in Figure 12-19.

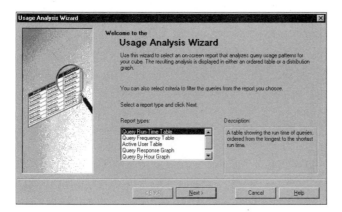

Figure 12-19.   *Choosing report type.*

Click Next. This brings you to the Select Criteria screen. This screen allows you to place numerous filters on the report. You place a filter on the date. Click Queries for the dates. Select Before in the first drop-down box and enter tomorrow's date in the second drop-down box (which is August 22 in this case), as shown in Figure 12-20. This gives you data on all the queries you have performed against the Sales partition.

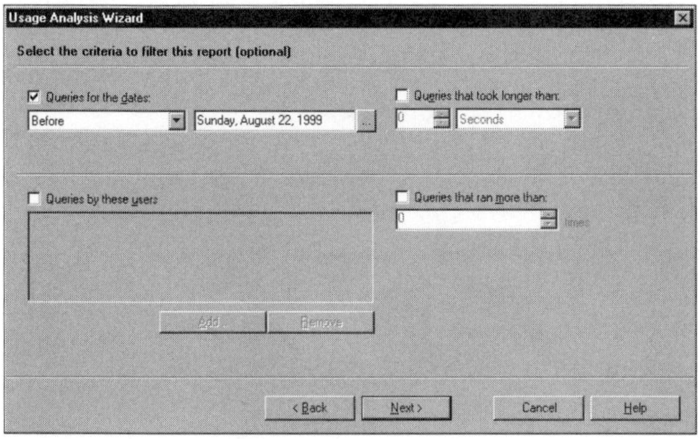

Figure 12-20.   *Filtering by time.*

Click Next. You should now see a report on the usage of your data warehouse. In the example in Figure 12-21, the longest any of the queries took was one second, and that was only for two of the queries.

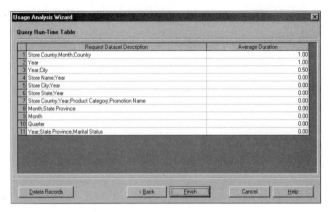

Figure 12-21.   *Final report.*

Click Finish to close the report.

Let's now take a look at the Usage-Based Optimization Wizard.

Usage-Based Optimization Wizard

The Usage-Based Optimization Wizard works just like the Aggregation Wizard, except it bases aggregations on the queries performed against the data warehouse. Right-click Sales and choose Usage-Based Optimization Wizard. This brings you to the Welcome screen for the wizard. Click Skip This Screen In The Future, because you do not need it. Click Next. This brings you to the Select Partition screen if you have the Enterprise edition. You should have the Sales partition selected. If not, select it. Click Next. This brings you to the Select Queries screen, which is the same screen for filtering as you saw in the Usage Analysis Wizard. Again, select Before in the first drop-down box and enter tomorrow's date in the second drop-down box. Click Next. This gives you essentially the same report that you saw before, as shown in Figure 12-22.

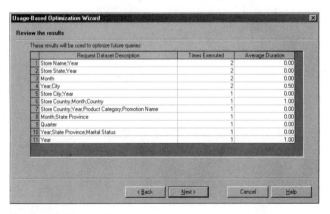

Figure 12-22.   *Sales report.*

Click Next. In this case, there are already aggregations on this partition, so you get the Aggregations Already Exist screen, as shown in Figure 12-23.

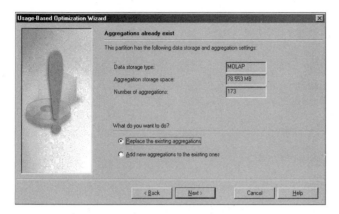

Figure 12-23.   *Aggregations Already Exist.*

Select Replace My Existing Aggregations and click Next. You must now choose your storage type. Choose MOLAP and click Next. Select Performance gain reaches and type 30 as shown in Figure 12-24. Although this looks like what you did before, this time the design of the aggregations are built on the data from the queries performed against the partition.

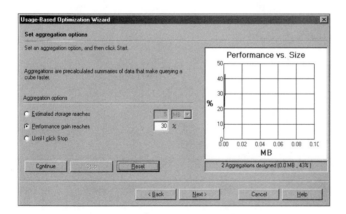

Figure 12-24.   *Choosing 30 percent performance.*

Click Next. This brings you to the Finish screen. Select Process and then click Finish.

Now that you have looked at the wizards that can optimize your cubes, let's look at best practices for making your cubes.

Best Practices for Designing Cubes

There is a wide range of good practices when designing your data warehouse that might improve the efficiency of your data warehouse. You begin with the basic structures of your cube: dimensions, the cubes themselves, and partitions.

Optimizing Dimensions

The three most important features of the dimension's design are the number of levels, the member key, and the Unique Members. Let's look at each of these.

Number of Levels

In regard to performance of your dimensions, the number of levels is a very critical factor for efficiency. The more levels there are in a dimension, the longer it takes to process a cube. By increasing the number of levels you do the following:

- Increase the amount of space required for storage (as both the level and index information on the level is stored in the physical hard drive)
- Increase the amount of memory required to work with the dimension on both the client and server
- Increase the amount of time it takes to update the dimension and/or cube

If you don't need a level, do not include it—do not project your time dimension years into the future. If a level will rarely be used but is required, make it a virtual dimension. Do not allow users to bloat the dimension with levels that are rarely going to be used or really not needed.

Reducing dimensions, though, should not be done at the expense of maintaining balanced levels. Imagine you have a hierarchy in which you have a customer dimension with Country, Region, StateProvince, and City. If you remove Region, you find that the United States may have many times more members than Luxembourg or Denmark. The indexes for these unbalanced members will not be very efficient and processing time on the server and client may be increased. By including a region, the United States can be broken into regions that are approximately the same size as the smaller countries. Of course, you should do such actions only if the corporation has regions defined as part of its business rules. If the idea of regions makes no sense, an alternate suggestion is to combine several of the smaller countries into one larger element such as Eastern Europe. Again, you should do this only if this fits within the definitions of the business.

Member Key

Properly defining your member key for each dimension is also an essential part of creating well-designed dimensions. OLAP Server uses the member key for identification of the rows of data in the dimension during processing.

Keeping the member key small, such as 32-bit integer, increases efficiency. Remember, this member key is used for all accesses to the dimension. Using a string for the member key is very inefficient. The Member Name property is used to give a key user-friendly values that the end user can understand. Avoid strings for your member key at all costs.

If you must use a string for the member key, it should be the same as the Member Name. A string member key should be as short as possible. The server performs comparisons based on the member key. These comparisons become more efficient when a short string value is used. The longer the string value, the slower and more inefficient the comparisons. When using the maximum string length of 255 characters, performance might be seriously affected. If you are using strings, choosing a short string and changing the SQL Server's method of string comparison to binary makes this an inefficient but workable solution. Of course, changing to a binary comparison affects the entire server and should only be done with careful consideration of the impact on other databases or data warehouses on the server.

Do not make the data type of the member key different from the data type of the underlying source in the informational table. Thus, if the field in the informational table used for the member key is a string in the informational table, it should be a string in the dimension.

Members and Virtual Dimensions

Earlier you learned about building virtual dimensions. These virtual members were placed under a level in the dimension. It is usually much better to associate a virtual dimension higher in the hierarchy than lower. Imagine that you have a customer dimension with Country, State, and City. If you wished to add a virtual dimension called Region with values NE, SE, NW, and SW, it would be more efficient to add this to Country than to either State or City.

Unique Members

Although the Unique Members have little effect on the time it takes to populate the dimension, they have a serious effect on the time it takes to process the overall partition that the dimension belongs to. The Unique Members also affect the time it takes to query a HOLAP or ROLAP cube.

Properly setting the Unique Members Flat to Yes if the member is unique reduces processing time. For a MOLAP cube, only the last level needs to be unique. For ROLAP all levels should be unique, if possible.

Number of Dimensions

Be careful not to include unnecessary dimensions in your cube. If there are more dimensions, the cube is larger and there are also more possible aggregations. A larger cube with more possible aggregations is slower than a smaller cube with fewer possible aggregations. Thus, always limit your number of dimensions to what is needed.

Optimizing Measures

The most important part of your measure is its byte size. Measures can be 4 bytes, which include data types such as integer and single, and 8 bytes, which include data types such as double, currency, and date. Not only are 4-byte data types smaller, but they also have a much higher rate of compression within OLAP Server. Thus, using the smaller data types as a measure can significantly improve the performance of your data warehouse.

Optimizing Partitions

Creating partitions is an important part of making your data warehouse. Once you have analyzed the business requirements, you can begin to make decisions on partitions. Let's look at how the design of partitions and the business requirements work together.

Dividing the Data into Partitions

In general, the rule for partitions is to group together data that is to be queried together. By doing a careful analysis of the business requirements, the needs of the users, and the expected usage of the data warehouse, you can determine what groups of data are to be accessed together. In the FoodMart data warehouse, you separated the years 1997 and 1998 into two partitions. In this case, you stated that the business requirement was that the 1997 data would rarely be accessed, and only for historical queries.

Dividing the data into partitions according to groups of data likely to be used together allows you to segment the data warehouse into smaller partitions. These smaller partitions can have fewer levels, which in turn increases efficiency. Data that is not likely to be included in queries is not part of the partition, and therefore is not included in processing queries.

Percentage of Aggregations and Partition Efficiency

Aggregations are perhaps the most important factor in how long it takes to process both the queries and the cube. You should start out with 30 percent aggregations and allow the data warehouse to be used long enough to gather data on usage. If you are working with a very large partition that is taking a very long time to process, you might want to reduce this to 5 percent or 10 percent, if possible. Then use the Usage-Based Optimization Wizard to get the best possible set of aggregations for your data warehouse. If you require better performance, run the Usage-Based Optimization Wizard and increase the percentage of aggregations. For a rough estimate, you should be able to process 15 to 20 million rows per hour.

Storage Method and Partition Efficiency

You have learned about ROLAP, HOLAP, and MOLAP throughout this book. MOLAP gives you the maximum level of efficiency and the best performance. Before choosing a ROLAP or HOLAP solution, make sure that there are good business reasons to make this choice.

Data Warehouse Advanced Properties

There are several advanced properties that can affect the performance of the data warehouse. Right-click the server name and select Properties. Select the Processing tab, as shown in Figure 12-25.

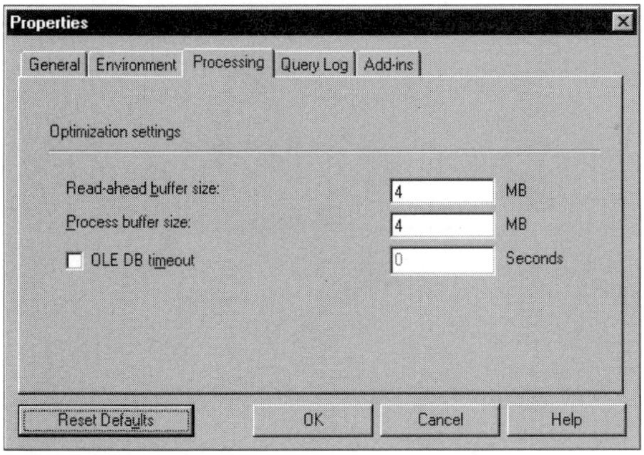

Figure 12-25.   *Processing tab.*

You see the Process Buffer Size, which is the size of the data that can be stored in memory before data begins being written to the disk. Thus, if you set the Process Buffer Size to 5 MB, data starts to be written to the disk when more than 5 MB of data needs to be used for processing a query. Because writing to the disk is a very slow process, having the Process Buffer Size too small seriously degrades performance. If you make the Process Buffer Size too large, there is not enough virtual memory and data is paged to disk and thrashing occurs. You should use Profiler to monitor the database if you make changes to the Process Buffer Size to make sure you have chosen the correct setting.

There is also the Read Ahead Buffer. When data is read from the data warehouse it is placed into a buffer in memory. The size of this buffer is determined by the size of the Read Ahead Buffer property. Making the value larger allows more data to be read in at a time decreasing I/O to the disk. If there is a large number of aggregations that need to be calculated, changing this value gives a very small change in performance in comparison to the time it takes to process the aggregations.

Hardware

No matter how well you design your cube, it can only run as fast as the underlying hardware allows it to run. When working with very large amounts of data, you find that the most common place for a bottleneck is I/O. Using Performance Monitor, you can find out if this is your problem. If I/O is slowing you down, get more hard drives, move from redundant array of independent disks (RAID) 5 to RAID 1 & 0 or RAID 0 if that fits within the business requirements, faster channels, and so forth.

Data Explosion

The explosion of data as you create aggregates was mentioned in earlier chapters. Data explosion is especially a problem with dimensions that have values in the fact table that are sparsely populated. Image that you had 25 base members in a dimension. These 20 base members can be rolled up into 4 groups containing 5 base members each. The 4 groups can be rolled up into 2 groups. This is shown in Figure 12-26.

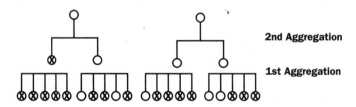

Figure 12-26. *Twenty base members.*

The circles with x's in Figure 12-26 represent null values (empty data). As you can see, the base level is very sparse. In the base level, there are 5 out of 20 values filled, or only 25 of the members have data. In the 1st aggregation 3 out of 4, or 75 percent, of the members have data. By the second aggregation 2 out of 2, or 100 percent, of the members have data. This brings out one of the properties of sparse data: If you perform 100 percent aggregations on sparse data, each aggregation will be denser than the level below it. Another important thing to notice is that there are only 5 base members and there are a total of 5 aggregated values. Thus, if you did 100 percent aggregations on this data, you would end up with as many aggregate values stored in the database as you have base data. When performing 100 percent aggregations, as the number of levels and dimensions increase the size of the aggregate data will become the largest portion of the information in the data warehouse.

This means that if you add a dimension that is only sparsely populated in the fact table, you can still get a large explosion in the data when the aggregates are performed. Actually, there is little increase in the amount of data explosion between a sparsely populated dimension and a densely populated dimension. This is especially true as you move beyond two or three levels. As Figure 12-26 shows, by the second level we already will have 100 percent data density for the aggregates. Generally, 100 percent will occur for the third or fourth level regardless of how sparse the data is when you are doing 100 percent aggregations.

When comparing the base data to the aggregated data for 100 percent aggregations, experimental results have shown that for up to 5 sparse dimensions the size of the aggregate data will increase by approximately a factor of 2 for each dimension. Thus, if you have 100 MB of base data, with 1 dimension and 100 percent aggregation, it will take 2 x 100 MB or 200 MB for the aggregations and base data. Add a second dimension and you will now have 200 MB x 2 or 400 MB for the base data and aggregations. A third dimension will now require 400 x 2 or 800 MB of data. This is an exponential growth. Five dimensions will require 3,200 MB of data or 3.2 GB. As you can see, even with a sparsely populated dimension the size of the aggregates quickly increases. Using 5 dimensions will result in a 32 fold increase in the data warehouse size. Beyond 5 dimensions the increase will be more than 2. Using 9 sparsely populated dimensions could result in an increase of the data by a factor well over 2,500. Creating 100 percent aggregations is rarely a good choice.

To avoid data explosion, there are two options. The first is using the Usage Optimization Wizard to find a minimum set of optimal aggregations for the data warehouse. The second is to keep the cubes small with fewer dimensions. You could use virtual cubes to create the specific cube that is required out of the smaller cubes. Try to find a balance between the nuMBer of aggregations, levels and dimensions that you create for the cubes and the performance of the data warehouse.

Conclusion

Using the tools that come with SQL Server and some basic good practices, you can substantially increase the efficiency of your fact and informational tables in your star schema, as well as the dimensions and measures in your cube. This increase in efficiency results in a decrease in the time it takes to perform queries against the data warehouse and the time it takes to process partitions. Based on a good understanding of the business requirements of the data warehouse and the types of queries that are to be performed against the data warehouse, you can fine-tune your star schema and your cubes for maximum performance.

Chapter 13
Conclusion

In the beginning of this book you learned that Microsoft SQL Server 7.0 was a key part of a knowledge management system. A complete SQL Server 7.0 data warehousing solution consists of an entire system that incorporates every component covered in this book. PivotTable Services, ADO MD, OLAP, MOLAP (or ROLAP or HOLAP) cubes, Visual Basic, Microsoft Excel, or Web component front ends and MDX all find their places in your corporation's knowledge management system.

Bill Gates has introduced the concept of a corporate Digital Nervous System (DNS). DNS can be considered to include every digital process that links the parts of the corporation and unites the knowledge, thoughts, and actions of the entire corporation. A central part of DNS is the knowledge worker, a person who works primarily with information and knowledge to make corporate decisions.

The brain of DNS is the data stores that contain the knowledge of the corporation. These data stores include exchange servers, legacy systems, SQL Server data warehouses, OLTP systems, and so forth. The digital nervous system that passes this information to the knowledge worker consists both of applications and the general infrastructure including hardware, Microsoft Back Office products, and SQL Server.

DNS should thus store the corporate knowledge and also give access to the right knowledge easily. A SQL Server data warehouse system is a critical, key element in any corporate DNS. When designing and building your data warehouse system, you must view it as part of the overall DNS of the corporation and research how it can fulfill the goal of providing the right information at the right time to the knowledge workers who need it.

A digital nervous system cannot be built haphazardly—it can only be built with the cooperation of all departments within the corporation. Standard formats must be created, data must be merged, and a unified view of the corporate knowledge must be made. Once this is accomplished, applications must be developed to give access to this knowledge.

There are many ways to develop applications that give access to corporate knowledge. One method is building Internet portals that allow knowledge workers to access information through the Internet. However, a portal requires that a connection be maintained; once a connection to the Internet is severed, the portal closes. The digital dashboard expands this concept by providing one interface to access all the information knowledge workers need to perform their jobs, but also gives them the ability to work offline. This information will come from all of the sources of data in the enterprise. A digital dashboard can work through the Internet or through Microsoft Outlook Express. There is more information about the digital dashboard on the CD.

The digital dashboard creates an interface that allows the knowledge worker to access group folders on an exchange server, view important information from the Internet, and view data warehouse data using pivot tables. In one interface, knowledge workers have access to everything they need. If the user needs to go offline, data can be cached locally. In regard to the data warehouse information, the data can be stored in a .cub file and accessed as discussed in the chapter on PivotTable Services.

Microsoft offers a wide range of tools that allows you to build a customized solution that meets the business needs of any corporation. Working as a team, the developers, system administrators, managers, and users can develop an enterprise-wide solution that can create an effective DNS. When building a SQL Server data warehouse, you should always be looking at how your system fits within the DNS and the enterprise as a whole. The greatest limitation you face is no longer the lack of tools at your disposal but your own ability to imagine the possibilities for using them to find innovative management solutions.

Appendix A
Multidimensional Extensions

This appendix provides some additional examples of Multidimensional Extensions (MDX). These examples should help clarify the information included in the three chapters on MDX.

> **Note** All the WHERE clause members are not specified. Microsoft SQL Server 7.0 OLAP Services will provide defaults. This keeps the sample simpler and makes it easier to focus on the subject matter being discussed.

These are the rules for your MDX queries:

- Curly brackets {} are used to delimit sets.
- Square brackets [] are used to delimit member names.
- Parentheses () are used in functions and to delimit tuples.

Once again, open the MDX sample application by following these steps:

1. Select Start, then Programs, then Microsoft SQL Server 7.0, and then OLAP Services.
2. Choose MDX Sample Application.
3. Select the server that has the FoodMart sample.

Begin by typing the following simple query:

```
SELECT
    {MEASURES.MEMBERS} ON COLUMNS,
    {[Gender].[All Gender]} ON ROWS
FROM Sales
```

Run the query. This query returns the values of all the measures over the All member of the dimension. When you are building dimensions with the dimension wizard, the All member is created by default and becomes the default member of the dimension. You can also give your All member a special name. In the case of Gender, the All member is called All Gender. If you change your query to the following, you get back all the measures for the All Gender member:

```
SELECT
    {MEASURES.MEMBERS} ON COLUMNS,
    {[Gender]} ON ROWS
FROM Sales
```

The reason this returns the All Gender member is that it is the default. Although defaults might be useful, they should be avoided. Always be explicit in your MDX queries.

You do not need to have a measure on the rows or columns. You can put dimensions on both the rows and columns as in the following query:

```
SELECT
 {[Gender].MEMBERS} ON COLUMNS,
 {[Promotion Media].MEMBERS} ON ROWS
FROM Sales
```

Type this query in and run it. You will see that you are getting the value of some measure on members of the Gender dimension on the Promotion dimension. The measure that is being evaluated is the default measure, which is Unit Sales. To see that this is really the case, change the query as follows:

```
SELECT
    {[Gender].MEMBERS} ON COLUMNS,
    {[Promotion Media].MEMBERS} ON ROWS
FROM Sales
WHERE MEASURES.[Unit Sales]
```

If you run the new query, you see that once again you get the same results as in the previous query without the WHERE clause. Using the WHERE clause, you can see any measure over Gender and Promotion Media. Change the query as follows:

```
SELECT
    {[Gender].MEMBERS} ON COLUMNS,
    {[Promotion Media].MEMBERS} ON ROWS
FROM Sales
WHERE MEASURES.[Store Sales]
```

This query returns the store sales for Gender and Promotion Media. When using the MEMBERS keyword, you are returning the set of all members of a dimension. Thus, your query is actually working with two sets, the first being the set of all members of the Gender dimension and the second, all the members of the Promotion Media dimension. Because these represent sets, they must be enclosed in curly brackets. Though you would not have an error raised if you left the brackets out, this is only because OLAP Services knows that the MEMBERS keyword returns a set. You should always use the brackets, even when OLAP Services figures out what you mean.

You can put any dimension into the WHERE clause. A query that finds the total profit for drink sales for married and unmarried females looks as follows:

```
SELECT
[PRODUCT].MEMBERS ON COLUMNS,
[Marital Status].MEMBERS ON ROWS
FROM SALES
WHERE  ([Gender].[F], MEASURES.[Profit])
```

This query answers the very detailed type of questions usually asked by someone doing analytical analysis.

[Gender].[F] is called a fully qualified name. A fully qualified name lists the parent level and the required dimension. You should always use qualified names to make sure you are getting the results you want and to make your MDX queries easy to understand and read.

Another commonly used set function is CHILDREN, which you use to return all the members of one level of the dimension. Thus, if you want to find the sales for all the customers living in the USA by city, you can use the following query:

```
SELECT
MEASURES.MEMBERS ON COLUMNS,
[Customers].[USA].CHILDREN ON ROWS
FROM SALES
```

You can get the results for the next level down as follows:

```
SELECT
MEASURES.MEMBERS ON COLUMNS,
[Customers].[CA].CHILDREN ON ROWS
FROM SALES
```

This allows you to drill down through different levels in the dimension.

Another powerful function that returns members from a particular level of a dimension is DESCENDANTS, which can return any level relative to one of the levels in the dimension. Thus, the following query returns the measures over all the cities in Washington:

```
SELECT
    {Measures.MEMBERS} ON COLUMNS,
    {DESCENDANTS ([Store].[Store State].[WA] , [Store].[Store City])} ON ROWS
FROM Sales
```

Enter and run this query and see how you get back all the cities in Washington. You can change this slightly so you can also see the sales on all of Washington and each of the stores in Washington as follows:

```
SELECT
    {Measures.MEMBERS} ON COLUMNS,
    {[Store].[Store State].[WA],
     DESCENDANTS ([Store].[Store State].[WA] , [Store].[Store City])} ON ROWS
FROM Sales
```

You created a set on the rows. You can change your original query to get the results for one level above by adding the BEFORE flag as follows:

```
SELECT
    {Measures.MEMBERS} ON COLUMNS,
    {
        [Store].[Store State].[WA], DESCENDANTS ([Store].[Store State].[WA] ,
[Store].[Store City], AFTER)
    } ON ROWS
FROM Sales
```

You can also use either the BEFORE flag or the BEFORE_AND_AFTER flag. Let's change the query to Before and After as follows:

```
SELECT
    {Measures.MEMBERS} ON COLUMNS,
    {
        [Store].[Store State].[WA], DESCENDANTS ([Store].[Store State].[WA] ,
[Store].[Store City], BEFORE_AND_AFTER)
    } ON ROWS
FROM Sales
```

One of the more powerful features of MDX is the creation of calculated members using the WITH clause. These queries can get fairly complex. To see the profit for the first and second halves of the year, write the following query:

```
WITH
MEMBER Measures.HalfProfit AS
    ' (Measures.[Store Sales] - Measures.[Store Cost])', FORMAT_STRING
='#.00%', SOLVE_ORDER =1
MEMBER [Time].[First Half] AS
    '[Time].[1997].[Q1] + [Time].[1997].[Q2]'
MEMBER [Time].[Second Half] AS
    '[Time].[1997].[Q3] + [Time].[1997].[Q4]'
Select
{ [Time].[First Half],  [Time].[Second Half] } ON COLUMNS,
{ [Store].[CA].CHILDREN } ON ROWS
FROM Sales
WHERE (MEASURES.[HalfProfit])
```

If you type and run this query, you see that it displays the results with the proper percentages.

For even more advanced examples of MDX queries, go to the *http://www.microsoft.com* site and search for the article, "Introduction to Multidimensional Expressions." This article gives many more examples of MDX queries using FoodMart, including several very advanced examples.

Appendix B
Microsoft Repository

An Enterprise solution is rarely made from a single tool or data source. A typical Enterprise solution might require using information from a Microsoft SQL Server 7.0 OLTP database and a SQL Server 7.0 OLAP database. Data might also come from a wide variety of other data sources such as an Oracle database, Microsoft Exchange Server, third-party data, and so forth. For the user portion of your Enterprise solution you can have custom applications built with Visual Basic, Microsoft Office 2000, and various third-party tools. The design of the application can be done with a modeling tool such as Rational Rose or Visio, the database design can be done with a modeling tool such as Erwin, and various project documents can be created with Microsoft Word and Microsoft Excel. Trying to get all these tools and data sources to work together to build a uniform Enterprise solution requires a standard language that they can all read and write to. The repository provides you with one place where all your applications can store information in one standard format.

Metadata

The repository standard format for storing information includes information such as Unified Modeling Language (UML) designs and database schemas. Many products can access this information. Although products may each speak their own internal language, they all speak one common tongue in the repository. The standard for the repository comes from the Metadata Coalition (MDC) and is called the Open Information Model (OIM). OIM is a product-neutral, technology-independent specification based on metadata. Metadata is a description of the structure of data, what the data means, information on the applications that work with this information, and the various processes that manipulate the data.

Metadata comes in two forms: technical and business. Technical metadata describes the structure of data, such as the structures of the tables in a database. The development team, administrators, and management can use technical metadata when they need to understand the structure of the data.

Business metadata describes the objects in the system, and how they communicate. Business metadata relates to the end users and the applications they use.

Benefits of the Repository

Using the repository allows you to use the best tool for a particular job, and then pass the information from that tool into another tool to do a different job. Thus, you can design your database using a database-modeling tool, and then export this model into the repository. You can next import this information from the repository into your UML tool, which can then generate a first approximation of the components of your system. When you are done building your UML diagrams using your UML tool, you can export the design of your project into the repository. You can then import this design into a custom-built Visual Basic application that reads the repository, and based on the UML class diagrams and other UML diagrams, creates the code for your Visual Basic project. Although this might seem futuristic, this is within the realm of what you can do today.

Corporations can now review all the available tools for building an Enterprise project, find the ones that best suit their projects, and then use the repository to pass information between these tools. This offers a corporation the ability to optimize the building of their Enterprise solutions. In addition to this, information on the structure of data stored in a variety of databases can be placed in the repository. Thus, the structure of data stored in an Oracle database can be placed in the repository, which can then be used by SQL Server to access the data.

The repository also offers the ability to track changes. Thus, a corporation can track changes to the structure of its data over time. This can be very useful information when trying to see how the corporate information has evolved.

Conclusion

The repository offers a place to store information in a standard format called OIM. The OIM is run by the MDC. Information can be exported from databases or development tools into the repository and then read in by other tools or databases. This allows Enterprise information to be passed through all the components of an Enterprise solution.

Appendix C
Visual Basic Components

Building the Visual Basic Components

In this appendix, you will create the components you learned about in Chapter 8. You will build the three components to wrap ADO MD, along with a control to view data in cubes. Let's begin with the connection object.

Cube Connection Object

Begin by opening a new Visual Basic ActiveX dll. Name the new project Cube Connection. Add the same references you added in the ADO MD project, that is, ADO 2.x, ADO MD, and the Data Services Object (DSO). Add a bas module to the project and call it basGlobal.

BasGlobal

You will need to code the basGlobal module first because it has a few private methods used by the clsCubeConnection object. Add the following code to the declarations section of basGlobal:

```
Private Declare Function GetComputerName Lib "kernel32" Alias _
        "GetComputerNameA" (ByVal lpBuffer As String, nSize As Long) _
        As Long
Private Const m_iBufferSize = 255
```

You use this function to get the server name. This function retrieves the correct name only when the component is running on the server. You can modify this function to read from a database or a file containing the names of the possible servers if this component is not running on the server where the data warehouse is located.

Next, you add a function called TrimNullChars to get rid of any null characters in a string. You use this because the GetComputerName function requires you to pass in a string of a certain size. The GetComputerName function places the name of the computer into the string and fills extra characters of the string with nulls. You need to remove the nulls. The function looks as follows:

```
Private Function TrimNullChars(sValue As String) As String
  Dim lngPos As Long
  lngPos = InStr(sValue, vbNullChar)
  If lngPos = 0 Then
    TrimNullChars = sValue
  Else
    TrimNullChars = Left(sValue, lngPos - 1)
  End If
End Function
```

Next, there is the GetServerNames function, which uses the GetComputerName function and the TrimNullChars function. GetServerNames gets the name of the server and is used by clsCubeConnection.

```
Public Function GetServerNames() As String
  Dim sBuffer As String
  sBuffer = String(m_iBufferSize, vbNull)
  GetComputerName sBuffer, m_iBufferSize
  GetServerNames = TrimNullChars(sBuffer)
End Function
```

Let's now look at the clsCubeConnection.

ClsCubeConnection

Let's begin with the declarations section.

Declarations

```
Option Explicit
Private m_sServerName As String
Private m_sDataWarehouseName As String
Private m_sCubeName As String
Private m_sProvider As String
Private m_sMDXQuery As String
Private m_sPassword As String
Private m_sUserID As String
Private m_sConnectionString As String
Private Const cnsProvider As String = "MSOLAP.1"
```

You will have to follow the standard practice for creating a Visual Basic component. In the declarations, you create private variables that are accessed through properties. You have also provided a default value for the provider name. Next, you will code the properties of this component.

Properties

These properties consist of a Get property that retrieves the private variable and a Let property that sets these properties. As mentioned earlier, there should also be error handling in these properties which we are leaving out to keep the code simple.

```
Public Property Get CubeName() As String
  CubeName = m_sCubeName
End Property

Public Property Let CubeName(ByVal v_sNewCubeName As String)
  m_sCubeName = v_sNewCubeName
End Property

Public Property Get UserID() As String
  UserID = m_sUserID
End Property

Public Property Let UserID(ByVal v_sNewUserID As String)
  m_sUserID = v_sNewUserID
End Property

Public Property Get Password() As String
  Password = m_sPassword
End Property

Public Property Let Password(ByVal v_sNewPassword As String)
  m_sPassword = v_sNewPassword
End Property

Public Property Get Provider() As String
  Provider = m_sProvider
End Property

Public Property Let Provider(ByVal v_sNewProvider As String)
  m_sProvider = v_sNewProvider
End Property

Public Property Get ServerName() As String
  ServerName = m_sServerName
End Property

Public Property Let ServerName(ByVal v_sNewServerName As String)
  m_sServerName = v_sNewServerName
End Property
```

```
Private Property Get ConnectionString() As String
  ConnectionString = m_sConnectionString
End Property

Private Property Let ConnectionString _
    (ByVal v_sNewConnectionString As String)

  m_sConnectionString = v_sNewConnectionString
End Property

Public Property Get DataWarehouseName() As String
  DataWarehouseName = m_sDataWarehouseName
End Property

Public Property Let DataWarehouseName(ByVal v_sNewDWName As String)
  m_sDataWarehouseName = v_sNewDWName
End Property
```

SetConnection

You use the SetConnection method when this is a stateful object. SetConnection allows you to set all the values of the connection object with a single method. This method sets the properties if the parameter is passed in. The reason the default is set to EMPTY is that the IsMissing function, which tells if value has been passed into an optional parameter, only works with variants. Because your parameters are all strings, you need to have some way to check if a value has been passed in. You use a default value to do this. If the value of the parameter is EMPTY, you know that the parameter was not passed in.

```
Public Sub SetConnection _
    (Optional ByVal v_sDataWarehouseName As String = "EMPTY", _
    Optional ByVal v_sCubeName As String = "EMPTY", _
    Optional ByVal v_sServerName As String = "EMPTY", _
    Optional ByVal v_sProvider As String = "EMPTY", _
    Optional ByVal v_sUserID As String = "EMPTY", _
    Optional ByVal v_sPassword As String = "EMPTY")

  If v_sDataWarehouseName <> "EMPTY" Then
    DataWarehouseName = v_sDataWarehouseName
  End If
  If v_sCubeName <> "EMPTY" Then
    CubeName = v_sCubeName
  End If
  If v_sServerName <> "EMPTY" Then
    ServerName = v_sServerName
```

```
  End If
  If v_sProvider <> "EMPTY" Then
    Provider = v_sProvider
  End If
  If v_sUserID <> "EMPTY" Then
    UserID = v_sUserID
  End If
  If v_sPassword <> "EMPTY" Then
    Password = v_sPassword
  End If

End Sub
```

Let's now look at GetDataWarehouseNames.

GetDataWarehouseNames

You can use this component as either a stateless or stateful component so it was given optional parameters. If the parameters are passed in, you must set the properties for these parameters. If the parameters are not passed in, this should be a stateful object and you should set the properties for the server name. If the userID and password are not passed in, you must set them to an empty string. You use a function called SetandGetProperties to check the parameters and to set the userID and password to empty strings if no value has been passed in or set. There is an error handler included to show how the error handler should look.

You use the DSO to get this information. The DSO is designed to get information on Microsoft SQL Server 7.0 and to perform administrative tasks with SQL Server. I do not go into the entire hierarchy. You need only one element of the DSO, the Server object's MDStores object. The Server object has an MDStores object which has information on all the multidimensional data stores on the server. You can use the MDStores object to get all the data warehouse names.

```
Public Function GetDataWarehouseNames _
  (ByVal v_sServerName As String, _
    Optional ByVal v_sUserID As String = "EMPTY", _
    Optional ByVal v_sPassword As String = "EMPTY") As String

  Dim objDSOServer As DSO.Server
  Dim Index As Integer
  Dim strServerList as String
  SetandCheckProperties v_sServerName:=v_sServerName, _
    v_sUserID:=v_sUserID, v_sPassword:=v_sPassword
  Set objDSOServer = New DSO.Server
  objDSOServer.Connect v_sServerName
  For Index = 1 To objDSOServer.MDStores.Count
```

```
        If strServerList = "" Then
            strServerList = objDSOServer.MDStores.Item(Index).Name
        Else
            strServerList = strServerList & ":" & _
            objDSOServer.MDStores.Item(Index).Name
        End If
    Next
    GetDataWarehouseNames = strServerList
```

Here is one technique:

```
GetDataWarehouseNames_Exit:
    On Error Resume Next
    objDSOServer.CloseServer
    Set objDSOServer = Nothing
    Exit Function
GetDataWarehouseNamesError:
    MsgBox "Error:" & Err.Description & vbCrLf & _
            "Error Number:" & Err.Number & vbCrLf & _
            "Error Source:" & Err.Source

    Resume GetDataWarehouseNames_Exit
End Function
```

Let's look at SetandCheckProperties.

SetandCheckProperties

The SetandCheckProperties method checks if a parameter has been passed in by checking if its value is equal to the word EMPTY. Notice that there is a different default here, that is, IGNORE, which is used for SetandCheckProperties and EMPTY, which is used for all public methods.

The SetandCheckProperties method is used by other public methods, such as GetDataWarehouseNames, that have optional parameters with a default value of EMPTY. You want to check if a value has been passed into the public function calling SetandCheckProperties (such as GetDataWarehouseNames), not if a value has been passed into the SetandCheckProperties method. If a parameter is not passed into SetandCheckProperties, its value is IGNORE and these parameters are ignored by this method.

```
Private Function SetandCheckProperties _
    (Optional ByVal v_sDataWarehouseName As String = "IGNORE", _
    Optional ByVal v_sCubeName As String = "IGNORE", _
    Optional ByVal v_sServerName As String = "IGNORE", _
    Optional ByVal v_sProvider As String = "IGNORE", _
    Optional ByVal v_sUserID As String = "IGNORE", _
    Optional ByVal v_sPassword As String = "IGNORE")
```

If the cube name was passed into SetAndCheckProperties (its value is not equal to IGNORE), you want to first check if the value is EMPTY. If it is not EMPTY, the cube name was passed into the public method calling SetandGetProperties. In this case, you want to update the CubeName property to the new value. If no value was passed into as a parameter and the CubeName property is not set, you consider this an error. If you raise an error, it is trapped by the calling function that then raises the error to the component that called the original method.

```
If v_sCubeName <> "EMPTY" AND v_sCubeName <> "IGNORE" Then
   CubeName = v_sCubeName
Else
  If CubeName = "" Then
      'Err.Raise
  End If
End If
```

Let's do the same for the DataWarehouseName, the Provider, and the ServerName.

```
If v_sDataWarehouseName <> "EMPTY" Then
  DataWarehouseName = v_sDataWarehouseName
Else
  If DataWarehouseName = "" Then
    'Err.Raise
  End If
End If
If v_sProvider <> "EMPTY" Then
  Provider = v_sProvider
End If
If v_sServerName <> "EMPTY" Then
  ServerName = v_sServerName
Else
  If ServerName = "" Then
    'Err.Raise
  End If
End If
```

For the password and userID, set them to the empty string if no value has been passed in or set.

```
If v_sPassword <> "EMPTY" Then
  Password = v_sPassword
Else
  Password = ""
End If
If v_sUserID <> "EMPTY" Then
  UserID = v_sUserID
```

```
    Else
      UserID = ""
    End If

End Function
```

GetServerName

GetServerName returns the names of the servers. It uses the GetServerNames function in your bas module, which in turn uses an application programming interface (API) call, to get the name of the server.

```
Public Function GetServerName(Optional ByVal v_sUserID As String = "EMPTY", _
    Optional ByVal v_sPassword As String = "EMPTY") As String
  GetServerName = GetServerNames
End Function
```

GetCubeNames

GetCubeNames uses the ADO MD catalog object hierarchy to get the names of the cubes. Again, you are allowing the user to either pass a parameter in or set properties, depending on whether the component has state. Error handling is not included here, but you should include it in the production code.

```
Function GetCubeNames _
    (Optional ByVal v_sServerName As String = "EMPTY", _
    Optional ByVal v_sDataWarehouseName As String = "EMPTY", _
    Optional ByVal v_sProvider As String = "EMPTY", _
    Optional ByVal v_sUserID As String = "EMPTY", _
    Optional ByVal v_sPassword As String = "EMPTY") As String
  Dim lngCubeDefCounter As Long
  Dim objCatalog As ADO MD.Catalog
  Dim objConnection As ADODB.Connection
  Dim strCubeNames As String

  Set objCatalog = New ADO-MD.Catalog
  Set objConnection = New ADODB.Connection

  SetandCheckProperties v_sDataWarehouseName, _
      "", v_sServerName, v_sProvider
  objConnection.Open "Provider=" & Provider & _
      ";Persist Security Info=False;Data Source=" & _
      ServerName & ";Location=" & DataWarehouseName & _
      ";Connect Timeout=60;Client Cache Size=25;" & _
      "Auto Synch Period=10000;User ID=" & UserID & _
      ";Password=" & Password & ";"
  Set objCatalog.ActiveConnection = objConnection
```

```
With objCatalog.CubeDefs
   For lngCubeDefCounter = 0 To (.Count - 1)
      If strCubeNames = "" Then
          strCubeNames = .Item(lngCubeDefCounter).Name
      Else
          strCubeNames = strCubeNames & "," & _
              .Item(lngCubeDefCounter).Name
      End If
   Next
End With
GetCubeNames = strCubeNames
Set objConnection = Nothing
Set objCatalog = Nothing
End Function
```

Initialize and Terminate

In the initialize event, you set the provider property to the default value:

```
Private Sub Class_Initialize()
   Provider = cnsProvider
End Sub
```

CubeData

You use CubeData to get a dataset from a cube. You can disconnect this dataset from the data warehouse and return it to a client from a middle tier data services component. Add a new project to make a Visual Basic dll project and create a Visual Basic group. Call the project CubeData and the new Visual Basic group grpCube. Call the class in project CubeData, clsTupleMember. Start at the bottom of the hierarchy and work up.

ClsTupleMember

The clsTupleMember class is a managed class and is composed only of properties. These properties are the same ones that are found in ADO MD. If you need additional properties from ADO MD or custom properties, you can add these, too.

```
Option Explicit
Private m_sMemberType As String
Private m_sMemberCaption As String
Private m_oMembersCollection As Collection
Private m_sMemberUniqueName As String
Private m_sMemberName As String
Private m_sMemberDescription As String
Private m_lMemberDepth As Long
Private m_lMemberChildCount As Long
Private m_lMemberAxisPosition  As Long
Private m_sMemberParent As String
```

Properties

```
Public Property Get MemberDescription() As String
  MemberDescription = m_sMemberDescription
End Property
Friend Property Let MemberDescription _
  (ByVal v_sNewMemberDescription As String)

  m_sMemberDescription = v_sNewMemberDescription
End Property
Public Property Get MemberUniqueName() As String
  MemberUniqueName = m_sMemberUniqueName
End Property
Friend Property Let MemberUniqueName _
  (ByVal v_sNewMemberUniqueName As String)
  m_sMemberUniqueName = v_sNewMemberUniqueName
End Property
Public Property Get MemberName() As String
  MemberName = m_sMemberName
End Property
Friend Property Let MemberName(ByVal v_sNewMemberName As String)
  m_sMemberName = v_sNewMemberName
End Property
Public Property Get MemberCaption() As String
  MemberCaption = m_sMemberCaption
End Property
Friend Property Let MemberCaption(ByVal v_sNewMemberCaption As String)
  m_sMemberCaption = v_sNewMemberCaption
End Property
Public Property Get MemberDepth() As Long
  MemberDepth = m_lMemberDepth
End Property
Friend Property Let MemberDepth(ByVal v_lNewMemberDepth As Long)
  m_lMemberDepth = v_lNewMemberDepth
End Property
Public Property Get MemberAxisPosition() As Long
  MemberAxisPosition = m_lMemberAxisPosition
End Property
Friend Property Let MemberAxisPosition _
  (ByVal v_lNewMemberAxisPosition As Long)

  m_lMemberAxisPosition = v_lNewMemberAxisPosition
End Property
```

```
Public Property Get MemberChildCount() As Long
  MemberChildCount = m_lMemberChildCount
End Property
Friend Property Let MemberChildCount _
  (ByVal v_lNewMemberChildCount As Long)

 m_lMemberChi`ldCount = v_lNewMemberChildCount
End Property
Public Property Get MemberType() As String
    MemberType = m_sMemberType
End Property
Friend Property Let MemberType(ByVal v_sNewMemberType As String)
  m_sMemberType = v_sNewMemberType
End Property
Public Property Get MemberParent() As String
  MemberParent = m_sMemberParent
End Property
Friend Property Let MemberParent(ByVal v_sNewMemberParent As String)
  m_sMemberParent = v_sNewMemberParent
End Property
```

ClsTuple

The clsTuple class is a managing class, which manages a collection of clsTupleMember objects. Add a new class to the project and call it clsTuple. Let's look at some of the methods in this class. The class begins with the following declarations:

Declarations

```
Option Explicit
Private m_lAxisLocation As Long
Private m_lNumberOfDimensions As Long
Private m_lCount As Long
Private m_oNameCollection As Collection
Private m_oTupleMemberCollection As Collection
Private m_bInitializedNames As Boolean
```

Properties

The properties once again just give access to the private variables.

```
Public Property Get Count() As Long
    Count = m_lCount
End Property

Friend Property Let Count(ByVal v_lNewCount As Long)
    m_lCount = v_lNewCount
End Property
```

```
Private Property Get InitializedNames() As Boolean
    InitializedNames = m_bInitializedNames
End Property
Private Property Let InitializedNames _
  (ByVal v_bNewInitializedNames As Boolean)

  m_bInitializedNames = v_bNewInitializedNames
End Property
```

TupleMember

The method TupleMember retrieves the clsTupleMember with either the index number or the name of the tuple passed in. In this object hierarchy, the standard Item for these methods is not used. However, they are used in the other hierarchy so you can see both options. Some think it is clearer to use a name that reflects what item is being returned, rather than using the Item, but it is up to you to decide what is best.

If an index number is passed in that does not exist within the clsTupleMember collection, a new clsTupleMember is added to the collection. This means that you can add members to the collection without explicitly calling a special function to create members. You may prefer to make the AddToTupleMemberCollection a friend property and add the collection members explicitly. Some find that coding it implicitly is simpler and cleaner.

Thus, the TupleMember function has to check if a numeric index that is passed in really exists, and if it does not, add a new clsTupleMember with that index. This does create one potential problem, though. If an application using the CubeData object inputs the wrong ID, it results in a new member being added instead of raising an error. To handle this, there should be a Friend Boolean parameter called CubeClosed. CubeClosed should be set to True when the object is initialized, and set to False after the data is placed into the collection. Additional code needs to be added to the functions, like TupleMember, to raise an error if CubeClosed is set to True if the index does not exist.

You also use a collection to map the names of each clsTupleMember to the numeric ID. The first time a string is passed in as the Index, the function InitializeNames is called to build the collection that makes the mapping. If a string is passed in again, the collection has been initialized and can be used to get the numeric ID. You use a private Boolean InitializedNames to check if the collection has been initialized yet.

```
Public Function TupleMember(ByVal v_vIndex As Variant) _
    As clsTupleMember


  On Error GoTo ItemError
```

First, you check if a string has been passed in by using the Visual Basic TypeName function. This works as long as none of the names of your TupleMembers is numeric. This again goes back to the system administrator and developers working together. Looking in FoodMart, you find the months in the time dimension are listed as 1,2, … If when trying to access month 1 you just passed the number 1 in, you get back the first item in the collection. Although this is probably month 1, it could also be something else. A simple workaround involves having the functions make sure that when they mean month 1, they pass the 1 in as a string, either by using quotes ("1") or the string function (Str(lngMonth)). In this case, TypeName returns String. Either way, bad naming conventions have resulted in the developer adding special code into the application. This is why it is so essential that the developer and the administrator work together.

```
If UCase(TypeName(v_vIndex)) = "String" Then
  If Not InitializedNames Then
    InitializeNames
    InitializedNames = True
  End If
  Set TupleMember = _
m_oTupleMemberCollection(Str(m_oNameCollection.Item(v_vIndex)))
```

If a string is not passed in, assume it is numeric. You can add additional checks to make sure it really is numeric, and raise an error if it is not numeric.

```
Else
  On Error Resume Next
```

If the numeric ID is not in the collection, error number 5 is raised when you try to retrieve that member from the collection. Shut off error handling and then check if error number 5 has been raised. If it was raised, add a new member to the collection with that numeric ID. AddTupleMember adds a new clsTupleMember to the m_oTupleMemberCollection.

```
  Set TupleMember = m_oTupleMemberCollection(Str(v_vIndex))
  If Err.Number <> 0 Then
    If Err.Number = 5 Then
      Dim objTupleMember As New clsTupleMember
      AddToTupleMemberCollection v_vIndex, objTupleMember
      Set TupleMember = m_oTupleMemberCollection(Str(v_vIndex))
    Else
```

If you have any error other than 5, you should raise the error:

```
      'Err.Raise
    End If
  End If
End If
Exit Function
ItemError:
  Err.Raise Err.Number, Err.Source & "  TupleMember.Item"
End Function
```

InitializeNames

InitializeNames goes through all the members in the collection and maps the unique name of these members to their numeric ID. An application can then use the unique ID of a member to retrieve the clsTupleMember associated with that member. The AddToNameCollection adds the name and numeric ID to the collection.

```
Private Sub InitializeNames()
    Dim lngCollectionCounter As Long
    For lngCollectionCounter = 0 To _
        m_oTupleMemberCollection.Count - 1
      AddToNameCollection 0, m_oTupleMemberCollection.Item _
          (Str(lngCollectionCounter)).MemberUniqueName
    Next
End Sub
```

AddToNameCollection

The private AddToNameCollection method adds the unique name of a tuple member and its numeric ID to a collection. This allows a mapping between the unique name and the numeric ID of the member tuple.

```
Private Sub AddToNameCollection _
  (ByVal v_lTupleMemberID As Long, ByVal v_sTupleMemberName As String)

    m_oNameCollection.Add v_lTupleMemberID, v_sTupleMemberName
End Sub
```

AddToTupleMemberCollection

The private AddToTupleMemberCollection method adds clsTuple objects to a collection and associates them with a numeric ID.

```
Private Sub AddToTupleMemberCollection(ByVal v_lTupleMemberID As Long,
ByVal v_oTupleMember As clsTupleMember)
    m_oTupleMemberCollection.Add v_oTupleMember, Str(v_lTupleMemberID)
End Sub
```

ClearNameCollection

Let's empty the collection before destroying it.

```
Private Sub ClearNameCollection()
  Dim lngCollectionCounter As Long
  If m_oNameCollection.Count = 0 Then
    Exit Sub
  End If
  lngCollectionCounter = m_oNameCollection.Count
  Do Until lngCollectionCounter = 0
```

```
     m_oNameCollection.Remove lngCollectionCounter
     lngCollectionCounter = lngCollectionCounter - 1
   Loop
End Sub
```

ClearTupleMemberCollection

Before destroying the clsTuple object, destroy the clsTupleMember objects in the collection. You do this by removing them from the collection.

```
Private Sub ClearTupleMemberCollection()
  Dim lngCollectionCounter As Long
  If m_oTupleMemberCollection.Count = 0 Then
    Exit Sub
  End If
  lngCollectionCounter = m_oTupleMemberCollection.Count
  Do Until lngCollectionCounter = 0
    m_oTupleMemberCollection.Remove lngCollectionCounter
    lngCollectionCounter = lngCollectionCounter - 1
  Loop
End Sub
```

Initialize and Terminate

The Intialize and Terminate events create and destroy the objects used by the clsTuple object.

```
Private Sub Class_Initialize()
  Set m_oNameCollection = New Collection
  Set m_oTupleMemberCollection = New Collection
End Sub
Private Sub Class_Terminate()
  ClearNameCollection
  ClearTupleMemberCollection
  Set m_oNameCollection = Nothing
  Set m_oTupleMemberCollection = Nothing
End Sub
```

With the exception of the clsCubeData class, the rest of the classes are either managing or managed classes and are coded in the same way as clsTuple and clsTupleMember.

ClsAxes

The clsAxes class manage a collection of clsAxis objects.

Declarations

```
Option Explicit
Private m_lCount As Long
```

```
Private m_bInitializedNames As Boolean
Private m_oNameCollection As Collection
Private m_oAxisCollection As Collection
Private Sub InitializeNames()
   Dim lngCollectionCounter As Long

   For lngCollectionCounter = 0 To m_oAxisCollection.Count - 1
     AddToNameCollection 0, _
         m_oAxisCollection.Item(Str(lngCollectionCounter)).AxisName
   Next
End Sub
```

Properties

```
Private Property Get InitializedNames() As Boolean
  InitializedNames = m_bInitializedNames
End Property
Private Property Let InitializedNames _
    (ByVal v_bNewInitializedNames As Boolean)

  m_bInitializedNames = v_bNewInitializedNames
End Property
Public Property Get Count() As Long
    Count = m_lCount
End Property
Friend Property Let Count(ByVal v_lNewCount As Long)
    m_lCount = v_lNewCount
End Property
```

Axis

```
Public Function Axis(ByVal v_vIndex As Variant) As clsAxis
    On Error GoTo ItemError
    If UCase(TypeName(v_vIndex)) = "STRING" Then
        If Not InitializedNames Then
            InitializeNames
            InitializedNames = True
        End If
        Set Axis = _
            m_oAxisCollection(Str(m_oNameCollection.Item(v_vIndex)))
    Else
        On Error Resume Next
        Set Axis = m_oAxisCollection(Str(v_vIndex))
        If Err.Number <> 0 Then
            If Err.Number = 5 Then
```

```
            Dim objAxis As New clsAxis
            AddToAxisCollection v_vIndex, objAxis
            Set Axis = m_oAxisCollection(Str(v_vIndex))
        Else
            'Err.Raise
        End If
    End If
    End If
    Exit Function
ItemError:
    Err.Raise Err.Number, Err.Source & "  Axis.Item"
End Function
```

AddToNameCollection

```
Private Sub AddToNameCollection _
    (ByVal v_lAxisID As Long, ByVal v_sAxisName As String)
    m_oNameCollection.Add v_lAxisID, v_sAxisName
End Sub

Private Sub ClearNameCollection()
    Dim lngCollectionCounter As Long
    If m_oNameCollection.Count = 0 Then
        Exit Sub
    End If
    lngCollectionCounter = m_oNameCollection.Count
    Do Until lngCollectionCounter = 0
        m_oNameCollection.Remove lngCollectionCounter
        lngCollectionCounter = lngCollectionCounter - 1
    Loop
End Sub
```

ClearAxisCollection

```
Private Sub ClearAxisCollection()
    Dim lngCollectionCounter As Long
    If m_oAxisCollection.Count = 0 Then
        Exit Sub
    End If
    lngCollectionCounter = m_oAxisCollection.Count
    Do Until lngCollectionCounter = 0
        m_oAxisCollection.Remove lngCollectionCounter
        lngCollectionCounter = lngCollectionCounter - 1
    Loop
End Sub
```

AddAxisCollection

```
Private Sub AddToAxisCollection _
    (ByVal v_lAxisID As Long, ByVal v_oAxis As clsAxis)
    m_oAxisCollection.Add v_oAxis, Str(v_lAxisID)
End Sub
```

Initialize and Terminate

```
Private Sub Class_Initialize()
  Set m_oNameCollection = New Collection
  Set m_oAxisCollection = New Collection
End Sub
Private Sub Class_Terminate()
  ClearAxisCollection
  ClearNameCollection
  Set m_oNameCollection = Nothing
  Set m_oAxisCollection = Nothing
End Sub
```

ClsAxis

For each axis in the cube we will have a clsAxis object containing information on the axis.

Declarations

```
Private m_sAxesName As String
Private m_lDimensionCount As Long
Private m_oTuples As clsTuples
```

Properties

```
Public Property Get AxesName() As String
  AxesName = m_sAxesName
End Property
Friend Property Let AxesName(ByVal v_sNewAxesName As String)
  m_sAxesName = v_sNewAxesName
End Property
Public Property Get DimensionCount() As Long
  DimensionCount = m_lDimensionCount
End Property
Friend Property Let DimensionCount(ByVal v_lNewDimensionCount As Long)
  m_lDimensionCount = v_lNewDimensionCount
End Property
Public Property Get Tuples() As clsTuples
  Set Tuples = m_oTuples
End Property
```

```
Friend Property Set Tuples(ByVal v_oNewTuples As clsTuples)
  Set m_oTuples = v_oNewTuples
End Property
Private Sub Class_Initialize()
  Set m_oTuples = New clsTuples
End Sub
Private Sub Class_Terminate()
  Set m_oTuples = Nothing
End Sub
```

ClsCubeData

The clsCubeData class must retrieve data based on an MDX query. The most complicated part of the code is the InitializeCube method, which you will explore in detail.

Declarations

```
Option Explicit
Private m_sMDXQuery As String
Private m_oAxes As clsAxes
Private m_vCubeValues() As Variant
Private m_sConnectionString As String
Private m_lCubeIndex As Long
Private Const cnsProvider As String = "MSOLAP.1"
Private m_sSlicerAxisTuple As String
Private m_oCubeConnection As CubeConnection.clsCubeConnection
```

Properties

```
Public Function GetCubeValues _
  (ByVal v_lAxis0Coordinate As Long, _
  ByVal v_lAxis1Coordinate As Long) As Variant

  GetCubeValues = m_vCubeValues(v_lAxis0Coordinate, v_lAxis1Coordinate)
End Function
Private Function SetCubeValues _
  (ByVal v_lAxis0Coordinate As Long, _
  ByVal v_lAxis1Coordinate As Long, ByVal v_vCubeValue As Variant)

  m_vCubeValues(v_lAxis0Coordinate, v_lAxis1Coordinate) = v_vCubeValue
End Function
Private Property Get ConnectionString() As String
    ConnectionString = m_sConnectionString
End Property
Private Property Let ConnectionString _
  (ByVal v_sNewConnectionString As String)
```

```
    m_sConnectionString = v_sNewConnectionString
End Property
Public Property Get MDXQuery() As String
    MDXQuery = m_sMDXQuery
End Property
Public Property Let MDXQuery(ByVal v_sNewMDXQuery As String)
    m_sMDXQuery = v_sNewMDXQuery
End Property
Public Property Get Axes() As clsAxes
  If m_oAxes Is Nothing Then
    Set Axes = Nothing
    Exit Property
  End If
  Set Axes = m_oAxes
End Property
Public Property Get SlicerAxisTuple() As String
  SlicerAxisTuple = m_sSlicerAxisTuple
End Property
Public Property Let SlicerAxisTuple(ByVal v_sNewSlicerAxisTuple As String)
  m_sSlicerAxisTuple = v_sNewSlicerAxisTuple
End Property
```

InitializeCubeData

Looking at the code, you see that this module looks very complicated. You can show what the code is doing using a Unified Modeling Language (UML) activity diagram, as shown in Figure C-1.

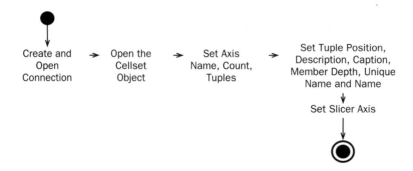

Figure C-1. *Activity diagram for IntializeCubeData.*

This complicated code module turns out to actually be a few simple steps. The diamonds represent decision points where the flow can go one way or the other. These can represent If statements, or in this case, the decision to continue a loop or exit the loop. The activity diagram maps out the code in pseudo-code format showing the steps and flow of the code. The diagram could have been made more detailed, but this one is just a general overview of the code. If you look through the code, you see that the diagrams cover the majority of what the code is doing. Activity diagrams are useful for mapping out how you are going to code modules. Using activity diagrams, teams discuss the best way to code difficult code modules and reach the best solution together.

Notice that you are not calling any explicit method to add members to the collections. You only need to call the item method associated with the managing classes, and the managing classes create the object and add it to the collection.

```
Public Sub InitializeCubeData _
  (ByVal v_oCubeConnection As CubeConnection.clsCubeConnection, Optional
ByVal v_MDXQuery As String)

  Dim lngMembersCounter As Long
  Dim lngAxesCounter As Long
  Dim lngPositionCounter As Long
  Dim objConnection As ADODB.Connection
  Dim objCellset As ADO-MD.Cellset
  Set objConnection = New ADODB.Connection
  Set objCellset = New ADO-MD.Cellset


  'Create and Open Connection
  ConnectionString = "Provider=" & v_oCubeConnection.Provider & _
      ";Persist Security Info=False;Data Source=" & _
      v_oCubeConnection.ServerName & ";Location=" & _
      v_oCubeConnection.DataWarehouseName & _
      ";Connect Timeout=60;Client Cache Size=25;" & _
      "Auto Synch Period=10000;User ID=" & v_oCubeConnection.UserID & _
      ";Password=" & v_oCubeConnection.Password & ";"
  objConnection.Open ConnectionString
  'Open Cellset Object
  Set objCellset.ActiveConnection = objConnection
  If v_MDXQuery <> "EMPTY" Then
    MDXQuery = v_MDXQuery
  End If
  objCellset.Open MDXQuery
  With objCellset.Axes
    'Set the name of Axis, Axis Count and the Tuples on the Axis
    Axes.Count = .Count
    For lngAxesCounter = 0 To (.Count - 1)
      With .Item(lngAxesCounter)
        Axes.Axis(lngAxesCounter).DimensionCount = .DimensionCount
        Axes.Axis(lngAxesCounter).AxesName = .Name
        With .Positions
          Axes.Axis(lngAxesCounter).Tuples.Count = .Count
```

```
        For lngPositionCounter = 0 To (.Count - 1)
'Set the position, description, caption, member depth. unique
name and name for each Tuple Member
        With .Item(lngPositionCounter)
          Axes.Axis(lngAxesCounter).Tuples. _
              Tuple(lngPositionCounter).Count = .Members.Count
          For lngMembersCounter = 0 To (.Members.Count - 1)
            With .Members.Item(lngMembersCounter)
              Axes.Axis(lngAxesCounter).Tuples. _
                  Tuple(lngPositionCounter). _
                  TupleMember(lngMembersCounter). _
                  MemberAxisPosition = _
                  objCellset.Axes.Item(lngAxesCounter). _
                  Positions(lngPositionCounter).Ordinal
              Axes.Axis(lngAxesCounter).Tuples. _
                  Tuple(lngPositionCounter). _
                  TupleMember(lngMembersCounter).MemberCaption = _
                  .Caption
              Axes.Axis(lngAxesCounter).Tuples. _
                  Tuple(lngPositionCounter). _
                  TupleMember(lngMembersCounter). _
                  MemberDescription = .Description
              Axes.Axis(lngAxesCounter).Tuples. _
                  Tuple(lngPositionCounter). _
                  TupleMember(lngMembersCounter).MemberDepth = _
                  .LevelDepth
              Axes.Axis(lngAxesCounter).Tuples. _
                  Tuple(lngPositionCounter). _
                  TupleMember(lngMembersCounter).MemberName = _
                  .LevelName
              Axes.Axis(lngAxesCounter).Tuples. _
                  Tuple(lngPositionCounter). _
                  TupleMember(lngMembersCounter). _
                  MemberUniqueName = .UniqueName
              Axes.Axis(lngAxesCounter).Tuples. _
                  Tuple(lngPositionCounter). _
                  TupleMember(lngMembersCounter). _
                  MemberChildCount = .ChildCount
            End With
          Next lngMembersCounter
        End With
```

```
            Next lngPositionCounter
         End With '.Positions
      End With '.Item(lngAxesCounter)
   Next lngAxesCounter
End With
Dim lngSlicerTupleCounter As Long
Dim strSlicerMembers As String
For lngSlicerTupleCounter = 0 To _
   objCellset.FilterAxis.Positions.Item(0).Members.Count - 1
   If strSlicerMembers = "" Then
      strSlicerMembers = objCellset.FilterAxis.Positions.Item(0). _
         Members.Item(lngSlicerTupleCounter).UniqueName
   Else
      strSlicerMembers = strSlicerMembers & "," & _
         objCellset.FilterAxis.Positions.Item(0).Members. _
            Item(lngSlicerTupleCounter).UniqueName
   End If
Next
SlicerAxisTuple = strSlicerMembers
Dim lngPosition0Counter As Long
Dim lngPosition1Counter As Long
With objCellset.Axes
   ReDim m_vCubeValues(.Item(0).Positions.Count, _
         .Item(1).Positions.Count)
   For lngPosition0Counter = 0 To .Item(0).Positions.Count - 1
      For lngPosition1Counter = 0 To .Item(1).Positions.Count - 1
         SetCubeValues lngPosition0Counter, lngPosition1Counter, _
         objCellset.Item(lngPosition0Counter, _
            lngPosition1Counter).FormattedValue
      Next
   Next
End With
End Sub
```

Initialize and Terminate

```
Private Sub Class_Initialize()
   Set m_oAxes = New clsAxes
End Sub

Private Sub Class_Terminate()
   Set m_oAxes = Nothing
End Sub
```

ClsTuples

The clsTuples object will manage a collection of clsTuple objects.

Declarations

```
Option Explicit
Private m_lAxisLocation As Long
Private m_lNumberOfDimensions As Long
Private m_lCount As Long
Private m_oNameCollection As Collection
Private m_oTupleCollection As Collection
Private m_bInitializedNames As Boolean
```

Properties

```
Public Property Get Count() As Long
    Count = m_lCount
End Property
Friend Property Let Count(ByVal v_lNewCount As Long)
    m_lCount = v_lNewCount
End Property
Private Property Get InitializedNames() As Boolean
    InitializedNames = m_bInitializedNames
End Property
Private Property Let InitializedNames _
  (ByVal v_bNewInitializedNames As Boolean)

  m_bInitializedNames = v_bNewInitializedNames
End Property
```

InitializeNames

```
Private Sub InitializeNames()
  Dim lngCollectionCounter As Long
  For lngCollectionCounter = 0 To m_oTupleCollection.Count - 1
    AddToNameCollection 0, _
      m_oTupleCollection.Item(Str(lngCollectionCounter)). _
        MemberUniqueName
  Next
End Sub
```

Tuple

```
Public Function Tuple(ByVal v_vIndex As Variant) As clsTuple
  On Error GoTo ItemError
  If UCase(TypeName(v_vIndex)) = "String" Then
    If Not InitializedNames Then
```

```
      InitializeNames
      InitializedNames = True
    End If
    Set Tuple = _
      m_oTupleCollection(Str(m_oNameCollection.Item(v_vIndex)))
  Else
    On Error Resume Next
    Set Tuple = m_oTupleCollection(Str(v_vIndex))
    If Err.Number <> 0 Then
      If Err.Number = 5 Then
        Dim objTuple As New clsTuple
        AddToTupleCollection v_vIndex, objTuple
        Set Tuple = m_oTupleCollection(Str(v_vIndex))
    Else
          'Err.Raise
      End If
    End If
  End If
  Exit Function
ItemError:
  Err.Raise Err.Number, Err.Source & "  Tuple.Item"
End Function
```

AddToNameCollection

```
Private Sub AddToNameCollection _
  (ByVal v_lTupleID As Long, ByVal v_sTupleName As String)
  m_oNameCollection.Add v_lTupleID, v_sTupleName
End Sub
Private Sub ClearNameCollection()
  Dim lngCollectionCounter As Long
  If m_oNameCollection.Count = 0 Then
      Exit Sub
  End If
  lngCollectionCounter = m_oNameCollection.Count
  Do Until lngCollectionCounter = 0
      m_oNameCollection.Remove lngCollectionCounter
      lngCollectionCounter = lngCollectionCounter - 1
  Loop
End Sub
```

ClearTupleCollection

```
Private Sub ClearTupleCollection()
  Dim lngCollectionCounter As Long
  If m_oTupleCollection.Count = 0 Then
```

```
        Exit Sub
    End If
    lngCollectionCounter = m_oTupleCollection.Count
    Do Until lngCollectionCounter = 0
        m_oTupleCollection.Remove lngCollectionCounter
        lngCollectionCounter = lngCollectionCounter - 1
    Loop
End Sub
```

AddToTupleCollection

```
Private Sub AddToTupleCollection _
    (ByVal v_lTupleID As Long, ByVal v_oTuple As clsTuple)
    m_oTupleCollection.Add v_oTuple, Str(v_lTupleID)
End Sub
```

Initialize and Terminate

```
Private Sub Class_Initialize()
    Set m_oNameCollection = New Collection
    Set m_oTupleCollection = New Collection
End Sub
Private Sub Class_Terminate()
    ClearNameCollection
    ClearTupleCollection
    Set m_oNameCollection = Nothing
    Set m_oTupleCollection = Nothing
End Sub
```

CubeMetaData

The CubeMetaData object holds all the metadata for the cube. This object can easily become very large, so you should add ways of limiting the records that are returned. Once again, this is an ideal job for a business services component. Eliminating the names of all the customers in the code reduces the time it takes to get the data by at least 10 seconds and substantially reduces the size of the data being returned. You begin with clsCubeMeta data because it has the InitializeCubeMeta data method that requires explaining. The rest of the classes are coded the same as in clsCubeData.

Add a new project called CubeMetaData to the Visual Basic group. Call the default class clsCubeMetaData and code it as follows.

ClsCubeMetaData

The clsCubeMetaData sits on top of the hierarchy and is responsible for maintaining access to all of the members of the hierarchy. The clsCubeMetaData will also be responsible for the initialization of all of the members of the hierarchy.

Declarations

```
Option Explicit
Private m_sCubeName
Private m_oDimensions As clsDimensions
Private m_sConnectionString As String
Private m_lCubeIndex As Long
```

Properties

```
Private Property Get CubeIndex() As Long
  CubeIndex = m_lCubeIndex
End Property
Private Property Let CubeIndex(ByVal v_lNewCubeIndex As Long)
  m_lCubeIndex = v_lNewCubeIndex
End Property
Public Property Get CubeName() As String
  CubeName = m_sCubeName
End Property
Public Property Let CubeName(ByVal v_sNewCubeName As String)
  m_sCubeName = v_sNewCubeName
End Property
Private Property Get ConnectionString() As String
  ConnectionString = m_sConnectionString
End Property
Private Property Let ConnectionString _
  (ByVal v_sNewConnectionString As String)

  m_sConnectionString = v_sNewConnectionString
End Property
Public Property Get Dimensions() As clsDimensions
  If m_oDimensions Is Nothing Then
    Set Dimensions = Nothing
  End If
  Set Dimensions = m_oDimensions
End Property
```

InitializeCubeMetaData

Once again, you can use an activity diagram to simplify the code, as shown in Figure C-2.

If the level name is CustomerName, you ignore this level and continue; otherwise you get the level information. The other diamonds represent a decision point to continue a loop or exit the loop. These diagrams are also very useful for the system administrator to understand the code without having to get into the actual code.

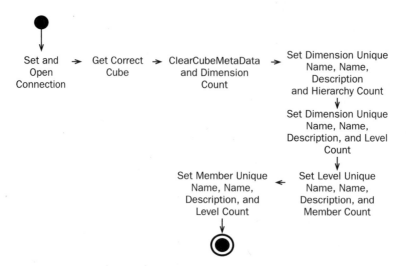

Figure C-2. *Activity Diagram for InitializeCubeMetaData.*

```
Public Function InitializeCubeMetaData _
    (ByVal v_oCubeConnection As CubeConnection.clsCubeConnection)

    Dim lngCubeDefCounter As Long
    Dim lngCubePropertiesCounter As Long
    Dim lngCubeDimensionCounter As Long
    Dim objCatalog As ADO-MD.Catalog
    Dim objConnection As ADODB.Connection
    Dim lngHierarchiesCounter As Long
    Dim lngLevelsCounter As Long
    Dim lngMembersCounter As Long


    Set objCatalog = New ADO-MD.Catalog
    Set objConnection = New ADODB.Connection
    'Set and Open Connection
    ConnectionString = "Provider=" & v_oCubeConnection.Provider & _
    ";Persist Security Info=False;Data Source=" & _
    v_oCubeConnection.ServerName & ";Location=" & _
    v_oCubeConnection.DataWarehouseName & _
    ";Connect Timeout=60;Client Cache Size=25;" & _
    "Auto Synch Period=10000;User ID=" & v_oCubeConnection.UserID & _
      ";Password=" & v_oCubeConnection.Password & ";"
    objConnection.Open ConnectionString
    Set objCatalog.ActiveConnection = objConnection
    CubeName = v_oCubeConnection.CubeName
    With objCatalog.CubeDefs
```

```
   CubeIndex = -1
   For lngCubeDefCounter = 0 To (.Count - 1)
     If UCase(CubeName) = UCase(.Item(lngCubeDefCounter).Name) Then
       CubeIndex = lngCubeDefCounter
       Exit For
     End If
   Next
   If CubeIndex = -1 Then
     'Err.Raise
   End If
 End With
 With Dimensions
```

If the object is being refreshed, you want to clear any old values. To do this call the ClearDimensionsCollection. This clears all the clsDimension objects from the clsDimensions collection. As each clsDimension is cleared, it clears all its clsHierarchy objects, which clear all their clsHierarchy objects in their clsHierarchy collection, and so forth. Thus, calling ClearDimensionCollection clears the entire CubeMetaData object of data.

```
'Clear any existing information out of the CubeMetaData object, set
'Dimension count
.ClearDimensionCollection
.ClearNameCollection
'Set Dimension Unique Name, Dimension Name, Dimension
'Description,Set Hierarchy count
.Count = objCatalog.CubeDefs(CubeIndex).Dimensions.Count
For lngCubeDimensionCounter = 0 To _
      (objCatalog.CubeDefs(CubeIndex).Dimensions.Count - 1)
    With .Item(lngCubeDimensionCounter)
      .DimensionName = _
         objCatalog.CubeDefs(CubeIndex).Dimensions. _
         Item(lngCubeDimensionCounter).Name
      .DimensionUniqueName = _
         objCatalog.CubeDefs(CubeIndex).Dimensions. _
         Item(lngCubeDimensionCounter).UniqueName
      .DimensionDescription = objCatalog.CubeDefs(CubeIndex). _
         Dimensions.Item(lngCubeDimensionCounter).Description
      With .Hierarchies
' Set Hierarchy Name, Hierarchy Unique name, Hierarchy Name and
' Hierarchy Description,Set Level Count
        .Count = objCatalog.CubeDefs(CubeIndex).Dimensions. _
           Item(lngCubeDimensionCounter).Hierarchies.Count
        For lngHierarchiesCounter = 0 To (.Count - 1)
          With .Item(lngHierarchiesCounter)
            .HierarchyName = _
```

```
objCatalog.CubeDefs(CubeIndex).Dimensions. _
    Item(lngCubeDimensionCounter).Hierarchies. _
    Item(lngHierarchiesCounter).Name
.HierarchyUniqueName = _
    objCatalog.CubeDefs(CubeIndex).Dimensions. _
    Item(lngCubeDimensionCounter).Hierarchies. _
    Item(lngHierarchiesCounter).UniqueName
.HierarchyDescription = _
    objCatalog.CubeDefs(CubeIndex).Dimensions. _
    Item(lngCubeDimensionCounter).Hierarchies. _
    Item(lngHierarchiesCounter).Description
With .Levels
' Set Level Name, Level Unique Name, Level Description,
' Level Depth,Set Member Count
  .Count = _
      objCatalog.CubeDefs(CubeIndex).Dimensions. _
      Item(lngCubeDimensionCounter).Hierarchies. _
      Item(lngHierarchiesCounter).Levels.Count
  For lngLevelsCounter = 0 To (.Count - 1)
  ' Move to Next Level
    If objCatalog.CubeDefs(CubeIndex).Dimensions. _
        Item(lngCubeDimensionCounter).Hierarchies. _
        Item(lngHierarchiesCounter).Levels. _
        Item(lngLevelsCounter).UniqueName = _
"[Customers].[Name]" Then
        .Count = .Count - 1
        Exit For
      End If
      With .Item(lngLevelsCounter)
        .LevelDescription = _
        objCatalog.CubeDefs(CubeIndex).Dimensions. _
            Item(lngCubeDimensionCounter).Hierarchies. _
            Item(lngHierarchiesCounter).Levels. _
            Item(lngLevelsCounter).Description
        .LevelName = _
        objCatalog.CubeDefs(CubeIndex).Dimensions. _
            Item(lngCubeDimensionCounter).Hierarchies. _
            Item(lngHierarchiesCounter).Levels. _
            Item(lngLevelsCounter).Name
        .LevelUniqueName = _
        objCatalog.CubeDefs(CubeIndex).Dimensions. _
            Item(lngCubeDimensionCounter).Hierarchies. _
            Item(lngHierarchiesCounter).Levels. _
            Item(lngLevelsCounter).UniqueName
```

```
.LevelCaption = _
objCatalog.CubeDefs(CubeIndex).Dimensions. _
    Item(lngCubeDimensionCounter).Hierarchies. _
    Item(lngHierarchiesCounter).Levels. _
    Item(lngLevelsCounter).Caption
.LevelDepth = _
objCatalog.CubeDefs(CubeIndex).Dimensions. _
    Item(lngCubeDimensionCounter).Hierarchies. _
    Item(lngHierarchiesCounter).Levels. _
    Item(lngLevelsCounter).Depth
With .Members
' Set Member Unique Name, Member Name, Member Caption
    .Count = _
      objCatalog.CubeDefs(CubeIndex).Dimensions. _
        Item(lngCubeDimensionCounter). _
        Hierarchies.Item(lngHierarchiesCounter). _
        Levels.Item(lngLevelsCounter).Members. _
        Count
  For lngMembersCounter = 0 To (.Count - 1)
    With .Item(lngMembersCounter)
      .MemberName = _
          objCatalog.CubeDefs(CubeIndex). _
          Dimensions.Item _
          (lngCubeDimensionCounter).Hierarchies. _
          Item(lngHierarchiesCounter).Levels. _
          Item(lngLevelsCounter).Members. _
          Item(lngMembersCounter).Name
      .MemberUniqueName = _
          objCatalog.CubeDefs(CubeIndex). _
          Dimensions. _
          Item(lngCubeDimensionCounter). _
          Hierarchies. _
          Item(lngHierarchiesCounter).Levels. _
          Item(lngLevelsCounter).Members. _
          Item(lngMembersCounter).UniqueName
      .MemberCaption = _
          objCatalog.CubeDefs(CubeIndex). _
          Dimensions. _
          Item(lngCubeDimensionCounter). _
          Hierarchies. _
          Item(lngHierarchiesCounter).Levels. _
          Item(lngLevelsCounter).Members. _
          Item(lngMembersCounter).Caption
      .MemberDescription = _
```

```
                              objCatalog.CubeDefs(CubeIndex). _
                              Dimensions. _
                              Item(lngCubeDimensionCounter). _
                              Hierarchies. _
                              Item(lngHierarchiesCounter).Levels. _
                              Item(lngLevelsCounter).Members. _
                              Item(lngMembersCounter).Description
                         End With '.Item(lngMembersCounter)
                      Next lngMembersCounter
                   End With ' .Members
                  End With '.Item(lngLevelsCounter)
               Next lngLevelsCounter
             End With '.Levels
           End With 'Item(lngHierachiesCounter)
         Next lngHierarchiesCounter
       End With '.Hierarchies
     End With '.Item(lngCubeDimensionCounter)
   Next lngCubeDimensionCounter
 End With '.Dimensions
 Set objConnection = Nothing
 Set objCatalog = Nothing

End Function
```

Initialize and Terminate

```
Private Sub Class_Initialize()

    Set m_oDimensions = New clsDimensions
End Sub

Private Sub Class_Terminate()
    Set m_oDimensions = Nothing
End Sub
```

ClsDimension

For each dimension in the data warehouse there will be a clsDimension object containing information on the dimension.

Declarations

```
Option Explicit
Private m_sDimensionName As String
Private m_oHierarchies As clsHierarchies
Private m_sDimensionUniqueName As String
```

```vb
Private m_sDescription As String
Private m_sDimensionDescription As String
```

Properties

```vb
Public Property Get DimensionUniqueName() As String
    DimensionUniqueName = m_sDimensionUniqueName
End Property
Friend Property Let DimensionUniqueName _
  (ByVal v_sNewDimensionUniqueName As String)

    m_sDimensionUniqueName = v_sNewDimensionUniqueName
End Property
Public Property Get DimensionDescription() As String
    DimensionDescription = m_sDimensionDescription
End Property
Friend Property Let DimensionDescription _
  (ByVal v_sNewDimensionDescription As String)

    m_sDimensionDescription = v_sNewDimensionDescription
End Property
Public Property Get DimensionName() As String
    DimensionName = m_sDimensionName
End Property
Friend Property Let DimensionName _
  (ByVal v_sNewDimensionName As String)
    m_sDimensionName = v_sNewDimensionName
End Property
Public Property Get Hierarchies() As clsHierarchies
    Set Hierarchies = m_oHierarchies
End Property
Friend Property Set Hierarchies _
  (ByVal v_oNewHierarchies As clsHierarchies)
    Set m_oHierarchies = v_oNewHierarchies
End Property
```

Initialize and Terminate

```vb
Private Sub Class_Initialize()
    Set m_oHierarchies = New clsHierarchies
End Sub
Private Sub Class_Terminate()
    Set m_oHierarchies = Nothing
End Sub
```

clsDimension

The clsDimensions class will manage a collection of clsDimension objects.

Declarations

```
Option Explicit
Private m_lCount As Long
Private m_oNameCollection As Collection
Private m_oDimensionCollection As Collection
Private m_bInitializedNames As Boolean
```

Properties

```
Private Property Get InitializedNames() As Boolean
    InitializedNames = m_bInitializedNames
End Property
Private Property Let InitializedNames _
  (ByVal v_bNewInitializedNames As Boolean)

    m_bInitializedNames = v_bNewInitializedNames
End Property
Public Property Get Count() As Long
    Count = m_lCount
End Property
Friend Property Let Count(ByVal v_lNewCount As Long)
    m_lCount = v_lNewCount
End Property
```

InitializeNames

```
Private Sub InitializeNames()
    Dim lngCollectionCounter As Long
    For lngCollectionCounter = 0 To m_oDimensionCollection.Count - 1
      AddToNameCollection 0, _
          m_oDimensionCollection.Item(Str(lngCollectionCounter)). _
              DimensionUniqueName
    Next
End Sub
```

Item

```
Public Function Item(ByVal v_vIndex As Variant) As clsDimension
  On Error GoTo ItemError
  If UCase(TypeName(v_vIndex)) = "STRING" Then
    If Not InitializedNames Then
      InitializeNames
      InitializedNames = True
    End If
```

```
      Set Item = _
        m_oDimensionCollection(Str(m_oNameCollection.Item(v_vIndex)))
    Else
      On Error Resume Next
      Set Item = m_oDimensionCollection(Str(v_vIndex))
      If Err.Number <> 0 Then
        If Err.Number = 5 Then
          Dim objDimension As New clsDimension
          Err.Clear
          On Error GoTo ItemError
          AddToDimensionCollection v_vIndex, objDimension
          Set Item = m_oDimensionCollection(Str(v_vIndex))
        Else
            'Err.Raise
        End If
      End If
    End If
    Exit Function
ItemError:
      Err.Raise Err.Number, Err.Source & " Dimension.Item"
End Function
```

AddToNameCollection

```
Friend Sub AddToNameCollection _
  (ByVal v_lDimensionID As Long, ByVal v_sDimensionName As String)

    m_oNameCollection.Add v_lDimensionID, v_sDimensionName
End Sub
```

ClearNameCollection

```
Friend Sub ClearNameCollection()
    Dim lngCollectionCounter As Long
    If lngCollectionCounter = 0 Then
        Exit Sub
    End If

    lngCollectionCounter = m_oNameCollection.Count
    Do Until lngCollectionCounter = 0
        m_oNameCollection.Remove lngCollectionCounter
        lngCollectionCounter = lngCollectionCounter - 1
    Loop
End Sub
```

ClearDimensionCollection

```
Friend Sub ClearDimensionCollection()
    Dim lngCollectionCounter As Long
    If m_oDimensionCollection.Count = 0 Then
        Exit Sub
    End If
    lngCollectionCounter = m_oDimensionCollection.Count
    Do Until lngCollectionCounter = 0
        m_oDimensionCollection.Remove lngCollectionCounter
        lngCollectionCounter = lngCollectionCounter - 1
    Loop
End Sub
```

AddToDimensionCollection

```
Friend Sub AddToDimensionCollection _
  (ByVal v_lDimensionID As Long, ByVal v_oDimension As clsDimension)

    m_oDimensionCollection.Add v_oDimension, Str(v_lDimensionID)
End Sub
```

Initialize and Terminate

```
Private Sub Class_Initialize()
    Set m_oNameCollection = New Collection
    Set m_oDimensionCollection = New Collection
End Sub
Private Sub Class_Terminate()
    ClearDimensionCollection
    ClearNameCollection
    Set m_oNameCollection = Nothing
    Set m_oDimensionCollection = Nothing
End Sub
```

ClsHierarchies

The clsHierarchies object will manage a collection of clsHierarchy objects.

Declarations

```
Option Explicit
Private m_lCount As Long
Private m_oNameCollection As Collection
Private m_oHierarchyCollection As Collection
Private m_bInitializedNames As Boolean
```

Properties

```
Private Property Get InitializedNames() As Boolean
    InitializedNames = m_bInitializedNames
End Property
Private Property Let InitializedNames _
  (ByVal v_bNewInitializedNames As Boolean)

  m_bInitializedNames = v_bNewInitializedNames
End Property
Public Property Get Count() As Long
    Count = m_lCount
End Property
Friend Property Let Count(ByVal v_lNewCount As Long)
    m_lCount = v_lNewCount
End Property
```

InitializeNames

```
Private Sub InitializeNames()
  Dim lngCollectionCounter As Long
  For lngCollectionCounter = 0 To _
      m_oHierarchyCollection.Count - 1
    AddToNameCollection 0, m_oHierarchyCollection. _
        Item(Str(lngCollectionCounter)).HierarchyUniqueName
  Next
End Sub
```

Item

```
Public Function Item(ByVal v_vIndex As Variant) As clsHierarchy
  On Error GoTo ItemError
  If UCase(TypeName(v_vIndex)) = "STRING" Then
    If Not InitializedNames Then
        InitializeNames
        InitializedNames = True
    End If

    Set Item = _
        m_oHierarchyCollection(Str(m_oNameCollection.Item(v_vIndex)))
  Else
    On Error Resume Next
    Set Item = m_oHierarchyCollection(Str(v_vIndex))
    If Err.Number <> 0 Then
      If Err.Number = 5 Then
```

```
                Dim objHierarchy As New clsHierarchy
                Err.Clear
                On Error GoTo ItemError
                AddToHierarchyCollection v_vIndex, objHierarchy
                Set Item = m_oHierarchyCollection(Str(v_vIndex))
            Else
                'Err.Raise
            End If
        End If
    End If
    Exit Function
ItemError:
    Err.Raise Err.Number, Err.Source & "  Hierarchy.Item"
End Function
```

AddToNameCollection

```
Friend Sub AddToNameCollection _
    (ByVal v_lHierarchyID As Long, ByVal v_sHierarchyName As String)

    m_oNameCollection.Add v_lHierarchyID, v_sHierarchyName
End Sub
Friend Sub ClearNameCollection()
    Dim lngCollectionCounter As Long
    If m_oNameCollection.Count = 0 Then
        Exit Sub
    End If
    lngCollectionCounter = m_oNameCollection.Count
    Do Until lngCollectionCounter = 0
        m_oNameCollection.Remove lngCollectionCounter
        lngCollectionCounter = lngCollectionCounter - 1
    Loop
End Sub
```

ClearHierarchyCollection

```
Friend Sub ClearHierarchyCollection()
    Dim lngCollectionCounter As Long
    If m_oHierarchyCollection.Count = 0 Then
        Exit Sub
    End If
    lngCollectionCounter = m_oHierarchyCollection.Count
    Do Until lngCollectionCounter = 0
        m_oHierarchyCollection.Remove lngCollectionCounter
```

```
      lngCollectionCounter = lngCollectionCounter - 1
   Loop
End Sub
```

AddToHierarchyCollection

```
Friend Sub AddToHierarchyCollection(ByVal v_lLevelID As Long, ByVal
v_oHierarchy As clsHierarchy)
   m_oHierarchyCollection.Add v_oHierarchy, Str(v_lLevelID)
End Sub
```

Initialize and Terminate

```
Private Sub Class_Initialize()
   Set m_oNameCollection = New Collection
   Set m_oHierarchyCollection = New Collection
End Sub
Private Sub Class_Terminate()
   ClearHierarchyCollection
   ClearNameCollection
   Set m_oNameCollection = New Collection
   Set m_oHierarchyCollection = New Collection
End Sub
```

ClsHierarchy

For each hierarchy within a dimension there will be a clsHierarchy object.

Declarations

```
Option Explicit
Private m_sHierarchyName As String
Private m_oLevels As clsLevels
Private m_sHierarchyUniqueName As String
Private m_sHierarchyDescription As String
```

Properties

```
Public Property Get HierarchyUniqueName() As String
    HierarchyUniqueName = m_sHierarchyUniqueName
End Property
Friend Property Let HierarchyUniqueName _
   (ByVal v_sNewHierarchyUniqueName As String)
   m_sHierarchyUniqueName = v_sNewHierarchyUniqueName
End Property
Public Property Get HierarchyName() As String
   HierarchyName = m_sHierarchyName
End Property
```

```
Friend Property Let HierarchyName(ByVal v_sNewHierarchyName As String)
  m_sHierarchyName = v_sNewHierarchyName
End Property
Public Property Get HierarchyDescription() As String
  HierarchyDescription = m_sHierarchyDescription
End Property
Friend Property Let HierarchyDescription _
  (ByVal v_sNewHierarchyDescription As String)

  m_sHierarchyDescription = v_sNewHierarchyDescription
End Property
Public Property Get Levels() As clsLevels
  Set Levels = m_oLevels
End Property
Friend Property Set Levels(ByVal v_oNewLevels As clsLevels)
  Set m_oLevels = v_oNewLevels
End Property
```

Initialize and Terminate

```
Private Sub Class_Initialize()
  Set m_oLevels = New clsLevels
End Sub
Private Sub Class_Terminate()
  Set m_oLevels = Nothing
End Sub
```

ClsLevels

The clsLevels object will manage a collection of clsLevels objects.

Declarations

```
Option Explicit
Private m_lCount As Long
Private m_oNameCollection As Collection
Private m_oLevelCollection As Collection
Private m_bInitializedNames As Boolean
```

Properties

```
Private Property Get InitializedNames() As Boolean
  InitializedNames = m_bInitializedNames
End Property
Private Property Let InitializedNames _
(ByVal v_bNewInitializedNames As Boolean)
  m_bInitializedNames = v_bNewInitializedNames
```

```
End Property
Public Property Get Count() As Long
  Count = m_lCount
End Property
Friend Property Let Count(ByVal v_lNewCount As Long)
   m_lCount = v_lNewCount
End Property
```

InitializeNames

```
Private Sub InitializeNames()
  Dim lngCollectionCounter As Long

  For lngCollectionCounter = 0 To m_oLevelCollection.Count - 1
   AddToNameCollection 0,
m_oLevelCollection.Item(Str(lngCollectionCounter)).LevelUniqueName
  Next
End Sub
```

Item

```
Public Function Item(ByVal v_vIndex As Variant) As clsLevel
  On Error GoTo ItemError
  If UCase(TypeName(v_vIndex)) = "STRING" Then
    If Not InitializedNames Then
      InitializeNames
      InitializedNames = True
    End If
    Set Item = m_oLevelCollection(Str(m_oNameCollection.Item(v_vIndex)))
  Else
    On Error Resume Next
    Set Item = m_oLevelCollection(Str(v_vIndex))
    If Err.Number <> 0 Then
     If Err.Number = 5 Then
       Dim objLevel As New clsLevel
       Err.Clear
       On Error GoTo ItemError
       AddToLevelCollection v_vIndex, objLevel
       Set Item = m_oLevelCollection(Str(v_vIndex))
     Else
        'Err.Raise
     End If
    End If
  End If
  Exit Function
```

```
ItemError:
  Err.Raise Err.Number, Err.Source & "  Level.Item"
End Function
```

AddToNameCollection

```
Friend Sub AddToNameCollection(ByVal v_lLevelID As Long, ByVal v_sLevelName
As String)
  m_oNameCollection.Add v_lLevelID, v_sLevelName
End Sub
```

ClearNameCollection

```
Friend Sub ClearNameCollection()
  Dim lngCollectionCounter As Long
  If m_oNameCollection.Count = 0 Then
    Exit Sub
  End If
  lngCollectionCounter = m_oNameCollection.Count
  Do Until lngCollectionCounter = 0
    m_oNameCollection.Remove lngCollectionCounter
    lngCollectionCounter = lngCollectionCounter - 1
  Loop
End Sub
```

ClearLevelCollection

```
Friend Sub ClearLevelCollection()
  Dim lngCollectionCounter As Long
  If m_oLevelCollection.Count = 0 Then
    Exit Sub
  End If

  lngCollectionCounter = m_oLevelCollection.Count
  Do Until lngCollectionCounter = 0
    m_oLevelCollection.Remove lngCollectionCounter
    lngCollectionCounter = lngCollectionCounter - 1
  Loop
End Sub
```

AddToLevelCollection

```
Friend Sub AddToLevelCollection _
  (ByVal v_lLevelID As Long, ByVal v_oLevel As clsLevel)

  m_oLevelCollection.Add v_oLevel, Str(v_lLevelID)
End Sub
```

Initialize and Terminate

```
Private Sub Class_Initialize()
  Set m_oNameCollection = New Collection
  Set m_oLevelCollection = New Collection
End Sub
```

ClsLevel

For each level in a hierarchy there will a clsLevel object.

Declarations

```
Option Explicit
Private m_sLevelName As String
Private m_oMembers As clsMembers
Private m_sLevelUniqueName As String
Private m_sDescription As String
Private m_sLevelCaption As String
Private m_lLevelDepth As Long
Private m_sLevelDescription As String
```

Properties

```
Public Property Get LevelUniqueName() As String
    LevelUniqueName = m_sLevelUniqueName
End Property
Friend Property Let LevelUniqueName _
  (ByVal v_sNewLevelUniqueName As String)

    m_sLevelUniqueName = v_sNewLevelUniqueName
End Property
Public Property Get LevelDescription() As String
    LevelDescription = m_sLevelDescription
End Property
Friend Property Let LevelDescription _
  (ByVal v_sNewLevelDescription As String)

    m_sLevelDescription = v_sNewLevelDescription
End Property
Public Property Get LevelName() As String
    LevelName = m_sLevelName
End Property
Friend Property Let LevelName(ByVal v_sNewLevelName As String)
    m_sLevelName = v_sNewLevelName
End Property
```

```
Public Property Get LevelCaption() As String
    LevelCaption = m_sLevelCaption
End Property
Friend Property Let LevelCaption(ByVal v_sNewLevelCaption As String)
    m_sLevelCaption = v_sNewLevelCaption
End Property
Public Property Get Members() As clsMembers
    Set Members = m_oMembers
End Property
Friend Property Set Members(ByVal v_oNewMembers As clsMembers)
    Set m_oMembers = v_oNewMembers
End Property
Public Property Get LevelDepth() As Long
    LevelDepth = m_lLevelDepth
End Property
Friend Property Let LevelDepth(ByVal v_lNewLevelDepth As Long)
    m_lLevelDepth = v_lNewLevelDepth
End Property
```

Initialize and Terminate

```
Private Sub Class_Initialize()
    Set m_oMembers = New clsMembers
End Sub

Private Sub Class_Terminate()
    Set m_oMembers = Nothing
End Sub
```

ClsMembers

The clsMembers class will manage a collection of clsMember objects.

Declarations

```
Option Explicit
Private m_lCount As Long
Private m_oNameCollection As Collection
Private m_oMemberCollection As Collection
Private m_bInitializedNames As Boolean
```

Properties

```
Private Property Get InitializedNames() As Boolean
    InitializedNames = m_bInitializedNames
End Property
Private Property Let InitializedNames _
```

```
   (ByVal v_bNewInitializedNames As Boolean)
      m_bInitializedNames = v_bNewInitializedNames
End Property
Public Property Get Count() As Long
      Count = m_lCount
End Property
Friend Property Let Count(ByVal v_lNewCount As Long)
        m_lCount = v_lNewCount
End Property
```

InitializedNames

```
Private Sub InitializeNames()
      Dim lngCollectionCounter As Long
  For lngCollectionCounter = 0 To m_oMemberCollection.Count - 1
      AddToNameCollection 0, _
         m_oMemberCollection.Item(Str(lngCollectionCounter)). _
         MemberUniqueName
   Next
End Sub
```

Item

```
Public Function Item(ByVal v_vIndex As Variant) As clsMember
   On Error GoTo ItemError
   If UCase(TypeName(v_vIndex)) = "STRING" Then
        If Not InitializedNames Then
            InitializeNames
            InitializedNames = True
        End If
        Set Item = _
            m_oMemberCollection(Str(m_oNameCollection.Item(v_vIndex)))
   Else
        On Error Resume Next
        Set Item = m_oMemberCollection(Str(v_vIndex))
            If Err.Number <> 0 Then
            If Err.Number = 5 Then
                Dim objMember As New clsMember
                Err.Clear
                On Error GoTo ItemError
                AddToMemberCollection v_vIndex, objMember
                Set Item = m_oMemberCollection(Str(v_vIndex))
            Else
                'Err.Raise
            End If
        End If
```

```
    End If
    Exit Function
ItemError:
    Err.Raise Err.Number, Err.Source & "  Member.Item"
End Function
```

AddToNameCollection

```
Friend Sub AddToNameCollection _
    (ByVal v_lMemberID As Long, ByVal v_sMemberName As String)

    m_oNameCollection.Add v_lMemberID, v_sMemberName
End Sub
ClearNameCollection
Friend Sub ClearNameCollection()
    Dim lngCollectionCounter As Long
    If m_oNameCollection.Count = 0 Then
        Exit Sub
    End If
    lngCollectionCounter = m_oNameCollection.Count
    Do Until lngCollectionCounter = 0
        m_oNameCollection.Remove lngCollectionCounter
        lngCollectionCounter = lngCollectionCounter - 1
    Loop
End Sub
```

ClearMemberCollection

```
Friend Sub ClearMemberCollection()
    Dim lngCollectionCounter As Long
    If m_oMemberCollection.Count = 0 Then
        Exit Sub
    End If
    lngCollectionCounter = m_oMemberCollection.Count
    Do Until lngCollectionCounter = 0
        m_oMemberCollection.Remove lngCollectionCounter
        lngCollectionCounter = lngCollectionCounter - 1
    Loop
End Sub
```

AddToMemberCollection

```
Friend Sub AddToMemberCollection(ByVal v_lMemberID As Long, ByVal v_oMember
As clsMember)
    m_oMemberCollection.Add v_oMember, Str(v_lMemberID)
End Sub
```

Intialize and Terminate

```
Private Sub Class_Initialize()
  Set m_oNameCollection = New Collection
  Set m_oMemberCollection = New Collection
End Sub
Private Sub Class_Terminate()
  ClearMemberCollection
  ClearNameCollection
  Set m_oNameCollection = Nothing
  Set m_oMemberCollection = Nothing
End Sub
```

ClsMember

Every level will have a collection of member objects. Member objects contain all of the information on each member of a level.

Declarations

```
Option Explicit
Private m_sMemberName As String
Private m_oMembers As clsMembers
Private m_sMemberUniqueName As String
Private m_sDescription As String
Private m_sMemberCaption As String
Private m_sMemberDescription As String
```

Property

```
Public Property Get MemberUniqueName() As String
    MemberUniqueName = m_sMemberUniqueName
End Property
Friend Property Let MemberUniqueName _
  (ByVal v_sNewMemberUniqueName As String)
    m_sMemberUniqueName = v_sNewMemberUniqueName
End Property
Public Property Get MemberName() As String
    MemberName = m_sMemberName
End Property
Friend Property Let MemberName(ByVal v_sNewMemberName As String)
    m_sMemberName = v_sNewMemberName
End Property
Public Property Get MemberCaption() As String
    MemberCaption = m_sMemberCaption
End Property
```

```
Friend Property Let MemberCaption(ByVal v_sNewMemberCaption As String)
    m_sMemberCaption = v_sNewMemberCaption
End Property
Public Property Get MemberDescription() As String
    MemberDescription = m_sMemberDescription
End Property
Friend Property Let MemberDescription _
  (ByVal v_sNewMemberDescription As String)
    m_sMemberDescription = v_sNewMemberDescription
End Property
```

Initialize and Terminate

```
Private Sub Class_Initialize()
    Set m_oMembers = New clsMembers
End Sub
Private Sub Class_Terminate()
    Set m_oMembers = Nothing
End Sub
```

Designing and Building a Generic Cube Browser

Once we have created ADO MD wrapper objects we will now want to use it. We will build a Visual Basic control that will use the ADO MD wrapper objects to provide data to the Visual Basic control.

PrjCubeGrid

PrjCubeGrid is a control that gives you all the functionality to browse and view data. Add a Visual Basic ActiveX Control project. Call the project prjCubeGrid. Go to the project explorer, right-click the prjCubeGrid project, and select Set as Start Up. Visual Basic 6 opens the project in the Internet Browser.

Go to project, and then references in the project menu. Add the CubeConnection, CubeData, and CubeMetaData as references. Open Project, Components, and select Microsoft Flex Grid and Microsoft Windows Common Control 5.0.

One of the key features allows a user to drill up and down the dimension hierarchies. The level that the user is at in the hierarchy is placed in the command button caption. Once the user has drilled up or down to the level they want, the user can drag the command button over to a grid box. If the user has selected the desired measures, the user sees the dataset in the gridbox. Thus, you must give your command buttons the ability to do object linking and embedding (OLE) drop and dragging. You also use a slider bar to move the command buttons up and down if there are too many dimensions to fit on the frame.

Open the control. Add the following controls onto the form with the following names, top, left, and height and width.

Table C-1. Control Object Properties

Type	Location	Left	Top	Height	Width	Name
Control cubeGridInformation	-	-	-	9045	12620	
Frame	CubeGridInformation	240	600	6975	4095	frmDimensions
Frame	frmDatabase	9960	1800	1275	3495	frmDatabase
Frame	CubeGridInformation	9960	360	1395	3495	frmServer
Label	frmDimensions	240	240	255	1455	lblDimension *
Command Button	frmDimensions	120	570	375	1575	cmdDimension *
Label	frmDimensions	1800	600	255	2175	lblValue *
Line	frmDimensions	(X1) 0	(X2) 4080	(Y1) 960	(Y2) 960	linDimension
Vertical Scroll Bar	CubeGridInformation	4440	720	6855	375	vscDimension
Treeview	CubeGridInformation	5040	720	2175	2295	tvwHierarchy
ListBox	CubeGridInformation	7440	720	2205	2295	lstMeasures
Flex Grid	CubeGridInformation	5040	3120	4335	8295	grdCubeValue
Textbox	frmServer	825	405	315	2415	txtServer
Textbox	frmServer	825	945	315	2400	txtProvider
Combo	frmDatabase	960	250	315	2415	cmbDatabase
Text	CubeGridInformation	240	8160	495	2275	txtMeasures
Text	CubeGridInformation	3120	8160	495	2775	txtDimensions
Command Button	CubeGridInformation	6420	7800	615	1215	cmdClear
Command Button	CubeGridInformation	7680	7800	615	1215	cmdHelp
Combo	frmDatabase	960	780	315	2415	cmbCube

The Project has the following declarations and properties:

```
Option Explicit
Private m_lDimensionCount As Long
Private m_sUniqueNameOfLastDragged As String
Private m_oCubeConnection As CubeConnection.clsCubeConnection
Private m_sMDXRow As String
Private m_sMDXColumn As String
Private m_oDimensionCollection As Collection
Private m_oMeasureCollection As Collection
```

```vb
Private m_oMemberCollection As Collection
Private m_o
Private m_sMDXQuery As String
Private m_dLastMouseX  As Double
Private m_dLastMouseY  As Double
Private Const c_ListSpacing = 800
Private Const c_CmdSpacing = 255
Private m_gMouseDownX As Single
Private m_gMouseDownY As Single
Private m_oCubeDef As CubeMetaData.clsCubeMetaData

Private Property Get CubeDef() As CubeMetaData.clsCubeMetaData
    Set CubeDef = m_oCubeDef
End Property

Private Property Set CubeDef _
  (ByVal v_oNewCubeDef As CubeMetaData.clsCubeMetaData)
  Set m_oCubeDef = v_oNewCubeDef
End Property

Private Property Get MDXRow() As String
    MDXRow = m_sMDXRow
End Property

Private Property Let MDXRow(ByVal v_sNewMDXRow As String)
    m_sMDXRow = v_sNewMDXRow
End Property

Private Property Get MDXColumn() As String
    MDXColumn = m_sMDXColumn
End Property

Private Property Let MDXColumn(ByVal v_sNewMDXColumn As String)
    m_sMDXColumn = v_sNewMDXColumn
End Property

Private Property Get DimensionCount() As Long
    DimensionCount = m_lDimensionCount
End Property

Private Property Let DimensionCount _
  (ByVal v_lNewDimensionCount As Long)
    m_lDimensionCount = v_lNewDimensionCount
End Property

Public Property Get CubeConnection() As _
    CubeConnection.clsCubeConnection
```

```
      Set CubeConnection = m_oCubeConnection
End Property

Property Set CubeConnection _
    (ByVal v_oNewCubeConnection As CubeConnection.clsCubeConnection)

    Set m_oCubeConnection = v_oNewCubeConnection
End Property

Private Property Get UniqueNameOfLastDragged() As String
    UniqueNameOfLastDragged = m_sUniqueNameOfLastDragged
End Property

Private Property Let UniqueNameOfLastDragged _
  (ByVal v_sNewUniqueNameOfLastDragged As String)

    m_sUniqueNameOfLastDragged = v_sNewUniqueNameOfLastDragged
End Property
```

InitializeCube

The InitializeCube method must get the information on the dimensions and the members of the dimensions from the data warehouse. To do this, this function uses the CubeMetaData to get the data. CubeMetaData can be running anywhere, including on a server. The activity diagram for InitializeCube looks as follows, as shown in Figure C-3.

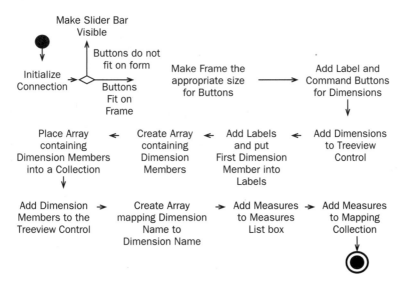

Figure C-3. *InitializeCube Activity Diagram.*

```
Private Function InitializeCube()
Dim lngDimensionCounter As Long
Dim lngLevelCounter As Long
Dim strDimensionName As String
Dim lngMeasureCounter As Long
Dim strCurrentDimensionName As String
Dim strMembers() As String
Dim lngMemberCounter As Long

'Initialize Cube Connection object
CubeConnection.SetConnection cmbDatabase, cmbCube.Text, txtServer
Set CubeDef = New CubeMetaData.clsCubeMetaData
CubeDef.InitializeCubeMetaData CubeConnection
With CubeDef.dimensions
```

The c_ListSpacing is a constant that is used to space the labels and command buttons with the dimension information. If c_ListSpacing times the number of dimensions is greater than the size of the frame the dimensions are on, you need the slider bar. If not, you size the frame to the height you need for all the dimensions.

You are creating an index to use as a reference for which dimension and which level is being referred to in each control. You are taking the unique name of the dimension, stripping off quotes and brackets, and adding a numeric for each level. Thus, the Customer dimension, All level, is Customer0, and the Customer dimension, Country, is Customer1. This unique ID is placed into the tree view as the key for each level in the tree. It is also placed in the tag of the command buttons to identify the current level of the command button. The identifier is also used as the key in the dimension array.

```
  If .Count * c_ListSpacing > frmDimensions.Height Then
    'Make Slider Bar visible and set Dimension Count Variable
    vscDimension.Visible = True
      DimensionCount = .Count - 1
  Else
      'Adjust size of frame for Dimension Command Buttons
    frmDimensions.Height = (c_ListSpacing + 10) * .Count
  End If
  For lngDimensionCounter = 0 To .Count - 1
    With .Item(lngDimensionCounter)
      If UCase(.DimensionName) <> "MEASURES" Then
      'Add Label and Command button for Dimension
        AddDimensionLabel .DimensionName
        strDimensionName = StripQuotes(.DimensionUniqueName)
        AddDimensions strDimensionName & "0", _
            .Hierarchies.Item(0).Levels.Item(0).LevelName
      'Add Dimension to treeview control
        tvwHierarchy.Nodes.Add , , strDimensionName, .DimensionName
```

```
        tvwHierarchy.Nodes.Add strDimensionName, _
        tvwChild, strDimensionName & "0", _
          .Hierarchies.Item(0).Levels.Item(0).LevelName
        AddDimensionUniqueName .Hierarchies.Item(0).Levels.Item(0). _
         LevelUniqueName, strDimensionName & "0"
        If lngDimensionCounter <> 0 Then
'Add New Label for the first member of the dimension and put the
'value of the first member, add line to separate dimension
          Load lblValue(lblValue.Count)
          Load linDimension(linDimension.Count)
          lblValue(lblValue.Count - 1).Top = _
            lblValue(lblValue.Count - 2).Top + c_ListSpacing
          linDimension(linDimension.Count - 1).Y1 = _
            linDimension(linDimension.Count - 2).Y1 + c_ListSpacing
          linDimension(linDimension.Count - 1).Y2 = _
            linDimension(linDimension.Count - 2).Y2 + c_ListSpacing
          lblValue(lblValue.Count - 1).Visible = True
          linDimension(linDimension.Count - 1).Visible = True
        End If
'Create an Array of all of the members of the Dimension
        ReDim strMembers(1 To _
          .Hierarchies.Item(0).Levels.Item(0).Members.Count)
        For lngMemberCounter = 1 To _
          .Hierarchies.Item(0).Levels.Item(0).Members.Count
          strMembers(lngMemberCounter) = _
            .Hierarchies.Item(0).Levels.Item(0).Members. _
              Item(lngMemberCounter - 1).MemberUniqueName
        Next
        'Place the array of members into a collection associated with the
        'dimensionsID
        AddMemberUniqueName strMembers, strDimensionName & "0"
        lblValue(lblValue.Count - 1).Caption = .Hierarchies.Item(0). _
          Levels.Item(0).Members.Item(0).MemberName
        With .Hierarchies.Item(0).Levels
          For lngLevelCounter = 1 To .Count - 1
          'Add Dimension members to tree view control
            tvwHierarchy.Nodes.Add strDimensionName & _
              Trim(Str(lngLevelCounter - 1)), tvwChild, _
              strDimensionName & Trim(Str(lngLevelCounter)), _
              .Item(lngLevelCounter).LevelName
          'Add to a collection that maps Dimension Unique name to
          dimensionID
            AddDimensionUniqueName .Item(lngLevelCounter).LevelUniqueName, _
              strDimensionName & Trim(Str(lngLevelCounter))
```

```
              ReDim strMembers(1 To .Item(lngLevelCounter).Members.Count)
              For lngMemberCounter = 1 To _
                .Item(lngLevelCounter).Members.Count
                strMembers(lngMemberCounter) = _
                  .Item(lngLevelCounter).Members. _
                    Item(lngMemberCounter - 1).MemberUniqueName
              Next
              AddMemberUniqueName strMembers, strDimensionName & _
                  Trim(Str(lngLevelCounter))
            Next
          End With
        Else
          With .Hierarchies.Item(0).Levels.Item(0).Members
            For lngMeasureCounter = 0 To .Count - 1
                'Add Measure to Measures List Box
                lstMeasures.AddItem .Item(lngMeasureCounter).MemberName
                'Add to a collection that maps Measure Unique name to Member
                Name
                AddMeasureUniqueName .Item(lngMeasureCounter). _
                    MemberUniqueName, .Item(lngMeasureCounter).MemberName
            Next
          End With
        End If
      End With
    Next
  End With

End Function
```

AddMemberUniqueName

The AddMemberUniqueName method adds a string array with the names of the members for a dimension.

```
Private Sub AddMemberUniqueName _
    (ByRef r_sMemberUniqueName() As String, _
     ByVal v_sMemberName As String)


  m_oMemberCollection.Add r_sMemberUniqueName, v_sMemberName
End Sub
```

AddUniqueName

The AddUniqueName adds the member unique name to the measure collection.

```
Private Sub AddMeasureUniqueName _
  (ByVal v_sMeasureUniqueName As String, _
```

```
  ByVal v_sMeasureName As String)


  m_oMeasureCollection.Add v_sMeasureUniqueName, v_sMeasureName
End Sub
```

GetMemberUniqueName

GetMemberUniqueName gets the unique name out of the collection using the numeric ID for the key. Because you are storing a string array, you need to retrieve the member by its unique numeric ID in the string array.

```
Private Function GetMemberUniqueName _
  (ByVal v_sLevelName As String, ByVal v_lkey As Long) As String

  Dim tempString() As String
  tempString = m_oMemberCollection.Item(v_sLevelName)
  GetMemberUniqueName = tempString(v_lkey)
End Function
```

AddDimensionUniqueName

This method adds the unique dimension to the collection so that you can map between the dimension name and the unique name.

```
Private Sub AddDimensionUniqueName _
  (ByVal v_sDimensionUniqueName As String, _
  ByVal v_sDimensionName As String)


  m_oDimensionCollection.Add v_sDimensionUniqueName, v_sDimensionName
End Sub
```

MemberCount

Each level is a count of member. This function returns the count of members for each level.

```
Private Function MemberCount(ByVal v_sLevelName As String)

    Dim tempString() As String
    tempString = m_oMemberCollection.Item(v_sLevelName)
    MemberCount = UBound(tempString)
End Function
```

GetMeasureUniqueName

GetMeasureUniqueName returns the unique name for a measure.

```
Private Function GetMeasureUniqueName _
  (ByVal v_sMeasureName As String) As String

  GetMeasureUniqueName = m_oMeasureCollection.Item(v_sMeasureName)
```

```
End Function
```

GetDimensionUniqueName

The GetDimensionUniqueName method gets the unique dimension name.

```
Private Function GetDimensionUniqueName _
  (ByVal v_sDimensionName As String) As String
    GetDimensionUniqueName = _
        m_oDimensionCollection.Item(v_sDimensionName)
End Function
```

BuildMDXString

Beside each textbox is a label with the current value of each dimension. For example, if the dimension command button is on Customer Country, the value can be USA, Mexico, or Canada. The values in these labels are used to build the WHERE clause. You have to get the unique name of the dimension so that you can properly declare your WHERE clause members with the value of the dimension and the dimension name. For example, if the dimension name is Customer and you have USA, you need [Customer].[USA] in your WHERE clause. You need the dimension name. The tag of the command button associated with the label has the unique dimension name plus a numeric, such as Customer0. The numeric has to be stripped off. The first part of the code strips off the numeric and then builds the WHERE clause. Once you have the WHERE clause, you use the MDXRow and MDXColumn properties to build the string.

```
Private Sub BuildMDXString()

  Dim lngWhereCounter As Long
  Dim strWhere As String
  Dim strDimensionName As String

  For lngWhereCounter = 0 To lblValue.Count - 1
    If IsNumeric(Right(cmdDimension(lngWhereCounter).Tag, 2)) Then
      strDimensionName = Left(cmdDimension(lngWhereCounter).Tag, _
      Len(cmdDimension(lngWhereCounter).Tag) - 2)
    End If
    If IsNumeric(Right(cmdDimension(lngWhereCounter).Tag, 1)) Then
      strDimensionName = _
        Left(cmdDimension(lngWhereCounter).Tag, _
        Len(cmdDimension(lngWhereCounter).Tag) - 1)
    End If

    If lblValue(lngWhereCounter).Caption <> "" Then
      If strWhere = "" Then
        strWhere = "[" & strDimensionName & "].[" & _
            lblValue(lngWhereCounter).Caption & "]"
```

```
      Else
        strWhere = strWhere & ",[" & strDimensionName & "].[" & _
            lblValue(lngWhereCounter).Caption & "]"
      End If
    End If
  Next
  MDXQuery = "SELECT " & _
    " {" & MDXColumn & "} ON COLUMNS, " & _
    " (" & MDXRow & ") " & _
    "      ON ROWS " & _
    " FROM Sales" & _
    " WHERE  (" & strWhere & ")"
  End Sub
Private Property Get MDXQuery() As String
  MDXQuery = m_sMDXQuery
End Property
Private Property Let MDXQuery(ByVal v_sNewMDXQuery As String)
  m_sMDXQuery = v_sNewMDXQuery
End Property
```

AddDimensionLabel

For each dimension, you add a label with the name of the dimension. The label with index number 0 is already on the form, so you not need to load (add) the first label.

```
Private Sub AddDimensionLabel(ByVal v_sCaption As String)
  If lblDimension(0).Caption <> "" Then
      Load lblDimension(lblDimension.Count)
  End If
  lblDimension.Item(lblDimension.Count - 1).Caption = v_sCaption
  If lblDimension.Count > 1 Then
      lblDimension(lblDimension.Count - 1).Top = _
          lblDimension(lblDimension.Count - 2).Top + c_ListSpacing
      lblDimension(lblDimension.Count - 1).Left = _
          lblDimension(lblDimension.Count - 2).Left
  End If
  lblDimension(lblDimension.Count - 1).Visible = True
End Sub
```

AddDimensions

The AddDimensions method adds a command button for every dimension. If the tag in the first element is empty, this is the first time you are calling this function. Otherwise, you need to load the command button.

```
Private Sub AddDimensions(ByVal v_sUniqueName As String, _
    ByVal v_sCaption As String)
```

```
   If cmdDimension.Item(0).Tag <> "" Then
     Load cmdDimension(cmdDimension.Count)
   End If


   cmdDimension(cmdDimension.Count - 1).Tag = v_sUniqueName
   If cmdDimension.Count > 1 Then
     cmdDimension(cmdDimension.Count - 1).Top = _
        lblDimension(cmdDimension.Count - 1).Top + c_CmdSpacing
     cmdDimension(cmdDimension.Count - 1).Left = _
        cmdDimension(cmdDimension.Count - 1).Left
   End If
   cmdDimension(cmdDimension.Count - 1).Caption = v_sCaption
   cmdDimension(cmdDimension.Count - 1).Visible = True
End Sub
```

StripQuotes

The StripQuotes method removes quotes and brackets from the parameter passed into
the method.

```
Public Function StripQuotes(ByVal v_sName As String) As String
    Dim strNoQuoteName As String
    Dim strFirstChar As String, strLastChar As String
    If InStr(1, v_sName, ".") > 0 Then
        strNoQuoteName = _
            Right(v_sName, InStr(1, StrReverse(v_sName), ".") - 1)
    Else
        strNoQuoteName = v_sName
    End If

    strFirstChar = Left(strNoQuoteName, 1)
    strLastChar = Right(strNoQuoteName, 1)

    If strFirstChar = "[" Or strFirstChar = Chr(34) _
        Or strFirstChar = "`" Or strFirstChar = "(" Then
      strNoQuoteName = Mid(strNoQuoteName, 2)
    End If
    If strLastChar = "]" Or strLastChar = Chr(34) Or strLastChar = "`" Or _
        strLastChar = ")" Then
      strNoQuoteName = Left(strNoQuoteName, Len(strNoQuoteName) - 1)
    End If
    StripQuotes = strNoQuoteName
End Function
```

FillGrid

The FillGrid method works the same as the FillGrid method did in the last chapter, except it uses the wrapper object CubeData instead of ADO MD.

```
Private Sub FillGrid()
  Dim lngColumnCounter As Long
  Dim lngRowCounter As Long
  Dim lngMemberCounter As Long
  Dim strLevelName As String
  Dim strMemberCaption As String
  Dim objCubeData As CubeData.clsCubeData

  Set objCubeData = New CubeData.clsCubeData
  objCubeData.InitializeCubeData CubeConnection, MDXQuery

  With grdCubeValues
    .Cols = objCubeData.Axes(0).Tuples.Count + _
        objCubeData.Axes(1).DimensionCount
    .Rows = objCubeData.Axes(1).Tuples.Count + _
        objCubeData.Axes(0).DimensionCount
    .FixedCols = objCubeData.Axes(1).DimensionCount
    .FixedRows = objCubeData.Axes(0).DimensionCount
    For lngRowCounter = 0 To .FixedRows - 1
      .MergeRow(lngRowCounter) = True
    Next
    For lngRowCounter = .FixedRows To .Rows - 1
      .MergeRow(lngRowCounter) = False
    Next
    For lngColumnCounter = 0 To objCubeData.Axes(1).DimensionCount - 1
      For lngRowCounter = 0 To objCubeData.Axes(1).Tuples.Count - 1
        .Col = lngColumnCounter
        .Row = lngRowCounter + .FixedRows
        .Text = objCubeData.Axes.Axis(1). _
            Tuples.Tuple(lngRowCounter). _
            TupleMember(lngColumnCounter).MemberCaption
        .ColWidth(lngColumnCounter) = 2000
        .CellAlignment = flexAlignCenterCenter
      Next
    Next
    For lngColumnCounter = 0 To objCubeData.Axes(0).Tuples.Count - 1
      For lngMemberCounter = 0 To _
          objCubeData.Axes(0).DimensionCount - 1
```

```
        strMemberCaption = _
            objCubeData.Axes(0).Tuples(lngColumnCounter). _
            TupleMember(lngMemberCounter).MemberCaption
        .Col = lngColumnCounter + .FixedCols
        .Row = lngMemberCounter
        .Text = strMemberCaption
      Next
    Next
    For lngColumnCounter = 0 To objCubeData.Axes(0).Tuples.Count - 1
      For lngMemberCounter = 0 To objCubeData.Axes(1).Tuples.Count
        .ColWidth(lngColumnCounter + .FixedCols) = 1500
        .Col = lngColumnCounter + .FixedCols
        .Row = lngMemberCounter
        .CellAlignment = flexAlignCenterCenter
      Next
      For lngRowCounter = 0 To objCubeData.Axes(1).Tuples.Count - 1
        .Col = lngColumnCounter + .FixedCols
        .Row = lngRowCounter + .FixedRows
        If IsNull(objCubeData.GetCubeValues _
            (lngColumnCounter, lngRowCounter)) Then
          .Text = 0
        Else
          .Text = objCubeData.GetCubeValues _
              (lngColumnCounter, lngRowCounter)
          If InStr(.Text, ".") > 0 Then
              .Text = Left(.Text, InStr(.Text, ".") + 2)
          End If
          If InStr(.Text, "-") > 0 Then
              .CellForeColor = &HFF&
          End If
        End If
      Next
    Next
  End With
  Set objCubeData = Nothing
End Sub
```

OLE Drag and Drop

You need code to allow the user to take a command button and drop it into the first row of the grid box. There are several parts to this. First, you want to see if the user is just clicking a command button, or if the user has held the mouse button down and actually moved the command button. You can check if the user moved the command button by storing the coordinates of the command button when the user pushes the mouse button down on the command button and comparing that to a new coordinate when the

MouseMove event fires. If the command button has moved at least three units, you call the OLEDrag method of the command button to signify that an OLE drag and drop has begun. This in turn triggers the OLEStartDrag event. You set the data, but you do not actually use it. You use a property called UniqueNameOfLastDragged, which is set in the MouseMove event, to trap the unique name of the command button that has been last dragged. The grid control uses this information to add the dimension to the grid.

```
Private Sub cmdDimension_MouseDown(Index As Integer, _
    Button As Integer, Shift As Integer, _
  X As Single, Y As Single)

  m_gMouseDownX = X
  m_gMouseDownY = Y
End Sub

Private Sub cmdDimension_MouseMove(Index As Integer, _
    Button As Integer, Shift As Integer, X As Single, Y As Single)
  UniqueNameOfLastDragged = cmdDimension(Index).Tag
  If Button <> 0 Then
    If Abs(X - m_gMouseDownX) > 3 Or Abs(Y - m_gMouseDownY) > 3 Then
      cmdDimension(Index).OLEDrag
    End If
  End If
End Sub

Private Sub cmdDimension_OLEStartDrag(Index As Integer, _
    Data As DataObject, AllowedEffects As Long)

    Data.SetData "test", vbCFText
    AllowedEffects = True
End Sub
```

When the command button is dragged, you must first determine what button was dropped by looping through the command buttons to find which one belongs to the tag in UniqueNameOfLastDragged. Once this is found, the command button is disabled, and the label with the value is emptied (as it can no longer contribute to the WHERE clause).

```
Private Sub grdCubeValues_OLEDragDrop _
    (Data As MSFlexGridLib.DataObject, _
    Effect As Long, Button As Integer, _
    Shift As Integer, X As Single, Y As Single)

  Dim lngCmdBtnCounter As Long
  Dim strDimension As String
```

```
For lngCmdBtnCounter = 0 To cmdDimension.Count - 1
  If cmdDimension.Item(lngCmdBtnCounter).Tag = _
     UniqueNameOfLastDragged Then
    cmdDimension.Item(lngCmdBtnCounter).Enabled = False
    lblValue(lngCmdBtnCounter).Caption = ""
    Exit For
  End If
Next
```

You have to get the name of the dimension out of the strUniqueLastDragged.

```
strDimension = UniqueNameOfLastDragged
If IsNumeric(Right(strDimension, 2)) Then
  strDimension = Left(strDimension, Len(strDimension) - 2)
End If
If IsNumeric(Right(strDimension, 1)) Then
  strDimension = Left(strDimension, Len(strDimension) - 1)
End If
```

You add the dimension to the text box that shows the selected dimensions.

```
If txtDimensions.Text = "" Then
  txtDimensions.Text = strDimension
Else
  txtDimensions.Text = strDimension & "," & txtDimensions.Text
End If
```

You select the node in the grid so the user can see what they have dragged onto the grid.

```
tvwHierarchy.SelectedItem = _
    tvwHierarchy.Nodes.Item(UniqueNameOfLastDragged)
```

If it was dropped into the first column, you add the row:

```
If grdCubeValues.ColWidth(0) > X Then
  AddRow
End If


End Sub
```

The AddRow adds a row into the row property using the UniqueNameOfLastDragged property to get the last dimension that was dropped into the grid.

```
Private Sub AddRow()

  If MDXRow = "" Then
    MDXRow = _
        "(" & GetDimensionUniqueName(UniqueNameOfLastDragged) & _
```

```
        ".MEMBERS" & ")"
    Else
      If InStr(1, MDXRow, "CROSSJOIN") > 1 Then
        MDXRow = " CROSSJOIN ({" & MDXRow & "}, {(" & _
            GetDimensionUniqueName(UniqueNameOfLastDragged) & ".MEMBERS)})"
      Else
        MDXRow = " CROSSJOIN ({" & MDXRow & "}, {(" & _
            GetDimensionUniqueName(UniqueNameOfLastDragged) & ".MEMBERS)})"
      End If
    End If
    If MDXColumn <> "" Then
      BuildMDXString
      FillGrid
    End If


End Sub
```

You use the MouseUp event for your click event. When the dimension command buttons are clicked, you use right-click if you want to move up the hierarchy and left-click if you want to move down the hierarchy.

If you hold down the shift key, you move up and down the values of the dimension value. Thus, if the dimension is currrently Customer Country, holding the shift key down and left-clicking on the customer button takes you through USA, Mexico, and Canada.

```
Private Sub cmdDimension_MouseUp(Index As Integer, _
    Button As Integer, Shift As Integer, X As Single, Y As Single)


Dim lngMemberKey As Long
Dim strLevelKey As String
Dim lngMemberCounter As Long
Dim lngLevelCounter As Long
```

If the shift key is down (Shift = 1), you must move through the members. First, you must determine what the numeric ID is for the current value in the label. If you click the left mouse, you go down one member. If you click the right mouse, you go up one level.

```
  If Shift = 1 Then
      For lngMemberCounter = 1 To _
          MemberCount(cmdDimension(Index).Tag)
        If InStr(1, GetMemberUniqueName(cmdDimension(Index).Tag, _
          lngMemberCounter), _
          "[" & lblValue(Index).Caption & "]") > 0 Then
          lngMemberKey = lngMemberCounter
          Exit For
        End If
```

```
      Next
      On Error Resume Next
      If Button <> vbKeyRButton Then
        lblValue(Index) = _
          StripQuotes(GetMemberUniqueName(cmdDimension(Index).Tag, _
          lngMemberKey + 1))
      Else
        lblValue(Index) = _
          StripQuotes(GetMemberUniqueName(cmdDimension(Index).Tag, _
          lngMemberKey - 1))
      End If
  Else
```

If the shift key was not held down, you move to the next level on the dimension. You must create a dimension index based on the next or previous dimension, depending on which mouse button was clicked. Thus, if the dimension identifier is Customer2 and you left-clicked, you want Customer3.

```
    If Button <> vbKeyRButton Then
      If IsNumeric(Right(cmdDimension(Index).Tag, 2)) Then
        strLevelKey = Left(cmdDimension(Index).Tag, _
        Len(cmdDimension(Index).Tag) - 2) & _
        Trim(Str(CInt(Right(cmdDimension(Index).Tag, 2)) + 1))
      End If
      If IsNumeric(Right(cmdDimension(Index).Tag, 1)) Then
        strLevelKey = Left(cmdDimension(Index).Tag, _
        Len(cmdDimension(Index).Tag) - 1) & _
        Trim(Str(CInt(Right(cmdDimension(Index).Tag, 1)) + 1))
      End If
    Else
      If IsNumeric(Right(cmdDimension(Index).Tag, 2)) Then
        strLevelKey = Left(cmdDimension(Index).Tag, _
        Len(cmdDimension(Index).Tag) - 2) & _
        Trim(Str(CInt(Right(cmdDimension(Index).Tag, 2)) - 1))
      End If
      If IsNumeric(Right(cmdDimension(Index).Tag, 1)) Then
        strLevelKey = Left(cmdDimension(Index).Tag, _
        Len(cmdDimension(Index).Tag) - 1) & _
        Trim(Str(CInt(Right(cmdDimension(Index).Tag, 1)) - 1))
      End If
    End If
    On Error Resume Next
```

Once you have all the required information, change the dimension command button labels, the value of the member in the value label, and the command buttons tag.

```
   cmdDimension(Index).Caption = _
     StripQuotes(GetDimensionUniqueName(strLevelKey))
   If Err.Number = 0 Then
     cmdDimension(Index).Tag = strLevelKey
     tvwHierarchy.SelectedItem = tvwHierarchy.Nodes.Item(strLevelKey)
   End If
   lblValue(Index).Caption = _
       StripQuotes(GetMemberUniqueName(cmdDimension(Index).Tag, 1))
 End If
 Screen.MousePointer = vbHourglass
```

If there were no errors and there is data in the grid box, you update the grid, because the value label is used in the WHERE clause. You might want to give the user a way of shutting this off because it creates a delay every time the user changes a value. You could add code such that pressing CONTROL and SHIFT at the same time will update the grid while moving through the hierarchy. This way, the user can adjust all the dimensions and then on the last one just press SHIFT and click to get the update.

```
 If Err.Number = 0 Then
   If MDXColumn <> "" And MDXRow <> "" Then
     BuildMDXString
     FillGrid
   End If
 End If
 Screen.MousePointer = vbDefault
 Err.Clear
 On Error GoTo 0


End Sub
```

Login Information

In the upper right of the control is the information the user needs to log in, including the cube name, the server name, and the database name. A userID and password is not included, because the FoodMart database does not have security. In a real application, you need to add the userID and password and use them to validate the users.

If a new server name is entered in the server textbox, you call the LoadDatabase method that retrieves the names of all the databases.

```
Private Sub txtServer_KeyUp(KeyCode As Integer, Shift As Integer)
  If KeyCode = vbCr Then
    LoadDatabases
  End If
End Sub
```

The LoadDatabase method uses the GetDataWarehouseNames method of the CubeConnection object and then parses out the database names.

```
Private Sub LoadDatabases()
  Dim strDatabaseNames As String
  strDatabaseNames = CubeConnection.GetDataWarehouseNames(txtServer.Text)
  Do Until strDatabaseNames = ""
   Dim lngCommaLocation As Long
   lngCommaLocation = InStr(1, strDatabaseNames, ",")
   If lngCommaLocation = 0 Then
     If strDatabaseNames <> "" Then
       cmbDatabase.AddItem strDatabaseNames
       cmbDatabase.ListIndex = 0
       LoadCubes
     End If
     Exit Do
   Else
     cmbDatabase.AddItem _
         Left(strDatabaseNames, lngCommaLocation - 1)
     strDatabaseNames = _
         Right(strDatabaseNames, _
         Len(strDatabaseNames) - lngCommaLocation)
   End If
  Loop

End Sub
```

If a new database is selected, you must get the cubes associated with the database. You call the LoadCubes method to do this.

```
Private Sub cmbDatabase_Change()
    LoadCubes
End Sub
```

The LoadCubes method gets the names of the cubes from the GetCubeNames method of the CubeConnsection object and then parses the names and places them in the list box.

```
Private Sub LoadCubes()
  Dim strCubeNames As String
  strCubeNames = CubeConnection.GetCubeNames _
      (txtServer, cmbDatabase.Text, txtProvider)
  Do Until strCubeNames = ""
    Dim lngCommaLocation As Long
    lngCommaLocation = InStr(1, strCubeNames, ",")
    If lngCommaLocation = 0 Then
      If strCubeNames <> "" Then
        cmbCube.AddItem strCubeNames
        cmbCube.ListIndex = 0
        InitializeCube
```

```
      End If
      Exit Do
    Else
      cmbCube.AddItem Left(strCubeNames, lngCommaLocation - 1)
      strCubeNames = Right(strCubeNames, Len(strCubeNames) - _
      lngCommaLocation)
    End If
  Loop
End Sub
```

cmdClear

The cmdClear method clears the grid box, restores the disabled command buttons, and places the value in the value label. When you select a measure, you remove it from the list box and place it into the selected members text box. You need to remove the members from the textbox and place them back into the list box. You also have to clear the MDXRow and MDXColumn properties.

```
Private Sub cmdClear_Click()
  Dim lngCommaLocation As Long
  Dim lngCommandCounter As Long
  grdCubeValues.Clear
  Do Until txtMeasures.Text = ""
    lngCommaLocation = InStr(1, txtMeasures.Text, ",")
    If lngCommaLocation = 0 Then
      If txtMeasures.Text <> "" Then
          lstMeasures.AddItem txtMeasures.Text
          txtMeasures.Text = ""
      End If
      Exit Do
    Else
      lstMeasures.AddItem Left(txtMeasures, lngCommaLocation - 1)
      txtMeasures.Text = Right(txtMeasures.Text, Len(txtMeasures.Text) - _
          lngCommaLocation)
    End If
  Loop
  txtDimensions.Text = ""
  For lngCommandCounter = 0 To cmdDimension.Count - 1
    cmdDimension.Item(lngCommandCounter).Enabled = True
    If lblValue.Item(lngCommandCounter).Caption = "" Then
        lblValue.Item(lngCommandCounter).Caption = _
        StripQuotes(GetMemberUniqueName _
        (cmdDimension(lngCommandCounter).Tag, 1))
    End If
  Next
  MDXColumn = ""
```

```
    MDXRow = ""

End Sub
```

cmdHelp

The cmdHelp button gives information on how to use the control.

```
Private Sub cmdHelp_Click()
    MsgBox "This control will allow you to select a server, " & _
        "database and cube" & vbCrLf & _
        "To use this, you must first connect to a server. " & _
        "The control will attempt to" & vbCrLf & _
        "connect automatically to a cube. If it cannot find " & _
        "either a server, database, or cube, the" & vbCrLf & _
        "user must make the connection" & vbCrLf & _
        "Click on the measures you want to view. " & _
        "Measures will be placed in columns" & vbCrLf & _
        "You can drill down into the dimensions by either clicking " & _
        "the buttons with the mouse or" & vbCrLf & _
        "by clicking on the treeview control. If you left & _
        "click on the dimension buttons, you will drill down the " & _
        "dimension, " & vbCrLf & _
        "right click to drill up the dimension." & vbCrLf & _
        "To the right of the button is the slicing values, " & _
        "the where clause. You can change these values by holding " & _
        "the shift button down and right" & vbCrLf & _
        "left clicking" & vbCrLf & _
        "Once you have clicked on the measures you want, " & _
        "you can drag and drop a dimension command button into the " & _
        "left column of the grid." & vbCrLf & "You can drop multiple " & _
        "dimensions into the grid." & vbCrLf & "When you change the " & _
        "value of the dimensions and there are values in the grid, " & _
        "they will be recalculated based on the new slice dimensions."
End Sub
```

lstMeasures_Click

When a measure is clicked in the lstMeasures list box it is selected as being part of the MDX query. Thus, when a measure is clicked it is removed from the list box and added to the measures that will be part of the MDX query.

```
Private Sub lstMeasures_Click()

    Dim lngColumnCounter As Long

    Screen.MousePointer = vbHourglass
```

```
   If MDXColumn = "" Then
      MDXColumn = "(" & _
        GetMeasureUniqueName _
            (lstMeasures.List(lstMeasures.ListIndex)) & ")"
   Else
      MDXColumn = MDXColumn & "," & _
          "(" & GetMeasureUniqueName _
          (lstMeasures.List(lstMeasures.ListIndex)) & ")"
   End If
   If txtMeasures = "" Then
     txtMeasures.Text = lstMeasures.List(lstMeasures.ListIndex)
   Else
     txtMeasures.Text = txtMeasures.Text & "," & _
         lstMeasures.List(lstMeasures.ListIndex)
   End If
     lstMeasures.RemoveItem lstMeasures.ListIndex
   If MDXRow <> "" Then
     BuildMDXString
     FillGrid
   End If
   Screen.MousePointer = vbDefault
End Sub
Private Sub tvwHierarchy_NodeClick(ByVal Node As ComctlLib.Node)
  Dim lngCommandCounter As Long

  For lngCommandCounter = 0 To cmdDimension.Count - 1
    If UCase(Left(cmdDimension.Item(lngCommandCounter).Tag, _
       Len(cmdDimension.Item(lngCommandCounter).Tag) - 3)) = _
      UCase(Left(Node.Key, Len(Node.Key) - 3)) Then
        cmdDimension.Item(lngCommandCounter).Caption = Node.Text
        cmdDimension.Item(lngCommandCounter).Tag = Node.Key
      Exit For
    End If
  Next
End Sub
```

UserControl Initialize

You need to initialize all your objects, set the default value for the slider control, set the
default value for the server, and call LoadDatabases. If the server name is the correct name,
LoadDatabases works. If it is not, LoadDatabases fails and the user has to enter the
required information. If a userID and password are required for the data warehouse or
for the application, you have to remove LoadDatabases from the initialize. The user has
to enter the information into the control. You could also include a userID and password
property and an InitalizeControl method (or a refresh method) that is retrieved by the

application using the control and passed to the control after the user has logged into the application.

```
Private Sub UserControl_Initialize()

    Set m_oCubeConnection = New CubeConnection.clsCubeConnection
    Set m_oMeasureCollection = New Collection
    Set m_oDimensionCollection = New Collection
    Set m_oMemberCollection = New Collection
    Set m_oCubeDef = New CubeMetaData.clsCubeMetaData
    vscDimension.Max = 100
    vscDimension.LargeChange = 20
    vscDimension.SmallChange = 5
    txtServer.Text = CubeConnection.GetServerName
    txtProvider.Text = "MSOLAP"


    LoadDatabases
End Sub
```

Slider Bar

The slider bar moves the command buttons up and down if there are more buttons than fit on the frame. In the control initialize, you set the units of the slider from 0 to 100. You must first calculate how far over the frame the command buttons go, which is the number of command buttons (DimensionCount) times the spacing needed for the label and the command button (c_ListSpacing) minus the height of the frame. If you divide the value of the slider by 100, you get the percentage of the distance you need to move the objects on the frame. Once you calculate this distance, you then need to move the dimension command buttons, the two labels, and the line this distance.

```
Private Sub vscDimension_Change()
  Dim lngMoveDistance As Long
  Dim lngDimensionControlCounter As Long
  lngMoveDistance = (DimensionCount * (c_ListSpacing + 10) - _
  frmDimensions.Height) * vscDimension.Value / 100
    cmdDimension.Item(0).Top = 570 - lngMoveDistance
    lblDimension.Item(0).Top = 240 - lngMoveDistance
    lblValue.Item(0).Top = 600 - lngMoveDistance
    linDimension.Item(0).Y1 = 960 - lngMoveDistance
    linDimension.Item(0).Y2 = 960 - lngMoveDistance
  For lngDimensionControlCounter = 1 To DimensionCount - 1
    lblDimension.Item(lngDimensionControlCounter).Top = _
        lblDimension.Item(lngDimensionControlCounter - 1).Top +
  c_ListSpacing
    cmdDimension.Item(lngDimensionControlCounter).Top = _
        lblDimension.Item(lngDimensionControlCounter).Top + c_CmdSpacing
```

```
    lblValue.Item(lngDimensionControlCounter).Top = _
        lblValue.Item(lngDimensionControlCounter - 1).Top + c_ListSpacing
    linDimension.Item(lngDimensionControlCounter).Y1 = _
        linDimension.Item(lngDimensionControlCounter - 1).Y1 +
c_ListSpacing
    linDimension.Item(lngDimensionControlCounter).Y2 = _
        linDimension.Item(lngDimensionControlCounter - 1).Y1 +
c_ListSpacing
    Next
End Sub
```

Appendix D
English Query

The Microsoft SQL Server 7.0 English Query is a tool that allows users to query a database using the English language instead of regular SQL statements. Thus, a typical English Query statement could be, "How many customers are there?" English Query allows users to ask ad hoc queries just like Microsoft SQL Server OLAP Services does. Thus, the two have much in common.

When building a data warehouse, you place the information in a star schema. The data is also cleaned and in one standard format. The data warehouse contains a great deal of knowledge from many sources and thus is a very valuable resource for the corporation. In addition to being used with online analytical processing (OLAP), it can be used to generate regular reports or used with English Query.

Star schemas are built around the idea of searching on descriptive words in the smaller informational tables, finding the primary key associated with that descriptive word, and then using that primary key to search the larger fact table. Thus, a star schema is designed for searches on text, which is what English Query is doing. English Query works best with a normalized database, but it can work with your informational tables as long as the rows in your informational tables are unique.

Note You cannot access the data in a multidimensional OLAP (MOLAP) storage scheme using English Query at this time. If you use a relational staging database to bring the cleaned, standardized data from many sources into one location before putting it in the multidimensional database, you can use this staging database as your source of data for English Query.

English Query uses an application called the Domain Editor to create the English queries. Before you look at the editor, let's cover domains, the most basic element of an English Query.

Domains

Domains are collections of information on the database you use for your English Queries. The domain is used to associate English words with objects in the database and uses these associations to make queries. Once a domain is created, an application can use the domain to make queries to the database using the English language.

The two main components of a domain are information on the structure of the database, which includes table and field names, joins, data types and keys, and the semantics of the objects in the database, which include the types of entities in the database and their relationships. An entity is something like a customer, a person, a shipment, an order, and so forth.

The structure of the database is, for the most part, done automatically for you. The semantics of the objects in the database, though, have to be created manually. Microsoft has provided English Query with a wide range of knowledge of the English language. This knowledge can be used to convert regular sentences into SQL queries. What English Query does not know is the relationships of the objects within your database. Thus, English Query may know that a customer places an order, but it cannot know what objects in your tables are customers and what objects are orders. You must tell English Query what object is associated with a customer and an order. Once you have done this, English query takes it from there.

There are three elements to an English Query:

- **Major entities**   These are the largest, most important entities in the database. They are usually tables in the database. Customer and Order are both major entities in English Query that would have a customer and orders table in the database.

- **Minor entities**   The fields within the tables become minor entities in English Query. Thus, customer name and customer address are both minor entities.

- **Relationships**   English query needs to have the relationships between entities clearly defined. There might be many ways to express the same concept. Thus, you can have the following relationships: Customers place orders and Orders are placed by customers.

Let's look at the process of making a domain using the Domain Editor.

The Domain Editor

You can open the Domain Editor by going to Start/Programs/Microsoft SQL Server 7.0/English Query/Microsoft English Query. Click Cancel on the New Project screen.

Note   Before you can use the English Query, you need to install it. It is a separate installation from both SQL Server and OLAP Services. If you have not installed it yet, install it now.

Let's do a simple example using the Northwind sample database in SQL Server. If you do not have a DSN (DataSourceName) for the Northwind database, go to Control Panel and open ODBC Data Sources. In the ODBC Data Source Administrator, click the System DSN tab. Click Add. Select SQL Server as the driver and click Finish. In the Create A New Data Source for SQL Server, use Northwind for the Name, and select either (local) or the server that has Northwind on it. Click Next and choose the correct security for your server. Click Next. Select

Change The Default Database To and select Northwind from the drop-down list box. Click Next and Finish. Finally, click OK.

Now, go back to the domain editor's menu and select File/Import New Tables. The Select Data Source screen comes up. Click the Machine Data Source tab and select the Northwind DSN you just created. Enter the appropriate information for login. On the New Database Tables, select the Customers table. Click OK. Click the Files tab and expand the tree. You should see dbo.Customers, as shown in Figure D-1.

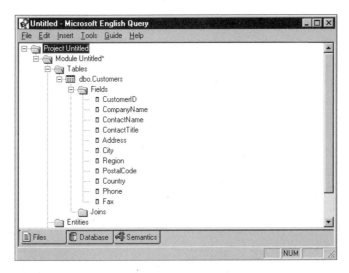

Figure D-1. *Domain editor with dbo.Customers.*

Click the semantics tab in the domain editor. You want to first add the major entity. Go to the menu and select Insert/Entity. For Words/phrases identifying entity, enter customer,client,Customer,Client. For Entity type, select None. Because this is a major entity, click Entire Table Is Associated With This Entity. Select dbo.Customer as the table.

You want to associate the company name with the customer. Using Autoname, you can associate a field with a major entity. Click Autoname. You are prompted to save. Click OK to save. Click Proper Name. Click Other. Select CompanyName in the drop-down list box next to Other. Click Accept. Click Apply. You should now be back in the editor with the new customer defined, a customer name associated with the new customer, and a relationship defined between these two entities.

You can add another entity related to customer. Once again go to the menu in the editor and select Insert/Entity. For Words/Phrases Identifying Entity, enter Contact,contact,ContactName,Contactname,contactname. For Entity type, enter Person. Use dbo.Customer for the table, ContactName for the Fields, and Proper Name (John Smith) for Name type. Click Apply. You get a warning about case sensitivity because you have not applied every possible combination of capitalizations. Ignore the warning and click OK.

Next you test your query. Select Tools/Test Application from the menu. Click Execute Query so you can see the results. Type and test the following questions:

- Show the customers and their customer names.
- Customer "Alfreds Futterkiste"?
- How many customers are there?
- Show customer names.
- What are the contacts?

If you look at the results, you see that some are very good and others are not quite what you expected. With additional relationships and entities, the results of your queries get better. Once you have done testing with a series of questions, you can save the questions to an ASCII file. Using a Regression Test you can run the questions again. In this way, you can see what questions did not work, make changes, and later run the questions again to see if there was an improvement.

Once you are done with all your testing, you can build an application file. Application files have an .eqd extension. Select Tools/Build Application from the menu. You get a message telling you that it might take a long time to complete. Click OK. COM components use the .eqd file to add English language ability.

To see how you can use these components, English Query comes with a complete set of applications. Look in the English Query folder (default install is Program Files/Microsoft English Query/Sample. There is a Visual Basic sample called EQVBUI.vbp that shows how to use English Query with the pubs and Northwind databases. You already built a DSN for the Northwind database. If you want to use it with pubs, you need to make a DNS connection to the pubs database. There are also Active Server Pages (ASP) and C++ examples.

English Query can offer the user additional ways to access and view the data in the data warehouse. As you work toward finding an enterprise-wide knowledge management system for your corporation, you might find that the features of English Query provide one more way to access corporate information.

Appendix E
Decision Support Objects

The Decision Support Objects (DSO) are a set of objects, interfaces, collections, and enumerations that you can use to programmatically administer Microsoft SQL Server 7.0 data warehouses. Instead of using OLAP Manager, you can create your own custom OLAP Manager with the DSO. More important, the DSO also provides you with the only way to perform certain tasks that are critical to properly administering your data warehouse. For example, you can set cell level security only with the DSO.

There is an extensive Help file on the DSO. You can find this Help file either in the platform software development kit (SDK) or in the product documentation for Microsoft SQL Server OLAP Services. Open Start/Programs/Microsoft SQL Server 7/OLAP Services/ Product Documentation. In the documentation, go to Building OLAP Services Applications/Decision Support Objects. You find detailed information on every aspect of the DSO there. Unfortunately, what you might not find is how all the information fits together and how to use the DSO. This appendix explains how to use the DSO to write applications that programmatically administer the SQL Server 7.0 data warehouse. The documentation explains what the different objects, interfaces, collections, and enumerations are.

Because you are primarily interested in using the DSO to program applications, you focus here on the object hierarchy you need to use to access information in the data warehouse. In this appendix, you explore objects and collections of objects. In a general sense, the hierarchy of the DSO looks like that in Figure E-1.

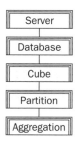

Figure E-1.   *General DSO object hierarchy.*

Looking at Figure E-1, you can see that you need to first create a server object. Next, you need to create a database object. Once you have a database object you can get access to cube objects. You access objects in this way all the way down to the bottom of the hierarchy.

As was the case in the ADO MD, the DSO has collections of objects. The standard method of building hierarchies has special objects that manage these object collections. The server object has a collection of database objects associated with it. A special object needs to manage this collection. Each database object has a collection of cube and virtual cube objects associated with it. The database objects need a special object to manage the collection of cube objects. Each cube object has a collection of partition objects associated with it. This continues down the hierarchy until you reach the bottom of the hierarchy, as shown in Figure E-2.

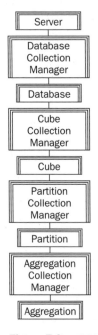

Figure E-2.   *DSO hierarchy with collection objects.*

If you look at all the collection objects, you find that they all have exactly the same set of methods and properties. The public methods and properties of an object are called the object's interface. You can therefore say that all the collection objects have the same interface. Because there is only one interface for all the collection objects, the DSO creates one object called MDStore to manage all the collections. Figure E-3 shows what this looks like.

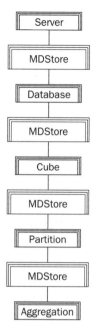

Figure E-3.   *DSO Hierarchy with MDStore.*

The DSO refers to an object with a common interface that is used by many different objects as Interfaces. The MDStore Interface's default function returns a member of the collection. When using the MDStore's default method with the server object, you get a database object. When you use the MDStore's default method with a database, you get a cube object. Thus, MDStore Interface always returns the correct objects when using the default method. This is called polymorphism.

Caution   The two scripting languages, VBScript and JavaScript, can only work with the default interface. In the case of the DSO, the MDStore Interface is not the default interface. This means you cannot currently access the MDStores Interface from the scripting languages. Because you can only move down the hierarchy by using the MDStores Interface, you cannot access the objects in the hierarchy using a scripting language. The best solution is to create a COM component with Visual Basic or C++ that uses the DSO and call the COM component from the scripting language.

There are also dimension, role, measure, command, and level interfaces. All of these, and the objects listed previously, are described in detail in the documentation.

Let's create a small Visual Basic application to see how to use the DSO and how to move through this hierarchy.

Create a new Visual Basic ActiveX dll project and call it DSOSample. Add the Microsoft Decision Support Objects to the references. Call the class DSOTest. Add the following code into the class module:

```
Option Explicit
Function TestDSO(ByVal v_sServerName As String)
Dim objDSOServer As DSO.Server
Dim objDSODatabase As DSO.MDStore
Dim objDSOCube As DSO.MDStore
Dim objDSOPartition As DSO.MDStore
Dim objDSOAggregation As DSO.MDStore
Dim objDSODimension As DSO.Dimension
```

Immediately, you should see something very interesting about these declarations. You are declaring the database, cube, partition, or aggregation objects using the MDStore Interface. This gives these objects all the properties and methods of the MDStore Interface. Let's see how this works when you actually begin to code with the DSO. Add the following two lines of code to initialize the DSO server object and to open a connection to the server.

```
Set objDSOServer = New DSO.Server
```

```
objDSOServer.Connect v_sServerName
```

Next you initialize all the rest of the objects:

```
Set objDSODatabase = New DSO.MDStore
Set objDSOCube = New DSO.MDStore
Set objDSOPartition = New DSO.MDStore
Set objDSOAggregation = New DSO.MDStore
```

You use the For Each … In … statement to move through the collections. You start with the database objects and print out the name of the database to the debug window:

```
For Each objDSODatabase In objDSOServer.MDStores
    Debug.Print "Database:" & vbCrLf & objDSODatabase.Name
```

The objDSOServer.MDStores returns a database object. The MDStores object has a dimensions object. Using objDSODatabase.Dimension returns a dimension associated with the database. Moving through the objDSODatabase.Dimension collection returns all the dimensions associated with the database. Add the following lines of code to do this:

```
    For Each objDSODimension In objDSODatabase.Dimensions
        Debug.Print "Dimension DW:" & objDSODimension.Name
    Next
```

You next move down the hierarchy and move through the cubes and the dimensions associated with each cube. To do this add the following code:

```
For Each objDSOCube In objDSODatabase.MDStores
    Debug.Print "Cube:" & vbCrLf & objDSOCube.Name
    For Each objDSODimension In objDSOCube.Dimensions
        Debug.Print "Dimension Cube:" & objDSODimension.Name
    Next
```

You finally move through the partitions and the aggregations:

```
    For Each objDSOPartition In objDSOCube.MDStores
        Debug.Print "Partition:" & vbCrLf & objDSOPartition.Name
        For Each objDSOAggregation In objDSOPartition.MDStores
            Debug.Print "Aggregation:" & vbCrLf & _
                    objDSOAggregation.Name
        Next
    Next
```

Finally, you put the rest of the Next statements in to close off the loops:

```
    Next
Next
End Function
```

You now have to add a new Standard Exe project creating a Visual Basic project Group. In the form load, add the following code:

```
Private Sub Form_Load()
Dim objDSOTest As New clsDSOTest
objDSOTest.TestDSO "IESMAIN"
End Sub
```

Replace IESMain with the name of your server. Make the Exe project the startup project and run the application. You should see the results in the immediate window.

Note If you are wondering what the numbers are for the aggregation, they are the levels of the dimension being used for the aggregation. Thus, if you have a Customer dimension with three levels and a Time dimension with two levels, you can have 11, 12, 21, 22, 31, 32. You should note that most of the aggregations are built from level 1 and 2. This is because of the 1/3 rule that limits aggregations only to combinations of levels that result in the total number of rows being less than 1/3 of the fact table. You can also adjust the aggregations and optimize them from the DSO.

With this basic understanding of the DSO, you can easily make your own cube editor. If you want to change the description property of a dimension, you can use the following function:

```
Public Function ChangeDescription(ByVal v_sServerName As String, _
                                  ByVal v_sDatabaseName As String, _
                                  ByVal v_sDimensionName As String, _
                                  ByVal v_sNewDescription As String)
Dim objDSOServer As DSO.Server
Dim objDSODatabase As DSO.MDStore
Dim objDSODimension As DSO.Dimension
Set objDSOServer = New DSO.Server
objDSOServer.Connect v_sServerName
Set objDSODatabase = objDSOServer.MDStores(v_sDatabaseName)
Set objDSODimension = objDSODatabase.Dimensions(v_sDimensionName)
objDSODimension.Description = v_sNewDescription
objDSODimension.Update
End Function
```

With minor modifications you can use this function to update all the properties of a dimension. You can also build a function to retrieve all the properties of the dimension. Using such functions, you can build a dll that provides all the data required by an application to view and edit cube properties.

There are many things you can do with the DSO. There is a white paper on Cell Level security on the CD that can only be done using the DSO. Another problem SQL Server data warehouse administrators face is building a virtual cube from two or more cubes that have the same measure. You cannot create a consolidated view of the measure. Let's look at this problem.

Go to OLAP Manager, create a regular cube, and call it CustomerCube. Using the shared dimensions as your source, add the dimensions Time and CustomerCube into CustomerCube. Also add the measure Store Sales from the Sales_1997 CustomerCube. Next, create another cube called ProductCube using the Products and Time dimensions and the Store Sales measure. Finally, create a virtual cube VirtualCustomerProduct built from the dimensions and measure in the CustomerCube and ProductCube. When making the CustomerProductCube you have to create two measures, Store Sales and Store Sales 1. OLAP Services cannot combine these two measures. This creates the problem that Store Sales will be associated with one dimension (either Products or Customers) and Store Sales 1 will be associated with the other dimension. There is no way the user can know which Store Sales goes with which dimension.

If you want to see the problem, open the MDX sample application. If you add customers first to the virtual cube, the following query gives the correct result:

```
SELECT
    {[Customers].[Country].MEMBERS} ON COLUMNS,
```

```
    {MEASURES.[Store Sales]} ON ROWS
FROM CustomerProductCube
```

The following query returns no values:

```
SELECT
    {[Customers].[Country].MEMBERS} ON COLUMNS,
    {MEASURES.[Store Sales 1]} ON ROWS
FROM CustomerProductCube
```

The solution is to create a new measure that knows what are the appropriate Store Sales. You need to build this new dimension using an IF Visual Basic statement. If you are querying against the Customer, use Store Sales. If you are querying against the Product, use Store Sales 1.

There is one other thing you need: ValidMember. The ValidMember function is not a standard MDX function. It is a SQL Server function that is useful for a Virtual Cube. ValidMember takes a measure and first finds out which cube it belongs to. Next, it tries to find the value of that measure based on the current cell.

Imagine that you are using ValidMeasure with Store Sales, the measure associated with CustomerCube. If your current cell in CustomerProductCube is the Time dimension equal to January 1997 and Customer Country equal to USA, ValidMeasure goes into the CustomerCube and finds the value of Store Sales at that point. Thus, ValidMeasure always returns the value of Store Sales from the cube the measure originated from.

If you are doing an MDX query using the Products dimension, the value of Store Sales in the virtual cube CustomerProductCube is Null. If you are doing an MDX query on Customers, the value of Store Sales in the virtual cube CustomerProductCube is the correct value. Thus, if ValidMeasure(Store Sales) is equal to MEASURES.[Store Sales] (the value of Store Sales in the virtual cube), you are doing an MDX query on Customers and need to use the Store Sales measure. If they are not equal, you are doing an MDX query on the Products dimension and need to use the Store Sales 1 measure. Thus, the following statement works:

```
CREATE MEMBER [CustomerProductCube].Measures.Store_Sales AS
'iif(ValidMeasure([Store Sales]) =
        [Store Sales], [Store Sales], [Store Sales 1])'
```

Unfortunately, at this point there is no way to do this with the cube editor. The solution is to do this using DSO. The following code creates the new Store_Sales member:

```
Public Function AddMeasure(ByVal v_sServerName As String, _
                           ByVal v_sVirtualCubeName As String, _
                           ByVal v_sDataBase As String, _
                           ByVal v_sCreateMemberString As String)
Dim objDSOServer As DSO.Server
Dim objDSODatabase As DSO.MDStore
```

```
Dim objDSOCube As DSO.MDStore
Dim objDSOCommand As DSO.Command

Set objDSOServer = New DSO.Server
Set objDSODatabase = New DSO.MDStore
Set objDSOCube = New DSO.MDStore
Set objDSOCommand = New DSO.Command

objDSOServer.Connect v_sServerName

Set objDSODatabase = objDSOServer.MDStores(v_sDataBase)
Set objDSOCube = objDSODatabase.MDStores(v_sVirtualCubeName)
objDSOCube.Commands.AddNew "Sales"
Set objDSOCommand = objDSOCube.Commands("Sales")
objDSOCommand.CommandType = cmdCreateMember
objDSOCommand.Statement = v_sCreateMemberString
objDSOCube.Update
End Function
```

You need to call this function from your VB Exe project as follows:

```
x.AddMeasure "IESMAIN", "CustomerProductCube", _
"FoodMart", _
"CREATE MEMBER [CustomerProductCube].Measures.Store_Sales AS " & _
" 'iif(ValidMeasure([Store Sales]) = " & _
" [Store Sales], [Store Sales], [Store Sales 1])'"
```

Once you run this code, you can enter the following MDX query and get the correct result.

```
SELECT
    {[Customers].[Country].MEMBERS} ON COLUMNS,
    {MEASURES.[Store_Sales]} ON ROWS
FROM CustomerProductCube
```

The following also works:

```
SELECT
    {[Product].[Product Family].MEMBERS} ON COLUMNS,
    {MEASURES.[Store_Sales]} ON ROWS
FROM CustomerProductCube
```

This gives you some idea as to what can be done with DSO. When it comes to administering your data warehouse, you will find the DSO an essential tool.

Index

Note to the Reader: Italicized page numbers refer to illustrations.

Symbols and Numbers

(), delimiting tuples, 127, 341
[], delimiting member names, 341
{}, delimiting sets, 127, 341
1stMeasures_Click, Cube browser, 414–15

A

ACID rules, 43
ActiveX control, 246
AddDimensionLabel, 403
AddDimensions, 403–4
AddDimensionUniqueName, 401
AddMemberUniqueName, 400
AddToDimensionCollection, clsDimension class, 382
AddToHierarchyCollection, clsHierarchies, 385
AddToLevelCollection, clsLevels, 388
AddToMemberCollection, clsMembers, 392–93
AddToNameCollection
    clsDimension class, 381
    clsHierarchies, 384
    clsLevels, 388
    clsMembers, 392
    clsTuple, 360
    clsTuples, 371
AddToTupleCollection, clsTuples, 372
AddToTupleMemberCollection, clsTuple, 360
AddUniqueName, 400–1
administrators
    designing data warehouse applications, 241
    optimizing data warehouse applications, 209
ADO connection object, 214
ADO Multidimensional (ADO MD), 209–40
    application design and, 241
    clsCubeConnection and, 248–50
    creating sample application, 211–14
    limitations of, 238–39

ADO Multidimensional (ADO MD) *(continued)*
    object hierarchy of, *210*
    overview of, 210–11
    PivotTable Services and, 291–92
    user, business, and data services and, 238–39
    Visual Basic controls and, 394
    wrapping with Visual Basic components, 347
ADO Multidimensional (ADO MD), catalog hierarchy, 214–25
    catalog object, 214–15
    CubeDef collection, 216
    CubeDef object, 216–17
    CubeDef properties, 217
    dimension object, 219–21
    dimensions collection, 219
    hierarchies collection, 221
    hierarchy object, 221–22
    level object, 222–24
    levels collection, 222
    member object, 224–25
    members collection, 224
    Property object, 218–19
ADO Multidimensional (ADO MD), cellset hierarchy, 226–40
    axes object, 226–27
    cell object, 234–37
    cellset object, 226
    objects properties, 237–38
    position object, 227–34
    positions collection, 227
AGGREGATE, MDX numeric functions, 204–5
aggregations, 62–64
    data explosion and, 62, 336–37
    data grain size and, 63–64
    definition of, 62
    HOLAP and, 79
    MOLAP and, 74–75
    partitions and, 81, 88, 334
    PivotTable Services and, 293
    ROLAP and, 66–68
Aggregation Wizard
    MOLAP and, 75
    ROLAP, 66–68
    Usage-Based Optimization Wizard and, 330
All Gender member, MDX, 341–42
analytical data
    creating systems for, 11

Jake Sturm The author has extensive experience throughout all levels of enterprise development. He has built a wide range of solutions, including Web applications, using Visual Basic, IIS, MTS, and SQL Server. Jake also helped develop a DNA workshop, and is the author of several technical books, including *VB6 UML Design and Development* and *Visual Basic Project Management*.

Jake presently works for Innovative Enterprise Solutions, Inc. as an Enterprise Systems Architect. He can be reached by email at jakes@gti.net and his personal Web site address is http://www.gti.net/ies. He resides in New Jersey with his wife, Gwen, her two daughters, Jill and Lynzie, his son, Will, and his daughter, Maya.

The manuscript for this book was prepared and submitted to Microsoft Press in electronic form. Text files were prepared using Microsoft Word 97 for Windows. Pages were composed by nSight, Inc., using Adobe Pagemaker 6.5 for Windows, with text in Garamond Light and display type in ITC Franklin Gothic. Composed pages were delivered to the printer as electronic prepress files.

Cover Designer:	Girvin Design
Layout Artist:	Joanna Zito
Project Manager:	Lisa Wehrle
Tech Editor:	Dennis Peterson
Copy Editors:	Susan Bradley, Bernadette Murphy
Proofreaders:	Elizabeth LeClerc, Rebecca Merz, and Denise Sadler
Indexer:	Jack Lewis

Gain work-ready expertise as you prepare for the Microsoft Certified Professional (MCP) exam.

Learn by doing—learn for the job—with official Microsoft self-paced training kits. Whether you choose a book-and-CD TRAINING KIT or the all-multimedia learning experience of an ONLINE TRAINING KIT, you'll gain hands-on experience building essential systems support skills—as you prepare for the corresponding MCP exam. It's Microsoft Official Curriculum—how, when, and where you study best.

Microsoft® Certified Systems Engineer Core Requirements Training Kit
ISBN 1-57231-905-4

MCSE Training Kit, Microsoft Windows® 2000 Server
ISBN 1-57231-903-8

MCSE Online Training Kit, Microsoft Windows 2000 Server
ISBN 0-7356-0954-3
COMING SOON

MCSE Training Kit, Microsoft Windows 2000 Professional
ISBN 1-57231-901-1

MCSE Online Training Kit, Microsoft Windows 2000 Professional
ISBN 0-7356-0953-5
COMING SOON

MCSE Training Kit, Microsoft Windows 2000 Active Directory™ Services
ISBN 0-7356-0999-3
COMING SOON

MCSE Online Training Kit, Microsoft Windows 2000 Active Directory Services
ISBN 0-7356-1008-8
COMING SOON

Microsoft SQL Server™ 7.0 Database Implementation Training Kit
ISBN 1-57231-826-0

Microsoft SQL Server 7.0 Database Implementation Online Training Kit
ISBN 0-7356-0679-X

Microsoft SQL Server 7.0 System Administration Training Kit
ISBN 1-57231-827-9

Microsoft SQL Server 7.0 System Administration Online Training Kit
ISBN 0-7356-0678-1

MCSE Training Kit, Networking Essentials Plus, Third Edition
ISBN 1-57231-902-X

MCSE Online Training Kit, Networking Essentials Plus
ISBN 0-7356-0880-6

MCSE Training Kit, Microsoft Windows 2000 Network Infrastructure Administration
ISBN 1-57231-904-6
COMING SOON

Microsoft Windows NT® Network Administration Training
ISBN 1-57231-439-7

Microsoft TCP/IP Training
ISBN 1-57231-623-3

Microsoft Press® products are available worldwide wherever quality computer books are sold. For more information, contact your book or computer retailer, software reseller, or local Microsoft Sales Office, or visit our Web site at mspress.microsoft.com. To locate your nearest source for Microsoft Press products, or to order directly, call 1-800-MSPRESS in the U.S. (in Canada, call 1-800-268-2222).

Prices and availability dates are subject to change.

Microsoft®
mspress.microsoft.com

Powerhouse resources to minimize costs while maximizing performance

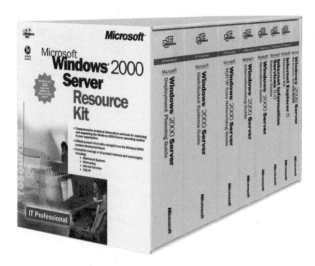

Deploy and support your enterprise business systems using the expertise and tools of those who know the technology best—the Microsoft product groups. Each RESOURCE KIT packs precise technical reference, installation and rollout tactics, planning guides, upgrade strategies, and essential utilities on CD-ROM. They're everything you need to help maximize system performance as you reduce ownership and support costs!

Microsoft® Windows® 2000 Server Resource Kit
ISBN   1-57231-805-8
U.S.A. $299.99
U.K.   £189.99 [V.A.T. included]
Canada $460.99

Microsoft Windows 2000 Professional Resource Kit
ISBN   1-57231-808-2
U.S.A. $69.99
U.K.   £45.99 [V.A.T. included]
Canada $107.99

COMING SOON

Microsoft BackOffice® 4.5 Resource Kit
ISBN   0-7356-0583-1
U.S.A. $249.99
U.K.   £161.99 [V.A.T. included]
Canada $374.99

Microsoft Internet Explorer 5 Resource Kit
ISBN   0-7356-0587-4
U.S.A. $59.99
U.K.   £38.99 [V.A.T. included]
Canada $89.99

Microsoft Office 2000 Resource Kit
ISBN   0-7356-0555-6
U.S.A. $59.99
U.K.   £38.99 [V.A.T. included]
Canada $89.99

Microsoft Windows NT® Server 4.0 Resource Kit
ISBN   1-57231-344-7
U.S.A. $149.95
U.K.   £96.99 [V.A.T. included]
Canada $199.95

Microsoft Windows NT Workstation 4.0 Resource Kit
ISBN   1-57231-343-9
U.S.A. $69.95
U.K.   £45.99 [V.A.T. included]
Canada $94.95

Microsoft®

mspress.microsoft.com

Practical, *portable* guides for **troubleshooters**

For hands-on, immediate references that will help you troubleshoot and administer Microsoft Windows NT Server 4.0, Microsoft SQL Server 7.0, or Microsoft Exchange 5.5, get:

Microsoft® Windows NT® Server 4.0 Administrator's Pocket Consultant
ISBN 0-7356-0574-2 $29.99 ($44.99 Canada)

Microsoft SQL Server™ 7.0 Administrator's Pocket Consultant
ISBN 0-7356-0596-3 $29.99 ($44.99 Canada)

Microsoft Exchange 5.5 Administrator's Pocket Consultant
ISBN 0-7356-0623-4 $29.99 ($44.99 Canada)

Ideal at the desk or on the go, from workstation to workstation, these fast-answers guides focus on what needs to be done in specific scenarios to support and manage mission-critical IT products. Great software and great learning solutions: Made for each other. Made by Microsoft.

Microsoft®
mspress.microsoft.com

There's no *substitute* for **experience.**

System Requirements

To use the Data Warehousing with Microsoft SQL Server 7.0 compact disc, you need a computer equipped with the following minimum configuration:

- 486 or higher processor

- Microsoft Windows 95, Windows 98, Windows NT 4.0, or later

- 32 MB of RAM

- CD-ROM drive

- Mouse or other pointing device (recommended)

- Microsoft Visual Basic 6.0

- Microsoft Word

- Microsoft SQL Server 7.0 installed on Windows NT 4.0 or later (for the Foodmart.mdb database file and the MDX files)

MICROSOFT LICENSE AGREEMENT

Book Companion CD

IMPORTANT—READ CAREFULLY: This Microsoft End-User License Agreement ("EULA") is a legal agreement between you (either an individual or an entity) and Microsoft Corporation for the Microsoft product identified above, which includes computer software and may include associated media, printed materials, and "on-line" or electronic documentation ("SOFTWARE PRODUCT"). Any component included within the SOFTWARE PRODUCT that is accompanied by a separate End-User License Agreement shall be governed by such agreement and not the terms set forth below. By installing, copying, or otherwise using the SOFTWARE PRODUCT, you agree to be bound by the terms of this EULA. If you do not agree to the terms of this EULA, you are not authorized to install, copy, or otherwise use the SOFTWARE PRODUCT; you may, however, return the SOFTWARE PRODUCT, along with all printed materials and other items that form a part of the Microsoft product that includes the SOFTWARE PRODUCT, to the place you obtained them for a full refund.

SOFTWARE PRODUCT LICENSE

The SOFTWARE PRODUCT is protected by United States copyright laws and international copyright treaties, as well as other intellectual property laws and treaties. The SOFTWARE PRODUCT is licensed, not sold.

1. GRANT OF LICENSE. This EULA grants you the following rights:

   a. Software Product. You may install and use one copy of the SOFTWARE PRODUCT on a single computer. The primary user of the computer on which the SOFTWARE PRODUCT is installed may make a second copy for his or her exclusive use on a portable computer.

   b. Storage/Network Use. You may also store or install a copy of the SOFTWARE PRODUCT on a storage device, such as a network server, used only to install or run the SOFTWARE PRODUCT on your other computers over an internal network; however, you must acquire and dedicate a license for each separate computer on which the SOFTWARE PRODUCT is installed or run from the storage device. A license for the SOFTWARE PRODUCT may not be shared or used concurrently on different computers.

   c. License Pak. If you have acquired this EULA in a Microsoft License Pak, you may make the number of additional copies of the computer software portion of the SOFTWARE PRODUCT authorized on the printed copy of this EULA, and you may use each copy in the manner specified above. You are also entitled to make a corresponding number of secondary copies for portable computer use as specified above.

   d. Sample Code. Solely with respect to portions, if any, of the SOFTWARE PRODUCT that are identified within the SOFTWARE PRODUCT as sample code (the "SAMPLE CODE"):

      i. Use and Modification. Microsoft grants you the right to use and modify the source code version of the SAMPLE CODE, *provided* you comply with subsection (d)(iii) below. You may not distribute the SAMPLE CODE, or any modified version of the SAMPLE CODE, in source code form.

      ii. Redistributable Files. Provided you comply with subsection (d)(iii) below, Microsoft grants you a nonexclusive, royalty-free right to reproduce and distribute the object code version of the SAMPLE CODE and of any modified SAMPLE CODE, other than SAMPLE CODE (or any modified version thereof) designated as not redistributable in the Readme file that forms a part of the SOFTWARE PRODUCT (the "Non-Redistributable Sample Code"). All SAMPLE CODE other than the Non-Redistributable Sample Code is collectively referred to as the "REDISTRIBUTABLES."

      iii. Redistribution Requirements. If you redistribute the REDISTRIBUTABLES, you agree to: (i) distribute the REDISTRIBUTABLES in object code form only in conjunction with and as a part of your software application product; (ii) not use Microsoft's name, logo, or trademarks to market your software application product; (iii) include a valid copyright notice on your software application product; (iv) indemnify, hold harmless, and defend Microsoft from and against any claims or lawsuits, including attorney's fees, that arise or result from the use or distribution of your software application product; and (v) not permit further distribution of the REDISTRIBUTABLES by your end user. Contact Microsoft for the applicable royalties due and other licensing terms for all other uses and/or distribution of the REDISTRIBUTABLES.

2. DESCRIPTION OF OTHER RIGHTS AND LIMITATIONS.

   • **Limitations on Reverse Engineering, Decompilation, and Disassembly.** You may not reverse engineer, decompile, or disassemble the SOFTWARE PRODUCT, except and only to the extent that such activity is expressly permitted by applicable law notwithstanding this limitation.

   • **Separation of Components.** The SOFTWARE PRODUCT is licensed as a single product. Its component parts may not be separated for use on more than one computer.

   • **Rental.** You may not rent, lease, or lend the SOFTWARE PRODUCT.

   • **Support Services.** Microsoft may, but is not obligated to, provide you with support services related to the SOFTWARE PRODUCT ("Support Services"). Use of Support Services is governed by the Microsoft policies and programs described in the user manual, in "on-line" documentation, and/or in other Microsoft-provided materials. Any supplemental software code provided to you as part of the Support Services shall be considered part of the SOFTWARE PRODUCT and subject to the terms and conditions of this EULA. With respect to technical information you provide to Microsoft as part of the Support Services, Microsoft may use such information for its business purposes, including for product support and development. Microsoft will not utilize such technical information in a form that personally identifies you.

- **Software Transfer.** You may permanently transfer all of your rights under this EULA, provided you retain no copies, you transfer all of the SOFTWARE PRODUCT (including all component parts, the media and printed materials, any upgrades, this EULA, and, if applicable, the Certificate of Authenticity), **and** the recipient agrees to the terms of this EULA.

- **Termination.** Without prejudice to any other rights, Microsoft may terminate this EULA if you fail to comply with the terms and conditions of this EULA. In such event, you must destroy all copies of the SOFTWARE PRODUCT and all of its component parts.

3. **COPYRIGHT.** All title and copyrights in and to the SOFTWARE PRODUCT (including but not limited to any images, photographs, animations, video, audio, music, text, SAMPLE CODE, REDISTRIBUTABLES, and "applets" incorporated into the SOFTWARE PRODUCT) and any copies of the SOFTWARE PRODUCT are owned by Microsoft or its suppliers. The SOFTWARE PRODUCT is protected by copyright laws and international treaty provisions. Therefore, you must treat the SOFTWARE PRODUCT like any other copyrighted material **except** that you may install the SOFTWARE PRODUCT on a single computer provided you keep the original solely for backup or archival purposes. You may not copy the printed materials accompanying the SOFTWARE PRODUCT.

4. **U.S. GOVERNMENT RESTRICTED RIGHTS.** The SOFTWARE PRODUCT and documentation are provided with RESTRICTED RIGHTS. Use, duplication, or disclosure by the Government is subject to restrictions as set forth in subparagraph (c)(1)(ii) of the Rights in Technical Data and Computer Software clause at DFARS 252.227-7013 or subparagraphs (c)(1) and (2) of the Commercial Computer Software—Restricted Rights at 48 CFR 52.227-19, as applicable. Manufacturer is Microsoft Corporation/One Microsoft Way/Redmond, WA 98052-6399.

5. **EXPORT RESTRICTIONS.** You agree that you will not export or re-export the SOFTWARE PRODUCT, any part thereof, or any process or service that is the direct product of the SOFTWARE PRODUCT (the foregoing collectively referred to as the "Restricted Components"), to any country, person, entity, or end user subject to U.S. export restrictions. You specifically agree not to export or re-export any of the Restricted Components (i) to any country to which the U.S. has embargoed or restricted the export of goods or services, which currently include, but are not necessarily limited to, Cuba, Iran, Iraq, Libya, North Korea, Sudan, and Syria, or to any national of any such country, wherever located, who intends to transmit or transport the Restricted Components back to such country; (ii) to any end user who you know or have reason to know will utilize the Restricted Components in the design, development, or production of nuclear, chemical, or biological weapons; or (iii) to any end user who has been prohibited from participating in U.S. export transactions by any federal agency of the U.S. government. You warrant and represent that neither the BXA nor any other U.S. federal agency has suspended, revoked, or denied your export privileges.

6. **NOTE ON JAVA SUPPORT.** THE SOFTWARE PRODUCT MAY CONTAIN SUPPORT FOR PROGRAMS WRITTEN IN JAVA. JAVA TECHNOLOGY IS NOT FAULT TOLERANT AND IS NOT DESIGNED, MANUFACTURED, OR INTENDED FOR USE OR RESALE AS ON-LINE CONTROL EQUIPMENT IN HAZARDOUS ENVIRONMENTS REQUIRING FAIL-SAFE PERFORMANCE, SUCH AS IN THE OPERATION OF NUCLEAR FACILITIES, AIRCRAFT NAVIGATION OR COMMUNICATION SYSTEMS, AIR TRAFFIC CONTROL, DIRECT LIFE SUPPORT MACHINES, OR WEAPONS SYSTEMS, IN WHICH THE FAILURE OF JAVA TECHNOLOGY COULD LEAD DIRECTLY TO DEATH, PERSONAL INJURY, OR SEVERE PHYSICAL OR ENVIRONMENTAL DAMAGE. SUN MICROSYSTEMS, INC. HAS CONTRACTUALLY OBLIGATED MICROSOFT TO MAKE THIS DISCLAIMER.

DISCLAIMER OF WARRANTY

NO WARRANTIES OR CONDITIONS. MICROSOFT EXPRESSLY DISCLAIMS ANY WARRANTY OR CONDITION FOR THE SOFTWARE PRODUCT. THE SOFTWARE PRODUCT AND ANY RELATED DOCUMENTATION ARE PROVIDED "AS IS" WITHOUT WARRANTY OR CONDITION OF ANY KIND, EITHER EXPRESS OR IMPLIED, INCLUDING, WITHOUT LIMITATION, THE IMPLIED WARRANTIES OF MERCHANTABILITY, FITNESS FOR A PARTICULAR PURPOSE, OR NONINFRINGEMENT. THE ENTIRE RISK ARISING OUT OF USE OR PERFORMANCE OF THE SOFTWARE PRODUCT REMAINS WITH YOU.

LIMITATION OF LIABILITY. TO THE MAXIMUM EXTENT PERMITTED BY APPLICABLE LAW, IN NO EVENT SHALL MICROSOFT OR ITS SUPPLIERS BE LIABLE FOR ANY SPECIAL, INCIDENTAL, INDIRECT, OR CONSEQUENTIAL DAMAGES WHATSOEVER (INCLUDING, WITHOUT LIMITATION, DAMAGES FOR LOSS OF BUSINESS PROFITS, BUSINESS INTERRUPTION, LOSS OF BUSINESS INFORMATION, OR ANY OTHER PECUNIARY LOSS) ARISING OUT OF THE USE OF OR INABILITY TO USE THE SOFTWARE PRODUCT OR THE PROVISION OF OR FAILURE TO PROVIDE SUPPORT SERVICES, EVEN IF MICROSOFT HAS BEEN ADVISED OF THE POSSIBILITY OF SUCH DAMAGES. IN ANY CASE, MICROSOFT'S ENTIRE LIABILITY UNDER ANY PROVISION OF THIS EULA SHALL BE LIMITED TO THE GREATER OF THE AMOUNT ACTUALLY PAID BY YOU FOR THE SOFTWARE PRODUCT OR US$5.00; PROVIDED, HOWEVER, IF YOU HAVE ENTERED INTO A MICROSOFT SUPPORT SERVICES AGREEMENT, MICROSOFT'S ENTIRE LIABILITY REGARDING SUPPORT SERVICES SHALL BE GOVERNED BY THE TERMS OF THAT AGREEMENT. BECAUSE SOME STATES AND JURISDICTIONS DO NOT ALLOW THE EXCLUSION OR LIMITATION OF LIABILITY, THE ABOVE LIMITATION MAY NOT APPLY TO YOU.

MISCELLANEOUS

This EULA is governed by the laws of the State of Washington USA, except and only to the extent that applicable law mandates governing law of a different jurisdiction.

Should you have any questions concerning this EULA, or if you desire to contact Microsoft for any reason, please contact the Microsoft subsidiary serving your country, or write: Microsoft Sales Information Center/One Microsoft Way/Redmond, WA 98052-6399.

OWNER REGISTRATION CARD   *Register Today!*   0-7356-0859-8

Return the bottom portion of this card to register today.

Data Warehousing with Microsoft® SQL Server™ 7.0 Technical Reference

FIRST NAME   MIDDLE INITIAL   LAST NAME

INSTITUTION OR COMPANY NAME

ADDRESS

CITY   STATE   ZIP

(   )

E-MAIL ADDRESS   PHONE NUMBER

U.S. and Canada addresses only. Fill in information above and mail postage-free.
Please mail only the bottom half of this page.

For information about Microsoft Press®
products, visit our Web site at
mspress.microsoft.com

Microsoft®Press